CPA's Guide to

Developing Effective

Business Plans

Fourth Edition

Tim Berry
Palo Alto Software

Aspen Law & Business
A Division of Aspen Publishers, Inc.
Gaithersburg   New York

(Formerly published by Harcourt Professional Publishing)

About Aspen Law & Business

Aspen Law & Business is a leading publisher of authoritative trea-
tises, practice manuals, services, and journals for attorneys, corporate and bank directors, accountants, auditors, environmental
compliance professionals, financial and tax advisors, and other business professionals. Our mission is to provide practical solution-
based how-to information keyed to the latest original pronounce-
ments, as well as the latest legislative, judicial, and regulatory developments.

We offer publications in the areas of accounting and
auditing; antitrust; banking and finance; bankruptcy; business and
commercial law; construction law; corporate law; criminal law; environmental compliance; government and administrative law; health
law; insurance law; intellectual property; international law; legal
practice and litigation; matrimonial and family law; pensions, benefits, and labor; real estate law; securities; and taxation.

Other Aspen Law and Business products treating accounting and auditing issues include:

> **Accounting Irregularities and Financial Fraud**
> **Audit Committees: A Guide for Directors, Management,**
>   **and Consultants**
> **Construction Accounting Deskbook**
> **CPA's Guide to Effective Engagement Letters**
> **CPA's Guide to E-Business**
> **Federal Government Contractor's Manual**
> **How to Manage Your Accounting Practice**
> **Medical Practice Management Handbook**
> **Miller Audit Procedures**
> **Miller Compilations and Reviews**
> **Miller European Accounting Guide**
> **Miller GAAP Financial Statement Disclosures Manual**
> **Miller GAAP Guide**
> **Miller GAAP Practice Manual**
> **Miller GAAS Guide**
> **Miller GAAS Practice Manual**
> **Miller Governmental GAAP Guide**
> **Miller International Accounting Standards Guide**
> **Miller Local Government Audits**
> **Miller Not-for-Profit Organization Audits**
> **Miller Not-for-Profit Reporting**
> **Miller Single Audits**
> **Professional's Guide to Value Pricing**

ASPEN LAW & BUSINESS
A Division of Aspen Publishers, Inc.
A Wolters Kluwer Company
www.aspenpublishers.com

SUBSCRIPTION NOTICE

This Aspen Law & Business product is updated on a periodic basis with supplements to reflect important changes in the subject matter. If you purchased this product directly from Aspen Law & Business, we have already recorded your subscription for the update service.

If, however, you purchased this product from a bookstore and wish to receive future updates and revised or related volumes billed separately with a 30-day examination review, please contact our Customer Service Department at 1-800-234-1660, or send your name, company name (if applicable), address, and the title of the product to:

ASPEN LAW & BUSINESS
A Division of Aspen Publishers, Inc.
7201 McKinney Circle
Frederick, MD 21704

CONTENTS

PART 2
GUIDE TO BUSINESS PLAN PRO
SOFTWARE 4.0

PREFACE

About the CD-ROM

The Fourth Edition of the *CPA's Guide to Developing Effective Business Plans* comes with Business Plan Pro software, Version 4, which is included on the CD-ROM attached to the inside back cover of this book. A key feature of this software is that it does *not* provide a cookie-cutter product intended to produce packaged business plans. It is based on the idea that every plan is unique and on the assumption that the plan belongs to its owner, not its consultant. With this software, you or your client can add or delete as many topics as you want in a flexible outline. You'll have a huge head start for developing a plan with complete linked financial tables already created and documented, and you also have extensive spreadsheet programmability and customizability. The software includes not just the dozen standard spreadsheet tables, but also three complete empty worksheets you can use as you or your client choose.

This software also has the facility to publish a business plan to a secure, password-protected business plan site at *www.liveplan.com*. Importantly, from the accountants' point of view, the Liveplan publishing facility includes the possibility of using the new collaborative features of the product, so that you and your client can work together, synchronizing your plan on the Liveplan secure site. With the collaborative features (which involve an extra monthly fee after 90 days), the secure website can manage changes, keep track of notes, and offer an easily accessible view of the plan for anybody to whom you give the login and password. You and your client can now work together on a collaborative plan, and then send it to bankers or investors in an e-mail with login and password. It is always available and always up to date. You can get all the information you need about this feature at the site, *www.liveplan.com*.

About the Book

As an accountant, you know that business is about money, and that the bottom line is profits. Business plans and business planning should also be about money, profits, and better business. Planning isn't about good plans or even accurate forecasts, much less conceptual brilliance, prescribed formats, or writing style. It is about money. It is about business plans that improve your accounting practice. It is also about business plans that improve your clients' businesses and a planning process that improves your relationship with your clients, without increasing your legal liabilities and reporting requirements.

Early in my career I realized that even if I got my invoices paid, I wanted nothing to do with unimplemented plans that were a waste of my time and my clients' money. I always hated those plans that went into drawers, never to be heard of again.

Business plans don't win investors or secure loans. People do. The plan is only as good as the people who implement it and the commitment it communicates. Business plans without "ownership" will fail. If it's the consultant's plan, it won't work. It must belong to the people who implement it.

This book has three objectives. The first is to encourage better business planning. It covers how to plan a business, what information to include, and how to put it together. More important, it covers the process of planning and how to make planning work to improve a business. We'll spend significant space on the human process, within a business or business group, that impact the implementation of a plan. We'll recommend a series of meetings and management practices that will help you develop, introduce, and manage a plan better. We also include Windows software you can use to develop and manage your plan as well as your clients' plans.

The second objective is to help you develop and implement a business plan for your practice. We'll look at how to improve your business planning within the practice, working with partners as professionals, and the rest of the practice's employees as well. The CPA business with its business plans is too often like the cobbler's children—without shoes. You are supposed to know how to create a business plan, and you should start with your own business. The software included with this book is based on the best available software for creating general business plans, a market leader in the U.S. retail market, further customized for use by CPAs. It includes everything in the retail version, plus additional commentary and sample plans related to the CPA practice.

The third objective of this book is to show you how to develop business plan consulting as part of your practice. I call this the business of business planning. If you are like most CPAs, you don't give your clients much help with business plans because you are concerned with the legal liabilities involved. You can't make projections for clients without taking on serious reporting requirements, so you avoid doing business plans. With this book and the software included, you'll be able to send your clients out for their own retail copy of Business Plan Pro, then provide them with the advice and suggestions they need, without having to write their plan yourself or even print out their projections. It will be their plan but will contain your expertise, optimized to maximize the results for you and your client.

The Business Plan Pro CD-ROM included with this book is a special version published by Palo Alto Software, customized for this book and Aspen Law & Business. The standard version of Business Plan Pro currently has a greater than 35% share of the U.S. retail market for Windows-based business planning software. Your clients can find it at any major retail store in the country, as well as in major mail-order catalogs and on the World Wide Web at www.palo-alto.com. The special version includes all the software in the standard retail version, plus additional sample plans and plan options customized to apply specifically to the CPA practice. The CD-ROM also contains a workbook for developing a business plan.

BUSINESS PLAN PRO QUICK START

Your copy of Business Plan Pro is a complete and full version of the software product, fully licensed for a single user, included on the CD-ROM attached to this book. That CD includes everything that is included in the boxes at the retail stores, and in addition:

1. Your CD includes a CPA-specific sample plan, CPAPLAN.SPD, that you can use as an example of a business plan for a CPA practice. You can load that plan as you would a finished plan, save it as a new file with a different name, and then modify it.

2. Your documentation is mainly this book. However, for good measure, the full documentation from the normal retail package is also included in its entirety on your CD, along with the software you need to read it easily on your computer monitor or print it onto your printer, or both. Details are included below.

Windows 95 Install

1. Click Start>Settings>Control Panel.

2. Click on the Add/Remove Programs icon in the Control Panel.

3. The Add/Remove Programs Properties dialog box displays. Click Install.

4. The Install Program from Floppy Disk or CD-ROM dialog box displays. Insert the Business Plan Pro CD into the appropriate drive. Click the Next button. Windows will search the disk, looking for the Business Plan Pro setup program. Click the Finish button.

5. The Registration dialog box displays. Click OK.

6. The default directory to install is C:\program files\pas\ business plan pro 4.0. Click OK, or change directories.

7. The default Start Menu group is called Palo Alto Software. Click OK, or change it.

Follow the screen prompts to complete the installation.

Troubleshooting

Remember, should you have questions or problems while working with the program, *Business Plan Pro* has online help.

A. Press F1 if *Business Plan Pro* is currently loaded, and the help file will load automatically.

B. If *Business Plan Pro* is not loaded, double-click on the *Business Plan Pro Help* icon in your program group.

C. If all else fails, double-click on bp.hlp in your *Business Plan Pro* home directory.

D. Each table and each topic has instructions and examples above it. When using a table, you also have the *Table Help* tab above the table to provide audio help and row-by-row help.

E. Use the *Text Manager* tab in text mode, and *Table Manager* in table mode, to work the links between topics, tables, and charts.

F. Use the Outline form to add and delete topics.

G. There's a database of support topics at *www.paloalto.com/su/*.

Technical Support Contact Information

Internet: World Wide Web, E-Mail FTP, and E-mail

World Wide Web:	*http://www.paloalto.com*
E-mail:	help@paloalto.com
Telephone Number:	1-541-683-6162
Fax Number:	1-541-683-6250
Address:	144 E. 14th Avenue, Eugene, OR 97401

Sample Plans

Your special CPA version includes CPAPLAN.SPD, which is on your CD-ROM with other sample plans. This plan appears only on the disk attached to this book, not in the normal retail versions.

The normal retail version includes more than 30 complete real-life plans (created with Business Plan Pro), many of which received financing from banks and the SBA. These sample plans illustrate the different types of plans that you can create with Business Plan Pro. The sample plans are available by choosing "Open a Sample Plan" from the Welcome Screen.

A list of file names and descriptions can be found in the Help file Contents Getting Started section.

Business Plan Pro Manuals in Portable Document Format (PDF)

The printed manuals for Business Plan Pro, Version 2.0 can also be found on your CD-ROM as PDF files. There are two PDF files. Main.pdf contains the first section of the manual, describing the process of creating a business plan. User.pdf contains step-by-step instructions on the features of the program, referred to in the second section of the manual as the Software Guide.

Installation files for Acrobat™ Reader are also included on your CD-ROM.

For Windows 3.1, the Reader install file is in the directory

Acrobat\Win3X\ar16e30.exe

For Windows95, the Reader install file is in the directory

Acrobat\Win95\ar32e30.exe

To Install the Reader Program

Double click on the reader file; follow the screen prompts to complete installation of the Acrobat™ Reader program to your hard drive.

To View a PDF File

Highlight the PDF file name, and double click. The Acrobat™ Reader program will open and display the PDF file.

Venture Capital Database

The Venture Capital Database is located in your Business Plan Pro directory. The tab-delimited text file is named vencap.txt. You can open and view this file in a word processor or a spreadsheet application like Microsoft Excel. You'll have an easier time dealing with the large file in a spreadsheet. Most spreadsheet applications will recognize the tab-delimited text file, allowing you to work with the file using spreadsheet commands.

ABOUT THE AUTHOR

Tim Berry has worked closely with CPAs for many years. As consulting director in Mexico for Business International, he worked with partners at Arthur Andersen and Touche Ross. While doing business planning for Apple Computer's Latin America, Pacific, and Japan groups, he worked with professionals from Peat Marwicke. During the 14 years he's owned and operated Palo Alto Software, Inc., he has worked with hundreds of CPAs on business planning and presented seminars for CPAs and other business groups in more than a dozen countries.

Berry developed a successful consulting practice dedicated to business plans and business planning. He prepared Apple Computer's annual and quarterly plans for Latin America from 1983 through 1987, and then again for its Japan group from 1991 through 1994. During his years with Apple Latin America, sales grew from $2 million to more than $30 million. While he was planning for Apple Japan, sales grew from less than $200 million to $1.5 billion. He worked with Philippe Kahn's business plan for Borland International and served on the board of directors of that company from the original founding in 1983 until it went public three years later. Sales grew from zero to more than $100 million during that period. Berry developed a seminar / software combination he delivered for four large clients to groups of their dealers in more than a dozen countries. In the meantime, he had three books on business planning and spreadsheets published, and for three years he wrote regular monthly columns in *Business Software* magazine.

The writing and business planning came together in 1988 when he developed his first version of *Tim Berry's Business Plan Toolkit*, a combination of spreadsheet templates, word templates, and readable documentation. Palo Alto Software was incorporated that same year and became the publisher of the Business Plan Toolkit. By 1994 the market had grown enormously, and Berry began to concentrate on Business Plan Pro, the descendent of Business Plan Toolkit. Today Business Plan Pro is a market leader in the United States. Experts and reviewers recommend it in articles published in *PC Magazine, Windows, PC Computing, Small Business Computing, Accounting Technology, Entrepreneur, Journal of Business Strategy,* and many other respected sources. More than 100 business schools either use it as part of their coursework or recommend it.

CPA's Guide to Developing Effective Business Plans

PART 1
DEVELOPING EFFECTIVE
BUSINESS PLANS

CHAPTER 1
BUSINESS PLANNING:
AN OPPORTUNITY FOR CPAS

Business plans have long had a special relationship to accounting and accountants. A business plan normally includes complete financial statements, an accustomed area for a business accountant. It also includes pro forma statements projecting the foreseeable future. These projections, because they come as pro forma income statement, cash flow, balance sheet, and ratios, are also a natural extension of the realm of the accountant. In many accounting practices, the CPA is a business's first resource for numerical analysis. In general, when a business needs a plan, an important business opportunity exists for an accountant.

It is hardly surprising, then, that CPAs frequently offer business planning as a service to their clients. The American Institute of CPAs (AICPA) offers its 330,000 members a steady stream of mini-courses on business planning as part of its programs in continuing education. It also offers a free brochure (which may be found on the AICPA website) selling business planning services to clients, a publication for sale called "Developing Business Plans," and a prepared speech that begins with the sentence: "As a CPA, one of the most important services I can provide to my clients is assisting them in preparing a viable business plan." As of January 2001, a simple Internet search for CPA and business plan produces dozens of websites in which CPAs offer business planning services.

What is surprising, however, is how many CPAs are *not* doing business planning for clients. This is hard to quantify. When asked directly, an accountant is not likely to decline to help with a business plan. As a presenter in AICPA events, however, I've run into countless accountants who do not often do plans, either for their clients or for their own practices. The same Internet search that turned up 100 CPA sites offering business plans turned up many times that many that did not say a word about it. Even the CPA societies go soft on the subject. The Massachusetts Society of CPAs, for example, says in its documentation that CPAs can do business planning "in addition to the traditional services."

When a business needs help with a plan, does it turn automatically to its accountant? Experts frequently recommend accountants, but not necessarily first. David Schmidt, Senior Vice President of Bank of Petaluma, writing to loan applicants, lists a number of sources of help with business plans, including the SBA and SCORE (Service Corps of Retired Executives). His list ends with, "You may also wish to solicit the help and advice of a CPA to assist you in the preparation of the loan package." In context, it seems like an afterthought. More to the point, what about you? Are you taking advantage of the opportunity to help clients with business plans? Are you doing your own business planning, for your practice, as well as you should?

THE OPPORTUNITY

Exactly how much opportunity is there? How many of your business clients will apply for a loan in the next few months? According to the federal Small Business Association (SBA), there are 23 million small businesses (fewer than 500 employees) in the United States. According to a 1994 SBA study, 56 percent of those used traditional financing from banks, including mortgage loan, leasing, or line of credit. How many of those loans involved business plans? Of companies with more than 100 employees, 60 percent had bank lines of credit. Did they submit business plans to their banks? Perhaps the most interesting statistic is from a study published by Global Entrepreneurial Monitor (GEM), which is sponsored by Babson College, the Kaufmann Center for Entrepreneuring, and London College of Business. The GEM study shows that 16 million adults, 8.4 percent of the U.S. adult population, are actively involved in starting a new business. SBA and banking statistics indicate that about 4 million new businesses are started each year, and roughly half of the 22 million existing small businesses apply for bank financing every year. How many of these different efforts result in creating business plans? My guess is 7 million.

What about your accounting practice? How many small business clients do you have? How many of them will apply for a business loan in the next few months? How many of them need a business plan? How many will develop a business plan? How many will implement a business plan? How many will ask you to be involved in the planning process?

THE PROBLEMS

If the opportunity is there, why don't accountants prepare more plans? Why don't you do more, in your practice? Why do bankers recommend going to SCORE or the local community college instead of to you? Why don't your clients come to you first? Or, if some of them do that already, why don't more of them?

Whose Plan Is It?

An important underlying problem is rooted in the nature of business plans and the need for ownership. As a professional giver of business advice, you must be hesitant to develop plans for clients. When you develop a plan for a client, whose plan is it? The danger is that it will be your plan, not your client's. If so, then its chance of implementation plummets. Your clients won't be committed, and their people won't be committed. Later, when things get tough (and sticking to a plan takes resolve), they abandon the plan and blame you for its failure.

Of course you can work around this problem—we'll deal with it at length in this book—but you have to start by recognizing the problem. Even if you do get paid for your services, if the plan isn't implemented, then the client loses, and on the longer term, if your client loses, then so do you.

Pricing and Comparative Costs

The first problem is pricing. As your client looks for help developing a business plan, he or she will find many options.

Any book store has half a dozen or more books on the subject, at prices ranging from $15 to $50. Computer and office supply stores have software to help, costing anywhere from $40 to $100. The local community college has courses at night and on weekends. The local Small Business Development Center (SBDC) has courses and low-cost consulting for entrepreneurs. As banker David Schmidt mentioned, there are also SCORE groups and the local SBA office. Business plan templates and business plan websites may be found on the Internet, with sample plans and outlines. All of these options are going to cost your client less than a single hour of your billing time.

The pricing problem is even tougher because of the nature of business planning. Unlike tax work, which has specific deadlines and obvious ending points, a business plan may never end. A real business plan is always alive and always under revision. Business is constant change. Can you develop a plan for a client and then pass it on to the client company for management? Or will your client always need you to revise the plan? How much will you bill to call up the plan on your computer system and modify the financial assumptions?

The pricing problem is much more a matter of never-ending jobs than of hourly billing rates. Accountants are generally quite comfortable with pricing and relative value and not concerned with competing against books, software, or community colleges. They also know, however, that clients are uncomfortable with open-ended jobs that have unlimited billing hours.

Competition in Business Planning

Aside from the lower-priced options, there are also powerful new competitors that have more aggressive sales and marketing. The past two decades have seen an explosion of professional services related to small business and entrepreneurship. No wonder the expert speakers, bankers, and magazine articles recommend so many advice providers other than accountants. Business plan consultants, financial planners, and general management consultants almost overwhelm the small business client with sales and marketing efforts.

Liabilities and Risk

Are there additional legal risks in business planning for professional accountants? There was a trend in the 1990s toward increasing legal accountability, particularly when projections are involved. Some CPAs recommend taking special care not to make projections for clients, simply because CPAs can be held liable for decisions made on the basis of those projections. It is even important that you do not print business plan documents on your own printer, because that increases your involvement. If you prepare a business plan for your client, you take on substantial additional reporting requirements and substantial additional legal risk. If things go wrong, you face legal responsibility. You can end up getting sued by your client, his or her bank, people who purchased the business, or your client's heirs, among others. If you even print the business plan in your office, you're responsible for it.

Other CPAs say the risk is negligible. After all, the most serious lawsuits that made headlines involved accountants being held liable for audits that failed to uncover problems, not for faulty projections. Even the AICPA itself, which has carefully followed risk management and legal liabilities for accountants for several years, recommends the business plan business.

As a professional, you must make the judgment yourself. You have a great deal of guidance available. Some of your clients need your help with business planning, some of them trust you to give it. You can choose to manage risk, following AICPA guidelines, with engagement letters, and professionalism. In Chapter 3 we'll go over additional suggestions in detail.

A PROFESSIONAL SOLUTION

Given the overwhelming presence of personal computers in business, even in home offices and small businesses, you can take advantage of business plan software to create the ideal business planning engagement. Your client purchases the software and develops the business plan on his or her own time.

You provide the additional benefits of guidance, reassurance, and security. In this case, you do not have the ownership problem. The end product is the client's plan, developed by the client. You also do not have the never-ending plan problem, so your client doesn't fear incurring too much cost at your hourly rate. Finally, you do not have the liability problem.

Of course, you should be billing less for this engagement than you would for developing a complete business plan. Remember, however, that you are also providing your client with a real benefit at an attractive cost while developing a deeper and longer-lasting relationship. You are serving as an advisor in a way that is likely to generate more business. You are also teacher and mentor, helping your client understand the realities of forecasting, cash projections, expenses, and working capital.

Software Specifics

A licensed copy of Business Plan Pro™, published by Palo Alto Software is included with this book. Your client can buy the same software at one of more than 3,000 stores in the United States for less than $100. The business plan discussion in this book applies to all business plans, not just those prepared with this specific software. However, many examples and some specific discussions refer to Business Plan Pro. Part 5 of this book is a reprint of the software-specific instructions normally included as documentation with Business Plan Pro. Also, information specific to Business Plan Pro is generally set aside in the text under the heading "Software Specifics." This is the first such topic.

CHAPTER 2
THE MARKETING OF BUSINESS PLANNING

INTRODUCTION

How will you market your business planning services? How will you build this new effort into your business? Will you develop a marketing plan for your business, or just add this into your existing client development efforts?

Contrary to commonly accepted myth, a website alone won't do it. The Internet alone won't do it. The web is best used as part of your marketing mix, a tool for strategy. It isn't a strategy in itself. We will look at the web in this chapter, but first we need to look at the underlying elements of marketing your professional services.

The first step is to determine your business goals. What role will the business planning business play in your business? Business planning means different things to different CPA practices. Consider some of the more obvious options:

- *New leads.* Use the business plan practice to bring in leads for more complete relationships. It's a fair assumption that people who need business plans are either starting a company, growing a company, or managing a company. These are people who may become new clients.

- *Enhanced client relationships.* Your existing clients need business plans to apply for new loans or investment or to improve management, or both. Offering business planning services to existing clients has the double benefit of building services for existing customers—the most cost-effective way to grow revenues—and also protecting the relationship. If your accounting clients go elsewhere for business planning, they might end up elsewhere for accounting services as well.

- *Consulting revenue.* Business planning and related services can be a source of revenue, as a line of business.

THE MARKETING PROCESS

As soon as you set your business objective, you then need to develop the marketing—or, if you prefer, client development or business development—to follow up. Figure 2–1, taken from Marketing Plan Pro, is a reminder of the basics of marketing, which apply to professional services as well as to any other business.

- Start with the target market.

- Understand the needs of the market.

- Develop your offering to meet those needs.

- Develop a strategy for communicating that offering.

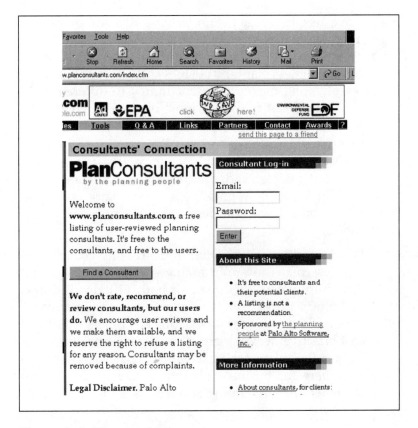

Figure 2–1. The marketing process.

- Create tactics to implement the strategy.

- Specify marketing program activities to make it all planned, budgeted, assigned, and real.

Start with the Target Market

Start with setting target markets. You can't aim anything without identifying a target. You've probably already identified the two most obvious targets, and I want to start with a third group for consideration, as a personal favorite:

- *Existing clients.* Existing clients are almost always the first and best target market for professional services. Figure 2–2 shows how providing more services to existing clients is by far the most profitable way to expand any professional business, and particularly accounting practices. The marketing expense per dollar of new business is almost zero, in this case, a fraction of the expense of finding new clients. Furthermore, you don't want your clients paying other experts to do what you also

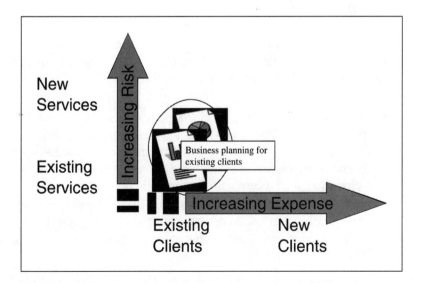

Figure 2–2. Business planning as healthy practice expansion.

can do; that potentially weakens your relationship. So this is important as a good defense and a good offense.

- *Start-up businesses.* Some 2–4 million new businesses start up every year, in the United States. At the high end, you have the 5,000 or so start-ups financed by 500 or so venture capital companies, some of them with healthy capitalization and excellent start-up management. At the low end, you have the millions of new home office businesses, sole proprietorships, and self-financed small businesses. Most of them either have a business plan or know they need one, or both. The best of them are real growth opportunities for professionals, and the worst of them are budget starved and dedicated to doing everything themselves.

- *Existing small businesses.* There are 11–22 million small businesses in the United States, the range depending mainly on definitions of experts and distinctions between large and small. These businesses need business planning as part of their ongoing management function. They may not all recognize that need, but they certainly do know they need business plans whenever they are looking for new investment and usually when they need new bank loans.

As you review these targets, remember your business objective. Some targets will fit your business objectives better than others. Here are some additional possibilities:

- *Entrepreneurs.* There are 15–20 million individual entrepreneurs (not companies) in the United States, according to a study published by the Kaufmann Center for Entrepreneuring (www.entreworld.org). Here too, there is a wide range of people and possibilities. At the upper end, you have wealthy individuals involved in starting new businesses as investors, catalysts, and co-owners. At the lower end, you have people without means who want to start businesses.

- *Nonprofit organizations.* Although the mystique of business planning hasn't spread quite as thoroughly to nonprofits, it is there. Many nonprofits recognize the need for planning. That includes some of the more prevalent types, such as schools.

- *Government agencies.* As with nonprofits, even though business plans are not as common in the governmental area, they are still needed. Some members of this group know that business plans are needed.

Another potentially attractive market focus is the specific vertical market. You might become an expert in business planning (and, by extension, accounting) for some specific type of business, such as construction and remodeling, architecture, auto repair shops, retail jewelers, restaurants, or any other. These so-called vertical markets give you a direct path into trade publications, websites, and industry-specific events that are a natural advantage for marketing your professional services. For example, my business planning practice focused mainly on personal computer manufacturers in Latin America and software publishers. That focus made it easier to understand where to find them, what to tell them, and how to fill their real market needs.

Some target markets might be part of your accounting practice that don't normally look for business planning services:

- *Individual taxpayers.* Some accounting practices focus on individual taxpayers. Normally, unless these individuals are entrepreneurs or looking to become investors in small business, they are not looking for business planning services. Financial planning, which often falls into similar space in people's minds, is quite different and not related to business planning in any way relevant to your practice.

- *Large corporations.* Fortune 1000 companies are not likely prospects.

Ultimately, this choice of target market is a strategic choice. It will shape your business and determine how you should reach that target group and what message you should be sending to that group.

Understand the Market Needs

Ideally, you want to research market needs as you develop target markets. Having spent some years in the business planning business, I can give you a head start from experience.

Business Plan Events

Even though every business needs a plan, I recommend starting with those who know they need it. Focus first on "business plan events," which force a business to create a plan. These include:

- *Starting a new business:* The start of a new business is the generally accepted time for developing a business plan. Books, websites, business classes, magazine articles, and thousands of experts tell millions of people that to start a business they need a business plan.

- *Loan applications:* An existing company needs a business plan to accompany a loan application. This might be a credit line, expansion loan, or debt consolidation.

- *Searching for capital:* An entrepreneur or start-up company needs a business plan as part of its search for start-up capital.

- *Buying or selling:* Either buyer or seller or, in many cases, both develop business plans to guide them through the transaction. This includes splitting of partnerships.

- *Valuation for taxes:* Professional valuations are required when small businesses look at estate planning, gifting (such as gifts to other family members), and divorces.

The Essential Intangibles

Nobody really wants a business plan; they really want the business benefits that come from developing and implementing that plan. Furthermore, instead of just doing it themselves, they go to an accountant or consultant for a plan for a number of very important reasons. Here are some of the intangible, but nonetheless critical, market needs you should keep in mind:

- *Reassurance*: Many of your potential clients want reassurance from you as a financial professional that their plan is good enough. They don't want to be embarrassed when they present it. They fear rejection and looking bad in front of the banker or investors.

- *Financial/mathematical expertise*: Many quite competent business owners and entrepreneurs mistrust their own ability to make acceptable financial projections. "Fear of finance," as I call it, is a definite factor in this business. Many otherwise competent business people break into a sweat when forced to estimate numbers or even to deal with numbers. They might be excellent salespeople and successful, but they can't deal with the numbers in business.

- *Jumping the hurdle*: The business plan often stands like a hurdle in the path to success. Without a plan, there is no loan application, no investment, and no moving forward. Many potential clients will see your services as a way to get over that hurdle.

DEVELOP YOUR SERVICE OFFERING

Your business offering is strategic. It should definitely flow logically from your choice of target markets and your understanding of market needs. A sampling of the wide range of common service offerings is presented below (some of which is reprinted, with permission, from the planning consultants website, www.planconsultants.com).

Business Plan Seminar

Starting point: Participants are interested in developing a business plan.

Deliverables: Normally from one to six hours, occasionally more than a single day, of seminar participation. Some seminars include software and hands-on experience, some include books or workbooks, and few are just oral presentations and responses.

Cost: Free seminars are suspected sales pitches. As little as $49 makes a seminar credible, $95 is still attractive, $295–$495 for a one-day seminar is steep but qualifies the participants' interest.

Pros: Seminars offer acceptable economics for both presenters and participants, with hours of available expertise offered to multiple people in a single session. A good way to offer questions and answers and product expertise.

Cons: The seminar is usually for the do-it-yourself audience, generally price sensitive, often attending a seminar precisely to avoid the expense of business plan consulting.

Business Plan Review

Starting point: A finished plan draft.

Deliverables: Suggest corrections, ranging from editing changes to wholesale changes of plan, strategy, and team.

Cost: Depends on how far along, how much plan development is already accomplished. Rarely less than $500, seldom more than $2,000. This might be proposed as a packaged price or at an hourly rate.

Pros: Cost-effective way to combine forces, optimize consultant's expertise and experience in relatively little time and with little expense.

Cons: Temptation to conclude a review with a pitch for more consulting.

Business Plan Revision

Starting point: A finished plan draft.

Deliverables: A revised, polished, completed plan.

Cost: Rarely less than $1,000 or more than $5,000. Depends on how much substance was added. This might be proposed as a packaged price or at an hourly rate.

Pros: Lever your own plan development with consultant's expertise and experience, saving the expense of starting from zero.

Cons: Expense; plan ends up as consultant's plan, not the owner's.

Complete Business Plan

Starting point: Ideas, management team, and raw financial data.

Deliverables: A completed plan, including financial projections, market analysis, sales forecast.

Cost: Rarely less than $2,500 or more than $10,000, depending on how much research and development is required. This might be proposed as a package price or at an hourly rate.

Pros: Turnkey service; business person can focus on business while an expert develops the plan.

Cons: Expense; plan ends up as consultant's plan, not the owner's.

Business Plan and Financial Implementation

Starting point: Ideas, management team, raw financial data.

Deliverables: The plan *and* the money. Consultant takes plan to investors and lands financing.

Cost: Rarely less than $10,000 or more than $25,000. This might be proposed as a packaged price or at an hourly rate.

Pros: This is what most entrepreneurs really want—the complete service. They don't want the plan; they want the results of the plan.

Cons: Disappointment is rampant. When the consultant can't deliver the money because the business doesn't merit financing, both sides have problems. Consultants may have promised more than they should have. The client's money may have been spent without results.

DEVELOP APPROPRIATE STRATEGY

Strategy is focus. Concentrate your resources on the areas of the business that make the most sense. Some target markets and some kinds of services fit your business better than others. As an accounting practice, you don't want to even try to be all things to all people.

Think of this as something like the artist squinting, trying to see just the highlights of the view. Consider your keys to success in the business planning business, the markets around you, and your customer's needs. Consider your strengths and weaknesses and how you might play toward your strengths and away from weaknesses.

CREATE THE TACTICS TO IMPLEMENT STRATEGY

Strategy is worthless without implementation. As soon as you develop your marketing strategy for the business planning portion of your business, think about tactics to make that happen.

As a professional service business, your tactics are likely to fall into some standard areas that develop your expertise and credibility while generating new leads. These include traditional service market tactics such as publications, speaking engagements, and seminars. You should also look into the development of your database and the optimal use of the power of the Internet.

Traditional Service Marketing

As you develop a marketing plan for business services, there is no need to move beyond the normal boundaries of professional service marketing. If you are not comfortable with marketing as a function of an accounting practice, then call it business development or even client development. At least at the beginning, you can normally make huge gains in this area by focusing on some of the most basic and traditional kinds of marketing programs for professionals. There are some classic ways to put your name into the world in the right context, as an expert in business planning. These include publications, speaking engagements, and seminars.

Publications

One of the three most traditional tactics for client development is appearing in print as an expert. You get two benefits at once: your name in front of potential clients and increased credibility as an expert.

For example, during the years I depended on business planning consulting, I wrote a monthly column about the software business in a software magazine. At the end of each column, a brief author's biography described me as an expert in business planning and included contact information. The column covered planning and strategy, and it generated leads. I also wrote reviews of accounting software in several computer magazines, and those reviews included author information at the bottom.

Ideally, you want the publication to appear where your target market groups can see it. One of the best placements by far, and frequently one of the easiest to achieve, is your local newspaper. Could you, or perhaps you and your partners, develop a once-a-month 600-word column on local business? How about a how-to article on the essentials of a business plan?

Once you have the idea, call the business editor and suggest the story. Most local newspapers are receptive to this kind of proposal. They want local coverage and they want more business coverage; and business coverage by a local professional is usually a good thing. The smaller the newspaper and the smaller the town, the more likely it will want to publish your column. The larger papers will be less likely. Of course, they can reject the story after it is submitted, so they have little to lose.

Assuming that your target market is local, then local business publications are also ideal. Do you have a *Business Journal* in a city near you? There are more than 40 such business newspapers, dailies or weeklies, focusing on business in their specific urban areas. They have even more space than the local newspaper. Does your local Chamber of Commerce have a monthly newsletter? How about the Junior Chamber of Commerce, the local economic development board, the Small Business Development Center in your area, the community college, the American Marketing Association, women in business, or local professional organizations? Many of these have publications with pages to fill. Sometimes you can use almost the same article to appear in different publications, with just some fine-tuning.

To find local organizations, I recommend starting with the "Yahoo! Get local" facility. Take your Internet web browser to www.yahoo.com, and look on that main page for a "Get Local" link, which is toward the bottom of the page. Type in your zip code and click the button. Figure 2–3 shows what the "Get Local" page looks like for Eugene, Oregon. These links will take you to local publications and local organizations.

If you've chosen to focus on a specific vertical market, then you'll be able to seek publication in industry-specific magazines and newspapers. These are usually ideal publica-

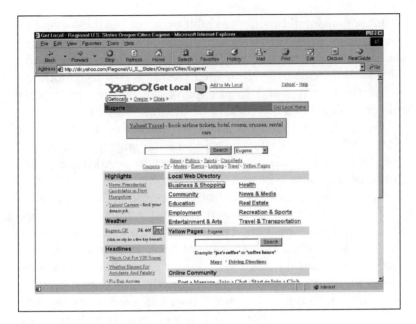

Figure 2–3. Yahoo! Get Local.

tions for client development, because their audience is your target market. Also, they can be easier to convince than a large local newspaper, particularly if you offer an article about business planning focused exactly on their target reader.

Speaking Engagements

The speaking engagement is another opportunity to appear as an expert in front of potential clients. The marketing works very much like publications, in that you choose your target market and look for opportunities to reach that group.

Your search for local organizations should turn up some speaking possibilities. The Chamber of Commerce, Small Business Development Center, and similar organizations have regular meetings, program committees, and business development goals. Local universities and community colleges try to serve the needs of business development and entrepreneurs. Offering a talk on real-world business planning is a good first step.

Is there a small business exhibit or small business event in your urban area? Local banks, chambers of commerce, and business publications may sponsor small-business trade shows and exhibits in your area. Vendors pay for booths to show their wares, and local experts can become presenters of scheduled talks or workshops during show hours.

Doug Wilson, Vice President of Marketing at Palo Alto Software, Inc., suggests preparing a letter stating your expertise in business planning and interest in speaking on that topic or appearing in panel discussions. Send the letter to your local organizations that might sponsor relevant events.

Radio talk shows need experts, and a guest appearance there offers you the same benefits as an appearance in print. Your name reaches many people at once, and your credibility goes up. Our local news radio station has an "ask an expert" series on rotating topics, including gardening, computers, investment, auto repair, and small business. One of my favorite shows, the "Small Business Advocate," is a three-hour daily small business show broadcast in dozens of local markets and over the Internet (www.smallbusinessadvocate.com).

If you've focused on a specific vertical market, then you have industry trade shows as speaking opportunities. Whether it's butchers, bakers, or candle manufacturers, they probably have one or two dates per year when they get together at a convention, association meeting, or similar event. They often need to fill those programs with expert workshops.

Seminars

Seminars are make-your-own speaker opportunities. The big advantage is that you can do it yourself, and the biggest disadvantage is that if you do it yourself then you have to market the seminar to draw participants.

Accounting practices frequently sponsor business seminars. Rent a meeting room in a local hotel, put advertisements in local media, and you have a seminar. To promote your business planning business, offer topics related to starting a business, finding investors, landing a business loan, or optimizing management with tracking and following up.

Sometimes you get the best of both worlds with this type of alliance. Join forces with a seminar sponsor who markets the seminar while you provide the delivery and expertise. Your sponsor might be a local business organization, a seminar marketing organization, a trade publication, a local business publication, even a Small Business Development Center, business school, or community college. If your marketing goals are awareness and leads generation, not revenue, then you can let the sponsor take all or most of the revenue and still achieve your objective.

The seminar business is a business in itself. Don't take it on lightly. A quick book search on the web in amazon.com (www.amazon.com) for the term *seminar marketing* turns up half a dozen solid books on how to develop and market a seminar business. If you are going to develop seminar programs, I recommend that you work with somebody (partner, employee, or allied organization) who has experience in this field.

The Marketing Machine

I first heard the term *marketing machine* in a seminar with Bruce Stuart, of Channelcorp (www.channelcorp.com), a Vancouver, British Columbia expert in channel development. Stuart's planning and consulting business is a good example of a focused vertical market, concentrated mainly on expertise related to channel development for computer companies.

The Database as an Asset

Stuart's concept of the marketing machine is essentially careful management of a database of clients and client prospects. Your database should include:

1. Present clients, with information about the people, the business, the nature of the work done, and the nature of the relationship.

2. Reference clients, which are a subset of the present clients who are willing to provide references to prospects.

3. Leads and prospects, who are people who call, write, or e-mail you about your services. The list should include as much information as possible about people who have attended your panel discussions, speeches, or seminars.

Contacting the Contacts

The marketing machine should generate a regular flow of contacts with prospective new clients and existing clients as well. Make your contacts professional and keep them useful to the people who receive them: a print or e-mail newsletter with useful information, a seminar or training schedule, or publication reprints. Do not contact a prospect unless you have something to say.

One objective is awareness. You send useful information to clients and prospects as reminders of your existence, your expertise, and your willingness to offer your services to help their business.

The underlying objective is turning prospects into clients. Contacts and reminders serve that purpose.

Website Marketing

The Internet, the world-wide web, adds a powerful new dimension to the marketing of business planning services. Now you can extend your client development way beyond your geographic area into a new world not as bound by physical presence. For example:

- Take your web browser to www.planconsultants.com, and explore that database of business planning consultants. Figure 2–4 shows an opening view of that website, and Figure 2–5 shows a typical consultant's search. Figure 2–6 shows one of the CPAs included in the database.

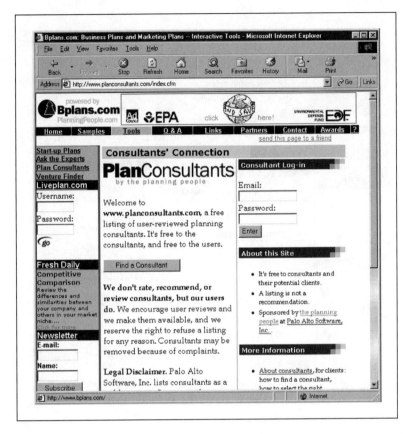

Figure 2–4. PlanConsultants Internet database.

- Your own website becomes one of your marketing tools. At the very least, it serves as sales literature, a powerful collateral that increases credibility. Figure 2–7 shows the corporate site of Jones & Roth, a regional CPA firm based in the Pacific Northwest (www.jrcpa.com). The website is part of that firm's marketing mix. Clients expect to find a website with partners' backgrounds, service offering, and additional information.

- Some business planning businesses have adapted to the web as their principal marketing tool. For example, visit www.bizplanit.com, a planning consulting business that markets its services via the Internet.

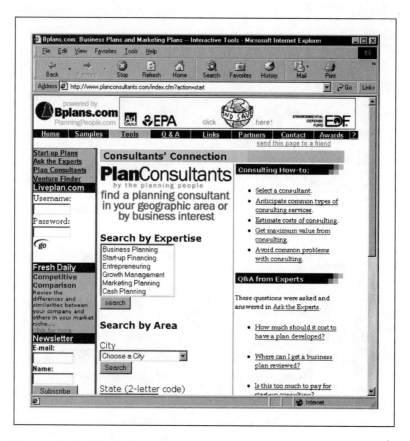

Figure 2–5. Finding a consultant.

BUILD PROGRAMS TO MAKE IT HAPPEN

Now that you have the strategy and tactics ready, develop realistic specific marketing activities. For each activity, assign a person responsible, start dates, and ending dates, all of which we call milestones. Start immediately to track implementation with plan vs. actual analysis.

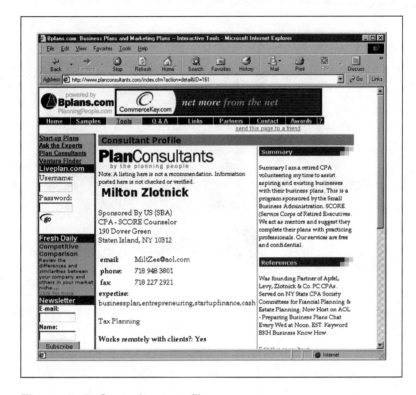

Figure 2–6. Consultant profile.

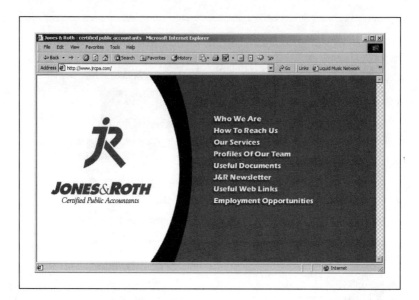

Figure 2–7. CPA website.

CHAPTER 3
THE ENGAGEMENT

A REAL EXAMPLE

My real example isn't a perfect example because it involves three parties: myself, my client company, and an entrepreneurial company in which the client company wanted to invest. In your practice you'll presumably have two-way consulting between you and your client. Still, this is a good example because it illustrates the underlying economics.

The engagement started on a Friday with a phone call from the client company's General Manager for the Pacific region, who we'll call GM.

"Tim," says GM, "I need you to do a business plan fast. Like in a week. It's for a couple of entrepreneurs who have word processing software in Japanese. We want to loan them money to get their software packaged and shipped, but we can't do that without a business plan."

"Not a problem," I answered. "Just send them to a store to buy Business Plan Pro." As this conversation took place I had almost stopped doing specific business plan consulting. My product business had taken off.

"No," he answered, "I need you to help them, because I really need a plan done, and these two are just not going to do it. They're totally lost in real business topics, focused on the quality of their software. I really need you to take it on for them."

We agreed on a $5,000 billing amount and a meeting on Monday. At the Monday meeting I gave a copy of the software to the two entrepreneurs, while the general manager watched. I explained the text elements, market analysis, and a sales forecast and set up one-hour meetings for Tuesday, Thursday, and Friday, plus a presentation meeting for the following Monday.

By the next day, at the Tuesday meeting, the entrepreneurs had already completed a sales forecast and most of the market analysis. They also had made substantial progress on their plan text. We went through the mechanics of the personnel plan and completing the profit and loss worksheet.

On Thursday they had the text finished and a good working feel for the full profit and loss. The market analysis was done. We explained the cash flow and break-even analysis.

By Friday the plan was done. With profit and loss and cash flow worked out, the balance sheet and business ratios were automatic. The text had been drafted and edited. The entrepreneurs presented the plan to GM that Monday, meeting the original schedule. Less than two weeks later, they called to share the news that the plan had been approved, the check had already cleared, and packages were being assembled. I billed my client, the software went to the market, successfully, and everybody won.

UNDERLYING CLIENT NEEDS

Even though this was a three-way business engagement, it illustrates the values underlying the normal two-way engagement between accountant and client. As a consultant I was able to reassure the entrepreneurs about the mechanics of the numbers and their ability to forecast. I provided them with a framework and guidance, a software environment with step-by-step help, and the reassurance that their plan made sense. The client, who paid for my time, got the benefit he wanted, which was a professional-looking plan created quickly. The entrepreneurs got the investment money they needed. And I was paid for my services.

Success in this business model lies in the understanding of the client's real needs. People in business understand that they need professional-looking business plans to communicate with banks, investors, partners, buyers, and team members. They may well need to develop a plan themselves, rather than have it developed, because ownership is critical to implementation. In this case they may also need reassurance from a professional that their plan is complete and acceptable. They may need guidance about what to include, where to find information, and how to present it. They need to reduce the fear of losing face, or looking insufficient, and their anxiety over the reaction to a plan when it is presented.

As a professional accountant, you are in a position to satisfy many of these underlying needs of clients, even if you don't develop and deliver a complete business plan. As in my example, you can help a client prepare a business plan, keeping it as the client's plan and not yours, while still providing the guidance, reassurance, and security the client wants as he or she turns that plan over to its eventual evaluator.

FACILITATING THE PROCESS

The extent of your role depends on your relationship with the client. In some cases, you may recommend software and nothing else. Usually you'll be asked to read and review a plan, probably more than once during the development process and at least once before it goes to a bank. Ideally, you'll be able to work with the client to facilitate the whole process, improving the results by guiding the steps. The AICPA literature on the subject, which is available for download at www.aicpa.org/members/tools/brochure/bussplan.htm, recommends facilitation as well.

If you do offer facilitation, work to build in the concrete hooks and specifics that will make the resulting plan more useful. There are ways to develop commitment and involvement in a plan, which enhance the chance of implementation.

Software Specifics

Facilitation eventually leads to texts in a business plan. Figure 3–1 illustrates the text treatment in Business Plan Pro. The plan includes more than four dozen business topics, organized into a logical outline. There are instructions and examples for each topic. In the illustration, the user has "instructions" checked in the button above the upper window, so it displays instructions. If you move your mouse and check the button labeled "example" in-

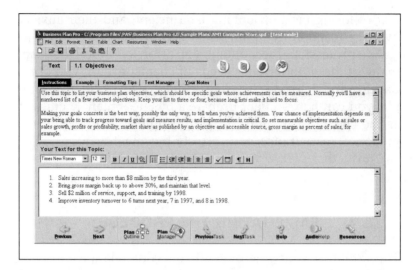

Figure 3–1. The Business Plan Pro screen as the user types text in the lower window and sees instructions in the upper window on the PC monitor.

stead, then that same upper window shows an example from a sample business plan, for the same topic. You type your text, for your own business plan, in the lower window. You can also hide the instructions window entirely, showing only a larger single window for your own text.

Text formatting should be simple. The software has built-in capabilities for bulleted and numbered lists, as well as tools to change fonts, sizes, and styles, but it isn't meant to be a full word processor. This is business planning, not page layout. The underlying editor is actually an HTML editor (the language used for text formatting on websites), because this is becoming the new standard for text. If you know HTML, you can click on the HTML tool and edit your text directly using simple HTML. The HTML tool is the H icon on the far right. Because of the importance of HTML text formatting, you may discover that your business plan formatting will be easier if your default text font is the same one you use in Internet Explorer.

You can customize that standard outline, adding or deleting topics as needed. Figure 3–2 shows how a dialog in the software selects outline topics and how it allows topics to be added or deleted to customize the outline. Please be careful, though, because when you delete an outline topic you also delete all the subtopics underneath it.

In steps 2 and 3 of the process below, you would probably use the Business Plan Pro milestones table, which is shown here as Figure 3–3 on page 34. The milestones table is a powerful list of specific business activities, called *programs*, each of which is assigned to a specific person, given a budget, and set for specific dates. The software is automatically set to record plan vs. actual results later on, during plan implementation.

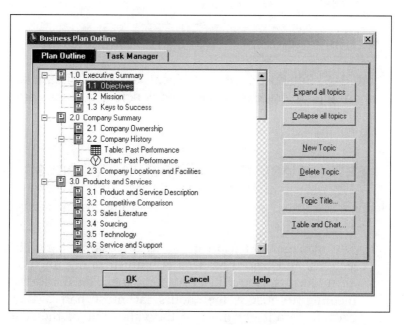

Figure 3–2. The Business Plan Pro screen as the user selects a topic from the suggested business plan outline. Note the buttons that allow adding and deleting topics.

Milestone	Mngr	Date	Dept.	Budget
Corporate Identity	TJ	12/16/97	Marketing	$10,000
Seminar implementation	IR	1/9/98	Sales	$1,000
Business Plan Review	RJ	1/9/98	GM	$0
Upgrade mailer	IR	1/15/98	Sales	$5,000
New corporate brochure	TJ	1/15/98	Marketing	$5,000
Delivery vans	SD	1/24/98	Service	$12,500
Direct mail	IR	2/15/98	Marketing	$3,500
Advertising	RJ	2/15/98	GM	$115,000
X4 Prototype	SG	2/24/98	Product	$2,500
Service revamp	SD	2/24/98	Product	$2,500
6 Presentations	IR	2/24/98	Sales	$0
X4 Testing	SG	3/6/98	Product	$1,000
3 Accounts	SD	3/17/98	Sales	$0
L30 Prototype	PR	3/26/98	Product	$2,500
Tech98 Expo	TB	4/12/98	Marketing	$15,000
VP S&M hired	JK	6/11/98	Sales	$1,000
Mailing system	SD	7/25/98	Service	$5,000
Other				
Totals				**$181,500**

Figure 3–3. Setting Specific Activities. The milestones table is where a plan includes specific and concrete business programs.

MEETINGS AND THE MANAGEMENT PROCESS

Here's a suggested step-by-step process to use with clients:

1. The management team meets to discuss strategy, objectives, and priorities. This is brainstorming. Include all managers who will implement the plan. Hold the meeting to just a few hours, at most half a day, because you'll get most of the value out of the first two hours of discussion. I've seen companies hold each issue to one-half hour. Deal with the critical questions suggested in Chapter 5, "Business Descriptions," such as:

- What are the keys to success in this business? Focus in on three or four key factors.

- Is there a value proposition? What benefits does this business offer, to what kinds of customers, at what relative price point?

- What business are you really in? People in the front-lines in business frequently lose sight of the benefits they actually sell. Railroads are in the business of transportation, not running railroads. More than any-thing else, accountants are in the business of tax man-agement.

- Is there a competitive edge? What is different about this company that sets it apart from the competition?

2. The first meeting produces a rough outline of strategy, priorities, and objectives. Sometimes they are clear at the end of the meeting, but usually they need to be fleshed out just afterwards. The process depends on the specific company, its management style, and ownership. Give the managers a week or two to suggest specific tactics and programs for sales, marketing, finance, and other functions. Each program needs a person responsi-ble, a suggested budget, due dates, and links to strategy and objectives. This is where the Business Plan Pro mile-stones table, shown in Figure 3–3, works very well. You can duplicate that, however, with a spreadsheet program.

3. Hold a second meeting to share the suggested programs. Ask the client to rent a computer projector or LCD screen for overhead display, so all the managers can share the proposals of all others. In years of business planning, I've discovered an interesting pattern: in almost all com-pany settings, the sum of the budgets of all the programs is almost always two or three times what can actually be spent. This is human nature and necessitates that groups and budgets work in companies. It is also ideal for the business planning process, because it sets the scene for managers to collectively discuss programs and budgets. Such a discussion builds commitment. Each manager must defend his or her proposals in front of

all others. An important evaluation of costs and benefits is inevitable. Better still, as they argue for budgets and programs, managers become committed to implementation. After all, if you argue for a program, you want to make it work. You're committed.

REVIEWING THE STRATEGY

After the second meeting is a good time to develop and review strategy. Figure 3–4 shows the strategy pyramid, a relatively simple tool for looking at a business strategy from a practical viewpoint.

I developed the pyramid to solve a common business problem rooted in strategy and implementation. Strategy is too often developed and explained, but not implemented. For example, a computer reseller business wants to focus on developing relationships with small and medium-sized businesses. That strategy means nothing unless accompanied by specific tactics like developing service, support, and training. Those tactics mean nothing without specific programs. Programs for training should include specific schedules and subject matter defined. Programs for service could include supplying white service robes, procuring additional counter space, and perhaps sending out some direct mail about up-

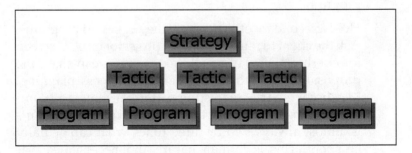

Figure 3–4. The strategy pyramid offers a simple framework for reviewing a business plan. Strategy is useless without tactics, and tactics are useless without programs. Programs are specific business activities, with ownership and budget dates.

grades. Programs for support should include installation and configuration, as well as phone calls to customers two weeks after delivery, making sure things are done correctly.

Don't get lost in definitions. You can debate the definitions of strategy and tactics later, but in the meantime, make the pyramid fit. I make strategy the higher level, the main focus, the important priority. Strategy is focus. Strategy can focus on target market, product line, marketing strategy, channel, or whatever works. Tactics implement strategy, and programs implement tactics, in detail, with specific dates, budgets, and responsibility assignments. I define the terms by making them work with each other in the pyramid.

Describe a strategy simply, in two or three sentences. Then describe the tactics used to implement the strategy. Then set specific programs that make those tactics real. When you're done, review the programs by relating them to tactics and strategies. Does your spending match your strategy? Does it reflect your business priorities? Does it look like the pyramid will be implemented?

A business strategy can involve one or more pyramids. In a sample computer reseller business, for example, there are three main points of strategy: (1) emphasize the company, not the product; (2) focus on the small business and high-end home office; and (3) develop customer relationships. Each main strategy is conceptually a separate pyramid. Each has related tactics and programs.

HELPING YOUR CLIENTS FORECAST

Accountants should be shy about forecasting, because clients tend to give accountants' forecasts too much weight. They misinterpret the level of uncertainty involved. In general, you don't want to forecast because clients can misinterpret the level of certainty when an accountant prepares a forecast. You can, however, help a client prepare his or her own forecast, and you can also help that client overcome the common fear of forecasting. Planning is impossible without forecasting. Furthermore, difficult as it is to forecast, it is even more difficult to plan a business without forecasting.

Software Specifics

Most of the tables in Business Plan Pro involve forecasting. They are programmed to calculate automatically, with proper links between sales forecast, personnel plan, income statement, cash flow, balance sheet, and ratios. Type your inputs into the green cells (or italic, depending on settings) and the black cells will calculate automatically. Black cells are protected because they contain formulas or links. For example, you can't type directly into the "Sales" or "Cost of Sales" lines of the income statement, because both come automatically from the Sales Forecast table. The same is true for personnel lines, which come from the Personnel table.

Many business people are afraid of forecasting. They don't realize that business forecasting is almost always educated guessing. To plan you have to make assumptions. To estimate next year's sales, cost of sales, travel expenses, or other items, you depend on good information and good judgment. Study past results, look for changed assumptions, research where you can, and make an estimate. People are most uncomfortable when they haven't had enough training to understand that it is all right not to know. There are rarely enough data for rigorous data analysis.

Many people view forecasting as guessing. A few days ago I sat with four managers guessing when a competitor would appear with new packaging. I asked each to give me a quick guess, as a number between 0 and 100, for the probability of the new packaging showing up within six months. The first guessed 60 percent, the second 40 percent, and the fourth 65 percent. The third one protested, "But we don't know. How can we possibly know that?" That is a typical reaction, which I call "fear of forecasting."

Unfortunately, such fear of forecasting gets in the way of planning. As you work with your clients to help them plan, you're going to have to deal with it. Here are some suggestions for overcoming fear of forecasting:

1. Understand the Past

The first step is to get a good grasp on recent past results. Your best guess about sales, salaries, and expenses should start with the immediate past. Specifically, look at what you spent last year and the year before, as you decide what you'll spend next year.

This is your reality check. If sales were $1.8 million last year, and $1.6 the year before, and nothing special is happening, they aren't going to jump to $4 million. You would have to suspect forecasts of much more than $2 million or of less than $1.7 million. If the company spent $12,800 on insurance in the most recent year, then $15,000 might be reasonable, $13,000 could be, but $8,000 isn't, and $20,000 probably isn't.

Don't expect much from statistical analysis, however. Although complex techniques exist that make projections on the basis of past data, they are rarely practical for business planning. Except for a rare sales forecast related to time series, smoothing, or regression analysis, these techniques based on past data are probably overkill. The past does predict the future in business, but mainly as a simple reality check, not at the level of sophistication found in technical data analysis.

2. Keep it Simple

The forecasting contained in a business plan is relatively simple. Advanced mathematics is not required. In your personnel plan, you guess salaries. In your profit and loss table, you estimate expenses. In your sales forecast, you estimate sales and cost of sales. You really don't need statistical analysis or econometrics—you need to take a good educated guess.

Figure 3–5 shows the first four months of a sample business plan spreadsheet, forecasting personnel expenses. For each row, guess what the salary amount will be. Every business owner should be able to estimate these amounts. Consult the present salary levels, consider the need for new personnel, and then make some educated guesses. Let the software calculate the totals.

Sales/Marketing Salaries	Jan-98	Feb-98	Mar-98	Apr-98
Manager	$6,000	$6,000	$6,000	$6,000
Technical sales	$5,000	$5,000	$5,000	$5,000
Technical sales	$3,500	$3,500	$3,500	$3,500
Salesperson	$2,500	$2,500	$2,500	$2,500
Salesperson	$2,500	$2,500	$2,500	$2,500
Salesperson	$2,500	$2,500	$2,500	$2,500
Salesperson	$2,000	$2,000	$2,000	$2,000
Other	$0	$0	$0	$0
Subtotal	**$24,000**	**$24,000**	**$24,000**	**$24,000**

Figure 3–5. A simple forecast that projects salaries by line per month, then adds up the totals.

When broken down like this, even a sufferer of "Fear of Forecasting" can do it.

3. Divide and Conquer

Figure 3–6 illustrates the divide and conquer rule, a variation on breaking things down into parts. Instead of simply forecasting sales by product line, the plan forecasts units sold and price per unit. The computer automatically calculates the resulting sales by multiplying units times price. Dividing things into parts usually makes it easier for the fear-of-forecasting business owner, because it focuses on the simplest form of the number.

In the illustration, which is taken from the first four months of a Business Plan Pro sample plan, the first section contains unit sales estimates. The second section contains revenue per units. The third section automatically calculates the product of units times price.

4. Use Simple Growth Formulas

Growth rates are not always quoted the same. For a single year, I use the simple calculation:

1-year growth rate = (next year/last year) − 1

Unit Sales		Jan-98	Feb-98	Mar-98	Apr-98
Executive desk oak	15.00%	40	55	60	60
Executive desk cherry	5.00%	20	30	33	30
Other furniture oak	5.00%	26	35	40	35
Other furniture cherry	5.00%	6	11	13	12
Other	20.00%	4	5	6	6
Total Unit Sales		**96**	**136**	**152**	**143**
Unit Prices					
Executive desk oak		$1,600	$1,600	$1,600	$1,600
Executive desk cherry		$1,750	$1,750	$1,750	$1,750
Other furniture oak		$900	$900	$900	$900
Other furniture cherry		$1,000	$1,000	$1,000	$1,000
Other		$2,500	$2,500	$2,500	$2,500
Total Sales					
Executive desk oak		$64,000	$88,000	$96,000	$96,000
Executive desk cherry		$35,000	$52,500	$57,750	$52,500
Other furniture oak		$23,400	$31,500	$36,000	$31,500
Other furniture cherry		$6,000	$11,000	$13,000	$12,000
Other		$10,000	$12,500	$15,000	$15,000
Total Sales		**$138,400**	**$195,500**	**$217,750**	**$207,000**
Direct Unit costs					
Executive desk oak	25.00%	$400	$400	$400	$400
Executive desk cherry	30.00%	$525	$525	$525	$525
Other furniture oak	20.00%	$180	$180	$180	$180
Other furniture cherry	30.00%	$300	$300	$300	$300
Other	25.00%	$625	$625	$625	$625
Total direct cost of Sales					
Executive desk oak		$16,000	$22,000	$24,000	$24,000
Executive desk cherry		$10,500	$15,750	$17,325	$15,750
Other furniture oak		$4,680	$6,300	$7,200	$6,300
Other furniture cherry		$1,800	$3,300	$3,900	$3,600
Other		$2,500	$3,125	$3,750	$3,750
Subtotal Direct Costs		**$35,480**	**$50,475**	**$56,175**	**$53,400**

Figure 3–6. Even this more complex sales forecast is easy to understand. We project units and revenue per unit to get sales and project cost per unit to get costs.

For example, growth from 75 to 100 is $(100/75) - 1$, which is 33.33 percent growth. Growth from 100 to 200 is $(200/100) - 1$, which is 100 percent growth.

To generate an average growth rate over several periods, use the standard formula for compound annual growth (CAGR) over a number (N) of years:

$$CAGR = (\text{last year}/\text{first year})^{(1/N)} - 1$$

For example, if unit sales were 115,000 in 1998, and are projected to grow to 128,323 in 2002, that is four periods of growth. The average annual growth is 27.8 percent, as calculated below:

$$CAGR = (128,323/115,000)^{(1/4)} - 1 = .0278$$

As another example, the growth in sales for the sample CPA plan, from $610,000 in the last full year to $915 million in the third year of the plan, is 14.47 percent. The actual formula is:

$$(915/610)^{(1/3)} - 1 = 0.1447$$

In this case, the *N* variable for the number of years is three, for three years of growth, although the sales are for 1997, 1998, 1999, and 2000. The forecast covers three years of growth.

These formulas are discussed in more detail in Chapter 8, "The Pro-Forma Financial Statements."

5. Use Business Charts

Many people understand numbers better when they're presented as charts rather than as numbers in financial tables. Figure 3–7 shows a simple Business Plan Pro chart illustrating

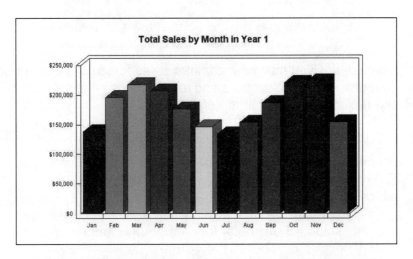

Figure 3–7. A simple Business Plan Pro chart showing a sample plan sales forecast by month.

a sample plan sales forecast by month. Just about anyone can look at that chart and understand the ups and downs of a business, as sales drop during the summer and go up again during the fall. In many cases, the chart helps people feel more comfortable with the numbers.

BUSINESS PLAN RESEARCH

There is a big difference between a blatant guess and an educated guess. The emphasis in business planning is on educated guessing. Planning demands realism. The difficulty of data analysis and simplicity of educated guessing is not intended as an excuse for simply guessing, glibly, without researching the background.

Software Specifics

Business Plan Pro includes 891 industry profiles for types of business as defined by the Standard Industry Classification (SIC) code. You can access these using the 891 Industry Profiles command in the Resource menu. It will give you a system to select the type of industry and will then automatically put standard data into the business ratios area. Figure 3–8 shows this form, from within the software, displaying data for a hotel business.

The industry data is supplied by Integra Information Systems, whose website is at www.privateco.com.

The Internet

It is interesting how much the business of gathering information has changed in the past 30 years. In the 1970s the problem was getting information. Raw data was valuable and often hard to come by. Since the 1990s, information is everywhere in overabundance, and the problem is sorting through it all. It is as if information were a metal that was precious 30 years

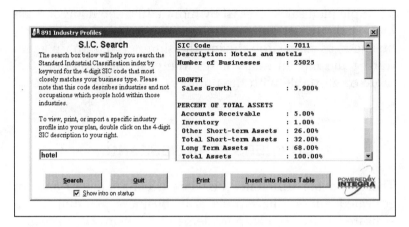

Figure 3–8: Standard Industry Profiles in Business Plan Pro.

ago and is now so oversupplied that we pay to sift through it all.

Earlier books about information gathering included advice about how to find forecasts from trade associations, trade magazines, market research companies, and reference libraries. Today you simply can't get through planning without understanding the internet and the world-wide web. There is so much to gain from this overwhelming new way to manage information that you simply can't afford to be without it. A large number of books have been published on this topic, magazines are dedicated to it, and consulting businesses have grown up around it. My strong recommendation is: If you're in the business of business planning, get on the Net.

The world-wide web is a wealth of information unlike anything a nonuser can imagine. Millions of different pages, all linked together, can be accessed from your computer. Special links, accessed by a click of the mouse, take you from one page to another. Some sites require payment and passwords, and others are free.

Without attempting to broach a subject that has generated an industry of experts and consultants, I can at least offer you some specific examples. Figure 3–9 shows the home page at Yahoo, an enormous catalog of sites by subject matter and content. The address is www.yahoo.com. Yahoo is one of the best on-line searchers, certainly the best known, but there are

Figure 3–9. The front page of the www.yahoo.com Internet site, which lists thousands of other sites according to useful categories.

many others. When you search for sites that include the words "Business Plan," for example, a good searcher will yield hundreds of different sites. Figure 3–10 shows the results of a search I was doing for additional information on demographic segmentation, which I needed for a chapter in this book. The shopping center whose site is shown in the illustration turned up as part of the search, because it offers "demographic" information. If I were doing a business plan for a retail store in that shopping center, this information would be quite valuable.

Figure 3–11 shows the Internet home page of the U.S. Census Bureau, at www.census.gov. If you were accessing that page on the Net, you would move the mouse over the different selections offered, then click to move to the related pages. The Census Bureau publishes a variety of statistical and demographic studies. It is also the main source of local demograph-

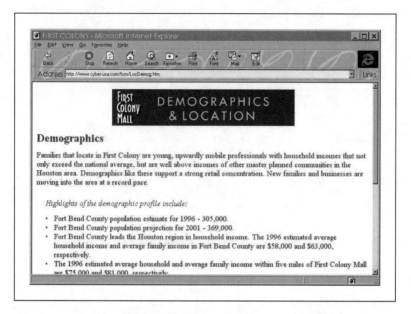

Figure 3–10. Sample Research Page. A random sample of information available through browsing.

ics that would be valuable for studying a retail site or service location.

The next three illustrations show home pages of companies offering commercial information services. Figure 3–12 shows the home page of the Lexis-Nexis on-line database service. Lexis-Nexis is one of the best known providers of on-line business information, generally for a hefty price. Figure 3–13 shows Knight-Ridder Information Service, and Figure 3–14 shows Integra Information Systems. These are all market research and business research firms; they have all offered such services for years, but now they offer them on the Internet.

Other Good Sources of Information

Although the Internet is by far the most useful, there are other sources of information available. Ideally, you will find market data published in trade magazines, trade association yearbooks, academic studies, or market research libraries. Many

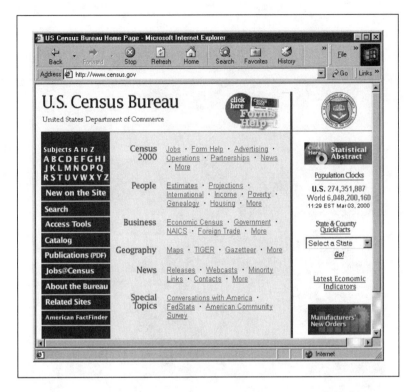

Figure 3–11. The main entrance page to the U.S. Census Bureau, at www.census.gov. The census offers a range of information and publications on U.S. statistics and demographics.

companies also conduct their own market research, in customer surveys, to find out more about customers and potential customers to corroborate market size, growth rates, and value. A company might use published research studies and market research consultants to establish market growth in various segments. It might even contract primary market research at times, when the information sought is particularly important.

Unfortunately, these days it is difficult to write about the old fashioned ways of gathering information. You won't use them. To survive in the business of business planning, you'll be working off the world-wide web. You won't purchase information that you can't buy off the web, and most of your information will be free. Your biggest problem will be not

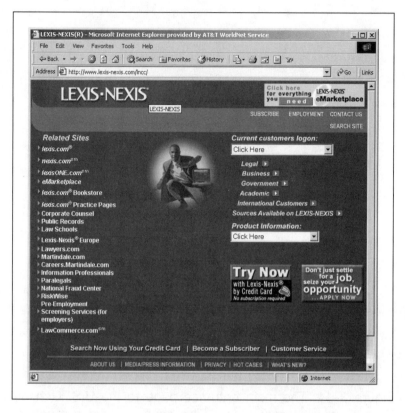

Figure 3–12. The Lexis-Nexis website is the front page for a major information provider.

where to find information, but how to sort through and digest the great amount of information you can find.

IMPLEMENTING THE PLAN

Once upon a time there were three small businesses, each of which set out to develop its business plan and use the plan to seek its fortune. The first entrepreneur built a plan of straw—wildly optimistic projections and canned text. The second entrepreneur built a plan of sticks, using standard templates for word processors and spreadsheet software, plus some books and loose-leaf binders, all of them working

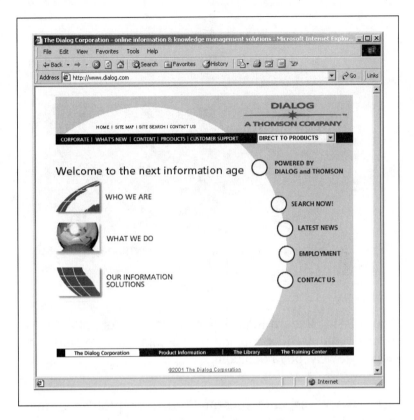

Figure 3–13. The Dialog Corporation offers a variety of information databases through its main website at www.dialog.com.

around unrealistic projections and vague objectives. The third entrepreneur built a plan of bricks. Bricks were action points, specific activities, or events. They were also specific responsibility assignments, deadline dates, and budgets. Bricks were concrete, measurable objectives. Each specific point in the plan that could be tracked and followed up, whose results could be measured, whose responsibility was assigned, each of those was a brick.

After the plans were published, the real world appeared, as threatening as the big bad wolf of the children's story. The real world blows business plans apart. The real world is full of fires to put out, phone calls to answer, and deadlines to

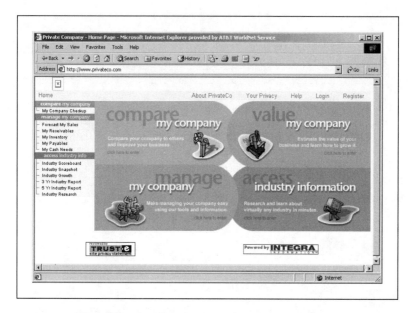

Figure 3–14. Integra Information Systems offers standard financial data by SIC code, industry profiles, and related information at www.privateco.com.

meet, as well as sales presentations, cash problems, unexpected changes, and crushing routine. People get excited, forget priorities, chase after new ideas, and forget to follow through with the plan.

The real world will blow apart that plan of straw without any hesitation. It will do the same for the plan of sticks. Bricks are our best hope for making a viable business plan. We need a backbone of measurable goals and specific activities, so we know whether we are implementing or not. We have to track results, analyze the difference between plan and action, and follow up with corrections and changes. The bricks—the specifics of the plan—give us something we can stand on when we get back into the fight for implementation.

Although much of the plan of bricks comes later, as you implement a plan, you need to begin with the quality of information you build into your personnel plan, sales forecast, profit and loss, and cash flow plan. Are your assumptions realistic? Can you track them and measure them later?

The Real Value of a Plan Is Its Implementation

A business plan should improve your business. Its value to your business, ultimately, is measured in the decisions it helps you make. It is about the real actions it creates (business activities) more than knowledge, insight, or strategy. This measure of value carries with it some important implications:

1. The business plan in the drawer—the one that is not implemented, perhaps is not even read, and certainly is not followed—is a complete waste of time and money.

2. If a business plan serves only to secure a loan for a business, then that is its full value. If the loan was good for the business, then so was the plan; but the plan in such a case is also no more than a long-winded loan application.

3. If this book and the planning process it recommends are to do you any good, you must progress all the way through the cycle from planning to implementation.

A good business plan should be focused on creating the tools and processes that lead to implementation. We'll talk about that—the bricks of business planning, the foundations of implementation—at length in this book. By bricks I mean concrete, measurable goals, specific responsibility assignments, specific dates, budgets, plan-vs.-actual analysis, and other elements that can be tracked and followed up later. The bricks of a plan are what lead to implementation later on. That's what makes a plan worth it.

Implementation Depends on the Whole Cycle

Figure 3–15 illustrates the complete cycle of business planning, and what makes a good plan. It starts with the qualities of the plan itself. Of course, it should be complete, concise, well written, properly formatted, and so forth. More important, however, are the plan qualities that lead to implementation:

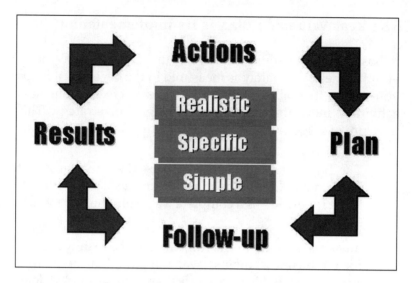

Figure 3–15. The *complete* planning process starts with a good plan and depends on follow up and tracking results.

- A plan should be *realistic*. If projections, objectives, responsibility assignments, and other elements are not realistic, they are useless. The people charged with implementing a plan won't do it. They know when it is not realistic.

- A plan should be *specific*. Objectives should be set in measurable terms, such as percentage sales increase, percent of gross margin, number of sales presentations, average inventory balance, or percent of sales on credit. Actions and objectives should be assigned to specific people who take responsibility for them. Dates of completion should be assigned.

- A plan should be *simple*. Limit the plan to three or four priorities, not ten or twenty. Summarize your financial projections so they are understandable. Focus on key elements. Sales forecasts and expense budgets should be understandable to all. Responsibility assignments must be clear and understandable. Because planning is about implementation, it is also about working with people and communicating ideas. The focus on priorities should emphasize a few major elements. The focus should be easy to understand and communicate to the people involved in implementing the plan. Three or four priorities are better than six or seven; ten is way too many. Financial projections should be easy to read and understand. Summarize where possible. A business plan is not a doctoral thesis.

The Cycle Depends on People More than Plans

The original plan is only the beginning of the process. A plan should make things happen. Business managers create business programs, sales and marketing activities, administrative improvements, productivity, and results. A good plan, well implemented, produces business results every day, every week, and every month. In the full cycle, those results are monitored and measured. You compare actual results to the original plan, watch for changes, make adjustments, revise the plan, and continue to improve management. The full cycle makes the business better. The plan is at best a tool, but its value depends on the management it causes.

In the next chapters we will talk about the specific elements of a business plan.

CHAPTER 4
OUTLINES AND ANALYSES

A business plan is hardly a new invention. Dozens of books are available, as well as three or four decent software packages and a dozen bad ones, sample plans, in-house masters, and plans taught in business schools and night schools in thousands of different institutions. Most of these sources offer similar basic views of what a plan is and what it should contain.

Software Specifics

In Chapter 3, with Figures 3–1 and 3–2, we looked at the Business Plan Pro standard outline. Remember, you can change this outline as needed to make sure the business plan you write covers the right topics—no more and no less. You can also print selected topics, with or without the associated tables and charts, for selected drafts and outputs. For example, a plan going to a bank to support a loan application might have just a selected collection of summary topics. Also, through the same dialog shown in Figure 3–2, you can choose to associate specific tables and charts with specific topics. Some associations are set by default, but you can change them.

A STANDARD PLAN OUTLINE

Chapter 1: Executive Summary

The classic beginning to a business plan contains objectives, mission statement, and other general statements. This is a good place to put a chart showing projected growth in sales and profits.

Chapter 2: Company Description

Chapter 2 describes the legal entity, its ownership, its history, and its basic business model. This is a good place to put a table showing either past financials or start-up costs, depending on whether the plan is for an existing business or a start-up business. Bar charts showing these numbers are also appropriate.

Chapter 3: Products or Services (or Both)

Chapter 3 includes a detailed description of whatever the company sells. It might include catalogs and price lists, descriptions, features and benefits, competitive comparison, bills of materials, sources and vendors, and other related information.

Chapter 4: Market Analysis

The market analysis focuses on real information for business decision making. It should not be too theoretical. It shows how many potential customers the business might have, where to find them, why they buy, how much they spend, and what they like. This is an excellent place to put a spreadsheet showing market analysis, with accompanying charts. It should also include an industry analysis, covering competitors, competitive factors, and industry economics.

Chapter 5: Strategic Plan

Rather than just describing a strategy, Chapter 5 turns the strategy into specific tactics and business activities, with dates listed and responsibilities assigned. This is also the best place for a detailed sales forecast, with related charts. It should always include a well-detailed list of specific action points, with names of people in charge, deadline dates, and budgets.

Chapter 6: Management Team

Chapter 6 includes management strategy, an organizational chart, and lists of key management team members, with biographical description and functions. This is a good place to offer a detailed table of personnel costs.

Chapter 7: Financial Plan

As a CPA, you know the financial plan portion quite well. You may refer to the term *pro forma*, the fancier way to refer to forecasts or projections. The financial plan includes all the essential pro forma financial projections, aside from those shown in other chapters. They should include at least a good projection of profit and loss, cash flow, balance, and ratios. Usually they also include tables for general assumptions and break-even analysis.

STANDARD TABLES AND NUMERICAL ANALYSIS

Expert opinions may vary, but in general, a business plan ought to have some standard analyses, regardless of specifics. We'll be looking at each of these in detail later on in this book, but let's discuss here what probably ought to be included in a business plan.

- *Cash flow.* This is the most important. Businesses run on cash. No business plan is complete without a cash flow plan.

- *Profit and loss,* incorporating sales, cost of sales, operating expenses, and profits. This, of course, is also a pro forma income statement. In most cases it should show sales less cost of sales as gross margin, and gross margin less operating expenses as profit before interest and taxes (also called gross profit and contribution to overhead). Normally there is also a projection of interest, taxes, and net profits.

- *Pro forma balance sheet.* Aside from cash and income, there is the balance of assets, liabilities, and capital.

- *Sales forecast.* The form may vary to suit the business, but it is difficult to imagine a plan without a sales forecast. Some plans forecast in excruciating detail, some summarize, but the forecast should be there. In the simplest of plans, the sales forecast might be a single line in the pro forma income statement.

- *Personnel plan.* Personnel costs are so intimately related to fixed costs that they should often be set aside and discussed. In some simple plans, they, too, like the sales forecast, can be just a line or two in the income statement.

- *Business ratios.* The numbers are there, when there is pro forma income, cash, and balance sheet, so the ratios can be calculated. This isn't as necessary for an internal plan as for one prepared for bankers and investors, but some key ratios are almost always a good idea. They should probably include some profitability ratios like gross margin, return on sales, return on assets, and return on investment, plus some liquidity ratios such as debt to equity, current ratio, and working capital. You already know which ratios you like to use and how to calculate them. A banker will have a similar view.

- *Break-even analysis.* You'll recognize the break-even as a classic financial analysis that determines the sales required to cover fixed costs. This one is included in a standard business plan more because it is expected than because it really provides business insight. While it is a useful exercise for many start-up companies, it doesn't always offer much insight to an ongoing company.

    The underlying analysis is simple. Calculate the unit's break-even point by dividing the fixed costs by the difference between unit price and unit variable cost (BE = fixed cost/(price − variable cost)). The sales break-even point is calculated by dividing fixed costs by one less variable cost divided by unit price (BE = fixed cost/(1 − (variable cost/unit price))). The break-even can be monthly or annual, but monthly is more common.

Many of the break-even analyses included with business plans have little real value because the underlying assumptions are so difficult to determine. Most businesses sell multiple lines of products or services, but the break-even requires a single unit price estimate and single variable costs estimate for the entire business. How many small businesses do you know that can estimate these inputs in any useful way?

Furthermore, the concept of fixed costs is questionable. Most business classes define fixed costs as costs that would be incurred even if the business failed, such as rent related to a term lease contract. It is more useful to use the running expenses instead of fixed costs, doing a modified break-even that shows what sales are required to support the standard running expense rate of the business. This produces a more useful analysis, but of course it also has the disadvantage of being a modified analysis that doesn't mean exactly what the experts think it does. Experts are sometimes slow to accept revisions of standard tools.

Finally, a third disadvantage of the break-even is that people frequently confuse the break-even analysis with an investment payback analysis. The latter records how long it takes for an investment to pay back its investor, which people sometimes think of as reaching a "break-even" point.

The break-even analysis is included in Business Plan Pro because plan readers tend to expect it. You may well advise your client to leave it out.

- *Market forecast.* Aside from the sales forecast, which is essential, a market forecast is also a good idea. How many potential customers are there? How does market growth stand to impact this business?

Software Specifics

Business Plan Pro includes its own spreadsheet software, basically compatible with Excel, to handle the tables shown on the Table menu: General Assumptions, Break-

even Analysis, Market Analysis, Sales Forecast, Personnel Plan, Income Statement, Cash Flow, Balance Sheet,
Business Ratios, either Start-up or Past Performance,
Long Term if options are set for it, and a setting for plan,
actual, or variance. In all of these tables, green cells (or
italics, depending on settings) are for data input, and
black cells are formulas or linked cells that can't be
changed. Your client does not need to program the
spreadsheets; they are already programmed correctly for
the business plan. However, you can add some sophistication with Excel-like formulas if you like. The green cells
can absorb standard spreadsheet formulas.

VARIATIONS: FUNCTIONALITY FIRST

The business plan should match its intended business purpose. Business plans are not all the same. Plans are used to
raise new money, back up loan applications, communicate
ideas, and explain or even just polish strategy. Some plans
are intended to focus resources on priorities, set objectives,
establish logical steps, and ultimately improve the businesses
for which they are written.

The purpose of the plan indicates its intended readership.
For concrete examples, let's take the two cases presented in
this book. The Briarpatch plan is one that is likely to be read
by bankers and possibly even outside investors. Therefore, it
should have a careful description of the company, polished
for viewing by outsiders. The readers of the CPA plan for a
sample accounting practice, on the other hand, are really just
the three partners involved. For that plan, they could have
skipped the company chapter altogether (although in the sample, they don't). The description of the management team will
also vary. Briarpatch needs to provide detailed background
information on its management team, including the owners'
résumés. For your accounting practice plan, you may need
to plan compensation and organizational concepts, but you
need not present résumés and detailed biographical information on every partner.

Always remember: form follows function. If it turns out that your accounting practice is planning to seek a merger with another practice, then you probably do want to describe the company quite carefully and provide detailed background information on the partners.

MORE VARIATIONS:
THE NATURE OF THE BUSINESS

Variations go beyond readership. Some follow the nature of the company. For example:

- The plan for a start-up company is different from a plan for an existing company. A business plan for a new company should include start-up costs such as legal costs, initial office equipment, and stationery and letterhead. It also needs to plan for initial assets at the start-up point and for the start-up investment. These elements determine the starting balance. They should be included in the plan, and the text discussion should explain the assumptions. When a plan is for an existing company, in contrast to a start-up, it should include details on company history and past performance. The starting balance is determined by the finishing balance of the most recent period.

- Some companies need to manage inventory and some don't. Some need to manage accounts receivable, and some—the lucky ones—don't. The business plan needs to accommodate these realities. The pro forma analysis shouldn't deal with inventory or accounts receivable unless the company does.

- The structure of the financial analyses should depend on the nature of the business, too. For example, most companies need to break down and include payroll and operating expenses in management categories, such as production, sales and marketing, general and administrative, and other categories. However, a simple service company or retail store may prefer to list operating expenses and personnel in a simpler form, without dividing them into categories. Some companies need to forecast sales by unit, setting a price and cost per unit, and multiplying unit sales to calculate sales and unit costs for cost of sales; others will prefer to forecast by simple dollar amounts. A business plan should not be a straightjacket for the planners. It must be sensitive to needs and practicality.

- Home office companies that do not have employees should probably have a simpler financial analysis of personnel costs than the more conventional company. While the home office company needs to plan as much as any other company, it does not need to plan for details that don't affect it.

Software Specifics

Business Plan Pro includes a plan wizard that manages many of the options. The plan wizard comes up when you start a new plan and is available at all times to change options. It manages settings for different types of plans and plan options, including the following:

- Is this plan for a start-up company or for an already-existing company (also called an "ongoing" company)? The software uses either a start-up worksheet or a past performance worksheet, but not both. One or the other will establish the starting balances in the balance sheet.

- What type of business is this? The software asks you to choose service, retail, distribution, manufacturing, or "Plan Wizard." The settings change for different types. For example, services and retail companies have simpler income statements, simpler sales forecasts, and simpler personnel plans. Services don't deal with inventory. If you choose the wizard, it asks a series of questions to determine preferences on forecasting detail, expenses by categories, and some other options.

- Does this company have sales on credit? This changes whether or not the plan deals with accounts receivable in the general assumptions, cash flow, and balance sheet.

- Is this a home office company? If so, the software changes the personnel treatment to its simplest mode, without payroll taxes.

- Do you want to input balances directly? You can override automatic estimates of accounts receivable, inventory, and accounts payable. The software has some complex formulas that estimate these balances on the basis of assumptions. Sometimes it is easier or better just to type in your own subjective estimates.

There are other obvious options about lines of sales, plan title, and starting months. The software-specific manual included at the end of this book has more details.

CHAPTER 5
BUSINESS DESCRIPTIONS

The description in a business plan is not there for the sake of description alone. As you work with your own or your client's business plan, make the planning process a time to look at the business strategically. Try to understand the flow from past to present and future. Take the opportunity to consider redirecting this company, changing its course, or improving its focus. In describing a company, try to focus attention on some critical questions. Figure 5–1 shows a sample topic in Business Plan Pro, with instructions and examples in one window as the user prepares a text in the other. This is the same illustration as shown in Figure 3–1.

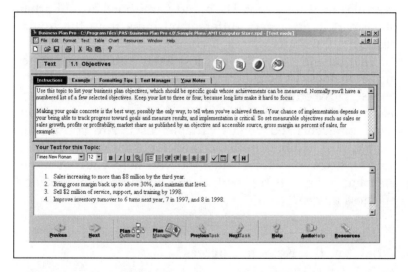

Figure 5–1. The Business Plan Pro screen as the user types a description of the business in the lower window and sees instructions in the upper window.

SOME CRITICAL QUESTIONS

What Business Are We In?

This classic business question is more symbolic than specific. Consider the classic example of railroads. The people who ran railroads thought their business was railroads, so as highway systems developed they failed to take advantage. They could have been in the business of transporting goods and people, but they failed to see it and lost out on an opportunity. A generation later, airlines jumped on air freight.

Think about your clients and the business they are in. Focus first on the benefits they offer to their customers. A restaurant, for example, is more likely selling service than selling food. It isn't the fish and chips they sell, it is the cooking, serving, and cleaning. A fast-food restaurant isn't in the same business as an elegant dining spot. The brand-name hotel in a suburban office park is in a very different business from the luxury beach hotel with its own golf course.

What business are you in? Most likely you are sometimes in the business of accounting, but do you keep your clients' books? How often do you consult on business issues, such as capital or working capital requirements, banking relationships, or even fixed versus variable costs? Are you also in the business of tax compliance and reporting, perhaps minimizing taxes for your clients? Do you help your clients to plan and budget? Is this perhaps the business of giving good business advice?

What Are the Keys to Success?

Take a step back from the business, yours or your client's, and consider what three or four factors are most important. Call these factors "keys to success." The exercise is a bit like the artist contemplating the subject, squinting to see only the highlights.

In the retail business, for example, the traditional joke is that the three keys to success for retailers are location, location, and location. Maybe that's really location, parking, and something else. In the McDonald's franchised hamburger business, according to a book published on the subject, keys to success are consistency and convenience. In a professional accounting business, one key to success is not losing clients, since it is so much more difficult to find new clients than to preserve existing clients. What's important here is focusing on priorities.

Remember to limit the keys to success to the short list, the main three or four priorities. More than three or four on the list makes the list less important, because a long list is not a focused list.

Consider at this point my own law of inverse focus: the more priorities in a business plan list, the slimmer the chance of implementation. Figure 5–2 illustrates the basic nature of an inverse relationship: one factor goes down when the other goes up. What happens is that as the list gets long people lose the emphasis. We're all just human, and when we're told that a new project doesn't fit priorities, if there are 20 priorities we don't pay attention; but if there are only three priorities, then we do.

Figure 5–2. The Law of Inverse Focus. If you have a priority list of three or four items, the list has power. Longer lists lose focus and have less impact.

Do We Have a Value Proposition?

Another way to look at a business is through its value proposition. The value proposition is benefit less price, for what kind of customer. The price is considered in relative terms. For example:

- The advertising of Michelin Tires stresses the benefit of safety by showing a baby sitting in the tire. The value proposition might be described as "more road safety for safety-minded consumers, at a slight price premium." That is a guess, by the way, not confirmed by Michelin. It is intended as an example only, not as a reference to company strategy or company secrets.

- The value proposition of a McDonald's outlet might be "reliable and fast lunch for convenience-minded consumers, at a slight price discount." That is also simple guess, by the way, not confirmed by the McDonald's corporation. It is intended as an example only, not as a reference to any proprietary information. As with Michelin, I am using an existing company with high brand awareness as a way to illustrate a point.

- The value proposition of a computer store might be "a small business' technology partner, stressing reliability and service and support in a relationship business, for a price premium."

When you work through a value proposition in a business plan, then you can evaluate the plan on the basis of how it helps the business communicate and fulfill the value proposition, in all areas of the business. In a computer reseller plan, for example, the value proposition suggested above would be communicated in ads and literature stressing the relationship, not the brand name of the computers sold. It might also be communicated by a large, clean, service area, staffed by people in white service coats. It might be fulfilled by programs to train and support customers, from installation, to upgrade, to daily use. That value proposition might also require some sensitivity from the administrative staff as it collects overdue bills.

Do We Have a Competitive Edge?

Another good review of a business is to consider its competitive edge. Compared with other businesses of the same type that seek the same customer, what if any is the competitive edge? In your own firm, your competitive edge is likely to be related to the clients you already have, your client loyalty, and your established relationships. With a McDonald's fast-food outlet, the competitive edge is related to consistency and convenience, plus brand name identity and, usually, location. A consumer products company might consider a national brand name and established shelf position in stores as a competitive edge. A software company is likely to have its proprietary software, its own technology, as a competitive edge. Every business ought to have some sort of competitive edge, even if it is simply the only store in town.

What Is Our Mission?

The mission statement is like a company's charter, its reason for existence. It should summarize the underlying goals, the business offering, and the target market. What is this business selling and to whom? Why? What are the benefits? You should also include an explicit statement about customer service or customer satisfaction and another about the company's goals for its employees and its workplace.

The mission statement should absorb the answers to some other key questions explored above. What business is this company in? What benefits does it offer to its customers? As you prepare your own mission statement, for example, think about what business you are really in. As a CPA firm, are you in the business of tax preparation, tax reporting, and auditing? Are you in the business of minimizing taxes legally or maximizing the worth of your clients? Can you provide additional service to your clients beyond what you currently provide?

Also think about what you want your firm to stand for. Do your goals for this practice include becoming a rewarding and pleasant place to work? Do your goals include your customers' goals for their businesses?

THE REST OF THE DESCRIPTION

A normal business plan includes an additional description of the company intended as background information. What subjects are covered depends on the kind of plan.

If you are writing a plan for a banker or investors, they want to know the legal details. You will normally have this at your fingertips for a client company. If not, then you should, and this is a good time to get it. Corporations are either subchapter C for the standard corporation or subchapter S for a smaller corporation owned by just one or a few owners. Corporate details vary by state and by the state in which the corporation was chartered, which of course isn't always the state of its home address. Companies may also be partnerships, professional corporations, limited liability partnerships, or "DBA" companies, which are essentially individuals who have registered their business name in their county seat.

When writing a plan for an existing company with a few years of history behind it, include a summary of past results and a description of company history. Usually this summary is keyed to financial results, explaining highs and lows. It should also talk about changes in products or services offered, moves to new locations, and other events that might be relevant. Of course, a plan for an existing company, when used to back a loan application or secure new investment, will have ample financial data included as an appendix or attachment.

A plan for a start-up company will include plans for legal formation and start-up expenses. The simplest way to deal with the difference between an existing company and a start-up company is to use the same place in your outline, where history and past performance might have been, to explain your start-up plans and start-up financing in detail.

Most plans will also discuss company facilities, proprietary intellectual or commercial property, and other basic information that is relevant to anybody looking to put money into a company.

CHAPTER 6
MARKET ANALYSIS

Know your market. The process of creating a business plan can be a reminder of the importance of understanding market needs and market growth. Obviously, market growth is critical to plans to be used to back loans or investments, but even for internal plans the market section is crucial. Do not try to plan a business without it. Sometimes owners and planners know their market extremely well, presumably by constantly gathering market information, so they can make plans without specific new market studies. More frequently, however, they take their market for granted, so a CPA who recommends some effort looking at the market is doing the business owner a favor. In your own practice, too, you want to take your business plan as a reminder of the importance of revisiting your market.

The market information should fit the needs of the plan. A local retail store needs local information, and a national consumer brand product needs national information. Most CPA practices need to understand their present and potential clients. Before determining your focus and priorities, you should look into the local community to consider your potential opportunities.

Your market research should also fit the needs of your plan. As discussed in Chapter 3, you cannot claim competence in this area without competence in searching the Internet. Lifetimes' worth of information is available, and the difficult part of the research is sorting through it all. You can also find trade associations, trade publications, government publications, databases of published information, and reference sources.

MARKET SEGMENTATION

Market segmentation can be delightfully creative. In its simplest form, *segmentation* is a marketer's jargon for dividing a market into its logical parts. If you sell to consumers, for example, you might segment by demographics, geography, or the more trendy psychographics.

- Demographics are basic population factors, such as age, gender, income levels, and households.

- Geography is location: zip code, town, state, nation, county, etc.

- Psychographics are consumer behavior factors, opinions, and preferences. The most famous psychographic classification used for marketing was the Yuppies of the 1980s, who were "young urban professionals." In its marketing literature, First Colony Mall of Sugarland, Texas, describes its local area psychographics as including "25% Kid & Cul-de-Sacs (upscale suburban families, affluent), 5.4% winner's circle (suburban executives, wealthy), 19.2% boomers and babies (young white-collar suburban, upper middle income), and 7% country squires (elite exurban, wealthy)." It describes that first group as "a noisy medley of bikes, dogs, carpools, rock music and sports." It describes the second group as "well-educated, mobile, executives & professionals with teen-aged families. Big producers, prolific spenders, and global travelers." The country squires are "where the wealthy have escaped urban stress to live in rustic luxury. No. 4 in affluence, big bucks in the boondocks." This is classic psychographics, a marketing technique that began in the early 1960s.

As a CPA firm, you might segment your market in a way that includes groups of businesses. Businesses are frequently classified by business demographics, including type of industry and size of company (measured in sales, number of employees, coverage, or number of locations). Segmentation can also divide businesses into geographic classifications, such as zip code or state.

Segmentation is supposed to help a company plan its business. Segmentation generates marketing ideas. For example, if you know you are marketing to the "kid & cul-de-sac" market in a local area, maybe sponsoring kids' athletic teams is a good idea. If you are concerned with people over 60, then you look for different marketing vehicles. In the more specific context of the CPA practice, a good segmentation might help you focus on certain customer types, such as successful locally owned retail businesses, or professionals approaching retirement age. During the years I was doing planning for Apple Computer, in the 1980s, we segmented the personal computer market by the type of buyer: home, academic, small business, large business, and government. This segmentation helped us plan channels of distribution, media spending, even computer configurations, software, and seminars.

Figure 6–1 shows the Business Plan Pro market analysis table for a sample office furniture company. In this example, the plan divides potential buyers into business executives, business owners, and home offices. In Figure 6–2, a different sample plan divides a different sample company's market into consumers, large business, small business, and government. The tables look similar in both cases, but the segmentations are different.

Both tables add up potential customers in the different segments, and estimate the annual growth rates of each segment. For the record, although there are a number of ways to calculate annual growth, these tables use the simple calculation that we introduced in Chapter 3:

1-year growth rate = (next year/last year) − 1

Potential Customers	Customers	Growth rate
Corporate executives	2,500,000	1%
Small business owners	11,000,000	4%
Home offices	36,000,000	10%
Other	1,000,000	3%
Total	**50,500,000**	**8.23%**

Figure 6–1. A simple market analysis, including several market segments with the estimated market size and growth rate for each.

Potential Customers	Total Cust's	Growth rate
Consumer	12,000	2%
Small Business	15,000	5%
Large Business	33,000	8%
Government	36,000	-2%
Other	19,000	0%
Total	115,000	2.78%

Figure 6–2. Another simple market analysis, for a different business.

For example, growth from 75 to 100 is $(100/75) - 1$, which is 33.33 percent growth. Growth from 100 to 200 is $(200/100) - 1$, which is 100 percent growth.

MARKET ANALYSIS

After segmentation comes analysis. A good plan explores market size, growth rates, market needs, buying patterns, competition, trends, and projections. For each market segment identified, the complete plan addresses most, if not all, of the following elements:

- *Sales in this segment in units or dollar value.* Or it examines both for the previous five years and the next five years. In a pinch, you can get by with less (last year and five future years, for example; or even last year and three future years), but when the information is available, you should include it.

- *Average price or dollar value of purchases.* This can be part of a market forecast or not, depending on how much detail is appropriate. One of the examples later in this discussion projects the market by multiplying potential customers by dollar spending per customer, in each year and each segment, to create a more detailed forecast.

To forecast laptop computers for five years, we would definitely want to include unit sales and dollars per unit, so we can calculate the total value as units times price.

- *The underlying market needs and requirements of this segment.* The sample CPA plan, for example, discusses the accounting needs of individuals vs. small business retail or service. The Briarpatch plan talks about the different needs of executive offices, high-end home office, as compared to small business. Marketing should always be based firmly on market needs, so they should be explored as part of a plan.

- *Distribution channels.* Where do customers go to buy? This may be irrelevant for some businesses, such as a local restaurant, but it is vital for others. In the packaged software business the consumer channel is vital and determines most of the programs in the plan. Where channels are important, describe the natural channels for each segment. Do customers buy through the mail, telephone orders, retail stores, Internet, or some other channel? Do you sell direct to customers as businesses, with a direct sales force? Explore the margins and trends in the channels and possible future developments.

- *Competitive forces.* What factors make potential customers choose one business over another? Is price more important than benefits or features, for example? Is rapid delivery or reliability more important? Consider how people choose a CPA, and compare that to how they choose a new car or a new computer. How important is price when buying a fax machine compared with billing rates when choosing an accountant? How important is price when people choose doctors, dentists, or lawyers? The factors are usually different for different types of business.

- *Communications.* Where do these customers see advertisements? Where do they go to look for product information or descriptions of services? Major national brands advertise on national TV, but local brands use newspapers and radio. Where does a CPA firm find potential new customers? Probably not through advertising at all—more likely through business organizations and events, seminars, newspaper columns, and professional business development.

- *Keys to success.* Rather than a repetition of your business's keys to success found in a different section of the plan, in this section you cover the keys to success for a particular market segment. For example, the sample plan for a CPA practice must recognize that the keys to success for dealing with wealthy individuals are different from those for dealing with retail stores or professional services. As Briarpatch, our sample company, looks at high-end home offices compared with small businesses, its keys to success for each business are different.

INDUSTRY ANALYSIS

You need to know and plan for the industry you're in. You must be realistic about the type of business. As a CPA, for example, you are in the business of professional service, with many smaller firms and only a few large ones. Although national brand names are relevant for many large national and international client companies, most accounting focuses on local markets and smaller, local firms. Accountants don't advertise the way car dealerships do. Gross margins are not a relevant variable. In the many product businesses, including computer furniture as in the Briarpatch example, there are national chains that are quite important players. Catalogs and local resellers are squeezed by price competition, and gross margins are declining. In the software business, when software is sold through national retail chains, gross margins are quite high, but sales and marketing expenses are also quite high. Selling through major distributors means the software company needs to carry two to three months' worth of receivables, so it needs working capital.

Some of the standard topics in the industry analysis are:

- *Industry participants.* How many companies are in this industry? Are they generally large, small, or in between?

Are there major brand names? Dry cleaning, for example, is a pulverized industry of many small participants, and auto manufacturing is a concentrated industry of a few very large companies.

- *Distribution patterns.* How does this industry generally sell its goods or services? In the market analysis, you look at where a particular market segment likes to shop, and in this section you look at where an industry likes to display its wares. Autos, for example, are distributed through dealer networks that provide sales and service, usually for only one or, at most, two or three manufacturers. Computers are sold through retail, direct mail, and direct corporate sales forces. Breakfast cereal is sold through grocery stores, including major brand name chain stores, smaller local stores, and convenience stores.

- *Competition and buying patterns.* Look at how this industry generally competes and what seem to be important factors in competition. Computers, for example, compete on price and power specifications, plus some product features. They also compete on retail shelf space and brand awareness. Autos compete on price and features and distribution patterns. Breakfast cereals probably compete on strength in distribution channels (shelf space) as well as content specifications and price. In the market analysis you looked at, what factors are important to a specific market segment; and in the industry analysis you look at, what factors are important to the competition in the whole industry.

- *Main competitors.* Having described competition within each market segment, and then within the industry, you should also list and discuss your main competitors. For the accountant partners in the CPA sample plan, the main competitors are other local accounting firms, but they also describe the national firms and the smaller firms. For Briarpatch, the main competitors are selling through the larger chain stores. For Palo Alto Software, my company, the competitors are a small group of competing software publishers offering products in the same product area, also through retail channels.

MARKET FORECAST

A good plan should normally include a specific market forecast, such as the ones shown in Figures 6–1 and 6–2 for two sample companies. The forecast includes real numbers. In these first two simple examples, the plan simply estimates the number of potential customers in each segment and the future growth rate of the number of customers.

The market projection shown in Figures 6–3 and 6–4 is another relatively simple example. This table isn't built into Business Plan Pro, by the way, but is included here as an examples of forecasting. You could duplicate it with any reasonable spreadsheet software, and it will be included in future versions of Business Plan Pro. For the total potential customers at the bottom, you simply do a sum of the numbers for the segments. To generate an average growth, I recommend a simple table such as the one shown in Figure 6–3 projecting growth in potential customers. Using the power of the computer, this table applies the projected growth rates to the starting estimates to calculate the actual numbers for each of the following four years, creating a five-year forecast. Once that is done, the average growth can be calculated using the standard formula, introduced in Chapter 3, for compound annual growth (CAGR) over a number (N) of years:

$$\text{CAGR} = (\text{last year}/\text{first year})^{(1/N)} - 1$$

Potential Customers	1998	1999	2000	2001	2002	CAGR
Local retail	1,200	1,260	1,323	1,389	1,459	5.01%
Local service	1,850	1,943	2,040	2,218	2,476	7.56%
Professional services	750	825	908	1,041	1,294	14.61%
Personal accounts	500	525	551	579	608	5.01%
Larger business	250	255	260	265	271	2.04%
Other	100	102	104	106	108	1.94%
Total	4,650	4,910	5,186	5,598	6,216	7.53%

Figure 6–3. A market forecast table projecting growth in customer segments over five years. This example uses the growth rates suggested in Figure 6–5, applying them equally over a five-year-period.

Potential Customers	1998	1999	2000	2001	2002	CAGR
Local retail	1,200	1,260	1,323	1,389	1,459	5.01%
Local service	1,850	1,943	2,040	2,218	2,476	7.56%
Professional services	750	825	908	1,041	1,294	14.61%
Personal accounts	500	525	551	579	608	5.01%
Larger business	250	255	260	265	271	2.04%
Other	100	102	104	106	108	1.94%
Total	4,650	4,910	5,186	5,598	6,216	7.53%

Billing per Customer	1998	1999	2000	2001	2002	CAGR
Local retail	$2,000	$2,050	$2,101	$2,154	$2,208	2.50%
Local service	$1,850	$1,924	$2,001	$2,081	$2,164	4.00%
Professional services	$2,400	$2,472	$2,546	$2,623	$2,701	3.00%
Personal accounts	$245	$247	$250	$252	$255	1.00%
Larger business	$7,500	$7,650	$7,803	$7,959	$8,118	2.00%
Other	$2,000	$2,050	$2,101	$2,154	$2,208	2.50%

Value ($ thousands)	1998	1999	2000	2001	2002	CAGR
Local retail	$2,400	$2,583	$2,780	$2,992	$3,221	7.63%
Local service	$3,423	$3,738	$4,082	$4,616	$5,359	11.86%
Professional services	$1,800	$2,039	$2,312	$2,730	$3,495	18.05%
Personal accounts	$123	$130	$138	$146	$155	6.06%
Larger business	$1,875	$1,951	$2,029	$2,109	$2,200	4.08%
Other	$200	$209	$219	$228	$238	4.49%
Total	$9,820	$10,650	$11,559	$12,821	$14,668	10.55%

Figure 6–4. A more detailed market forecast table projecting growth in customer segments over five years, by forecasting the growth in customers and in billings per customer, following up with the mathematics to calculate value as per-cusomer billings times customers, in each segment.

The numbers in the sample table offer a specific example:

$$\text{CAGR} = (6216/4650)^{(1/4)} - 1 = .0753$$

Figure 6–4 shows a more detailed market forecast, based on projecting unit sales and price per unit, then calculating the market value by multiplying units times price. In the example we use "billings per customer," an estimate of annual spending on accounting by type of customer, to stand for unit price. This example is usually a better way to forecast, because it divides the forecast into logical parts. Therefore, we can look at the assumptions for how much each type of client spends, on average, for accounting services, and how this annual spending might change over time, as well as how the number of clients in each segment changes. The local retail business, to cite one specific segment, is worth $2.4 million in 1998, because it is 1,200 businesses each spending on average $2,000 per year. Although the professional services segment is worth less than three other segments in 1998, it is expected to grow much faster than the others in both potential customers and billings per customer, so it is the most interesting opportunity. The resulting forecast is valuable for the hypothetical accountants as they plan the growth of their practice.

Graphics can help bring a forecast to life. Figure 6–5 is a simple pie chart illustrating the local market analysis in Figure 6–3, with the segments shown as pieces of the pie. It offers a clear picture of the preponderance of local service businesses. Figure 6–6 charts the more detailed forecast in Figure 6–4, showing the growth of the different segments.

Software Specifics

Business Plan Pro automatically creates the tables shown in Figures 6–1 and 6–2, as well as the pie chart in Figure 6–5. Use the Tables menu or the Task Wizard to reach the Market Analysis table, and the Charts menu

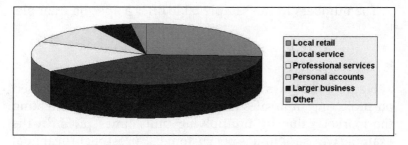

Figure 6–5. A simple market pie chart showing the market segments as total potential customers over a five-year period in each segment of the pie.

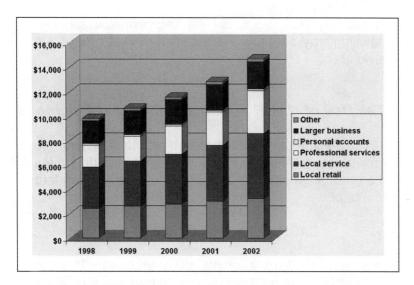

Figure 6–6. A market forecast bar chart projecting growth in customer segments over five years. This example uses the growth rates suggested in Figure 6–4, applying them equally over a five-year period.

to reach the Market Analysis chart. Type your estimates into the green areas in the software; the rest is automatic.

Business Plan Pro's market analysis looks at the total potential market, usually divided into segments. Figure 6–7 shows a specific example. Normally this is total potential market, not total actual customers. For example, in the sample market analysis shown in Figure 6–7, the total market is 115,000 possible customers. This might be a local community. Normally, the accompanying text

	A	B	C	D	E	F	G	H
	H3	=IF(C3<>0,(G3/C3)^(1/4)-1,0)						
1	Market Analysis							
2	Potential Customers	Growth	2001	2002	2003	2004	2005	CAGR
3	Consumer	2%	12,000	12,240	12,485	12,735	12,990	2.00%
4	Small Business	5%	15,000	15,750	16,538	17,365	18,233	5.00%
5	Large Business	8%	33,000	35,640	38,491	41,570	44,896	8.00%
6	Government	-2%	36,000	35,280	34,574	33,883	33,205	-2.00%
7	Other	0%	19,000	19,000	19,000	19,000	19,000	0.00%
8	Total	2.78%	115,000	117,910	121,088	124,553	128,324	2.78%

Figure 6–7. The Market Analysis Table in Business Plan Pro

in the plan has to explain the segmentation scheme, detailing why and how the potential market groups are divided.

The Use of CAGR Formula in the Final Column

The Market Analysis table uses the compound average growth rate (CAGR) formulas in column H to determine the average growth rate. The CAGR formula is a standard formula:

$$CAGR = (last/first)^{(1/years)} - 1$$

So in cell H3, for example, the formula for CAGR in that cell is "$= (G3/C3)^{(1/4)} - 1$." There are four years of growth in this forecast, even though it includes five years. The growth years are 2002, 2003, 2004, and 2005.

The CAGR formula counts only the first and final values, without regard to the intervening values.

The ROUND Function

The formula shown also illustrates the ROUND function to round the result to the nearest whole number. For example, the formula "= round(3/5,0)" would produce as its result the whole number 1, while the formula "= round(2/5,0)" would produce the value 0.

Unprotected Formulas in Columns D through G.

The illustration shows the formula for column D. It calculates this second-year value using simple math from the first-year value and the growth rate assumption in column B. In this table, the unprotected formula calculates an estimation for the second through the fifth year if you type in values for the first year and the growth rate.

This is an excellent example of an unprotected formula. It is there for your convenience, but is not required. If you type data and assumptions on your own, you can overwrite the formulas and type in your own numbers to create a different growth pattern. In Figure 6–8, the line labeled "Straight" is built using the preprogrammed growth formulas. Each column represents 78 percent growth from the previous column. In the line labeled "Natural," in contrast, although the growth to 2004 is the same, none of the intervening columns follows the straight line. All of the values were typed into the cells as estimates, changing the formula.

In this case, it is important to treat the growth rate in column B, cell B4, as we did for the example. By making its growth rate equal to the growth in the last column, we avoid a logical contradiction. The overall growth rate is what's shown in column H, the CAGR column.

In Figure 6–9 you can see how different the two forecasts are. The straight-line forecast is the lower of the two (marked with +), curving up with a steady increase. The estimated forecast is the upper of the two lines (marked with X), growing faster at first and then slower later on. Notice that both forecasts get to the same endpoint, and they both have the same growth rate for the full period.

No Fewer Than Two Rows

In the market forecast, you can't have fewer than two rows. The logic involves SUM formulas that need to have a top row and a bottom row. If you want to delete a row

B4	=H4						
Market Analysis							
Potential Customers	**Growth**	**2000**	**2001**	**2002**	**2003**	**2004**	**CAGR**
Straight	78%	1,000	1,778	3,162	5,623	10,000	77.83%
Natural	78%	1,000	5,400	7,700	9,300	10,000	77.83%
Total	77.83%	2,000	7,178	10,862	14,923	20,000	77.83%

Figure 6–8. Straight Line vs. Estimated Market Growth.

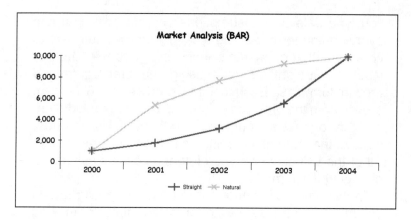

Figure 6–9. The Market Contrast.

in the market forecast, delete the middle row of the three starting rows.

Problems Deleting Rows

You can't delete either the top or the bottom row because of the underlying SUM formulas. You can, however, transfer data from the middle row (or any middle row if you added rows) to the top or bottom, and then delete that middle row.

CHAPTER 7
SALES FORECAST

For forecasting sales we need to focus on the basics of forecasting, which we discussed in Chapter 3. Avoid fear of forecasting by breaking a forecast into its logical components. Remember to maintain the CPA's role in the client plan, helping with advice and feedback, letting your client do his or her own forecast. The goal is to maintain the plan as the client's plan, not yours.

Software Specifics

Business Plan Pro varies the structure of the sales forecast depending on user options. The simpler sales forecast projects sales and cost of sales as simple dollar (or other currency) amounts. It has two blocks, one for sales and one for cost of sales, like the one shown in Figure 7–1. The more complex sales forecast projects units first, then price per unit, then sales as a function of price times units, then cost per unit, then cost of sales as a function

Sales	Jan-98	Dec-98	1998	1999	2000
Coffee	$3,550	$5,820	$48,840	$315,000	$350,000
Bakery	$2,343	$3,841	$32,234	$260,000	$260,000
Deli	$1,775	$2,910	$24,420	$260,000	$260,000
Other	$500	$500	$6,000	$10,000	$12,000
Total Sales	$8,168	$13,071	$111,494	$845,000	$882,000
Direct Costs	Jan-98	Dec-98	1998	1999	2000
Coffee	$533	$873	$7,326	$47,250	$52,500
Bakery	$1,172	$1,921	$16,117	$130,000	$130,000
Deli	$444	$728	$6,105	$65,000	$65,000
Other	$125	$125	$1,500	$2,500	$3,000
Subtotal Direct Cost of Sales	$2,273	$3,646	$31,048	$244,750	$250,500

Figure 7–1. In the simple dollar-based forecast, you estimate sales and cost of sales for each item you sell. This should be done by the business owner, not the CPA. Most months are omitted for purposes of illustration.

of cost times units. This one is shown in Figures 7–2 and 7–3. When you have a single line of sales, the software automatically uses an even simpler one-line forecast, not shown in this book.

A SIMPLE FORECAST

Figure 7–1 shows a simple sales forecast, projecting the sales of a coffee shop by line of sales: coffee, bakery, and deli. Business Plan Pro selects this forecast if you choose not to forecast by units, as part of the plan wizard options. The months between January and December are not shown in the

Sales Forecast				
Unit Sales	**Jan-98**	**Feb-98**	**Mar-98**	**Apr-98**
Executive desk oak	40	55	60	60
Executive desk cherry	20	30	33	30
Other furniture oak	26	35	40	35
Other furniture cherry	6	11	13	12
Other	4	5	6	6
Total Unit Sales	96	136	152	143
Unit Prices				
Executive desk oak	$1,600	$1,600	$1,600	$1,600
Executive desk cherry	$1,750	$1,750	$1,750	$1,750
Other furniture oak	$900	$900	$900	$900
Other furniture cherry	$1,000	$1,000	$1,000	$1,000
Other	$2,500	$2,500	$2,500	$2,500
Total Sales				
Executive desk oak	$64,000	$88,000	$96,000	$96,000
Executive desk cherry	$35,000	$52,500	$57,750	$52,500
Other furniture oak	$23,400	$31,500	$36,000	$31,500
Other furniture cherry	$6,000	$11,000	$13,000	$12,000
Other	$10,000	$12,500	$15,000	$15,000
Total Sales	$138,400	$195,500	$217,750	$207,000

Figure 7–2. A unit-based sales forecasting example, which breaks sales into units and dollar prices, multiplying units times price to calculate sales.

Sales Forecast				
Unit Sales	Jan-98	Feb-98	Mar-98	Apr-98
Executive desk oak	40	55	60	60
Executive desk cherry	20	30	33	30
Other furniture oak	26	35	40	35
Other furniture cherry	6	11	13	12
Other	4	5	6	6
Total Unit Sales	96	136	152	143
Direct Unit costs				
Executive desk oak	$400	$400	$400	$400
Executive desk cherry	$525	$525	$525	$525
Other furniture oak	$180	$180	$180	$180
Other furniture cherry	$300	$300	$300	$300
Other	$625	$625	$625	$625
Total direct cost of Sales				
Executive desk oak	$16,000	$22,000	$24,000	$24,000
Executive desk cherry	$10,500	$15,750	$17,325	$15,750
Other furniture oak	$4,680	$6,300	$7,200	$6,300
Other furniture cherry	$1,800	$3,300	$3,900	$3,600
Other	$2,500	$3,125	$3,750	$3,750
Subtotal Direct Costs	$35,480	$50,475	$56,175	$53,400

Figure 7–3. Another view of the unit-based forecast, showing how units are multiplied by cost per unit to calculate cost of sales.

illustration because of page limitations. To fill out a forecast like this, let the software sum the totals for each month and for the first year. The rest is data entry, essentially educated guessing. The forecasting will be as good as the estimates of the person responsible. The forecast includes an area for sales and an area for cost of sales. Both cases are basically educated guessing. For an accounting practice, for example, cost of sales would be zero in rows for which the main cost is the salary of the professionals or of the staff, which is kept as an operating expense.

UNITS-BASED SALES FORECAST

Figures 7–2 and 7–3 show two views of a more detailed sales forecast, based on units and price per unit. Business Plan Pro selects this forecast when you tell the plan wizard you want to forecast by units. In Figure 7–2, the first block of the forecast projects unit sales, with the software summing the sales in units per month and per year. The second block projects the price per unit for each line of sales. The third block multiplies units times price, to calculate actual sales.

In Figure 7–3, we see a fourth block projecting per-unit cost for each line of sales, and a fifth and final block that multiplies the units (shown in Figure 7–2) times the cost per unit, calculating direct cost of sales.

The advantage of this sales forecast structure, which is more detailed than the simple sales forecast, is that it breaks down the problem into logical parts. For most people the educated guess is more likely to be correct when it is set into its component parts instead of calculated back to totals. This is called breaking down the forecast.

With sales forecasting you can also use business charts, as shown in Figure 7–4, to guide your forecast. In the example, the monthly sales chart provides a picture of the ebb and flow of sales during the year.

Software Specifics

Switching Between Two Sales Forecasts

When you have an existing business plan started with numbers already in the Sales Forecast, and you then go to the Plan Wizard and switch to the other option, it appears as though data has disappeared. In fact, what happens is that there are two separate forecasts embedded within the plan. When you go from one to the other, you make one active and the other inactive.

As a helpful option, this facility can be used to create two alternative sales forecasts and to switch quickly between the two for comparisons. This can help you look at alternatives and develop a sense for how either of the two would affect other areas of the plan.

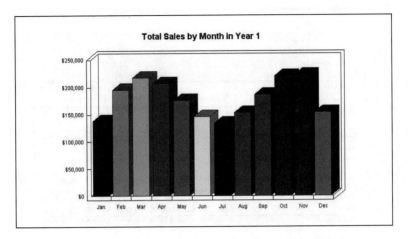

Figure 7–4. This bar chart of monthly sales shows how sales are expected to go up and down during different months of the year.

Problems Deleting Rows

As with the Market Analysis table discussed in the previous chapter, in the Sales Forecast you can't delete either the top or the bottom row because of the underlying SUM formulas. You can, however, transfer data from the middle row (or any middle row if you added rows) to the top or bottom then delete that middle row.

The Average Price Calculation

Figure 7–5 shows what happens when a sales forecast contains prices but no sales. The average price of zero in the first-year column looks wrong, because the price assumption is $25 per unit. However, look again: the average price is zero, because Business Plan Pro calculates average price by dividing sales by units. If there are no sales—as is the case here—then the average price is zero.

In Figure 7–6 we see why Business Plan Pro has to calculate the average price from sales and units. In this

O20	=IF(O15<>0,O24/O15,0)					
	A	**M**	**N**	**O**	**P**	
13	**Sales Forecast**					
14	**Unit Sales**	**Nov**	**Dec**	**2000**	**2001**	
15	example	0	0	0	4,000	
16	Other	2,300	3,100	15,200	24,000	3!
17	**Total Unit Sales**	2,300	3,100	15,200	28,000	
18						
19	**Unit Prices**	**Nov**	**Dec**	**2000**	**2001**	
20	example	$25.00	$25.00	$0.00	$25.00	$;
21	Other	$50.00	$50.00	$50.00	$50.00	$!
22						
23	**Sales**					
24	example	$0	$0	$0	$100,000	$20(
25	Other	$115,000	$155,000	$760,000	$1,200,000	$1,75(
26	Total Sales	$115,000	$155,000	$740,000	$1,300,000	$1,95

Figure 7–5. No Sales, No Price.

O20	=IF(O15<>0,O24/O15,0)					
	A	**L**	**M**	**N**	**O**	**P**
13	**Sales Forecast**					
14	**Unit Sales**	**Oct**	**Nov**	**Dec**	**2000**	**2001**
15	example	200	300	700	1,200	4,000
16	Other	1,600	2,300	3,100	15,200	24,000
17	**Total Unit Sales**	1,800	2,600	3,800	16,400	28,000
18						
19	**Unit Prices**	**Oct**	**Nov**	**Dec**	**2000**	**2001**
20	example	$25.00	$25.00	$15.00	$19.17	$15.00
21	Other	$50.00	$50.00	$50.00	$50.00	$50.00
22						
23	**Sales**					
24	example	$5,000	$7,500	$10,500	$23,000	$60,000	$
25	Other	$80,000	$115,000	$155,000	$760,000	$1,200,000	$1,
26	Total Sales	$85,000	$122,500	$165,500	$783,000	$1,260,000	$1,

Figure 7–6. Average Price, Second Case.

example, volume changes with price. To calculate the average, you have to divide total sales for the year by total units for the year. The average price isn't the mathematical average of 12 price assumptions in 12 columns, it is sales divided by units. In the example, if you made $23,000 in sales on a volume of 1,200 units, the average is $19.17 per unit.

Handling Direct Labor as Cost of Sales

Many companies have salaried employees whose compensation should be included in the cost of sales. The Personnel Plan has facilities for this. Set your plan to break expenses into categories, and put these salaries into the first category. They will automatically flow into cost of sales, without affecting inventory.

Programming a Growth Rate in Column B

Figure 7–7 shows a sample sales forecast in which a growth rate assumption, in column B, automatically calculates sales projections for annual sales in the second and third year.

That illustration has some of the columns hidden (using the Hide Column command in the format menu) so you can see columns B, O, and P. The formula in P (shown in the illustration) calculates service unit sales in 2002 by applying the growth rate in column B. The phrase "$B16" in that formula will always refer to the value in the B column, regardless of which other column it appears in. The "$" in "$B" makes that an absolute reference, not a relative reference. The formula also uses the ROUND function to round the result to the nearest whole number.

P16	=ROUND(O16*(1+$B16),0)						
	A	B	C	N	O	P	Q
13	Sales Forecast						
14	Unit Sales			Jan	Dec	2001	2002	200
15	Systems			85	275	2,251	3,134	4,323
16	Service	20.00%		200	343	3,128	3,754	7,50C
17	Software			150	490	3,980	5,000	6,50C
18	Training			145	200	2,230	4,000	8,00C
19	Other			160	200	2,122	2,500	3,00C
20	Total Unit Sales			740	1,508	13,711	18,388	29,32

Figure 7–7. Working with a Growth Rate Variable in Sales.

Programming a Straight Cost of Sales Percentage

In Figure 7–8, the sales forecast programmed Business Plan Pro to use a similar straight-line assumption for cost of sales related to sales price. The underlying assumption is that cost of sales will be a constant percentage of the sales price, regardless of what the sales price is. The spreadsheet example shows how to program this in one cell, then you can copy that formula into all the cells in the row. The illustration shows the constant percentage as 80%, but of course the value of programming these formulas is that if you decide to change the percentage, you have to type it into a single cell.

Linking to Sales from User-Defined Tables

Of course you can also create different sales models and link your sales to different tables within Business

	A	B	C	D	E	
13	Sales Forecast					
14	Unit Sales		Jan	Feb	Mar	
22	Unit Prices		Jan	Feb	Mar	
23	Systems		$2,000.00	$1,900.00	$1,900.00	$1,
24	Service		$75.00	$69.00	$58.00	:
25	Software		$200.00	$200.00	$200.00	$
26	Training		$37.00	$35.00	$39.00	
27	Other		$300.00	$300.00	$300.00	$1,
36						
37	Direct Unit Costs		Jan	Feb	Mar	
38	Systems	80.00%	$1,600.00	$1,520.00	$1,520.00	$1
39	Service		$30.00	$60.00	$60.00	:
40	Software		$120.00	$120.00	$120.00	$
41	Training		$11.10	$11.10	$11.10	
42	Other		$90.00	$90.00	$90.00	:
43						
44	Direct Cost of Sales		Jan	Feb	Mar	

D38 =$B38*D23

Figure 7–8. Constant Cost Percentage Formula.

Plan Pro, using formulas that link tables. Details about table linking are included in the Business Plan Pro advanced table help (on the web at www.paloalto.com/support/bpwprogramming.htm). You can use that document, a companion to this one, for some specific step-by-step examples of linking user-defined tables into the Sales Forecast. For example:

> Some business plans link annual sales to the potential market forecast, using percentage assumptions. To establish this kind of link, we'd recommend using a user-defined table to hold assumptions for market share as a percent of total market, and then linking from the user-defined table for share into the Sales Forecast table.

You can calculate whatever details are appropriate in the user-defined table and link to the Sales Forecast. Figure 7–9 shows a link formula from sales to the user-

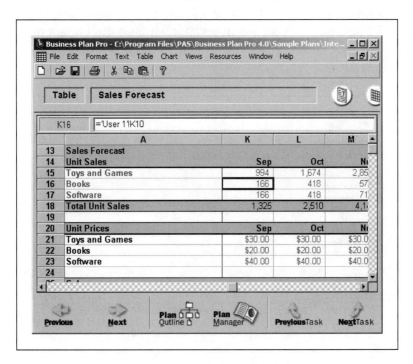

Figure 7–9. Linking Tables in Sales Forecast.

defined table in the Intelichild.com sample plan, which is included with Business Plan Pro. In that case, the source table projects Internet traffic, so that the resulting sales forecast is dependent on Internet traffic.

Dealing with Subscriptions (Churn Rate)

Figure 7–10 shows the first portion of a subscription sales model, also called Churn Rate model. It calculates subscriber sales for a $19.95 monthly membership business. The Plan Wizard sets the Sales Forecast for a units-based forecast, not value-based. In the units area, one row shows new subscribers, one row shows cancellations (attrition), and one shows total subscribers. In the unit prices, a subscriber pays $19.95 on a monthly basis and a cancellation causes a single-month credit. You can see the resulting sales forecast.

You can see in the illustration how the cancellation formula uses a percentage assumption (3% in Column B), so you can vary the assumption to see the impact of different cancellation rates. The formula shown in the

	D16	=ROUND($B16*C18,0)						
		A	B	C	D	E	F	G
13	Sales Forecast							
14	Unit Sales			Jan	Feb	Mar	Apr	May
15	New subscriptions			100	150	250	300	400
16	Cancellations		3.00%	0	3	7	15	23
17	Total subscribers			100	247	490	775	1,152
18	Subscriber Months			100	247	490	775	1,152
19	Total Unit Sales			300	647	1,237	1,865	2,727
20								
21	Unit Prices			Jan	Feb	Mar	Apr	May
23	Cancellations			$0.00	($19.95)	($19.95)	($19.95)	($19.95)
25	Subscriber Months			$19.95	$19.95	$19.95	$19.95	$19.95
26								
27	Sales							
29	Cancellations			$0	($60)	($140)	($299)	($459)
31	Subscriber Months			$1,995	$4,928	$9,776	$15,461	$22,982
32	Total Sales			$1,995	$4,868	$9,636	$15,162	$22,524
33								

Figure 7–10. Subscription Sales (Churn).

illustration uses the ROUND function to set the cancellations to single user numbers.

This is another good example of an input variable programmed into column B of the sales forecast. That makes changing assumptions easier. You can change the rate of cancellation in this sales forecast by changing that single cell.

Hiding Unused Rows with Zero Values

This illustration is also a good example of hiding rows you don't need. Although this Sales Forecast needs to keep track of new subscribers and total subscribers, there are no price or sales implications. We used the Hide Row command in the format menu to hide those rows that we didn't need.

Subscriber months are fairly easy for monthly projections, but the system gets more complex when you need to translate subscriber months into annual forecasts. Figure 7–11 shows a detailed treatment of the subscription

P18	=((N17+P17)/2)*12			
	A	N	O	P	Q
13	**Sales Forecast**				
14	**Unit Sales**	Dec	2001	2002	2003
15	New subscriptions	700	4,700	10,000	12,500
16	Cancellations	108	497	2,557	4,346
17	Total subscribers	4,203	20,757	11,646	19,800
18	Subscriber Months	4,203	20,757	95,097	243,343
19	**Total Unit Sales**	9,214	46,711	119,300	279,989
20					
21	**Unit Prices**	Dec	2001	2002	2003
23	Cancellations	($19.95)	($19.95)	($19.95)	($19.95)
25	Subscriber Months	$19.95	$19.95	$19.95	$19.95
26					
27	**Sales**				
29	Cancellations	($2,155)	($9,915)	($51,003)	($86,710)
31	Subscriber Months	$83,850	$414,102	$1,897,180	$4,854,685
32	**Total Sales**	$81,695	$404,187	$1,846,177	$4,767,975
33					

Figure 7–11. Subscription (Churn) Model Years Formulas.

or churn Sales Forecast for years instead of months. Some of the formulas require detailed explanation.

The new subscriptions estimated for 2002 (column P, cell P15) is an input estimate. Be careful, if you are doing this kind of forecast, to build in the growth. In this forecast, the 10,000 new subscribers model may look ambitious, but at the end of the first year the business was picking up 700 new subscribers per month. At that rate, the next year would bring in 8,400 subscribers (700*12). Therefore, the 10,000 estimate is not as ambitious as it might seem at first glance.

Cancellations in cells P16 and Q16 are also estimates, based on percentage cancellations from the subscriber base. How many people will cancel in a given year? If your business has a history, you might be able to turn to that history for an estimate. If not, you might be able to research cancellations from other similar businesses (publicly traded, perhaps, so that they have to release such information). In either case, you need to make these assumptions clear, and row 16 allows you to do that.

Cell P17 presents total subscribers at the end of the year, as a result of the formula: "= N17 + P15 − P16." The cell N17 in that formula contains the total subscribers at the end of the last month of the previous year. Cell P15 contains new subscribers for the year, and P16 contains dropouts. This isn't the number used to calculate revenue, but it is still an important number for marketing and benchmarking. A subscription business needs to know how many subscribers it adds and loses. Many similar businesses, subscription-based or not, need to estimate their monthly "churn," as this is called in some circles.

The formula in P17 needs to be adjusted for Q17, because of the impact of the annual numbers in column O. The correct formula for Q17 is "= P17 + Q15 − Q16."

The formula for cell P18 needs to account for subscription months. These are paying months, and they are critical to calculating revenue. If you have 1,000 subscribers for a full year, they contribute 12,000 subscriber months. The formula in P18 is "= ((N17 + P17)/2)*12." This formula takes the average between the total subscribers at the beginning of the year and total subscribers at the end of the year and multiplies that average number of subscribers by 12 to calculate subscriber months.

This is not a perfect calculation. It creates a reasonable estimate. You could make it more exact by developing another complete year of months. This approximation is good enough for planning purposes, however. In the end, no matter how detailed you make your future estimates, they are still estimates. We prefer to leave that fact obvious by not trying to bury estimated guesses in overwhelming detail.

As with row 17, there is a difference between column P and column Q in these formulas because of the impact of the annual column O intervening. The correct formula for cell Q18 is "= ((O17 + Q17)/2)*12."

The effect of taking averages for these columns is appropriate to the level of certainty in predicting subscriptions two and three years into the future.

CHAPTER 8
PLANNING FOR PERSONNEL

A good next step is the personnel plan. This should normally include a detailed projection of personnel costs plus an analysis of management structure, organizational issues, gaps and, of course, in a plan intended to sell investors, detailed résumés of the founders.

DEFINING THE TEAM

The most important single variable for venture capital is the quality of the management team. Many new companies have been financed by outsiders solely because of the quality of the founders and their professional backgrounds. While this is rare these days, there is no underestimating the importance of the management team in the success of a business.

Give your plan a thorough analysis of management and personnel. Describe its organizational structure, its important functions, and how the key people manage the key functions. Make sure you provide detailed background on each of your managers and enough job and organizational description to guide you towards your future objectives.

Look honestly for management gaps. Especially in smaller businesses and start-up companies, some important functional areas usually need stronger management. CPA firms are frequently weak in marketing, for example, and sometimes in technical computer-focused consulting. In the Briarpatch business, the partners needed to discuss sales, marketing, manufacturing, and administration. In my business at Palo Alto Software, we need to look at sales, marketing, development, support, and administration.

Software Specifics

This chapter of the business plan should also contain a detailed personnel plan, showing wages and salaries and cost of benefits for the three years in the plan. Figure 8–1 shows how a simple personnel plan lists employees by job title, projecting the monthly salaries for each for the first year and annual salaries for the second and third. This is another good example of simple forecasting. The software adds up the totals for each month and the totals for the year. Business Plan Pro uses this format when you choose not to divide expenses by categories, which is a choice you make in the plan options.

Figure 8–2 shows a more detailed personnel plan, in which personnel costs are divided into functional categories. Here, too, the software supplies the obvious additions. Dividing personnel by category is important when operating expenses are to be divided by category in the income statement. Without this distinction, you could not look at, say, sales and marketing expenses as a percent of total expenses, or of total revenue. Business Plan Pro uses this forecast structure when you divide expenses into categories, by selecting the appropriate options.

Software Specifics

If you use the more detailed expense breakdowns, as we explained for the Sales Forecast in Chapter 6, your personnel will appear in different spots in your Profit and Loss statement. The first category, regardless of its name, goes into the cost of goods or cost of sales section at the

Job Title	Jan-98	Dec-98	1998	1999	2000
Owner	$2,500	$2,500	$30,000	$35,000	$40,000
Clerk	$1,700	$1,700	$20,400	$24,000	$27,000
Clerk	$1,500	$1,500	$18,000	$21,000	$24,000
Clerk	$1,300	$1,300	$15,600	$18,000	$21,000
Other	$250	$250	$3,000	$3,000	$4,000
Total Sales	$7,250	$7,250	$87,000	$101,000	$116,000

Figure 8–1. A simple personnel plan listing employees for a small store. Some months are left out for the sake of page size.

Personnel Plan							
Professional	Jan-98	Feb-98	Nov-98	Dec-98	1998	1999	2000
Abbott	$10,000	$10,000	$10,000	$10,000	$120,000	$132,000	$145,000
Baker	$9,000	$9,000	$9,000	$9,000	$108,000	$119,000	$131,000
Collins	$9,000	$9,000	$9,000	$9,000	$108,000	$119,000	$131,000
Other partners			$7,500	$7,500	$15,000	$110,000	$250,000
Associates	$18,000	$18,000	$18,000	$18,000	$216,000	$227,000	$238,000
Other	$6,000	$6,000	$6,000	$6,000	$72,000	$79,000	$87,000
Subtotal	$52,000	$52,000	$59,500	$59,500	$639,000	$786,000	$982,000
Sales and Marketing Salaries							
Director of Marketing	$6,000	$6,000	$6,000	$6,000	$72,000	$83,000	$95,000
Marketing Assistant	$2,500	$2,500	$2,500	$2,500	$30,000	$33,000	$36,000
Other	$0	$0	$0	$0	$0	$25,000	$40,000
Subtotal	$8,500	$8,500	$8,500	$8,500	$102,000	$141,000	$171,000
Administrative Salaries							
Controller	$5,000	$5,000	$5,000	$5,000	$60,000	$66,000	$73,000
Office Manager	$3,500	$3,500	$3,500	$3,500	$42,000	$46,000	$51,000
Admin. Staff	$12,000	$12,000	$12,000	$12,000	$144,000	$158,000	$174,000
Other	$1,000	$1,000	$1,000	$1,000	$12,000	$13,000	$14,000
Subtotal	$21,500	$21,500	$21,500	$21,500	$258,000	$283,000	$312,000
Other Salaries							
Systems and support	$5,000	$5,000	$5,000	$5,000	$60,000	$66,000	$73,000
Other	$0	$0	$0	$0	$0	$0	$0
Subtotal	$5,000	$5,000	$5,000	$5,000	$60,000	$66,000	$73,000

Figure 8–2. A more detailed personnel plan listing employees taken from the ABC Partners sample plan. Employees are listed by function.

top of the income statement. The other three categories of personnel go into the operating expenses. Figure 8–3 shows how the first personnel category (in this case named "Production") automatically appears in Profit and Loss as "Production Payroll."

Headcount is Simple Data Input

Headcount stands for total number of employees. As with all green cells in Business Plan Pro, the headcount row near the bottom of the Personnel Plan is simple data entry. Business Plan Pro doesn't calculate headcount automatically because there is no way to know how many people are included. In column O of that row, the first-year total automatically links from the end of the last month.

D5	=IF(PERS=3,Payroll3P,0)					
	A	B	C	D	E	F
1	Profit and Loss (Income Statement)					
2			Jan	Feb	Mar	Apr
3	Sales		$268,365	$342,025	$415,635	$701,590
4	Direct Cost of Sales		$184,510	$249,061	$307,612	$398,087
5	Production Payroll		$9,500	$9,500	$9,500	$9,500
7						
8	Total Cost of Sales		$194,010	$258,561	$317,112	$407,587
9	Gross Margin		$74,356	$83,465	$98,524	$294,003
10	Gross Margin %		27.71%	24.40%	23.70%	41.91%
11	Operating expenses:					
12	Sales and Marketing Expenses					
13	Sales and Marketing Payroll		$24,000	$24,000	$24,000	$24,000
14	Ads		$5,000	$5,000	$7,000	$10,000
15	Catalog		$2,000	$3,000	$2,000	$2,000
16	Mailing		$3,000	$11,800	$5,500	$10,500
17	Promo		$0	$0	$0	$0
18	Shows		$0	$0	$0	$0

Figure 8–3. Personnel in Cost of Sales.

Formula for Sales Commission in Personnel

Figure 8–4 shows one way a commission structure can be built into the Personnel Plan. The formula for the cell is shown in the edit bar in that illustration. It applies whatever percentage is typed into column B in that row to the gross margin for that same month. This is also

D28	=6000+($B28*Gross_margin)					
	A	B	C	D	E	F
15	Personnel Plan					
16	Production Personnel		Jan	Feb	Mar	Apr
23	Fulfillment		$1,500	$1,500	$1,500	$1,500
24	Other		$0	$0	$0	$0
25	Subtotal		$9,500	$9,500	$9,500	$9,500
26						
27	Sales and Marketing Personnel					
28	Manager	1.00%	$6,744	$6,835	$6,985	$8,940
29	Technical sales		$5,000	$5,000	$5,000	$5,000
30	Technical sales		$2,500	$2,500	$2,500	$2,500

Figure 8–4. Setting Commissions for Personnel.

an example of using a named variable in a formula, as explained in the Business Plan Pro Advanced Table Help section on named ranges.

Deleting Rows in Personnel

The Personnel Plan is one of several tables (including Market Analysis and Sales Forecast) that doesn't allow row deletion to fewer than two rows in sections of three. This limitation is because of the nature of summation formulas in a spreadsheet. If you want to delete the third or the first row of a group of three, copy the data from a middle row and delete the middle row instead. You can also change its name to match a middle row.

CHAPTER 9
PRO FORMA FINANCIAL STATEMENTS

BUSINESS ESSENTIALS

It would be hard to imagine a business plan that didn't contain at least income statement, cash flow, and balance sheet. These should normally be pro forma statements projecting the future for at least three years, with monthly pro forma statements for at least the next 12 months. Some plans go for five and even 10 years, with monthlies for two or even three years, but these are unusual. The Business Plan Pro software discourages plans for longer than three years and doesn't offer monthlies for more than the first 12 months. This isn't because there aren't some cases that demand longer time periods and more detail, but it's because most don't. When in doubt, look at the function of the plan and think about its value as a guide to decision making. We all agree that companies should plan for longer terms. However, such planning might not take form in as much detail as in standard pro forma statements.

Certainly the existence of personal computing has changed business planning forever. The detail of financial analysis, once reserved for an elite, calculation-rich and education-rich few, now comes in software.

As we suggested in Chapter 3, you may need to educate clients about forecasting as educated guessing. You should normally insist that the client make his or her own educated guesses. Important data come from the sales forecast and personnel plan tables, and the balance sheet influences the interest rates. For most of the rest of the pro forma statements, educated guessing is about the best you can hope for. Difficult as it is to guess, it is still more difficult to run a company without a plan or a budget.

PROFITS ARE NOT CASH

Cash flow is the single most important element of a business plan. Cash flow is not intuitive, and people don't think in terms of cash flow, but cash is what makes or breaks a business. This contrast between what really matters and the way most people think—cash really matters, but people think about profits—is one of the biggest problems in business. It is also the area in which a business plan can be most helpful to a business.

What do I mean when I say that people think in profits but spend cash? In business lore, for example, the three founders of Compaq Computer sketched a plan on a napkin in a restaurant. Do you think they thought about cash—working capital, inventory management, accounts receivable? Or about profits—how much it costs to build one computer, how much we make when we sell one? Whenever people get together to discuss a business idea, they think about sales price less cost, that is, profits. They rarely think about cash until they don't have any.

For sure, part of your contribution to your clients' business planning is likely to be explaining the critical concept of cash vs. profits. There is no underestimating how important this is and how easily it is misunderstood.

The following discussion of software specifics includes some powerful examples. In one specific example, a 15-day change in collection days costs a sample company several hundred thousand dollars of working capital. The impact of this example is much more than simple financial concepts. Can this be an issue of business survival? Quite possibly. Even if we assume this company does have enough history and financial strength to support the additional liabilities, the bank is going to want credit applications well in advance of this company needing the money. So the business plan here is critical, because it manages and foresees the difference between cash and profits.

Software Specifics

Business Plan Pro automatically prepares pro forma standard Income Statement, Balance Sheet, and Cash Flow Statement. The key difference between these and standard statements is that the pro forma statements project the future, while financial statements normally show what has already happened.

These pro forma statements are automatically linked up and preprogrammed in the Business Plan Pro software. You can add and delete rows as required for expenses and personnel plan. Any changes made to any of the statements are set to automatically record correctly in all others.

Figure 9–1 shows the underlying links within a standard financial analysis.

The Pro Forma Income Statement, also known as the Profit and Loss Table, incorporates a sales forecast and personnel plan. The standard statement starts with sales, subtracts cost of sales to show gross margin, then subtracts operating expenses for earnings before interest and taxes (EBIT). Then it subtracts interest and taxes to create net income. Figure 9–2 shows a simple example. Figure 9–3 has a more detailed example.

The Pro Forma Balance Sheet shows assets, liabilities, and capital. The balance sheet starts with a starting balance set either by start-up costs or by past results. Changes in the balance sheet can be critical to a business because they affect

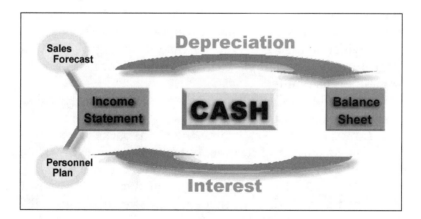

Figure 9–1. The linked financials pull information together to create a fully linked system. All assumptions lead to the most critical element, cash in the bank.

Pro-forma Income Statement					
	Jan-98	Dec-98	1998	1999	2000
Sales	$10,000	$55,000	$592,000	$875,000	$1,100,000
Cost of Sales	$2,500	$19,000	$159,000	$219,000	$289,000
Other	$0	$0	$0	$0	$0
	-----------	-----------	-----------	-----------	-----------
Total Cost of Sales	$2,500	$19,000	$159,000	$219,000	$289,000
Gross margin	$7,500	$36,000	$433,000	$656,000	$811,000
Gross margin percent	75.00%	65.45%	73.14%	74.97%	73.73%
Operating expenses:					
Advertising/Promotion	$3,000	$3,000	$36,000	$40,000	$44,000
Public Relations	$2,500	$2,500	$30,000	$30,000	$33,000
Travel	$7,500	$7,500	$90,000	$60,000	$110,000
Miscellaneous	$500	$500	$6,000	$7,000	$8,000
Payroll expense	$12,000	$27,250	$194,750	$377,000	$432,000
Leased Equipment	$500	$500	$6,000	$7,000	$7,000
Utilities	$1,000	$1,000	$12,000	$12,000	$12,000
Insurance	$300	$300	$3,600	$2,000	$2,000
Rent	$1,500	$1,500	$18,000	$0	$0
Depreciation	$0	$200	$200	$450	$600
Payroll Burden	$1,680	$3,815	$27,265	$52,780	$60,480
Contract/Consultants	$0	$0	$0	$0	$0
Other	$0	$0	$0	$0	$0
Total Operating Expenses	$30,480	$48,065	$423,815	$588,230	$709,080
Profit Before Interest and Taxes	($22,980)	($12,065)	$9,185	$67,770	$101,920
Interest Expense ST	$0	$400	$3,600	$12,800	$12,800
Interest Expense LT	$417	$417	$5,000	$5,000	$5,000
Taxes Incurred	($5,849)	($3,220)	$146	$12,493	$21,030
Net Profit	($17,548)	($9,661)	$439	$37,478	$63,090
Net Profit/Sales	-175.48%	-17.57%	0.07%	4.28%	5.74%

Figure 9–2. A simple profit and loss statement, as built into the Business Plan Pro software. This is one of two optional models. Months are omitted to save space.

cash flow. For example, when accounts receivable increases, the increase has the effect of absorbing cash. An increase in inventory absorbs cash. Changes in debt also affect interest costs, which influence the Income Statement. Figure 9–13, on page 128, shows a simple example of a balance sheet, with some months omitted.

The Pro Forma Cash Flow is the most important, because cash flow is the most critical analysis possible in business. The cash flow starts with Net Income, then adds back Depreciation (that was taken out of income, but is a noncash item). Then it accounts for other changes in cash that reflect on the balance sheet, instead of the Income Statement. We'll look in great detail at the cash flow in this section, after explaining the income statement. Examples are included in Figures 9–4 to 9–12, with detail about how the cash flow works and how to work with it.

Pro-forma Income Statement							
	Jan-98	Feb-98	Nov-98	Dec-98	1998	1999	2000
Sales	$138,400	$195,500	$223,000	$154,500	$2,155,425	$2,378,500	$2,642,500
Direct Cost of Sales	$35,480	$50,475	$56,900	$39,100	$552,518	$608,750	$676,100
Production	$12,750	$12,750	$12,750	$12,750	$153,000	$229,000	$311,500
Other	$0	$0	$0	$0	$0	$0	$0
	----------	----------	----------	----------	----------	----------	----------
Total Cost of Sales	$48,230	$63,225	$69,650	$51,850	$705,518	$837,750	$987,600
Gross margin	$90,170	$132,275	$153,350	$102,650	$1,449,908	$1,540,750	$1,654,900
Gross margin percent	65.15%	67.66%	68.77%	66.44%	67.27%	64.78%	62.63%
Operating expenses:							
Sales and Marketing Expenses							
Sales and Marketing Sa	$14,000	$14,000	$14,000	$14,000	$168,000	$177,000	$186,000
Advertising/Promotion	$15,000	$25,000	$30,000	$15,000	$264,000	$280,000	$310,000
Events			$15,000		$40,000	$42,000	$44,000
Public Relations	$3,000	$3,000	$3,000	$3,000	$36,000	$38,000	$40,000
Travel	$0	$5,000	$5,000	$0	$31,000	$33,000	$35,000
Miscellaneous	$2,000	$2,000	$2,000	$2,000	$24,000	$25,000	$26,000
Other	$1,000	$1,000	$1,000	$1,000	$12,000	$13,000	$14,000
	----------	----------	----------	----------	----------	----------	----------
Total Sales and Market	$35,000	$50,000	$70,000	$35,000	$575,000	$608,000	$655,000
Sales and Marketing Pe	25.29%	25.58%	31.39%	22.65%	26.68%	25.56%	24.79%
General and Administrative Expenses							
General and Administra	$22,500	$22,500	$22,500	$22,500	$270,000	$284,000	$299,000
Leased Equipment	$3,000	$3,000	$3,000	$3,000	$36,000	$36,000	$36,000
Utilities	$1,000	$1,000	$1,000	$1,000	$12,000	$12,000	$12,000
Insurance	$500	$500	$500	$500	$6,000	$6,000	$6,000
Rent	$2,500	$2,500	$2,500	$2,500	$30,000	$30,000	$30,000
Depreciation	$0	$0	$0	$3,000	$3,000	$3,000	$3,000
Payroll Burden	$8,138	$8,138	$8,138	$8,138	$97,650	$112,950	$129,525
Profit sharing				$20,000	$20,000	$25,000	$30,000
Other	$1,000	$1,000	$1,000	$1,000	$12,000	$12,000	$12,000
	----------	----------	----------	----------	----------	----------	----------
Total General and Adm	$38,638	$38,638	$38,638	$61,638	$486,650	$520,950	$557,525
General and Administra	27.92%	19.76%	17.33%	39.89%	22.58%	21.90%	21.10%

Figure 9–3. The more detailed structure of the pro forma income statement, another of the options in Business Plan Pro. You can always add and delete expense item rows.

FILLING OUT THE PRO FORMA INCOME STATEMENT

As you know, the income statement projects profits and losses, and in a business plan it's about forecasting, not reporting. In the standard income statement shown in Figure 9–2, taken from Business Plan Pro, sales and cost of sales come from the sales forecast, like the one shown in Figure 7–1. The personnel data are taken from the personnel plan table, like the one shown in Figure 8–1.

The difficult part is the educated guessing. When that's done, the calculations are simple. Gross margin is the result

C47	=Tax_rate_percent*(Profit_before_int_and_taxes-(Interest_expense_ST+Interest_expense_LT))					
	A	C	D	E	F	G
1	**Profit and Loss (Income Statement)**					
2		Jan	Feb	Mar	Apr	May
36	Development Expenses					
37	Development Payroll	$5,000	$5,000	$5,000	$5,000	$5,000
38	Software & Equipment	$2,000	$2,000	$2,000	$10,000	$2,000
39		------------	------------	------------	------------	------------
40	Total Development Expenses	$7,000	$7,000	$7,000	$15,000	$7,000
41	Development %	0.00%	0.00%	0.00%	1449.28%	242.05%
42		------------	------------	------------	------------	------------
43	Total Operating Expenses	$39,450	$49,850	$60,275	$200,375	$183,275
44	Profit Before Interest and Taxes	($39,450)	($49,850)	($62,275)	($208,393)	($190,425)
45	Interest Expense Short-term	$0	$0	$0	$0	$0
46	Interest Expense Long-term	$0	$0	$0	$0	$0
47	Taxes Incurred	($9,863)	($12,463)	($15,569)	($52,098)	($47,606)
48	Net Profit	($29,588)	($37,388)	($46,706)	($156,294)	($142,819)
49	Net Profit/Sales	0.00%	0.00%	0.00%	-15100.91%	-4938.41%

Figure 9–4. Negative Taxes.

24	Calculating new accounts payable				
25	Operating expenses	$39,450.00	$49,850.00	$60,275.00	$200,375.00
26	Less non-payables operating expenses				
27	Payroll in operating expenses	($20,000.00)	($20,000.00)	($25,500.00)	($29,000.00)
28	Payroll burden	($3,000.00)	($3,000.00)	($3,825.00)	($5,325.00)
29	Depreciation	$0.00	$0.00	$0.00	$0.00
30	Subtotal	$16,450.00	$26,850.00	$30,950.00	$166,050.00
31	Plus additional payables				
32	taxes incurred, if they are positive	$0.00	$0.00	$0.00	$0.00
33	Inventory purchase	$0.00	$0.00	$0.00	$1,552.50
34	Interest expense	$0.00	$0.00	$0.00	$0.00
35	Purchased assets, if they are positive	$0.00	$0.00	$0.00	$0.00
36	Other costs of sales	$0.00	$0.00	$2,000.00	$2,035.00
37	Subtotal	$16,450.00	$26,850.00	$32,950.00	$169,637.50
38	Amount paid immediately	$1,645.00	$2,685.00	$3,295.00	$16,963.75
39	*Remainder (new accounts payable)*	$14,805.00	$24,165.00	$29,655.00	$152,673.75
40	Include negative taxes (true/false)	FALSE			

Figure 9–5. Tax Toggle in Cash Details.

of subtracting cost of sales from sales. Gross profit, also called contribution margin, also called EBIT (earnings before interest and taxes), is the result of subtracting operating expenses from gross margin. Subtract interest and taxes, and you have net profit.

The simple income statement shown in Figure 9–2 doesn't divide operating expenses into categories. Figure 9–3 contains an example of a more detailed income statement, one that divides operating expenses into three standard categories: Sales and Marketing Expenses, General and Administrative Expenses, and Other Expenses. The use of these standard

	A	O	P	Q
	C3	0.1		
1	General Assumptions			
2		2000	2001	2002
3	Short-term Interest Rate %	10.00%	10.00%	10.00%
4	Long-term Interest Rate %	10.00%	10.00%	10.00%
5	Payment Days Estimator	30	30	30
6	Collection Days Estimator	45	45	45
7	Inventory Turnover Estimator	6.00	6.00	6.00
8	Tax Rate %	0.00%	0.00%	0.00%
9	Expenses in Cash %	10.00%	10.00%	10.00%
10	Sales on Credit %	3.75%	3.75%	3.75%
11	Personnel Burden %	15.00%	15.00%	15.00%

Figure 9–6. Zero Tax Rate for Loss Periods.

	A	B	C	D	E	F
	D15	=$B15*Sales				
1	Profit and Loss (Income Statement)					
2			Jan	Feb	Mar	Apr
10	Gross Margin %		17.71%	14.40%	13.70%	31.91%
11	Operating expenses:					
12	Sales and Marketing Expenses					
13	Sales and Marketing Payroll		$24,475	$24,493	$24,570	$26,238
14	Ads		$5,000	$5,000	$7,000	$10,000
15	Outside reps	6.00%	$16,102	$20,522	$24,938	$42,095
16	Mailing		$3,000	$11,800	$5,500	$10,500

Figure 9–7. Expense as Percent of Sales.

categories makes it easier to compare projected results with standards for an industry or with past results. Also, the structure of this income statement matches the structure of the detailed personnel plan shown in Figure 8–2.

PLANNING VS. ACCOUNTING

There is a clear distinction between planning and accounting. Planning begins today and goes forward into the future. Ac-

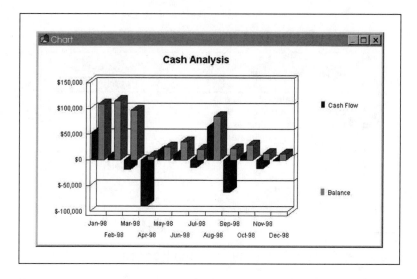

Figure 9–8. The cash flow chart for AMT set at standard, 45 days average collection days, 7 inventory turns per year. The dark bar shows the cash balance, and the light bar shows the cash flow.

General Assumptions					
	Jan-98	Dec-98	1998	1999	2000
Short Term Interest Rate	8.00%	8.00%	8.00%	8.00%	8.00%
Long Term Interest Rate	8.50%	8.50%	8.50%	8.50%	8.50%
Payment days	45	45	45	45	45
Collection days	45	45	45	45	45
Inventory Turnover	7.00	7.00	7.00	7.50	8.00
Tax Rate Percent	20.00%	20.00%	20.00%	20.00%	20.00%
Expenses in cash%	14.00%	14.00%	14.00%	14.00%	14.00%
Sales on credit	70.00%	70.00%	70.00%	70.00%	70.00%
Personnel Burden %	16.00%	16.00%	16.00%	16.00%	16.00%

Figure 9–9. Assumptions used for the cash flow chart in Figure 9–8.

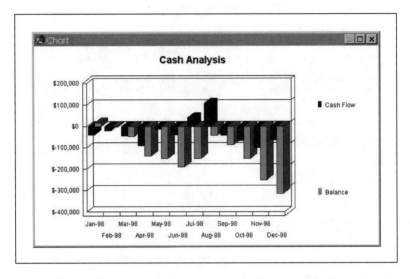

Figure 9–10. Revised cash flow scenario, showing how badly the cash projection looks when some key assumptions change only slightly.

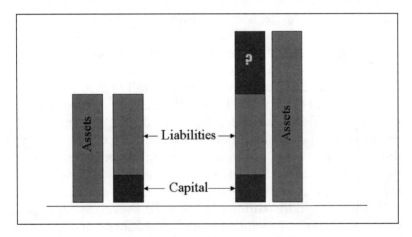

Figure 9–11. A critical business problem: Growing assets without capital.

Pro-Forma Cash Flow					
	Jan-98	Dec-98	1998	1999	2000
Net Profit:	($17,548)	($9,661)	$439	$37,478	$63,090
Plus:					
Depreciation	$1,500	$1,500	$18,000	$0	$0
Change in Accounts Payable	$9,475	($5,005)	$26,068	$1,434	$11,035
Current Borrowing (repayment)	$0	$0	$60,000	$100,000	$0
Increase (decrease) Other Liabilities	$0	$0	$0	$0	$0
Long-term Borrowing (repayment)	$50,000	$0	$50,000	$0	$0
Capital Input	$0	$0	$0	$0	$0
Subtotal	$43,428	($13,167)	$154,507	$138,911	$74,125
Less:	Jan	Dec	1905	1905	1905
Change in Accounts Receivable	$10,000	($32,500)	$100,000	$97,072	$50,676
Change in Inventory	$0	$0	$0	$0	$0
Change in Other ST Assets	$0	$0	$0	$0	$0
Capital Expenditure	$0	$0	$0	$0	$0
Dividends	$0	$0	$0	$0	$0
Subtotal	$10,000	($32,500)	$100,000	$97,072	$50,676
Net Cash Flow	$33,428	$19,333	$54,507	$41,839	$23,449
Cash balance	$58,428	$79,507	$79,507	$121,346	$144,796

Figure 9–12. The cash flow table from Business Plan Pro, with some months omitted. The cash projection first groups items that normally add cash when they are positive, then items that normally absorb cash when they are positive.

counting ends today and goes backward into the past. Planning is for making decisions, setting priorities, and assisting management. Accounting is also for information and management, of course, but there are legal obligations related to taxes. Accounting must necessarily go very deep into detail. Planning requires a balance between detail and concept, because there are times when too much detail is not productive.

Many people fail to understand this distinction, and they put disproportionate attention into accounting details as they develop a plan. For example, tax reporting and proper accounting requires detailed lists of assets and depreciation, whereas for planning purposes a good estimate is more efficient.

To understand this difference, consider the relative proportion of uncertainty in a forward-looking estimate of depreciation versus a sales forecast. The AMT computer store, one of our Business Plan Pro sample plans, projects depreciation of approximately $13,000 per year. It expects sales to rise from $5 million to $9 million in three years. AMT could develop a plan that lists future assets purchases and uses depreciation functions to depreciate each future asset according to accepted formulas. Doing that would probably reduce the uncertainty built into the depreciation estimate, but how much uncertainty would be reduced, and for how much effort? A 50% variation in the projected depreciation, either way, comes to less than $10,000, while a 10% variation in the sales forecast in the last year is worth $900,000. A good business plan process maintains the proportion between effort and value. Accounting needs detailed depreciation in this company, after the fact, but the business plan, looking three years ahead, doesn't.

SIMPLIFYING ASSUMPTIONS

Business Plan Pro does follow the general model of business planning, as opposed to accounting, when it comes time to make simplifying assumptions. We want to call your attention to several of the more important assumptions we make. We'll also explain why we make them, why they work in most cases, when they don't work, and what to do when they don't work.

The Government Doesn't Pay for Losses

As the Business Plan Pro documentation explains in several places, taxes are based on simple mathematics. Your estimated tax in the Profit and Loss table is the product of multiplying pretax profits by the tax rate you typed into your General Assumptions.

This simple, powerful estimator is excellent in most cases. However, if you have a string of steady losses, it requires special attention. In that case, you need to be aware of tax treatments and tax toggles. You do have a potential problem if you leave everything in default mode: you'll end up with a projection that treats taxes as if the government paid back money to you when you lose money.

The Simplifying Assumption

The simplifying assumption in this case is taxes as simple mathematics. Business Plan Pro multiplies pretax profits by the tax rate percentage in your General Assumptions table, and that gives it its estimate for taxes.

This is rather simple. We could make it a lot more complex with lookup functions for graduated tax rates. We could do formulas to change tax treatment in different countries. We could automatically change the treatment for loss situations. The tax rate forms specify pages of different rates. Furthermore, the real rates depend on specific deductions and specific situations.

Still, this is about planning, not accounting, and simple is good. The estimated tax rate is easy to understand and easy to apply. You get a lot more planning power from a simple and obvious estimated input than from a complex, hard-to-follow formula. There is a real danger of automating assumptions to the point at which users don't realize how much is involved and how critical those assumptions are.

Software Specifics

Figure 9–4 shows a perfect example from one of our better sample plans. The InteliChild.com sample plan projects steady losses throughout the three years in the plan. The first look, as you see in Figure 9–4, indicates negative taxes throughout.

The problem, however, is that government doesn't pay companies to lose money. We could end up with a negative tax rate unless we're careful with the plan.

Figure 9–5 shows the quick solution for conservative cash flow estimates. Find the tax toggle cell in the Cash Details worksheet and type the word "false" into it. The tax toggle is C40. When the tax toggle is false, the cash flow estimate ignores negative taxes. They are not added to Accounts Payable.

The Recommended Solution

The solution to the potential problem is the tax rate assumption in the General Assumptions table, and your own follow-up. Figure 9–6 shows the key point, which is a zero tax rate.

Specifically, to handle taxes for a business plan that has a long string of losses:

1. Set the tax rate to zero for the period of losses. Figure 9–6 shows the General Assumptions table, with the years columns displaying a zero tax rate.

2. If your plan includes making a profit later on, then you'll have a "loss carried forward" tax advantage that will reduce the tax rate when there are profits.

3. Therefore, your tax rate in the profitable periods should be less than it would have been otherwise. This should be a simple educated guess; you are not doing tax accounting here, just planning. Take whatever your tax rate would have been, and make it lower.

4. If you insist on detailed mathematical calculations— and only because you insist—here's more detail:

5. Take the sum of the losses. For example, $100K.

6. Multiply that by your estimated tax rate when you make profits. For example, $100K * .25 = $25K. Call that the loss carried forward.

7. Subtract that amount ($25K) from the tax estimate of the first profitable year. For example, if the tax estimate was $50K at an estimated 25% rate, $50K minus $25K is $25K. Don't worry about making this an exact calculation, an estimate is good enough for planning purposes.

8. Change your estimated tax rate in the profitable year to make the estimated tax equal to the reduced estimate. For example, if the estimated tax was $50K at 25%, and your target tax is $25K, then make your tax rate 12.5% for that first profitable year.

9. Explain the adjustment in text. The explanation can be this simple: "taxes are set at zero during the loss periods. The loss carried forward impact reduces the estimated tax rate during the profitable periods." This

should be in the text accompanying the General Assumptions table.

Depreciation as a Single Row of Simple Input

Business Plan Pro uses a single row of data input to contain your estimated depreciation. This simplifying assumption is much better than a complex set of depreciation formulas, for several good reasons:

- Government tax authorities set strict rules for when and how assets can be depreciated.

- These rules are not always logical.

- Different assets are allowed to be depreciated according to different formulas: there is straight-line depreciation, double-declining balance, sum-of-the-years digits, and several other formulas.

- The formulas can't be applied to groups of assets; each asset generally has its own set of rules, according to which type of asset it is.

If we decided to apply detailed formulas to future assets, we'd have to estimate the purchase of those assets, and keep track of each significant asset and its depreciation formula separately. The detail required would produce an artificially difficult data problem without really reducing uncertainty in any practical way.

An educated guess is a better option. If you take a percent of assets value per year, based on past years' depreciation, that's a good option. If you don't have past data to use, then ask somebody who does. Ask your accountant. In the worst case, you can take 10% of assets value per year and not go too far wrong.

If you do have a business that depends on high-price capital assets, for which depreciation and purchase of assets is very significant, you can get detailed instructions and even examples of depreciation functions from Chapter 10. That chapter also has illustrations of programming the user-defined tables, so you can create a new depreciation and assets table and link that into the main tables.

Interest Rates as Simple Mathematics

Business Plan Pro treats loan interest and principal payments according to standard accounting: interest, which is deductible against income as an expense, is in the Profit and Loss table. Principal repayment, which is not deductible, affects the Cash Flow and the Balance Sheet, but not the Profit and Loss.

Following the accounting standard, it calculates monthly interest expenses by multiplying the balance for any given month by the interest rate assumption in General Assumptions. It calculates annual interest by taking the average balance and multiplying that by the interest rate in the General Assumptions. Both of these calculations are logical and easy to understand.

However, as easily understood and as logical as these calculations may be, they may not be nearly as exact as you'd want them for accounting purposes after the fact.

One potential problem is that the bank might calculate interest based on the beginning balance, while Business Plan Pro calculates based on the ending balance.

Another problem is the timing of the loan: a loan taken out on January 28 produces the same interest estimate in Business Plan Pro as a loan taken out on January 3.

Furthermore, Business Plan Pro will take a loan taken out at any time during the second, third, fourth, or fifth year of a plan and calculate its average balance as ending balance plus beginning balance divided by two. Since the beginning balance was zero, that calculation divides the loan amount by half, for planning purposes. That means that interest will be as if the loan were taken out on June 30, the middle of the year, regardless of whether it was planned for the first month or the last month.

Most of these problems are not really problems in business plans. Good practical estimates, easy to explain, are more valuable than detailed exact calculations based on uncertain assumptions.

If your business plan should require more detailed interest calculations because of the significance of the amounts, you can adjust the estimated interest rates in the General Assumptions table to produce exactly the interest you want. Then all you need to do is explain the reason for the interest rate assumptions in the text that accompanies the General Assumptions table.

Profit and Loss Variations

As explained earlier in this chapter, the Profit and Loss table in Business Plan Pro has two forms, the simple form and the more complex one that breaks expenses into categories. What isn't discussed is the underlying logic and implementation: both variations exist within the same spreadsheet region. Business Plan Pro automatically hides the more complex rows and sets some values to zero when you choose the simpler form.

You can experiment with this difference by going to the Plan Wizard and switching between breaking expenses into categories and not. When you break into categories, you see more rows in Profit and Loss. When you don't, you see fewer rows, but they are some of the same rows.

This can be particularly disconcerting if you use the Format menu to show all the rows in the table. You don't have to hide them again after you've done this; simply use your Table menu to go to any other table and then return to Profit and Loss.

Links from Other Tables

One of the most common errors with Profit and Loss is the failure to realize how extensively it gets data from other tables. Sales and Costs of Sales come from the Sales Forecast. Payroll and Payroll Burden come from the Personnel Plan. Interest expenses are calculated automatically, from the balance of liabilities in the Balance Sheet and the interest rates in General Assumptions.

Interest expenses generate more than their share of questions, so those are discussed in detail later in this same section.

Make an Expense a Percent of Sales

Figure 9–7 shows another common use of named variables in formulas, as the Business Plan Pro Profit and Loss table sets an expense to be a percent of sales. The formula is shown in the illustration. The percent rate is set as a variable in column B, and all the cells in the row apply that percentage to the named variable "Sales." There is a list of more than 100 named variables included in the Advanced Table Programming Help.

Problems Deleting Rows

Within the Profit and Loss, there are some green rows, presumably unprotected and unlinked, that can't be deleted. This can be especially tricky with the simpler Profit and Loss table, because it hides rows from the more complex table. Underneath, harder to see, you can't delete either the top or the bottom row because of the underlying SUM formulas. You can, however, transfer data from the middle row (or any middle row if you added rows) to the top or bottom, and then delete that middle row.

When you run into this constraint involving deleting rows in the Profit and Loss, try moving data from a deletable row somewhere else among the expenses and changing the row name.

HANDLING CASH FLOW

Software Specifics

The Business Plan Pro cash model is powerful, and it can help you explain cash flow to your clients. For example, consider some scenarios taken from the AMT sample plan, which is on your CD-ROM as AMT Computer Store.spd (details on sample plan files are in the software guide, which is Part 2 of this book).

In its business plan AMT expects to make $167,000 net profits in year 1, on sales of $6.3 million. Figure 9–8 shows the Business Plan Pro chart for its cash flow with collection days set for 45 days. The light bars in that illustration show the cash balance, which in a business plan means the assumed balance in checking and similarly liquid cash. The dark bars show the cash flow, which is the change in the cash balance every month. A business plan needs to have its cash balance (the light bars) above zero at all times, although its cash flow (the dark bars) can go below. The chart shows the next 12 months of the cash plan. As shown in Figure 9–8, the plan looks acceptable. The cash balance is always above zero. Figure 9–9 shows a view (without all months showing) of the general assumptions related to the cash flow chart in Figure 9–8.

Figure 9–10 highlights the importance of cash flow and cash management. In the chart for this second scenario for the same time period, only one variable has changed: collection days go from 45 days to 60 days. The difference in cash balances, with that one change, is more than $300,000. You can see this in the illustration by noting how far below zero the cash balance goes at its lowest point. This means that with only a 15-day decline in collection days, that same company now needs more than $300,000 of new money—loans or investments—that it didn't need before.

This is a stunning example of the dramatic difference between profits and cash. There is no change in costs, prices, expenses, payroll, or anything else except 15 days of wait for money. The difference in real money available to the owners of the company is more than $300,000, but in theory at least (in fact there may be some capital expense or interest expense implications) profits haven't changed a single penny!

Figure 9–11 shows the background, the underlying problem, in graphic terms. As collection days increase, assets—accounts receivable—increase relative to sales and expenses.

Given the basic rule of assets being equal to capital plus liabilities, when you increase those assets, you need more capital or more liabilities to support your working capital.

The impact here is much more than simple financial concepts. If the collection problems require an additional $300,000 of working capital, business planning can mean the difference between disaster and survival. The sample company probably has enough assets to borrow additional working capital but only if it foresees its needs in advance. Even if we assume this company does have enough history and financial strength to support the additional liabilities, the bank is going to want credit applications well in advance of this company needing the money. So the business plan here is critical.

Cash Flow Inputs

Figure 9–12 shows a basic view of the cash flow analysis, which is probably the most important analysis in the plan— certainly the most important financial or numerical analysis. This powerful table absorbs other important assumptions and data and provides a centralized table for managing the business cash plan. This illustration omits some months so you can see the way cash flow works in months first and then for years.

I use a cash flow model based on the sources and uses of cash, optimized for linking to the other tables in the plan. As you can see in the illustration, this model starts with net income, adds a set of items—increase in accounts payable, new loans, new capital—that add cash when they are positive and subtract cash when they are negative. Then it subtracts a set of items that absorb cash when positive, including any increase in accounts receivable and inventory, new assets, and dividends.

The model shown here is hardly the only way to project cash. We recommend it because it offers a powerful tool for understanding and projecting cash, particularly in a software mode. It allows a direct link and immediate feedback on the impact of borrowing money and paying loans and, in general, the cash impact of changes in the balance sheet.

SOME KEY FORMULAS IN DETAIL

The method discussed here, which is the one used in Business Plan Pro, rests on some interesting assumptions about how forecasts are made. For example, if we know cost of sales and inventory turnover assumptions, we can calculate the balance in inventory. Also, if we know collection days and sales on credit, we can calculate the resulting accounts receivables balance. If we know about expenditures going into accounts payable and we have an assumption for payment days, then we can calculate the accounts payable balance. The mathematics are correct but sometimes confusing. Furthermore, the software includes an automatic override facility so you can choose to ignore the mathematics and formulas for estimating and just type in your own estimate. As good as the mathematical estimates are, in some situations it is better to directly estimate your balances for these items and type them into the model directly. You are the accountant, so it is worth taking the effort to understand the details. Let's look in detail at each of the three key items in the cash model: accounts payable, inventory, and accounts receivable.

Dealing with Accounts Payable

Changes in accounts payable are important to cash flow. If you owed $100,000 last month, and you now owe $200,000, and everything else is unchanged, then your cash has increased by $100,000. A new dollar in accounts payable is a dollar that was spent in the profit and loss but is still in the bank. The software calculates the accounts payable balance automatically, using some key assumptions. Although you don't need to go into the algebra in detail, your relationship with your client—who is doing his or her own plan—may require some familiarity. Here is how the software estimates accounts payable: The software calculates a "new accounts payable" value in each column, month or year. This is an estimate of the amount added to accounts payable each time period, regardless of what was paid out. It uses the "expenses in cash%" assumption from the general assumptions table and the planned costs and expenses to estimate the amount added to accounts payable. The detailed formula is:

$$= (1 - \text{expenses in cash } \%)(\text{Total Operating Expenses} + \text{Cost of Sales} - [\text{Payroll} + \text{Payroll Burden}])$$

For ongoing companies, Accounts Payable in the balance sheet is estimated using the formula:

$$= \text{Payment Days} \times \text{New accounts payable} \times (12/365)$$

This is simple algebra, reworked from the standard formula for calculating payment days. Normally you know your new accounts payable and your payables balance, so you calculate payment days. In this case, because we are looking at the future instead of reporting the past, we assume payment days and expenses, so we calculate the payables balance.

For start-up companies, accounts payable is a more complicated formula that guards against accidentally estimating more money in accounts payable than has been spent in total since the company started. It is based on the same formula used for ongoing companies, with some additional nuances to calculate the lowest value possible.

For accounts payable in the second and third year, the estimate takes the percentage of payables to new accounts payable in the previous year and applies it to the calculated new accounts payable in the present year, then applies a mathematical factor for the estimated change in accounts payable assumptions. Specifically, the formula in year 2 is:

$$= (\text{Accounts payable}[\text{Yr1}]/\text{New accounts payable}[\text{Yr1}]) \times \text{New accounts payable} \times (\text{Payment days}/\text{Payment days}[\text{Yr1}])$$

Calculating Inventory Balances

The software calculates inventory using assumptions for inventory turnover and cost of sales. Normally we calculate inventory turnover as a function of average balances and cost of sales. For the plan, however, we calculate the average balance using the assumption for turnover and cost of sales.

The monthly inventory formula for ongoing companies is:

$$= (\text{Cost-of-sales} \times 12)/\text{Inventory-turns}$$

For start-ups, in which start-up inventory is more likely to be a factor, the formula used is:

$$= \text{MAX}([\text{Cost-of-sales} \times 12]/\text{Inventory-turns, previous-} \\ \text{inventory-Cost-of-sales})$$

To calculate inventory for the second and third year, the formulas calculate the percentage of inventory to total cost of sales for the previous year and apply it to the cost of sales for the next year and factor in a mathematical factor for the change in the inventory turnover estimator. Specifically, the formula for inventory in year 2 is:

$$= \text{Cost of sales} \times \text{Inventory}[\text{Yr1}]/\text{cost of sales}[\text{Yr1}] \times \\ \text{Inventory-turns}[\text{Yr1}]/\text{Inventory-turns}$$

Calculating Accounts Receivable

The accounts receivable calculation is one of the most important and, unfortunately, one of the most complex in the software model.

In the first three months, the problem is that the software doesn't know amounts of previous receivables balances or sales on credit. The business plan has to start somewhere, and it doesn't ask the user for these values from the past as it starts. It has only your opening accounts receivable from the start-up worksheet or the past performance worksheet.

To create a reasonable estimate, it calculates accounts receivable using estimates for sales on credit and collection days. Normally you, the accountant, calculate collection days as a function of accounts receivables balance and sales on credit. Business Plan Pro uses algebra to rework the formula, calculating the balance from the collection days assumption and sales on credit. So for the first three months of the plan, the calculated accounts receivable balance is:

$$= (\text{Collection-days} \times \text{Sales-on-credit} \times 12)/365$$

That is adjusted for start-up companies with some minimums to avoid having more in the receivables balance than total sales on credit for the history of the company. For example, if a start-up company sells $10,000 on credit in its first month and estimates 60 collection days, the formula above would estimate $20,000 in receivables after a single month. In fact, some additional formulas make sure the receivables won't be higher than $10,000 in this special case.

By the fourth month in the model, the software has sales history for three previous months, including sales on credit. For that and all following months it drops the algebraic formula above and calculates receivables on the basis of the collection days and past sales on credit, using specific sales on credit numbers from previous months.

THE IMPORTANCE OF HANDLING EXCEPTIONS

Despite the elegance of the software's formulas for calculating balances from assumptions, they don't always work better than simple human educated guessing. All of the formulas for the three key balance items (payables, receivables, and inventory) assume a reasonably steady-state business, so that one month's sales, costs, and expenses are a reasonable estimate of the recent past and near future. That assumption is simply not valid for all businesses. The software has an override facility so that, if your client's business is different from the norm and isn't estimating balances well, he or she can type over the formulas with estimated guesses. This is an area that will require real substantive input from the accountant in the relationship, because whether the formulas or a person provides estimates, the estimated levels of balance items are critical to future cash flow.

CASH ESTIMATIONS IN PRACTICE

You could, of course, use any of several other methods, depending on your preference and your clients. My recommendation is to stick with what you have in the software, because it is financially correct and does a good job projecting the real implications of business decisions that affect working capital. As you work with a plan, if the assumptions project a negative cash balance, then go to the cash area and add new loans or new capital to bring in additional working capital. If the cash balance generates a great deal of cash (hooray), then you can go into the cash flow table and type in dividends or purchase of additional assets. The response to cash behavior is centralized in the cash table and mimics the response in the real world, borrowing money, investing, or taking money out of the company.

For a better illustration, let's look at the way the cash flow works in an actual example, showing how we change and adjust. Figure 9–13 shows the cash flow chart again, with an unacceptable balance. The dark bars in the chart, which is

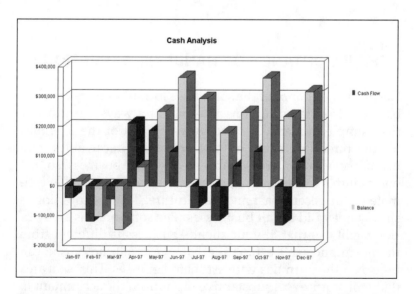

Figure 9–13. This cash chart, from Business Plan Pro, is a warning. The cash balance falls below zero in the first three mohths, which means that checks would bounce. The business plan is not finished yet.

taken from Business Plan Pro, shouldn't extend below zero. If they do, checks bounce. A plan without a working cash flow, which is what we see here, is not a finished plan.

Figure 9–14 shows the associated cash table for the first four months of the business plan year. Notice that the projected cash balance is negative, dropping to a deficit of close to $150,000 in March. This cash flow needs fixing.

Using the cash flow model in Business Plan Pro, we correct the cash flow problems in the plan much like we do in real life: invest more money or borrow more money. In Figure 9–15 we see the adjusted cash flow for this case, and the adjustments are significant:

In February we borrow $100,000 in short-term credit and invest $25,000 in new capital. Compare Figures 9–14 and 9–15 and notice the changes in February, with borrowing and investment showing up as positive numbers in the cash flow table. The borrowed money shows up as a positive entry in the "Current Borrowing (Repayment)" row.

In March we had to borrow even more from the credit line, another $30,000. This is another positive entry in the "Current Borrowing (Repayment)" row.

Pro-Forma Cash Flow				
	Jan-98	**Feb-98**	**Mar-98**	**Apr-98**
Net Profit:	$595	($3,782)	$17,450	$162,719
Plus:				
Depreciation	$1,000	$1,010	$1,020	$1,030
Change in Accounts Payable	$44,672	$101,743	$59,705	$133,150
Current Borrowing (repayment)	$0	$0	$0	$0
Increase (decrease) Other Liabilities	$0	$0	$0	$0
Long-term Borrowing (repayment)	($2,942)	($2,962)	$97,017	($3,005)
Capital Input	$0	$25,000	$0	$0
Subtotal	$43,325	$121,008	$175,191	$293,895
Less:	$35,810	$35,840	$35,871	$35,901
Change in Accounts Receivable	($24,543)	$102,835	$102,392	($72,935)
Change in Inventory	$82,433	$111,687	$101,505	$156,232
Change in Other ST Assets	$0	$0	$0	$0
Capital Expenditure	$25,000	$0	$15,000	$0
Dividends	$0	$0	$0	$0
Subtotal	$82,890	$214,522	$218,897	$83,298
Net Cash Flow	($39,565)	($93,514)	($43,706)	$210,597
Cash balance	$15,867	($77,647)	($121,352)	$89,245

Figure 9–14. The cash flow table related to Figure 9–13. It shows how the cash balance is projected to fall below zero in several months.

Pro-Forma Cash Flow				
	Jan-98	Feb-98	Mar-98	Apr-98
Net Profit:	$595	($4,316)	$16,756	$162,719
Plus:				
Depreciation	$1,000	$1,010	$1,020	$1,030
Change in Accounts Payable	$44,672	$101,743	$59,705	$133,150
Current Borrowing (repayment)	$0	$100,000	$30,000	($130,000)
Increase (decrease) Other Liabilities	$0	$0	$0	$0
Long-term Borrowing (repayment)	($2,942)	($2,962)	$97,017	($3,005)
Capital Input	$0	$25,000	$0	$0
Subtotal	$43,325	$220,475	$204,498	$163,895
Less:	$35,810	$35,840	$35,871	$35,901
Change in Accounts Receivable	($24,543)	$102,835	$102,392	($72,935)
Change in Inventory	$82,433	$111,687	$101,505	$156,232
Change in Other ST Assets	$0	$0	$0	$0
Capital Expenditure	$25,000	$0	$15,000	$0
Dividends	$0	$0	$0	$0
Subtotal	$82,890	$214,522	$218,897	$83,298
Net Cash Flow	($39,565)	$5,953	($14,399)	$80,597
Cash balance	$15,867	$21,820	$7,421	$88,018

Figure 9–15. The cash flow has been adjusted by borrowing. Compare this illustration to Figure 9–14.

In April, when profits are up and cash is up, we pay back the $130,000 borrowed in February and March. This is a negative entry in the same current borrowing row.

Figure 9–16 shows the result of the adjustments, which is another acceptable cash chart. Notice that the projected balance is no longer negative.

THE BALANCE SHEET IS ALREADY CALCULATED

Figure 9–17 shows a sample plan balance sheet, with months omitted to show the first and last month and the years. The balance sheet is a picture of a business's assets, liabilities, and capital—its overall financial picture—on a given date, at a given time. In Business Plan Pro, the software automatically calculates the balance sheet from other worksheets that affect it: starting balances from either the start-up worksheet or past performance; income statement; and cash flow.

Figures 9–18 and 9–19 give you a way to track the relationship between the balance sheet and cash flow. Figure 9–18 shows the balance sheet associated with the situation shown

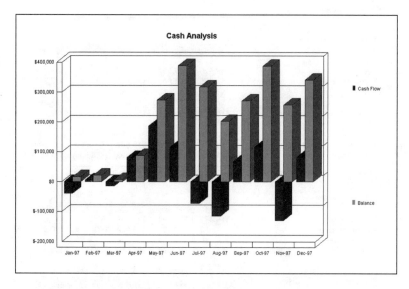

Figure 9–16. The adjusted cash chart after the cash flow was corrected. Compare this chart to Figure 9–13.

in Figure 9–14, with the cash flow still incomplete. Figure 9–19 shows the balance sheet associated with Figure 9–15, with the financial adjustments to correct the cash flow.

The Business Plan Pro software calculates all the balance items automatically. Net profit and depreciation come from the income statement. Accounts receivable, accounts payable, and inventory are calculated from assumptions. Starting balances come from either the start-up worksheet or past performance. Other changes, such as new borrowing or debt repayment, or new capital or dividends, or changes in other assets and liabilities, go into the cash flow first. For example, when you borrow money you set the borrowed amount into the cash flow, and the balance changes automatically.

Ultimately, your business plan must treat its pro forma statements much like you are used to treating financial statements in standard accounting and reporting. Balance sheet items in the plan mean exactly what they mean in reporting past results. In the initial balance, the software recalculates retained earnings as a plug amount, forcing retained earnings to make sure that assets are always equal to capital plus liabilities. Retained earnings remain unchanged through the

Pro-forma Balance Sheet					
	Jan-98	Dec-98	1998	1999	2000
Short-term Assets					
Cash	$58,428	$79,507	$79,507	$121,346	$144,796
Accounts receivable	$10,000	$100,000	$100,000	$197,072	$247,748
Inventory	$0	$0	$0	$0	$0
Other Short-term Assets	$7,000	$7,000	$7,000	$7,000	$7,000
Total Short-term Assets	$75,428	$186,507	$186,507	$325,418	$399,543
Long-term Assets					
Capital Assets	$0	$0	$0	$0	$0
Accumulated Depreciation	$1,500	$18,000	$18,000	$18,000	$18,000
Total Long-term Assets	($1,500)	($18,000)	($18,000)	($18,000)	($18,000)
	----------	----------	----------	----------	----------
Total Assets	$73,928	$168,507	$168,507	$307,418	$381,543
Debt and Equity					
	Jan-98	Dec-98	1998	1999	2000
Accounts Payable	$14,475	$31,068	$31,068	$32,502	$43,537
Short-term Notes	$0	$60,000	$60,000	$160,000	$160,000
Other ST Liabilities	$0	$0	$0	$0	$0
Subtotal Short-term Liabilities	$14,475	$91,068	$91,068	$192,502	$203,537
Long-term Liabilities	$50,000	$50,000	$50,000	$50,000	$50,000
Total Liabilities	$64,475	$141,068	$141,068	$242,502	$253,537
Paid in Capital	$50,000	$50,000	$50,000	$50,000	$50,000
Retained Earnings	($23,000)	($23,000)	($23,000)	($22,561)	$14,916
Earnings	($17,548)	$439	$439	$37,478	$63,090
Total Equity	$9,453	$27,439	$27,439	$64,916	$128,006
Total Debt and Equity	$73,928	$168,507	$168,507	$307,418	$381,543
Net Worth	$9,453	$27,439	$27,439	$64,916	$128,006

Figure 9–17. Sample pro forma balance sheet from Business Plan Pro. The balance sheet is normally calculated automatically from other assumptions in other tables.

12 monthly columns, then at the end of the year the software moves earnings into retained earnings.

RATIOS AND THE BUSINESS PROFILE

When you have a linked software system developing financial tables, business ratios can be automatic. By the time you've got tables for important assumptions, profit and loss, cash flow, and balance sheet, you have the information required to calculate all of the business ratios shown in Figure 9–19. These include the standard financial profile information provided by Business Plan Pro.

Pro-forma Balance Sheet				
	Jan-98	**Feb-98**	**Mar-98**	**Apr-98**
Short-term Assets				
Cash	$15,867	($102,647)	($146,352)	$64,245
Accounts receivable	$370,564	$473,399	$575,791	$502,857
Inventory	$333,445	$445,132	$546,637	$702,869
Other Short-term Assets	$25,000	$25,000	$25,000	$25,000
Total Short-term Assets	$744,876	$840,884	$1,001,076	$1,294,970
Long-term Assets				
Capital Assets	$375,000	$375,000	$390,000	$390,000
Accumulated Depreciation	$51,000	$52,010	$53,030	$54,060
Total Long-term Assets	$324,000	$322,990	$336,970	$335,940
	--------------	--------------	--------------	--------------
Total Assets	$1,068,876	$1,163,874	$1,338,046	$1,630,910
Debt and Equity				
	Jan-98	**Feb-98**	**Mar-98**	**Apr-98**
Accounts Payable	$268,569	$370,312	$430,017	$563,167
Short-term Notes	$90,000	$90,000	$90,000	$90,000
Other ST Liabilities	$15,000	$15,000	$15,000	$15,000
Subtotal Short-term Liabilities	$373,569	$475,312	$535,017	$668,167
Long-term Liabilities	$281,920	$278,958	$375,974	$372,970
Total Liabilities	$655,489	$754,270	$910,992	$1,041,137
Paid in Capital	$500,000	$500,000	$500,000	$500,000
Retained Earnings	($87,208)	($87,208)	($87,208)	($87,208)
Earnings	$595	($3,188)	$14,262	$176,981
Total Equity	$413,387	$409,604	$427,054	$589,773
Total Debt and Equity	$1,068,876	$1,163,874	$1,338,046	$1,630,910
Net Worth	$413,387	$409,604	$427,054	$589,773

Figure 9–18. This balance sheet is related to the cash flow before adjustments in Figure 9–14.

You can explain to your client the use and importance of standard ratios. The software automatically calculates more than a dozen standard ratios, including breakdowns of expenses and costs of sales into percent of sales, and breakdowns of balance sheet items into percent of total assets. The ratios also include standard ratios such as quick ratio, current ratio, and return on sales. You will probably be called on to explain these to your client, and there may be discussion of whether the projected ratios are acceptable to lenders or investors. As you already know, what is acceptable varies by industry, and depends on past results and other factors. The change in the ratios is often as important as the raw numbers.

Business Plan Pro provides information for the fourth column, as shown in Figure 9–19, containing standard financial

Ratio Analysis				
	2001	2002	2003	Industry Profile
Sales Growth	121.39%	132.83%	142.72%	10.50%
Percent of Total Assets	**2001**	**2002**	**2003**	**Industry Profile**
Accounts Receivable	30.60%	33.56%	33.15%	19.20%
Inventory	33.28%	38.02%	35.50%	38.00%
Other Short-term Assets	2.72%	2.24%	1.55%	20.80%
Total Short-term Assets	86.34%	83.14%	80.34%	78.00%
Long-term Assets	13.66%	16.86%	19.66%	22.00%
Total Assets	100.00%	100.00%	100.00%	100.00%
Other Short-term Liabilities	0.54%	0.45%	0.31%	44.60%
Subtotal Short-term Liabilities	44.37%	40.53%	35.58%	39.70%
Long-term Liabilities	12.61%	9.66%	5.27%	14.10%
Total Liabilities	56.98%	50.19%	40.85%	58.70%
Net Worth	43.02%	49.81%	59.15%	41.30%
Percent of Sales	**2001**	**2002**	**2003**	**Industry Profile**
Sales	100.00%	100.00%	100.00%	100.00%
Gross Margin	29.13%	23.82%	26.31%	37.20%
Selling, General & Administrative Expenses	20.57%	18.23%	16.53%	22.30%
Advertising Expenses	1.94%	1.64%	1.43%	4.10%
Profit Before Interest and Taxes	11.28%	7.79%	12.75%	1.50%
Ratios	**2001**	**2002**	**2003**	**Industry Profile**
Current	1.95	2.05	2.26	1.78
Quick	1.20	1.11	1.26	0.75
Total Debt to Total Assets	56.98%	50.19%	40.85%	58.70%
Pre-Tax Return on Net Worth	64.27%	44.08%	56.68%	3.80%
Pre-Tax Return on Assets	27.65%	21.95%	33.53%	9.30%

Figure 9-19. Standard Industry Ratios.

profiles from Integra Information. These numbers are standard industry ratios, occasionally required by banks as part of loan applications.

Business Plan Pro also offers a fourth column, not shown in Figure 9–21, for inputting RMA numbers. The RMA numbers are standard industry ratios published by the RMA association, a membership organization of banks and credit managers. The standard ratios come from more than 140,000 businesses as small as $1 million per year in sales, listed by standard industry code (SIC) and published annually in the RMA's *Annual Statement Studies*. Many banks require borrowers to include RMA numbers on loan applications, so Business Plan Pro leaves a place in the ratios table for printing them out. Usually when a bank requires these numbers, the loan manager has access to them from an in-house library and is able to provide them for business planning. You may also want to have the annual study in house, for use by clients. As of this writing, the cost of the *Annual Statement Studies* for nonmembers is as little as $29.00 for a hard copy, or $125 for a disk copy. You can contact RMA directly at (800) 677-7621,

Pro-forma Balance Sheet	Jan-98	Feb-98	Mar-98	Apr-98
Short-term Assets				
Cash	$15,867	$21,820	$7,421	$88,018
Accounts receivable	$370,564	$473,399	$575,791	$502,857
Inventory	$333,445	$445,132	$546,637	$702,869
Other Short-term Assets	$25,000	$25,000	$25,000	$25,000
Total Short-term Assets	$744,876	$965,351	$1,154,849	$1,318,744
Long-term Assets				
Capital Assets	$375,000	$375,000	$390,000	$390,000
Accumulated Depreciation	$51,000	$52,010	$53,030	$54,060
Total Long-term Assets	$324,000	$322,990	$336,970	$335,940
Total Assets	$1,068,876	$1,288,341	$1,491,819	$1,654,684
Debt and Equity	Jan-98	Feb-98	Mar-98	Apr-98
Accounts Payable	$268,569	$370,312	$430,017	$563,167
Short-term Notes	$90,000	$190,000	$220,000	$90,000
Other ST Liabilities	$15,000	$15,000	$15,000	$15,000
Subtotal Short-term Liabilities	$373,569	$575,312	$665,017	$668,167
Long-term Liabilities	$281,920	$278,958	$375,974	$372,970
Total Liabilities	$655,489	$854,270	$1,040,992	$1,041,137
Paid in Capital	$500,000	$525,000	$525,000	$525,000
Retained Earnings	($87,208)	($87,208)	($87,208)	($87,208)
Earnings	$595	($3,721)	$13,035	$175,755
Total Equity	$413,387	$434,071	$450,827	$613,547
Total Debt and Equity	$1,068,876	$1,288,341	$1,491,819	$1,654,684
Net Worth	$413,387	$434,071	$450,827	$613,547

Figure 9–20. This balance sheet is related to the cash flow after adjustments in Figure 9–11.

or via the Internet at the website www.rmahq.org. Another good source for this kind of information is Integra Information Systems, whose websites are www.integrainfo.com and www.privateco.com.

Business Plan Pro doesn't print RMA numbers as part of a standard plan. Instead, RMA users will print the ratios table separately, from Table mode, setting print options to include that last column.

Profitability Ratios:	1998	1999	2000
Gross margin	22.55%	26.13%	28.03%
Net profit margin	2.66%	5.57%	6.96%
Return on Assets	6.38%	13.39%	16.15%
Return on Equity	15.45%	27.85%	29.28%
Activity Ratios	1998	1999	2000
AR Turnover	3.64	3.64	3.64
Collection days	67	92	92
Inventory Turnover	6.86	4.97	5.80
Accts payable turnove	5.90	5.58	5.45
Total asset turnover	2.40	2.40	2.32
Debt Ratios:	1998	1999	2000
Debt to net Worth	1.42	1.08	0.81
Short-term Debt to Lia	0.77	0.82	0.88
Liquidity ratios			
Current Ratio	1.89	1.92	1.92
Quick Ratio	0.91	1.12	1.16
Net Working Capital	$1,060,442	$1,225,477	$1,390,392
Interest Coverage	4.68	9.73	15.35
Additional ratios	1998	1999	2000
Assets to sales	0.42	0.42	0.43
Debt/Assets	59%	52%	45%
Current debt/Total As:	45%	43%	39%
Acid Test	-0.11	0.04	0.02
Asset Turnover	2.40	2.40	2.32
Sales/Net Worth	5.81	5.00	4.21
Dividend payout	0.00	0.00	0.00

Figure 9–21. The Business Plan Pro software automatically calculates key ratios from numbers already calculated in other tables.

CHAPTER 10
FINANCIALS IN EXPERT MODE

Business Plan Pro includes preprogrammed financial tables, already linked together for optimal use, so that the average user can create correct financials without having to program. If you do know spreadsheets and financial analysis, however, then those tables are also programmable with many of the same formulas and even some of the functions used in standard Windows spreadsheets. This chapter focuses on some of the spreadsheet details, flexibility, and expert options.

Our assumption is that you know spreadsheets and you know finance, so you want to have more background on the spreadsheets in Business Plan Pro. You can make some powerful additions and modifications to the standard product.

SPREADSHEET PROTECTION AND FLEXIBILITY

Business Plan Pro protects many of its formula cells to protect them from accidental user error. For example, the row named "Sales" in the Profit and Loss table draws its information from the sales forecast table. If that row were not protected, then users could accidentally destroy the conceptual link by typing their sales numbers directly into the profit and loss. Cost of sales, salaries, and interest expenses are similarly protected, because they too draw information from other tables. Summary rows and columns are protected to prevent accidental overtyping that would change the math.

Normally, Business Plan Pro shows programmed formula cells in black and data cells in green. Black cells are protected and cannot be changed. Green cells—even some that contain formulas—are not protected and can be changed.

Some people are frustrated by protection of definitions in row labels. For example, the row named "Cost of Sales" cannot be changed to anything else. The labels are locked in these cases because the programming involved puts specific information into the row. We would not want the user to be able to take "Total Operating Expenses," for example, and rename that label, because the formulas in that row add up total operating expenses.

Other row labels are built for easy changing. The names of sales lines, personnel rows, expense rows, and implementation milestones, for example, are easy to change. Use the Edit Row Label command. Business Plan Pro allows unlimited rows in personnel, sales forecast, expenses in profit and loss, and in the milestones table. You can add and delete as many rows as you want within the areas intended to contain those rows. This allows you to exactly match sales classifications and charts of accounts.

SPREADSHEET LINKING

Chapter 9 introduced the links between the important financial tables included. All of these are set up so that a change in any one will logically and immediately produce corresponding changes in all the linked tables.

- The starting date in the plan wizard sets the dates that show on all tables, months, and years. When you change the starting date, all the dates change, but the financial numbers do not. Business Plan Pro was created that way on purpose, so that starting dates could slide without such sliding destroying the plan.

- The general assumptions table sets assumptions used in personnel plan, profit and loss, cash flow, balance sheet, and ratios.

- Every plan has either a past performance table or a start-up table to set starting balances in the cash flow and balance sheet.

- The sales forecast creates sales and costs of sales lines that feed the income statement, which in turn affects the cash flow, balance sheet, and ratios.

- The personnel plan creates assumptions used by the profit and loss table. It gets the payroll burden from general assumptions.

- Profit and loss draws assumptions from general assumptions, sales, personnel, and balance sheet (to determine interest expense).

- Cash flow draws from the profit and loss, balance, and general assumptions.

- The balance sheet calculates itself, without user intervention, on the basis of assumptions made everywhere else, unless you choose to use the Input Balances option. That option gives you the ability to override the algebraic formulas involved in calculating certain key balance sheet items and to use your own estimated balances instead. The rows involved are accounts receivable, accounts payable, and inventory, all of which are critical to cash flow.

- The software calculates business ratios automatically.

Finally, specific marketing program activities are included to make it all planned, budgeted, assigned, and real.

PERCENT OF SALES AND SIMILAR FORMULAS

Business Plan Pro includes several convenient variables in English so you can use them in formulas. For example, the total sales row in the profit and loss is named "sales," so you can use it in formulas. To see how that works, find an empty green (data input) cell in the Profit and Loss table, among the expenses. Type the formula

$$=.01*sales$$

into that cell and press <Enter>. You now have an operating expense programmed to automatically calculate as 1% of sales.

"Sales" is just one of several useful variables that are already programmed for use in the tables. Here are some others:

- Gross margin: sales less cost of sales

- Cost of sales: includes the unit cost of sales from your Sales Forecast, plus additional costs of sales added into the Profit and Loss

- Depreciation: from the Profit and Loss sheet

- Dividends: from the Cash Flow

- Earnings: from Profit and Loss

- Inventory: from the Balance Sheet

- Liabilities: from the Balance Sheet

- Indexer: a useful variable that can be used anywhere, tells you which month of the plan. For example, in the fourth monthly column, regardless of starting date, the formula = INDEXOR will show up the number 4.

Any of these can be used in a spreadsheet formula, as variables. They mean exactly what you would expect them to mean, as standard accounting terms.

CASH FLOW AND SENSITIVE BALANCE OVERRIDE

Chapter 9, "Pro Forma Financial Statements," includes important details on how Business Plan Pro combines net income and changes in the balance sheet to project cash flow. This is critical to a useful business plan.

Please remember, as you deal with the automatic and linked cash flow, that the algebraic formulas involved don't work for all companies. They are financially and mathematically correct, however. Some examples follow.

- You estimate sales, sales on credit, and collection days, and the software predicts your balance of accounts receivable.

- You estimate expenses, cost of sales, payment days, and percent of payments made immediately, and the software predicts your balance of accounts payable.

- You estimate cost of sales and inventory turnover, and the software predicts your inventory balance.

Remember, however, that there are some important weaknesses to this methodology:

- There is no conceptual link between your starting balances of accounts receivable, accounts payable, and inventory. The first month is calculated on the basis of the factors you predict. The starting balance is typed data. You can calculate balances on the basis of assumptions and algebra or on the basis of previous balances, but you can't do both. We use assumptions and algebra.

- The algebra involved assumes each month is a reasonable estimate of all months. That works best in steady-state companies, not so well in high-growth or highly seasonal businesses.

Just as important, there is a critical override facility to allow you to choose to ignore the algebra and estimate balances directly. You can find this override in the Table Manager area of your Balance Sheet Table. Set the override, and protected cells will be unprotected for your balance sheet rows for Accounts Receivable, Accounts Payable, and Inventory. Then you can type your balances directly into these rows. The rest of the model remains intact; you lose only the automatic balance estimation for these rows.

MANAGING THE TAX TREATMENT

The standard Business Plan Pro uses very simple tax assumptions. You select a tax rate percentage in General Assumptions. Profit and Loss calculates taxes by simply multiplying that percentage times the profits before taxes. There is no graduated tax rate, and no sales tax. While this is the only practical way to set the default to handle all cases, you can easily make some modifications.

For a business in a loss situation, the simple mathematics of the tax treatment, a before-tax loss with a positive tax rate creates a negative tax. Taxes actually reduce the amount of loss. While this makes sense for a going company that has some profitable and some losing months during the year, it probably doesn't make sense for a start-up company with steady losses.

The underlying issue is the tax loss carryforward. As every accountant knows, a tax loss can usually be carried forward to reduce taxes in later years, when there are profits. As a business planner, you can keep track of that loss carryforward as if it were an asset, but you don't want to pretend that the government is actually paying it back to you, because that would create a false boost to cash flow.

The simplest and probably the best way to handle this problem, within Business Plan Pro, is to set zero tax rates during the loss period, and then artificially lower tax rates when profits start. Explain the tax rate assumptions in the text for the General Assumptions and the Profit and Loss tables. For example, if the start-up generates a $100K loss during its first 12 months and then a $100K profit the next year, you might set taxes to zero for both years and explain in the text the impact of loss carryforward.

Another more sophisticated way to handle this preserves the numbers of the loss carryforward but compensates for it in cash flow. Add your tax loss back into the cash flow as an additional asset, and the software will assume you are buying it, which will adjust the cash flow while preserving the display of the tax loss in profit and loss. You could do that with a formula, within the spreadsheet, as follows:

1. Go to the Cash Flow table and find the row named "Change in Other ST Assets."

2. For the first month of a string of losses, type the equals key (=).

3. Use the Table menu to move to the Profit and Loss table. Find the row for taxes in the same month, click the

appropriate cell with the mouse, and press the <Enter> key.

4. Business Plan Pro will bounce you back to the cash flow, and the formula for your new short-term assets cell will be linked automatically to the loss in profit and loss. The cash flow is adjusted now, but the system still shows the tax impact of the loss.

The result of this adjustment is a more detailed treatment of taxes during the loss situation.

If you want to create a detailed business model within Business Plan Pro, you could use the lookup function to create a lookup table for tax rates. The lookup function works in Business Plan Pro exactly as it does in Microsoft Excel, but it is an undocumented, unsupported feature. If you want to try it, use the User-defined table for a lookup rates table, add another row in that table to calculate profit before taxes, and make the tax rate in general assumptions a lookup. For example, if the lookup table is in the user-defined table cells $B$2:$C$7, and the profit before taxes is in row 10 of that user-defined table, then the tax rate in the general assumptions column C would be calculated with the formula:

$$= \text{VLOOKUP(User1!C10,User 1!\$B\$2:\$C\$6,2)}$$

Remember, as you deal with these assumptions, that the business plan is not for tax accounting; it is a guide to decisions. The goal is a reasonably accurate projection of future financials.

LOAN REPAYMENTS

Business Plan Pro follows accounting standards in separating loan payments into interest expense and repayment of principal. Interest expense appears as an expense in profit and loss, and principal repayment should be typed into the cash flow as an input.

As with tax treatment, the business plan uses simple mathematics. Interest goes into your profit and loss automatically as the product of multiplying the interest rate times the out-standing balance, of either short-term or long-term borrowing. Principal outstanding is reduced only by typing principal repayment assumptions as negative amounts into the cash flow rows assigned to changes in debt, long term or short term.

One problem with this is that some users want the software to calculate interest and principal payments as components of a steady loan repayment. If this comes up, as you deal with your business-planning client, the best answer is to take the repayment schedule straight out of the existing loan documents. The second best option is to use existing tools—you have them, you use them all the time—to calculate an estimated repayment schedule. The third option is to use the built-in financial functions (another set of functions that are there but not documented and not supported) within Business Plan Pro.

For an example of a payment function implemented within Business Plan Pro, view the included sample business plan for AMT, the computer reseller (Chapter 14). Go to the cash flow table and look at the formula for column C in the row labeled "long-term borrowing (repayment)." That formula is:

= PPMT (Assumptions!C4/12,Indexor + 46,120,400000)

The technical specifications of that payment function are:

PPMT (interest rate, period, total periods, loan amount)

In that sample plan, the payment function is used to derive the principal payment for a $400,000 loan at the assumed interest rate, in the 47th month of a 10-year loan. Note the use of the Indexer, the variable for which month of the plan. Including the Indexer variable means the formula can be copied to the right.

You should look at column E as well of that same plan, same table, same row. The formula is:

= PPMT(Assumptions!E4/
12,Indexor + 46,120,400000) + 100000

In that cell, the plan continues to pay the existing loan but also borrows an additional $100,000.

MANAGING DEPRECIATION

Business Plan Pro doesn't calculate depreciation for you. It does leave a single row in the Profit and Loss table for depreciation, but that row is data entry only. There are no formulas for depreciation.

As with the lookup function above, Business Plan Pro will also recognize the same standard depreciation functions used in Microsoft Excel. That includes the db(), ddb(), sln(), and syd(). They aren't documented or supported, but they work exactly the same as in Excel.

- db() gives you declining balance depreciation. The format is db(cost,salvage,life,period,month).

- ddb() gives you double declining balance depreciation. The format is db(cost,salvage,life,period,factor).

- sln() gives you straight-line depreciation. The format is db(cost,salvage,life).

- Syd() gives you sum-of-years-digits depreciation. The format is syd(cost,salvage,life,period)

The problem with all of these depreciation functions is that they require more detailed tracking of assets than you would normally do for a business plan. Each formula is intended to calculate depreciation on a single asset, and of course, in a business plan you want to summarize all of depreciation in a single row in the Profit and Loss table. Here again, as elsewhere in the plan, there is a big difference between business plan and tax report. The business plan needs to summarize, while the tax report needs to lay out detail.

AN EXAMPLE WITH ASSETS AND DEPRECIATION

Although we recommend a much simpler treatment of assets and depreciation, Figure 10–1 shows how you can use a user-

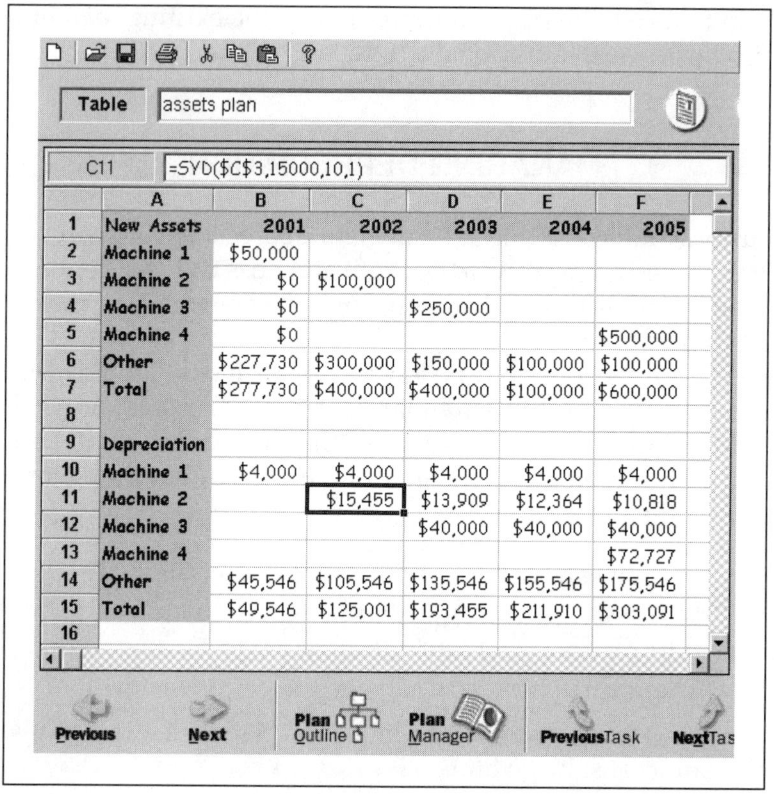

	A	B	C	D	E	F
1	New Assets	2001	2002	2003	2004	2005
2	Machine 1	$50,000				
3	Machine 2	$0	$100,000			
4	Machine 3	$0		$250,000		
5	Machine 4	$0				$500,000
6	Other	$227,730	$300,000	$150,000	$100,000	$100,000
7	Total	$277,730	$400,000	$400,000	$100,000	$600,000
8						
9	Depreciation					
10	Machine 1	$4,000	$4,000	$4,000	$4,000	$4,000
11	Machine 2		$15,455	$13,909	$12,364	$10,818
12	Machine 3			$40,000	$40,000	$40,000
13	Machine 4					$72,727
14	Other	$45,546	$105,546	$135,546	$155,546	$175,546
15	Total	$49,546	$125,001	$193,455	$211,910	$303,091
16						

Figure 10–1. Assets and Depreciation.

defined table with depreciation functions to help manage assets. In this case, capital assets are so important to the business's overall financial position that we used a user-defined table to track them directly. We also used the built-in depreciation functions to handle depreciation automatically:

- We depreciate Machine 2 with the sum-of-the-years' digits depreciation method, a built-in depreciation function compatible with Microsoft Excel depreciation functions. The syntax is as shown:

  =SYD(purchase price, salvage value,
  years of life, period)

  We copied that formula to the rest of the row to calculate depreciation for that machine for five years.

- We depreciated Machine 1 according to the straight-line method, which is another built-in function. The syntax for that depreciation function is:

  =SLN(purchase price, salvage value, years of life)

  which means that the actual formula in cells B10:F10 is

  " =SLN($B$2,10000,10)."

- We purchase Machines 3 and 4 according to the assumptions shown in the illustration, using the depreciation functions as well. Machine 3 gets straight-line depreciation and Machine 4 gets SYD depreciation.

- For the last line, which summarizes all other capital expenses for the various years, we depreciate by taking 20% of the value of the purchase in each year for each of the successive years. The underlying assumption is that all purchases are assets good for five years, depreciated straight-line at 20% per year, with no salvage value.

We Don't Recommend Depreciation in This Much Detail

Remember, as we discussed earlier, that planning is not accounting. A normal business plan for a normal company doesn't benefit from treatment of depreciation in this much detail. This example is for instruction purposes only.

BUILDING YOUR OWN LINKS

You can use the spreadsheet power to build your own links to fit your planning needs. Here are some examples:

Simple Link from Sales to Profit and Loss

Assume AMT plans on paying royalties equal to 10% of sales of software. We can build a formula that does that automatically. The formula is in Figure 10–2. We can take a row in Profit and Loss named "Royalties" and link it to the row in the Sales Forecast that contains software cells.

The formula for cell C6 in the illustration is "=Sales Forecast!C25*0.1." You could just type that formula into your worksheet, or you could follow these steps:

1. Select cell C6 in the Profit and Loss table. This is going to be the target cell for the link formula.

2. Use the Edit Row Label command in the Format menu to change its row label from "Other" to "Royalties."

3. Type the equals sign (=, just the "=" key, no quotations or parentheses) into the cell.

4. Go to the Table menu and choose the Sales Forecast table.

5. Find the cell you want to be the source cell, in this case cell C25, and click to select it. Your formula edit bar should at this point show the formula "=Sales Forecast!C25."

6. At this point you could just press the <ENTER> key and your formula would put whatever is in cell C25 of the Sales Forecast into cell C6 in Profit and Loss. However, in this case we want to make royalties equal to

C6	='Sales Forecast'!C25*0.1			
	A	C	D	E
1	Profit and Loss (Income Statement)			
2		Jan	Feb	Mar
3	Sales	$268,365	$334,025	$415,635
4	Direct Cost of Sales	$176,010	$231,161	$293,112
5	Production Payroll	$9,500	$9,500	$9,500
6	Royalties	$20	$20	$20
7		-----------	-----------	-----------
8	Total Cost of Sales	$185,530	$240,681	$302,632
9	Gross Margin	$82,836	$93,345	$113,004
10	Gross Margin %	30.87%	27.95%	27.19%

Figure 10–2. Simple Link from Sales to Profit and Loss.

only 10% of sales of software, so we type into the formula "*.1".

7. Press <ENTER>. Your formula is now correct, as " = Sales Forecast!C25*0.1." You are probably looking at Profit and Loss at this point, with cell C6 selected.

8. Even if you are looking at Profit and Loss, go back to the Table menu and choose Profit and Loss. This puts your Business Plan Pro back into the right table, the same one you're in.

9. To put this same link into the whole row, copy cell C6 and paste its formula into cells D6:N6, and P6:S6.

Linking from User-Defined into Sales Forecast

Business Plan Pro uses the user-defined tables to give you more spreadsheet power and more flexibility with your business plan.

Here's how that works in detail:

1. Select the target cell in the Sales Forecast.

2. Type the equals sign, " = ", into the cell (without quotation marks, just press the key that has = on it).

3. Use the Table menu to go to the user defined table that has the source cell.

4. Select the source cell by clicking on it.

5. Press <ENTER>.

6. Even though you are seeing the Sales Forecast table, use the Table menu to return the system pointer to the Sales Forecast table.

An IF Function in Profit and Loss Linked to a Sales Row in Sales

Figure 10–3 shows an expense row from Profit and Loss linked to a sales row, with a simple IF function to make the link

C21	=IF('Sales Forecast'!C33>10000,5000,2000)								
	A	C	D	E	F	G	H	I	J
1	Profit and Loss (Income Statement)								
2		Jan	Feb	Mar	Apr	May	Jun	Jul	Aug
18	Shows	$0	$0	$0	$0	$0	$0	$3,200	$0
19	Literature	$0	$7,000	$0	$0	$0	$0	$0	$0
20	PR	$0	$0	$0	$1,000	$0	$0	$0	$0
21	Seminar	$2,000	$2,000	$2,000	$2,000	$5,000	$2,000	$2,000	$2,000
22	Service	$2,000	$1,000	$1,000	$500	$2,500	$500	$500	$500
23	Training	$450	$450	$450	$450	$450	$450	$450	$450
24									
25	Total Sales and Marketing Expenses	$38,450	$54,250	$41,950	$50,450	$59,450	$52,450	$54,650	$51,450
26	Sales and Marketing %	14.33%	16.24%	10.09%	7.19%	9.23%	10.79%	15.08%	16.81%

Figure 10–3. The IF Function in a Linking Formula.

more effective. What the formula does is check whether training sales (in cell C33 of the Sales Forecast) are greater than $10,000. If they are, then the seminar expense is $5,000. If not, then the seminar expense is $2,000.

Here's how you would create that formula link, in your own plan, step-by-step and in detail:

1. Select the target cell. In this case it is cell C21 in the Profit and Loss.

2. Type "=IF(" into the cell (without the quotation marks).

3. Go to the Table menu and choose the Sales Forecast table.

4. Find the source cell in the Sales Forecast table and click on it to select it. In this case that cell is C33 in the Sales Forecast, the first month of estimated sales of training in the AMT sample plan. At this point the edit bar shows the formula "=IF(Sales Forecast!C33."

5. Type into the edit bar the rest of the formula as shown in the example, so it ends up ">10000,5000,2000)" and then press <ENTER>.

6. Use the Table menu to select the Profit and Loss again—even though it's showing—to set the system pointer back to Profit and Loss.

7. Copy the formula in C21 to the rest of the unprotected cells in the row, D21:N21 and P21:R21.

THE USER-DEFINED TABLES

Business Plan Pro's user-defined tables give you the option of developing your own complete tables to add to your business plan.

Pasting to User-Defined Table from an Excel Worksheet

You can copy a range from an Excel worksheet and paste it into a user-defined table. If you want to preserve the formulas within the worksheet, this is a two-step process.

Here are the details:

1. First, in Microsoft Excel, make sure that the spreadsheet area you want to paste contains only unprotected cells.

2. If you have any doubts, select the area you want to copy and paste, then use the Format menu, Cells command, and Protection tab to make sure those cells are not protected. IMPORTANT: if you copy protected cells from Excel to Business Plan Pro, they remain protected. You cannot access them to change them after they are copied.

3. From within Excel, select and copy the source area you want to use within Business Plan Pro.

4. Select Business Plan Pro. Choose the User-Defined table in the Table menu. Select the cell you want to have as the upper left cell in the target range. Remember, those cells should be unprotected in Excel.

5. Use Paste Special in the Edit menu, and choose the Paste All command. Your Excel spreadsheet will now be pasted into your Business Plan Pro user-defined table.

Tips and Traps with Pasting from Excel to Business Plan Pro

1. A simple copy and paste from Excel to Business Plan Pro copies values only, not formats or formulas. To copy

and paste spreadsheet information completely, you need to use the Paste Special command in Business Plan Pro and choose Paste All to paste both formulas and formats.

2. If you paste a formula from one worksheet containing an erroneous reference, you'll get a #REF error in the target worksheet. That's true in Excel alone, and it's also true when you paste from Excel into Business Plan Pro. For example:

- If you copy the formula "=C9" from cell C10 in Excel into cell C1 in Business Plan Pro (or Excel), you get a #REF error. Business Plan Pro wants to reinterpret the formula to refer to the relative row number (9 is 1 less than 10) but when you paste into row 1 you don't have the possibility of a lower row number.

- Copy a formula "=XYZ" (referring to a range name not already in Business Plan Pro) from Excel and paste it into Business Plan Pro. Business Plan Pro will behave like Excel does in this instance. It creates a new range named XYZ located in a position relative to the target cell.

- Copy the formula "=sales" from Excel and paste it into Business Plan Pro. Business Plan Pro will create a new range named "=sales_2" and will give the target cell the formula "=sales_2". To make the cell refer to the Business Plan Pro range named sales, you have to edit the formula manually.

An Investment Analysis with IRR, NPV, and Valuation

The InteliChild.com sample business plan, which is included on the Business Plan Pro main disk, includes an investment analysis in its User-Defined Table that uses the built-in functions for Net Present Value (NPV) and Internal Rate of Return (IRR). Figures 10–4 and 10–5 show this table.

- In 1999, the first-round investors purchase 500,000 shares of a total 1 million, for $1 per share. In row 10 they own 50% of the company at that point. The initial

B14   =NPV($B$19,B15:F15)

	A	B	C	D	E	F	G
2		1999	2000	2001	2002 2003 IPO		
3							
4	Total Shares Issued	1,000,000	1,500,000	1,800,000	2,000,000		
5	Valuation	$1,000,000	$6,000,000	$60,000,000	$125,000,000	$200,000,000	
6	Founders	500,000					
7	New Investment Amount	$500,000	$2,000,000	$10,000,000	$12,500,000		
8	Shares Purchased	500,000	500,000	300,000	200,000		
9	Dollars per Share	$1.00	$4.00	$33.33	$62.50		
10	Equity Purchased	50.00%	33.33%	16.67%	10.00%		
11	Ending Equity	25.00%	25.00%	15.00%	10.00%		
12	Ending Value	$50,000,000	$50,000,000	$30,000,000	$20,000,000		
13	Years Held	3					
14	NPV	$15,984,000	$18,880,000	$7,360,000	$2,800,000		IRR
15	Investor A IRR Calc	($500,000)	$0	$0	$0	$50,000,000	216.23%
16	Investor B IRR Calc		($2,000,000)	$0	$0	$50,000,000	192.40%
17	Investor C IRR Calc			($10,000,000)	$0	$30,000,000	73.21%
18	Investor D IRR Calc				($12,500,000)	$20,000,000	60.00%
19	Discount Rate	25.00%					

Figure 10–4. Investment Analysis Table.

G15   =IRR(B15:F15,$B$19)

	A	B	C	D	E	F	G
2		1999	2000	2001	2002 2003 IPO		
3							
4	Total Shares Issued	1,000,000	1,500,000	1,800,000	2,000,000		
5	Valuation	$1,000,000	$6,000,000	$60,000,000	$125,000,000	$200,000,000	
6	Founders	500,000					
7	New Investment Amount	$500,000	$2,000,000	$10,000,000	$12,500,000		
8	Shares Purchased	500,000	500,000	300,000	200,000		
9	Dollars per Share	$1.00	$4.00	$33.33	$62.50		
10	Equity Purchased	50.00%	33.33%	16.67%	10.00%		
11	Ending Equity	25.00%	25.00%	15.00%	10.00%		
12	Ending Value	$50,000,000	$50,000,000	$30,000,000	$20,000,000		
13	Years Held	3					
14	NPV	$15,984,000	$18,880,000	$7,360,000	$2,800,000		IRR
15	Investor A IRR Calc	($500,000)	$0	$0	$0	$50,000,000	216.23%
16	Investor B IRR Calc		($2,000,000)	$0	$0	$50,000,000	192.40%
17	Investor C IRR Calc			($10,000,000)	$0	$30,000,000	73.21%
18	Investor D IRR Calc				($12,500,000)	$20,000,000	60.00%
19	Discount Rate	25.00%					

Figure 10–5. Investment Analysis Table, IRR.

founders hold 500,000 shares, the other 50% (in cell B6). The valuation at that point is $1 million (in cell B5).

- The company goes public in 2003 with a market cap of $200 million (cell F5). By that time those first-round investors hold 25%, because their initial 50% has been diluted by new shares and new investors. Their yield at that point is $50 million (cell B12, repeated in cell

F15), 25% of $200 million. They invested $500K and received $50 million just a few years later.

- The cash stream for them is in cells B15:F15, which results in the NPV of $15.984 million, shown in B14. Figure 10–4 shows the formula that produces the NPV calculation, using the built-in NPV function. The function goes:

=NPV(discount rate, cash stream)

so you can see how it is applied in this case. The formula shows in the illustration.

- Their IRR is in cell G15, a healthy 216.23%. The exact formula for calculating IRR following the function syntax is:

=IRR(cash stream, starting discount rate)

- In 2000 the company issues 500,000 new shares (note the total increase in cell C4) and sells them to the second-round investors for $4 per share. Total valuation is then $6 million (cell C5, multiplying total shares in C4 by value per share in C9). These investors purchase ⅓ of the company (C10) for $2 million (C7).

- When the company goes public in 2003, if all goes according to plan, these investors will have 25% ownership, worth $50 million. That means their investment yields NPV of $18.88 million (C14) and IRR of 192.4% (G16). Business Plan Pro produces those values using the NPV and IRR functions.

- The third- and fourth-round investors purchase additional shares at higher valuations, as shown in the rest of the worksheet.

The Net Present Value (NPV) Function

Business Plan Pro offers a built-in Net Present Value (NPV) function as shown in detail in Figure 10–4. The formula shows in the edit bar, for the cell selected in the illustration. The normal way to put this function is:

$$=NPV(\text{discount rate, cash stream})$$

In the example, both the discount rate and the cash stream are references to a cell and a block of cells. However, you could also use the function:

$$=NPV(.25, -500000,0,0,0,50000000)$$

to generate the same results shown in Figure 10–4.

The Internal Rate of Return (IRR) Function

Business Plan Pro offers a built-in Internal Rate of Return (IRR) function as shown in detail in Figure 10–5. The formula shows in the edit bar, for the cell selected in the illustration. The normal way to put this function is:

$$=IRR(\text{cash stream, starting discount rate})$$

In the example, both the starting discount rate and the cash stream are references to a cell and a block of cells. However, you could also generate the same results by citing the block of cells containing the cash flow, and typing the discount rate, as in

$$=IRR(B15:F15,.25)$$

LINKING USER-DEFINED TABLES TO OTHER TABLES

The Personnel Plan, Start-up, Sales Forecast, Profit and Loss, and Cash Flow have many unprotected cells, expecting data entry, which you can link to the user-added tables if you choose. Here are some specifics:

1. Make sure your table preferences are set to show row and column headings. Look in the Table menu for the preferences view.

2. Go to the table that will receive the information linked from the user table, and select the target cell. For example, go to the sales forecast and click on the first row, first month.

3. Type the = key. Go to the Table menu and select User Defined. Find the cell in the user added that has your source information, in this example sales for the first month. Select that cell, and when you click you'll see that it is creating a formula. For example, if that cell in the user-defined table is C10, the formula will be

$$"=\text{User added!C10}"$$

4. Type the <Enter> key. The software will jump back to the original target table, and you'll see that the value in User Defined C10 is now showing there. In this example, it would be in your sales forecast in the cell you started in.

5. If you want, if you have a whole row of assumptions to link, you can use the Copy Right command in the Edit menu to copy that cell from column C across to column N.

This method works well with any of the User-defined tables, linking into any unprotected cell in any of the standard tables. Some of the examples we see in the experts area are:

- Linking a detailed list of capital investments into the start-up investment cell of the start-up worksheet.

- Providing more detail about specific cost of sales or sales units in the sales forecast.

- Building more detail about depreciation into the depreciation row of the Profit and Loss table.

- Building more detail about expense breakdowns into the Profit and Loss table.

CHAPTER 11
FINAL STEPS IN CREATING THE BUSINESS PLAN

MAKE IT CONCRETE AND SPECIFIC

You'll recall from Chapter 4 the need for a business plan to be specific. Far too many plans have way too much general promise and way too few specific plans. One can even write a complete plan with complete financial analysis without assigning any specific dates or responsibilities, and certainly without tracking results later. That kind of planning may read well and might even get money from a loan or an investor, but it isn't good planning.

The milestones table, shown in Figure 11–1, is my favorite business plan table. This table can be as simple as a spreadsheet list of activities. It pulls a business plan back into reality. With milestones, you set specific responsibilities for specific activities, with specific dates and specific budgets. This is what is really going to happen in a business, because it is what people are committed to. It is what you know you can follow through with. The milestones table is one of the things that makes a business plan of bricks instead of straw or sticks.

Figure 11–1 shows a milestones table as it would look after the fact, after the year has run its course and the plan-vs.-actual analysis is completed. The columns on the right of the table automatically calculate the variance between planned completion and actual completion and between planned spending and actual spending.

The real implementation follows with the process surrounding the plan, the following up and tracking, recording actual results, and making course corrections, which is the subject of the following sections.

REVIEW AND REVISE

Don't expect to ever really finish a business plan. Every new version brings on new revisions. Also, don't expect to start

Milestone	Mngr	Date	Dept.	Budget	Act date	Act $	Date P-A	$ P-A
Corporate Identity	TJ	12/16/97	Marketing	$10,000	1/14/98	$12,004	(29)	($2,004)
Seminar implementation	IR	1/9/98	Sales	$1,000	12/26/97	$5,000	14	($4,000)
Business Plan Review	RJ	1/9/98	GM	$0	1/22/98	$500	(13)	($500)
Upgrade mailer	IR	1/15/98	Sales	$5,000	2/11/98	$12,500	(27)	($7,500)
New corporate brochure	TJ	1/15/98	Marketing	$5,000	1/14/98	$5,000	1	$0
Delivery vans	SD	1/24/98	Service	$12,500	2/25/98	$3,500	(32)	$9,000
Direct mail	IR	2/15/98	Marketing	$3,500	2/24/98	$2,500	(9)	$1,000
Advertising	RJ	2/15/98	GM	$115,000	3/6/98	$100,000	(19)	$15,000
X4 Prototype	SG	2/24/98	Product	$2,500	2/24/98	$0	0	$2,500
Service revamp	SD	2/24/98	Product	$2,500	2/24/98	$2,500	0	$0
6 Presentations	IR	2/24/98	Sales	$0	1/9/98	$1,000	46	($1,000)
X4 Testing	SG	3/6/98	Product	$1,000	1/15/98	$0	50	$1,000
3 Accounts	SD	3/17/98	Sales	$0	3/17/98	$2,500	0	($2,500)
L30 Prototype	PR	3/26/98	Product	$2,500	4/11/98	$15,000	(16)	($12,500)
Tech98 Expo	TB	4/12/98	Marketing	$15,000	1/24/98	$1,000	78	$14,000
VP S&M hired	JK	6/11/98	Sales	$1,000	7/25/98	$5,000	(44)	($4,000)
Mailing system	SD	7/25/98	Service	$5,000	7/14/98	$7,654	11	($2,654)
Other							0	$0
Totals				$181,500		$175,658	11	$5,842

Figure 11–1. The milestones table, where specific and concrete business programs are specified for the business plan.

at the beginning and go through to the end, then publish. The process is not by nature sequential. When the profit looks good, the cash doesn't. You might revise sales and personnel, then profit looks bad. Research an issue and you'll often find that it changes your focus. A good plan is never really done.

As you think about finishing a plan, remember the discussion of form and function in Chapter 5. The finished plan may require presentation in color, special bindings, legal notices about confidentiality, disclaimers regarding offering of investment, and other formalities. You may need to prepare a two- or three-page summary memo to accompany the plan, tailored to the needs of banker, broker, or potential investors.

Software Specifics

The Business Plan Pro software included with this book will automatically create a business plan text with table of contents, cover page, legal page, and appendixes for displaying 12-month projections horizontally. Text, tables, and charts are automatically merged onto the page in an attractive professional format. You also have the option of exporting the plan's text, tables, and charts into a document format (RTF, or rich text format) that other Windows 95 software will read, and of exporting the tables to a Microsoft Excel–compatible spreadsheet file.

The use of the completed business plan is another area for close cooperation between accountant and client. Your client will look to you for guidance in the appearance and presentation. Does the plan look professional? Will the banker like it? You'll find yourself being able to reassure the client about the look and feel of the plan. Of course it has to be the client's plan, not yours, but presentation is important and you are in the business world.

IMPLEMENTING THE PLAN

Figure 11–2 is a reproduction of Figure 3–15. Here it serves as a reminder, after we've been through the process of creating a business plan, about the complete package for implementation. The plan itself must be realistic, specific, and simple. The milestones table (Figure 11–1) helps make a plan specific, so it can be tracked and followed. "Realistic" depends on the plan's objectives and forecasts. "Simple" depends on the focus

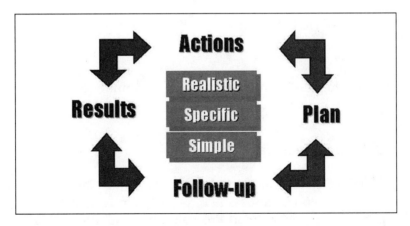

Figure 11–2. The *complete* planning process starts with a good plan and depends on follow up and tracking results.

and establishing priorities. The good plan includes these qualities that lead to implementation.

Once a plan is complete, the real management starts. Your role as accountant shifts from financial consultant to management consultant. The next sections of this chapter are about the care and feeding of business plans and business plan systems.

RECORD ACTUAL RESULTS

A plan should never lie untouched for more than a single month. As soon as the first month closes, the plan needs to record actual results.

The job of recording actual results is not difficult, and it is a vital part of implementation. Because a business plan is simplified on purpose, unlike accounting reports, there should not be a lot to type in. However, this vital job is almost always forgotten. Plans go into drawers and are never seen again. Avoid this for your own practice and for your clients' businesses. Make sure the actual results are available.

Remember that following up is a vital part of the planning process. Unless managers know that results will be tracked, they are not likely to implement. That's human nature.

Question: What is the difference between involvement and commitment in ham and eggs?

Answer: The hen is involved, the pig is committed.

Software Specifics

Specifically, for the sales forecast, income statement, cash flow, and balance sheet, you want to type into the plan—the Business Plan Pro software is set up for this automatically, when menu commands for it—the actual results. Figure 11–3 shows the Business Plan Pro screen

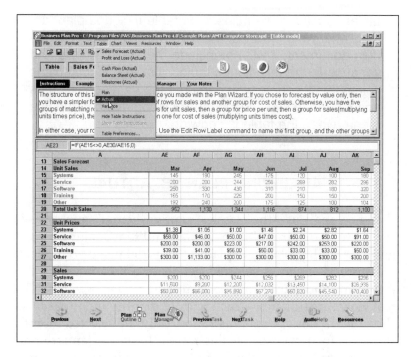

Figure 11–3. The menu settings in Business Plan Pro that switch the plan mode from plan to actual to variance.

when you select "Actual" in the Tables menu, instead of "Plan" or "Variance."

In the view shown in the illustration, if you were involved in that session, you would type actual sales units and dollar amounts into the indicated columns. The illustration omits most monthly columns for display purposes, but all 12 months are available for input.

The tables are set in advance for easier input of actual results. For example, in the plan view, you type in assumed units and price per unit, and the software calculates sales by multiplying price times units. In the Actual view, you type in units and dollar results—because this is the information you are likely to have—and the software calculates unit prices.

Pay careful attention to the milestones table, too. Milestones work differently than the other actual results tables, because the milestones table includes plan, actual, and variance in one single view. If you print the plan document, it will not include the actual results and variance in the milestones table—just the original plans columns. Of course, you can print the variance columns and the entire table, using the Print command in the File menu, when the table is showing.

ANALYZING PLAN VS. ACTUAL

Variance analysis—the classic "plan-vs.-actual" analysis—is critical to managing a business plan and to managing a business. You will probably explain specific details to your client.

Figure 11–4 shows selected details of a Business Plan Pro pro-forma income in plan, actual, and variance views. The real views are full views, each with 12 months and three years showing. In this special illustration, only the selected months show up for purposes of illustration. It shows January and February results completely for all three views, and March variance as well.

Plan			Actual			Variance		
	Jan-97	Feb-97	Jan-97	Feb-97	Mar-97	Jan-97	Feb-97	Mar-97
Sales	$200,000	$400,000	$202,404	$507,410	$250,000	$2,404	$107,410	$25,000
Direct Cost of Sales	$20,000	$40,000	$27,247	$74,861	$25,000	($7,247)	($34,861)	($2,500)
Freight	$7,000	$14,000	$6,523	$14,000	$7,500	$477	$0	($3,563)
Fulfillment	$3,000	$6,000	$2,871	$6,201	$2,750	$129	($201)	($1,063)
Royalties	$20,000	$40,000	$20,240	$50,741	$25,000	($240)	($10,741)	($20,680)
Total Cost of Sales	$50,000	$100,000	$56,881	$145,603	$60,250	($6,881)	($45,603)	($27,805)
Gross margin	$150,000	$300,000	$145,522	$361,807	$189,750	$9,285	$153,013	$52,805
Gross margin percent	75.00%	75.00%	71.90%	71.30%	75.90%	386.29%	142.46%	211.22%
Operating expenses:								
Sales/Marketing Expense	Jan-97	Feb-97	Jan-97	Feb-97	Mar-97	Jan-97	Feb-97	Mar-97
Sales/Marketing Salaries	$12,800	$12,800	$12,800	$12,800	$12,800	$0	$0	$0
Advertising - trade	$0	$6,500	$0	$6,500	$0	$0	$0	$6,500
Advertising - coop - retail		$0		$0	$30,000	$0	$0	($11,000)
Direct Mail Expenses	$0	$0	$0	$0	$0	$0	$0	$0
Graphics and collaterals	$1,500	$10,000	$1,362	$10,320	$25,000	$138	($320)	$0
Merchandising	$0	$10,000	$0	$9,960	$0	$0	$40	$8,630
Promotion	$120		$120		$0	$0	$0	$500
Public relations	$2,000	$2,000	$1,846	$2,000	$2,000	$354	$0	$1,000
Trade Shows and Events	$0	$2,400	$0	$2,400	$0	$0	$0	$3,000
Meals		$300		$300	$0	$0	$0	$300
Travel	$1,900	$2,000	$1,900	$2,000	$3,000	$0	$0	$1,000
Websites	$245	$250	$245	$250	$250	$0	$0	$0
Other	$1,000	$1,000	$2,345	$27,000	$1,000	($1,345)	($26,000)	$0
Total Sales/Marketing Exp	$19,565	$47,250	$20,418	$73,530	$74,050	($853)	($26,280)	$9,830

Figure 11–4. Selected columns of the plan, the actual, and the variance worksheets that are built into Business Plan Pro.

The variance analysis is set to correctly record favorable and unfavorable variances properly. In sales rows, the variance is positive when sales exceed plan, negative when they fall below the plan. In cost and expense rows, the variance is positive when expenses are less than plan, negative when expenses are greater than the plan.

Variance analysis needs case-by-case specifics. Spending less than budget on advertising, for example, could be smart buying or failure to implement. Maybe ads weren't submitted, and advertising wasn't done. Selling less than planned is normally bad news, but not always—maybe margins went up as sales fell below plan. Always, variance analysis demands human judgment and, ultimately, good management.

Variance analysis should take place every month. The software shows the variances automatically when actual results are typed in. Whether it's for your own practice or your clients, make sure actual results get into the plan every month and that somebody looks at the variances.

ONGOING REVISIONS

Revisions are literally vital to a plan. *Vital* means life-giving, and what keeps a plan alive is its revisions. It's not about forecasting so well that your plan stays correct for an entire year; it is about catching changes quickly and responding to them with management decisions.

Obviously, you don't want to revise your strategy every month. Strategy requires long-term consistency and patience. You need to stick to a strategy to make it work, and sometimes instant revisions and constant changes are the same as no strategy at all.

You do, however, need to stay constantly on top of changes in your ongoing forecasts for sales, costs, expenses, and most important, cash flow. We've seen in previous chapters how much a cash condition can change when economic conditions change and customers delay paying invoices, or conditions require more inventory than planned. You don't change strategy but you do respond to these changes with revised plans. If sales of product A are well above plan and sales of product

B well below plan, you absolutely need to see the changes quickly with good plan-vs.-actual analysis. Then you need to consider the significance in strategy terms. Do you stick with product B regardless, or do you revise budgets to emphasize Product A? Make your decisions strategic, but keep your antennae up all the time.

The most crucial monthly revisions are those that relate to cash flow. You cannot afford to run a company on a long-term plan when the short-term cash runs out. You must always revise for conditions that threaten the basic balance in the bank, which cannot go below zero.

Figure 11–5 shows how I recommend managing ongoing revisions to a plan, in the worksheet area intended for actual results. If you are using Business Plan Pro, you have this facility built into your plan software. This system automatically gives you a perfect area for revised budgets in the same worksheet area you also use for actual results. In the illustration, you see a sample in June 1998. The information in the April and May columns is real information, actual results. The numbers in the June, July, and August columns are revised forecasts based on the results for January through May. As the year goes on, the revised budgets disappear into the actual results as you type actual results into the proper months as

	Actual Results		Latest revised budget			
	Apr-98	May-98	Jun-98	Jul-98	Aug-98	Sep-98
Sales	$202,404	$507,410	$250,000	$275,000	$300,000	$275,000
Direct Cost of Sales	$27,247	$74,661	$25,000	$27,500	$30,000	$27,500
Freight	$6,523	$14,000	$7,500	$8,000	$8,500	$8,000
Fulfillment	$2,871	$6,201	$2,750	$3,000	$3,250	$3,000
Royalties	$20,240	$50,741	$25,000	$27,500	$30,000	$27,500
Total Cost of Sales	$56,881	$145,603	$60,250	$66,000	$71,750	$66,000
Gross margin	$145,522	$361,807	$189,750	$209,000	$228,250	$209,000

Figure 11–5. Using the "Actual" as "Latest Budget"—the actual worksheet includes real results in past months and revised budgets in future months.

the months close. This system gives you continuity with actual results and revised budgets, and you also get an automatic plan-vs.-actual analysis that maintains the integrity of your original plan and the true actual results.

Use the worksheet area intended for actual results to put in actual results for closed months and revised budgets and forecasts for future months. This then is the proper place for keeping a revised and up-to-date budget in the same area that you record the actual results, separate from the planned results.

SUMMARY AND CONCLUSIONS

In the end, helping your clients with business planning can be for you what it has been for me, a source of satisfaction as well as revenue. All businesses need to plan, but few do. That's a shame. Our business lore in this country associates business plans mainly with raising capital and applying for loans. Many people assume that they don't need a plan if they are already in business. Many others admit they need a plan, but think they don't have time, and if they are not forced to develop one, they postpone forever. Meanwhile, by postponing their planning, businesses fail to properly manage cash flow, miss opportunities, and waste resources.

Business planning, as a service offered to clients, is an important business opportunity for accountants. Many accountants offer this service, but many others worry about problems, including the cost to the client, the difficulty in managing hours spent, and the diminished likelihood of implementation when the accountant creates the plan instead of the managers.

We recommended working with business plan software as a standard tool for managing the business plan engagement. The client owns a copy, the accountant owns a copy, and the client does as much of the planning as possible. The accountant serves as expert advisor. Billing hours are reduced, so the costs are easier for the client to absorb. The resulting plan is more the client's plan than the accountant's plan, which means it is much more likely to achieve its business objectives.

The value of business planning depends on the resulting implementation. The process of developing a plan should be one that leads to commitment ahead of time and tracking and proper following up after the fact. Objectives should be concrete and measurable. Following up with variance and variance analysis, and regular revisions, is very important.

Long-term business survival depends to some extent on providing value. As an accountant, you should be good for your clients. If you are, you develop a better business for yourself in the long term. Business planning can help you provide real value because you encourage your clients to manage their businesses better. Improve their businesses and you improve your own.

The satisfaction comes, ultimately, from doing a good job for your clients. The best businesses believe in the value of what they do for their customers. The best professionals believe in the value of what they do for their clients. Helping clients develop business plans is that kind of opportunity. It can make you feel better at the end of the day, when you walk out of the office, for what you've done for your clients.

CHAPTER 12
INTERNATIONAL BUSINESS PLANS

A RAINY DAY IN RIO

I looked out the window of a parked plane, at a dark, drizzly airport, in Rio de Janeiro. Whatever spectacular views there might have been were obscured in low-hanging clouds. I was half a day from my starting point and still several hours from my eventual destination, Buenos Aires.

The memory sticks because as I looked into the dampness outside the plane, more than ten years ago, I worried about exactly the same subject as discussed in this chapter—business planning for the international company. Apple Computer, which was then riding the height of its success in the late 1980s, had hired me to travel to Argentina to instruct its local dealers on business planning.

Why not? I had lived in Mexico, spoke fluent Spanish, and had written books on business planning. As a consultant, I had helped Apple develop its annual Latin American business plan for four years running. I had developed the specialized software Apple dealers were using to create annual business plans.

What I worried about, however, that particular morning at the airport, was exactly that same question: why not? How about because I had never been in Argentina, hadn't studied its local tax laws and accounting practices, wasn't ready to predict its volatile currency exchange rates, and didn't know its standard business practices? So I worried.

I know now that I needn't have worried. Even though accounting practices and tax treatments vary widely from country to country, the techniques of business planning are far more international than country-specific. That Buenos Aires occasion was the first of many. In the following three years I gave business planning seminars in eight different Latin American countries, as well as five in Asia, for four different computer manufacturer sponsors. At each one, I dealt with a few dozen computer dealers who ran their small businesses in their local markets. As I presented business planning and we discussed the specifics of their markets and their businesses, the techniques held up. A good plan is essentially a good plan or not depending on a lot of factors besides tax treatments and accounting practices.

YOUR BUSINESS, YOUR CLIENT'S BUSINESS: WHAT'S DIFFERENT?

Let's assume you or your client are in the United States developing a business plan for an international business. How different is that business plan from a business plan developed for a strictly domestic business? The first answer, you've probably already guessed, is: not that much. However, we can be more specific than that. We can look at what kinds of differences there might be, and how you might accommodate those differences.

Currency Exchange Rates

Currency exchange rates are the first thing that concerns most people as they consider an international-oriented business plan. How do I handle currency exchange rates? How much does this influence my plan? Can I do a standard plan when I deal with currency exchange rates?

A Big Deal in International Business

Of course, currency fluctuations can be critical in international business. Changes in currency can mean changes in your costs and expenses, your sales, and even the value of your assets and liabilities.

For example, suppose you are importing handicrafts from Mexico. Your costs are mainly in Mexican pesos. When the peso trades at 3 pesos per dollar, then the hand-painted bowl from Oaxaca that costs you 15 pesos per unit costs you $5 per unit. When the peso exchange rate changes and the peso drops to 5 pesos per dollar, then the same bowl costs you only $3 per unit. If you think the peso is going to increase in value, you want to buy bowls and convert them to inventory quickly. If you think the peso is going to decrease in value, then you want to postpone your purchases to reduce the ultimate cost.

The problem with currency fluctuations, however, is the classic problem of guessing the future. Like prices in the stock market, currency exchange rates are a guessing game. Guess right, and you make money. Guess wrong, and you lose.

In the larger international businesses, predicting and managing currency exchange can be critical. When I was consulting to Apple Japan in the early 1990s, chief financial officer Judy David produced substantial profits, occasionally comparable to the profits from the computer business, with astute currency management, which involved detailed programs to keep assets in whichever currency seemed likely to increase in value, and liabilities in currencies likely to decrease in value. When I was with McKinsey Management Consulting in Mexico City in 1981, I saw major companies lose millions of dollars when the peso devalued, catching them with assets in pesos and liabilities in dollars.

Simple Mechanics in the Plan

As critical as currency exchange may be in your business, however, its specific treatment in your business plan is not much different from the way a wheat farmer would treat fluctuations in the market price of wheat. To understand that, you should first recognize that regardless of how international your business might be, you are still going to do your books and report your numbers to the tax authorities in a single currency. If you are based in the United States, your business plan should be in dollars. It doesn't matter how many countries you deal with, you still do your plan in dollars because you pay your taxes in dollars.

So where does the currency exchange come in? That depends on your business. Some businesses buy products in foreign markets and bring them into the United States to sell. Some export products made in the United States and sell them in foreign markets. You can sometimes be involved in multiple currencies, three or four in a single transaction. For example, you can buy computer circuit boards made in three countries and other hardware made in a fourth and a fifth, and then manufacture computers somewhere else and sell them in more than one country. In all these cases, however, if you are based in the United States then you are still going to have to translate all your currencies into dollars for your plan, your accounting, and your taxes.

Figures 12–1 to 12–3 show a simple example of how an import business handles its foreign currency costs in a start-up business plan, using Business Plan Pro's User Added and its Sales Forecast tables.

In Figure 12–1 the sales forecast consists of projections for unit sales, dollar revenues per unit sold, total dollar sales, dollar costs per unit sold, and of course total dollar costs of sales.

Figure 12–2 shows a simple two-row table for handling the currency exchange rates in the Business Plan Pro User Added table. Use the Table menu to select the User Added worksheet table.

- You can use copy and paste to copy the dates in the top row by selecting the date areas in any other table, copying them with the "Copy" command in the Edit menu, then returning to the User Added table and using the "Paste" command in the Edit menu.

- Use your "Custom Number" command in the format menu to change currency format display from dollars to any other number format. When the dialog for formats appears, use your mouse to select the bottom option ("Custom"). Then click the indicated area on the upper right and type in your new currency format, using quotation marks for currency symbols. In the illustration, for example, the format for the rows showing Mexican pesos is "MN"$#,##0.00_); ("MN"$#,##0.00). The format for the rows showing quetzals is "Q"$#,##0.00_); ("Q"$#,##0.00). Figure 12–3 shows that detailed custom format dialog.

Going back then to the sales forecast in Figure 12–1, focus on the second group from the bottom, the dollar costs per

Sales Forecast				
Unit Sales	Jan	Feb	Mar	Apr
Pottery Forecast (Mexico)	300	300	300	300
Weaving etc. (Mexico)	100	100	100	100
Weaving Etc. (Guatemala)	200	200	200	200
Woodstuff (Guatemala)	100	100	100	100
Other	0	0	0	0
Total Unit Sales	700	700	700	700
Unit Prices	Jan	Feb	Mar	Apr
Pottery Forecast (Mexico)	$15.00	$15.00	$15.00	$15.00
Weaving etc. (Mexico)	$20.00	$20.00	$20.00	$20.00
Weaving Etc. (Guatemala)	$25.00	$25.00	$25.00	$25.00
Woodstuff (Guatemala)	$5.00	$5.00	$5.00	$5.00
Other	$0.00	$0.00	$0.00	$0.00
Sales				
Pottery Forecast (Mexico)	$4,500	$4,500	$4,500	$4,500
Weaving etc. (Mexico)	$2,000	$2,000	$2,000	$2,000
Weaving Etc. (Guatemala)	$5,000	$5,000	$5,000	$5,000
Woodstuff (Guatemala)	$500	$500	$500	$500
Other	$0	$0	$0	$0
Total Sales	$12,000	$12,000	$12,000	$12,000
Direct Unit Costs	Jan	Feb	Mar	Apr
Pottery Forecast (Mexico)	$8.33	$8.33	$5.00	$5.00
Weaving etc. (Mexico)	$11.67	$11.67	$7.00	$7.00
Weaving Etc. (Guatemala)	$12.50	$12.50	$16.67	$16.67
Woodstuff (Guatemala)	$4.00	$4.00	$5.33	$5.33
Other	$0.00	$0.00	$0.00	$0.00
Direct Cost of Sales	Jan	Feb	Mar	Apr
Pottery Forecast (Mexico)	$2,500	$2,500	$1,500	$1,500
Weaving etc. (Mexico)	$1,167	$1,167	$700	$700
Weaving Etc. (Guatemala)	$2,500	$2,500	$3,333	$3,333
Woodstuff (Guatemala)	$400	$400	$533	$533
Other	$0	$0	$0	$0
Subtotal Direct Cost of Sales	$6,567	$6,567	$6,067	$6,067

Figure 12–1. The sales forecast consists of projections for unit sales, dollar revenues per unit sold, total dollar sales, dollar costs per unit sold, and total dollar costs of sales.

Currency Exchange Rate	Jan	Feb	Mar	Apr
Mexican Peso	MN$3.00	MN$3.00	MN$5.00	MN$5.00
Guatemalan Quetzal	Q$2.00	Q$2.00	Q$1.50	Q$1.50

Figure 12–2. A simple two-row table for handling currency exchange rates in the Business Plan Pro User Added table.

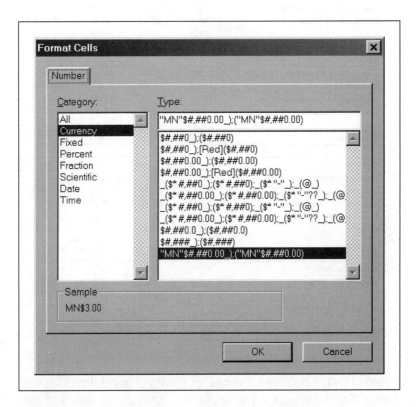

Figure 12–3. The detailed custom format dialog.

unit sold. These costs have to deal with the Mexican peso (MN$) and the Guatemalan quetzal (Q$). Notice how these costs change in March when both currencies (looking at Figure 12–2 again) change. You can work this into your business plan with some simple formula mechanics:

- The formula for the first row in costs refers directly to the peso exchange rate in the User Added table. To make that work, start with your mouse selecting in the first column, then type the equals (=) sign, then the number 25. You are saying that the average price in this row is 25 pesos. Then type the divided by sign (/) to indicate you want to divide that 25 by something else. Then use your Table menu to select the User Added table, find the peso rate for the first month, and click on it. Press Return, and Business Plan Pro entered your formula for you: " =25/'User added'!C2." In practice that formula means that you are paying MN$25 per unit, which is worth (in this specific example) $8.33. The dollar cost is exactly 25 divided by 3. The peso rate below indicates that it takes 3 pesos to make up a dollar.

- With that formula entered in that cell, you can copy to the right (using the command in your Edit menu) to copy it to all the other monthly columns in that same row. From then on, when you go to the User Added table to change your exchange rate forecasts, you will see your dollar cost forecast also changing automatically.

- You deal with the Quetzal prices with similar formulas, referring to the number of Quetzals required to equal a dollar.

Currency and Expenses

Figure 12–1 shows an example of currency rates affecting costs of goods sold. Even without the specific details, you can imagine how to handle a business in which currency rates affect expenses instead of costs of goods. In this case, for Business Plan Pro purposes, your expenses are included in the Profit and Loss table instead of the sales forecast. You can use a formula similar to the one in the example above to make expenses in the Profit and Loss change when the peso or quetzal rates change.

What's the difference? It's about standard accounting conventions. Accountants talk about costs as the cost of what you sold, and expenses are the operating expenses related to running the business. In the import example, an operating expense running in pesos might be the rental of an office suite in Mexico City, with a voice mail box, for 250 pesos per month. Exactly as with the products in the detailed example, the dollar value would change when the peso rate changes.

Foreign Currency in Sales

Looking at these examples, you can imagine how to handle a situation in which you are exporting U.S. goods to other markets. For example, if you're selling computers in Mexico your costs might be in dollars and your sales in pesos. You would take your unit price estimate in the second block of the sales forecast and create a formula calculating dollars from pesos, much like your formula that calculates dollars for pesos in costs.

Currency Exchange: Planning Decisions

In all of the above examples, the business plan mechanics are relatively simple. The thinking can be quite complex, and the significance of planning and forecasting is huge. At this point in the example, the mechanics end and the planning begins. The problem is not a problem of software or formulas. It is a problem of projecting rate fluctuations in the future. Guessing currency exchange rates is a major field of study and investment, every bit as much as guessing the future of interest rates. Factors affecting a change in currency exchange include political factors, economic factors, market factors, and even psychological factors.

As an example, in the 1970s I was living in Mexico and writing for *Business Week* magazine. The Mexican peso had traded at 12.5 to the dollar since the 1940s, In 1971 the United States dropped the gold standard, and currencies began to fluctuate more than they had previously. By 1976 the peso was still stuck at 12.5 to the dollar despite growing capital flight (Mexicans investing their money outside the country in dollars) and balance of trade problems (Mexico was buying much more than it was selling). The economics suggested a devaluation by 1975, but politics kept the peso unchanged until the presidency changed hands in 1976. The peso dropped about half its value, meaning it took more than 20 pesos to equal a dollar. To guess the timing of the devaluation that eventually took place, one had to guess the flow of dollars and pesos and political will as well.

The business plan in the example needs to deal with the possibility of changes in exchange rates affecting costs. How do you price your goods in dollars when your costs are in other currencies? Do you commit to steady unchanging prices? This is not an unusual problem. The business plan mechanics are easy, but the related decisions are not.

Taxation and Accounting Environment

Aside from currency exchange, some international business plans must also deal with different tax and accounting practices. Still, the business plan for a U.S. company has to remain in dollars, and taxes paid outside the United States serve as a credit against U.S. taxes.

For example, the value-added tax (VAT) is a major factor in most European markets, as well as in Mexico and Japan. It is quite significant for accounting and calculating tax burdens. In business planning, however, you are looking ahead and planning business decisions, not reporting to tax authorities. While you might use additional formulas to calculate your taxes, for planning purposes they are still going to be summarized in a single line toward the bottom of your profit and loss statement. Using Business Plan Pro, you could use the User-added worksheet to calculate the VAT or other taxes in more detail, and then run the results over to the tax line in your Profit and Loss. The form of the Profit and Loss doesn't change for taxes: sales less cost of sales is gross margin, and gross margin less operating expenses is gross profit, also called Earnings before Interest and Taxes, or EBIT. Then you subtract interest and taxes to calculate net profits.

Added Uncertainty

In general, as you plan the international business there is more uncertainty than with the strictly domestic business. You have the immediate impact of currency exchange rates to start with. Then you add in some extra problems with estimating costs, sales, and expenses. Also, there are factors affected by when you translate your foreign currency elements into dollars.

Costs, Sales, and Expenses

The problems of estimating your business numbers are relatively easy to understand. When you buy your goods in Mexico and Guatemala, you are farther away from your suppliers. When you sell your goods in Japan or Europe, you have a different view of the same problem. The markets in Mexico might change because Japanese buyers are affecting supply and demand, which raises prices. Maybe the government needs to focus its weaving industry on producing low-cost basic goods instead of export items for international markets. Maybe a group of U.S. weavers gets the U.S. government to restrict imports from Mexico to prevent competition. Any of these changes in the local economy can change your business. Local politics, national politics, and international politics can affect import and export policies, availability, and pricing. Because you are farther from the market, you can expect more trouble estimating future trends.

Translation Factors and Timing of Translation

As currencies fluctuate, the timing of your transactions can change your business. For example, if you are importing goods from Mexico and Guatemala, at what point do you translate their foreign-currency costs into dollars? Your accountant should be able to help you decide when—and at what exchange rate—to transfer your values to and from dollars. The timing can make a difference to profitability.

Market Factors

Although the business planning mechanics don't change as a result, the information gathering for international business is more complex. When doing business in multiple countries, you also have to deal with multiple markets and market trends. This makes your business plan preparation harder, even if it doesn't change the mechanics of business planning. If you are selling in Europe, you need to know about your European customers. If you are buying in Central America, you need to know about market factors that could affect your costs.

INTERNATIONAL PLANNING IS STILL PLANNING

When preparing this chapter, I was struck by an irony related to planning the international business. Despite having lived in three countries and worked in more than a dozen others, I had to remind myself first how planning an international business might be different. I had the privilege of doing the annual business plans for Apple Computer's Latin America group from 1984 to 1987, and for Apple's Japan subsidiary from 1991 through 1994. I was also involved in smaller start-up companies, mostly high tech, some of them focused almost entirely on the U.S. domestic market. In each case, there was always much more similarity than difference. Planning is still planning, not accounting.

CHAPTER 13
BUSINESS VALUATION

Your client wants to buy or sell a business. You are likely to be the first place a client looks for advice about valuation. How much is this business worth? The problem is valuation, determining the value of the business.

Business valuation is a big issue for buyers, sellers, the Internal Revenue Service, inheritance taxes, mergers, breaking up partnerships, and lawsuits. The IRS demands what it calls "fair market value" for establishing the value ownership. So do judges and juries, and partners, and buyers and sellers.

Valuation is a big topic, obviously. Let's assume that for the real valuations you'll be calling on a Certified Valuation Analyst (CVA, sanctioned by the National Association of Certified Valuation Professionals). The legal and tax implications generally demand CVA participation.

Still, for purposes of this book, we'd like to look at how a plan affects valuation, how you can influence valuation with a plan, and how to make a preliminary guess at valuation as a service to your client.

Of course we can't talk about valuation any more without noting that the whole science of valuation has been changed by the Internet. Internet traffic is now a critical factor in market valuation. A company that has established a leading position in a major Internet area can be worth millions and even billions of dollars, even without revenues. However, that runs outside of the general analysis in the rest of this chapter.

THE BUSINESS PLAN IS NOT THE MOST
IMPORTANT FACTOR

Valuation depends a lot more on the business than the business plan. Factors such as past performance, financial position, competitive advantage, market share, and management team are much more important than future projections and business plans.

Ultimately, most valuation jobs end up quoting a business's value in terms of multiples of sales or earnings. Publicly traded companies are valued by the stock market in multiples of earnings or sales. Some high growth companies are worth four or five times sales, and 20 or 30 times earnings. Private companies are generally smaller, have less growth, and are somewhat more risky. One or two times sales, or 5 or 10 times earnings, is a lot for a small privately owned business. Here are some examples:

1. Briarpatch Furniture, the sample company whose business plan is included with this book (see Chapter 16), was purchased by Jim and Susan Graham in 1992 for $100,000. In its present situation it's worth as much as $3 million, even $3.5 million, if its owners stay on. It has a strong balance sheet and attractive competitive advantage. However, it could be worth as little as $1 million if it were sold without its owners, in a declining market, or at a time of rising new competition. Note that the difference between $1 million and $3 million is an enormous range and depends on detailed conditions of the company at the time of sale. The 1992 purchase price was divided among the nine existing members of the cooperative. In 1991 the cooperative recorded slightly less than $350,000 in sales and lost about $25,000. It had no debt, no cash, and very few assets.

2. The American Technology Management (AMT) computer business is a detailed business plan that is included on your Business Plan Pro CD. Figure 15–5 shows its past performance table as included in the plan, and Figure 15–6 shows its past performance chart. AMT has had sales growing from $3.7 million to $5.3 million in the past three years, which is average growth of more than 14% per year. Profits, however, have been marginal at best—the balance sheet includes negative retained earnings. The market has become more competitive. Collection days are up, and inventory turns down. AMT is probably worth about $5 million, as much as it sells in a year. With its business plan to help guide a transfor-

mation, it could be worth more like 1.5 times sales if it manages to improve its performance as viewed in the business plan.

3. Ascend! Seminars offers 2-day motivational and training workshops to the upscale baby-boomer who "wants it all." The workshops are based on a series of popular self-help books written by the company's charismatic owner, Leticia Marvelous. The company has downtown offices in Seattle, 12 employees, and monthly sales averaging $80,000 on expenses running at $75,000. The business plan calls for cutting expenses to $60,000 and increasing revenues by moving into other markets.

    Ms. Marvelous began her career as a writer in 1983. The packed studios of the TV talk-show publicity tour for her 1990 bestseller, *You Can Have It All*, convinced her that there was a market hungry for live, interactive presentations of her ideas. Encouraged and exhausted by the success of her 1991 speaking schedule, Ms. Marvelous grew the company beyond her early home office in Mt Vernon, Washington, moving to Seattle offices overlooking Puget Sound, Ms. Marvelous now presides over a company of 12 employees, including 3 other workshop presenters. The company was recently buoyed by the release of a new book, *Sell Yourself!* in early 1997. Now Leticia has decided to return to writing and to sell the workshop business to someone with the capital and vision to promote it to a broader audience in cities all over the country.

    In this case the valuation problem is similar to Briarpatch, in that the value of this business depends very much on the involvement of the owners. With Briarpatch it depends on the owners' skills and backgrounds, and with Ascend! it depends on the owner's books and charisma. Even with sales of almost $1 million per year, Ascend! Seminars is difficult to leverage for any new owner without the continued contribution of the present owners.

Because valuation depends much more on present position than on future prospects, careful financial audits and the detailed research (normally referred to as "due diligence") are critical.

THE PLAN IS VITAL DOCUMENTATION

Still, even if it isn't the key factor in setting valuation, the business plan is likely to be the main working document. frequently the main working document in a valuation project. The plan is the seller's way of communicating the nature of the business, its recent past, its products, its strategies, strengths and weaknesses, management team, and future projections.

For example, look at the factors included in specific IRS guidelines for establishing "fair market value." As you look at each factor, consider how much it is influenced by the business plan. Consider also how to best deal with it in the plan.

1. *The history of the firm.* This is Chapter 2 of a business plan and appears in the past performance table and chart. As you develop a plan, emphasize stability, growth, and challenges overcome. You want the history of the company to strengthen its valuation.

2. *Its earnings potential.* The earnings potential is the core of a plan. You have a competitive analysis, strengths and weaknesses, keys to success, market analysis, sales forecast, management team, and profitability forecast. A good business plan should document a company's earnings potential. The plan is the seller's forum for explaining its value to the buyer. Make sure, as you work with your client's plan, that assertions made in the plan are defensible.

3. *Book value.* This is a matter of record, in the financials of the company.

4. *Dividend paying potential.* The apparent redundancy with "earnings potential" is in the specifics of IRS's revenue ruling 59-60, defining "fair market value." The resolution, perhaps, is the difference between generating earn-

ings and generating cash to pay dividends. Many growing companies need to maintain working capital to support growth. Focus here on the cash plan portions of the business plan.

5. *General economic conditions, business trends.* This should be covered in the market analysis chapter. Be careful, though, because you don't want a plan that oversells prospects. Optimism must be backed up with facts. Lacking facts, good subjective opinion from quotable experts is a good substitute.

6. *Investment market conditions and momentum.* In the summer of 1998 when the stock market fell by more than 10%, most business valuations went down with it. This is not a factor you can easily influence in a business plan. A professional valuation is going to take market conditions into account, just as a home appraisal takes real estate market conditions into account. It is part of the equation.

7. *Pertinent industry conditions.* This is another element communicated by the market analysis chapter of the business plan. If AMT is being valued at a time when computer resellers are struggling with increasing competition and declining margins, that affects valuation. At best, the plan may be able to react to industry conditions, as AMT does by shifting its business towards service and training.

8. *Relevant market conditions.* This presumably refers to local market conditions, economic growth, availability of investment capital, and other factors that are normally outside the business's control. This is probably outside of the business plan as well.

9. *Treatment of publicly traded comparable companies.* If Briarpatch Furniture wants to sell at a time when the publicly traded furniture manufacturers have depressed earnings, or lowered price/earnings ratios, then it has to affect its valuation. Although outside the business plan, this is an important factor. Most professionals will look at this factor and recommend changing the timing of a sale or purchase to respond to temporary conditions.

However, in many cases (for example, owner is retiring, or lawsuits, divorce, etc.) the timing of a sale is not affected.

10. *The firm's competitive posture.* This is business plan material, part of Chapters 3 (company analysis) and 5 (strategy). A business plan can articulate a strategy to enhance the value of a company. For example, Palo Alto Software, Inc., developer and publisher of Business Plan Pro, is probably worth a lot more with an internet strategy than with a purely retail strategy. How are we planning to take advantage of our strengths? How can we work around weaknesses? What is the real competitive advantage? These are questions a business plan should answer.

BENCHMARKS FOR BUYERS; READING A PLAN FOR VALUATION

On the other side of the fence, what if your client is the purchaser and has asked you to read a business plan? Now you put yourself on the other side of the fence.

I recommend starting with the benchmarks chart, as shown in Figure 13–1 from the AMT sample plan on your Business Plan Pro CD. You can read the whole AMT plan using Business Plan Pro. Figure 13–2 shows the underlying numbers so you can read the chart better.

The benchmarks chart is a personal favorite because it puts key information into an immediately visible format and compares trends over time. Let's look at the specifics in the chart in the example.

1. The first set of bars shows sales for 6 years in a row, 3 years of past history and 3 years of the future, according to the plan. Sales is presented as an index value, so that the last full year is set to 1. In this illustration, that means a value of 1 in sales is equal to the $5.3 million sales of 1998, the last full year. The $9 million sales forecast for 2001 is almost twice the size of $5.3 million, so the chart shows a value of nearly 2. As you look at

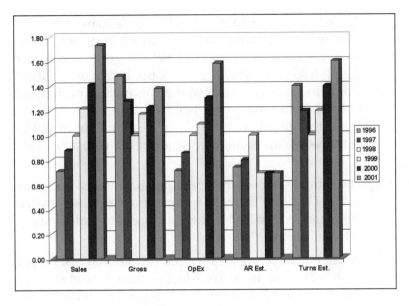

Figure 13–1. The benchmarks chart.

	1996	1997	1998	1999	2000	2001
Sales	0.71	0.88	1.00	1.23	1.41	1.73
Gross	1.48	1.28	1.00	0.95	1.25	1.40
OpEx	0.71	0.86	1.00	1.05	1.23	1.49
AR Est.	0.74	0.80	1.00	0.69	0.69	0.69
Turns Est.	1.40	1.20	1.00	1.20	1.40	1.60

Figure 13–2. Benchmark comparison showing the underlying numbers.

the sales growth in the chart, is the growth of the last 3 years realistic? Does the growth of the previous 3 years make the growth of the next 3 years reasonable? You'll have to look at the plan in detail and talk to the managers, but at least at first glance the growth seems reasonable.

2. The second set of bars shows the gross margin, in percent. The 1998 value was 21%, which becomes a 1 as an index value. The margin has been going down, but the plan suggests it will go back up. Is this reasonable? Does the plan contain justification of that optimism? Does the plan make you believe it can happen? Here again the visual comparison of past and future gives most people an immediate sense of the realism or lack of it.

3. The third set shows the operating expenses as an index value. Does the increase in operating expenses match the increase in sales? Is there a reasonable relationship between them?

4. In the fourth set of bars we see collection days, one of the keys to cash flow. Reading the chart we can see that collection days have been increasing, which is bad news. In Figure 13–2 we see that average collection days have increased in the past 3 years from 48 to 52 and 65, which is a dangerous trend. However, the plan calls for improving collection days back to 45. Is this realistic? Does the plan justify this improvement?

5. The last set focuses on inventory turnover, another key to cash flow. It shows that inventory turnover has been slowing steadily, but in the plan, it is supposed to improve. Does the plan explain how? Are there programs to make that happen?

Figure 13–3 shows a different benchmarks chart, illustrating the progress of a different kind of company. Notice the lack of growth. Stability is good for cash flow, but does this company have the same growth prospects as AMT? Not for most buyers. Most buyers would pay more for the growth prospects in Figure 13–1 than for the steady-state business in Figure 13–3.

Figure 13–4 shows the skeptic's view of the AMT plan, with the key elements set for pessimism. Obviously you'd need to read the business plan in great detail to decide which of these is realistic.

To read a business plan from a buyer's point of view, you need a healthy skepticism. I'd recommend starting with the

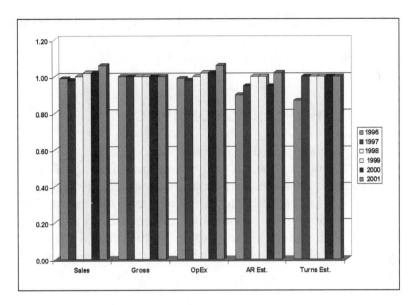

Figure 13–3. Stability is easy to manage but valuation would be higher with more growth.

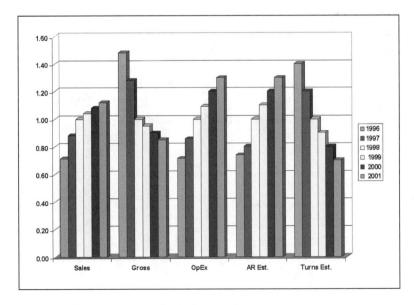

Figure 13–4. The pessimistic version.

management team background and resumés. Then look hard at the financials, looking for holes, unanswered questions, and hidden problems. Have the ratios changed, and why?

THE PLAN AS COMMUNICATION

Even though the plan doesn't determine valuation, the information it contains does. It is the communicator of value. It can influence how ideas and information are perceived and recognized. In the end, the distinction is a fine point. The value of a company is what somebody chooses to pay for it. If the plan puts ideas in their best light, the seller wins. If the plan reader catches the hidden problem, then the buyer wins.

NOTE ABOUT DATES IN SAMPLE PLANS

The AMT business plan shown here was originally done for the real company (its name and location are disguised) in the mid-1990s. As we reviewed this and other sample plans included in this edition, in 2001, we saw that they are still real and still very good examples. We've chosen not to revise the dates because what was true about the market in 1994 would not be true in 2001. This and other sample plans included with this book are valuable as examples of real business plans, not for the market research or strategic information they contain. To pretend they were developed in 2001 would make them less realistic, not more realistic.

CHAPTER 14
AMERICAN MANAGEMENT TECHNOLOGIES, INC., SAMPLE PLAN

This sample business plan has been made available to users of *Business Plan Pro*™ business plan software published by Palo Alto Software. It is based on a real business plan of an existing company. Names and numbers have been changed, and substantial portions of text may have been omitted to preserve confidential information.

You are welcome to use this plan as a starting point to create your own, but you do not have permission to reproduce, publish, distribute, or even copy this plan as it exists here.

Requests for reprints, academic use, and other dissemination of this sample plan should be addressed to the marketing department of Palo Alto Software.

AMERICAN MANAGEMENT TECHNOLOGIES (AMT), INC.

Confidentiality Agreement

The undersigned reader acknowledges that the information provided by ＿＿＿＿＿＿ in this business plan is confidential; therefore, reader agrees not to disclose it without the express written permission of ＿＿＿＿＿＿.

It is acknowledged by reader that information to be furnished in this business plan is in all respects confidential in nature, other than information which is in the public domain through other means and that any disclosure or use of same by reader, may cause serious harm or damage to ＿＿＿＿＿＿.

Upon request, this document is to be immediately returned to ＿＿＿＿＿＿.

Signature ＿＿＿＿＿＿＿＿＿＿ Date ＿＿＿＿＿＿＿

＿＿＿＿＿＿＿＿＿＿
Name (typed or printed)

This is a business plan. It does not imply an offering of securities.

AMERICAN MANAGEMENT TECHNOLOGIES (AMT), INC.

Table of Contents

AMERICAN MANAGEMENT TECHNOLOGIES (AMT), INC.

AMERICAN MANAGEMENT TECHNOLOGIES (AMT), INC.

1.0 Executive Summary

By focusing on its strengths, its key customers, and its underlying values, American Management Technology will increase sales to more than $9 million in three years, while also improving the gross margin on sales and cash management and working capital.

This business plan leads the way. It renews our vision and strategic focus: adding value to our target market segments, the small business and high-end home office users, in our local market. It also provides a step-by-step plan for improving our sales, gross margin, and profitability.

This plan includes this summary and chapters on the company, products and services, market focus, action plans and forecasts, management team, and financial plan.

Business Plan Highlights

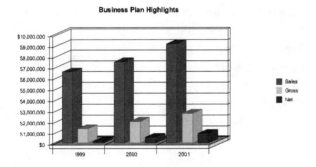

1.1 Objectives

1. Increase sales to more than $9 million by the third year.
2. Bring gross margin back up to above 29% and maintain that level.
3. Sell $2 million of service, support, and training by 2001.
4. Improve inventory turnover to six turns next year, seven in 2000, and eight in 2001.

Comments

A good executive summary communicates the most important points of the rest of the plan, so that a reader who reads just the summary will still get the most important information. In this case, the AMT summary notes the projected increase in sales and the change in strategy to reflect a changing market.

I note going through this plan that we had an earlier draft that had sales cited as "almost $10 million," instead of "more than $9 million." Either way is acceptable, but I personally like the more conservative. Some of the authors wanted to hike the reference to $10 million because $9 million rounds to 10, and "rounding is common." However, I say the $9 million figure is still very strong growth, and more accurate.

Note how the highlights chart gives the business plan reader an immediate view of the size of the company, in sales and profits. You know instantly that this company has sales between $5 and $10 million. That helps you place the plan in your mind, by size of company.

These objectives are all concrete and measurable, which is essential. Vague and hard-to-measure concepts like "market leadership" or "excellence" are hard to measure, and AMT chooses to put down specific objectives. They could improve that by adding more first-year objectives, which could help serve for plan-vs.-actual measurement in the first year of the plan.

AMERICAN MANAGEMENT TECHNOLOGIES (AMT), INC.

1.2 Mission

AMT is built on the assumption that the management of information technology for business is like legal advice, accounting, graphic arts, and other bodies of knowledge in that it is not inherently a do-it-yourself prospect. Smart businesspeople who are not computer hobbyists need to find quality vendors of reliable hardware, software, service, and support. They need to use these quality vendors as they use their other professional service suppliers, as trusted allies.

AMT is such a vendor. It serves its clients as a trusted ally, providing them with the loyalty of a business partner and the economics of an outside vendor. We make sure that our clients have what they need to run their businesses as well as possible, with maximum efficiency and reliability. Many of our information applications are mission critical, so we give our clients the assurance that we will be there when they need us.

1.3 Keys to Success

1. Differentiate from box-pushing, price-oriented businesses by offering and delivering service and support—and charging for it.
2. Increase gross margin to more than 25%.
3. Increase our non-hardware sales to 20% of the total sales by the third year.

2.0 Company Summary

AMT is a computer reseller based in the Uptown area. It was founded as a consulting-oriented VAR, became a reseller to fill the market need for personal computers, and is emphasizing service and support to differentiate itself from more price-oriented national chains.

Comments

This is a particularly strong mission statement because it links so well to the underlying change in strategy. AMT needs to change the business it's in. Where it used to be a "box pusher," selling computer products as brand-name boxes, it needs to become a strategic ally to small business clients. The mission statement emphasizes and highlights this new mission. It isn't just fluff, it is critical to strategy.

The keys to success match the change in business strategy. Once upon a time, AMT's keys to success would have been easy parking and price-oriented newspaper advertising. The new strategy has very different focus, and the keys to success reflect and emphasize that new focus. This is a good example of how Keys to Success develop a plan's focus.

The summary should contain all the important points in the rest of the chapter, particularly since it may be used as a single topic in an investment summary memo.

AMERICAN MANAGEMENT TECHNOLOGIES (AMT), INC.

2.1 Company Ownership

AMT is a privately held C corporation owned in majority by its founder and president, Ralph Jones. There are six part owners, including four investors and two past employees. The largest of these (in percent of ownership) are Frank Dudley, our attorney, and Paul Karots, our public relations consultant. Neither owns more than 15%, but both are active participants in management decisions.

2.2 Company History

AMT founder Ralph Jones, President, 46 years old, founded AMT in 1989 to focus on reselling high-powered personal computers to small business. Jones had been 15 years with Large Computer Company, Inc. in positions ending with project manager.

The business grew quickly in its first few years, as it served a real need in the local community. There was relatively little competition until the major chain stores moved in during the middle 1990s.

Lately, AMT has been caught in the vise grip of margin squeezes that have affected computer resellers worldwide. Although the chart titled "Past Financial Performance" shows that we have had healthy growth in sales, it also shows declining gross margin and declining profits.

The more detailed numbers in Table 2.2 include other indicators of some concern:

- The gross margin percent has been declining steadily, as we see in the chart.
- Inventory turnover is getting steadily worse.

All of these concerns are part of the general trend affecting computer resellers. The margin squeeze is happening throughout the computer industry worldwide.

Comments

This is a matter of fact, and a matter of public record in most cases. However, this topic can be easily left out when a plan is printed for use by employees of a closely held corporation. Frequently owners don't feel comfortable with sharing this information with all.

This same topic number and same place in the outline would be applied to a Start-up Plan if this plan were for a new or start-up company, rather than an ongoing company.

In this case, although there is some company history in this topic, there is also a serious note of growing problems. AMT ownership is not concerned about or interested in selling the company, as this plan is prepared, so there is little temptation to gloss over problems that have to be solved. This makes for a better plan.

AMERICAN MANAGEMENT TECHNOLOGIES (AMT), INC.

Past Performance

	1996	1997	1998
Sales	$3,773,889	$4,661,902	$5,301,059
Gross Margin	$1,189,495	$1,269,261	$1,127,568
Gross % (calculated)	31.52%	27.23%	21.27%
Operating Expenses	$752,083	$902,500	$1,052,917
Collection period (days)	48	52	65
Inventory Turnover	7	6	5

Balance Sheet

Short-term Assets	1996	1997	1998
Cash	$11,308	$47,603	$55,432
Accounts Receivable	$247,976	$311,074	$395,107
Inventory	$521,132	$694,098	$841,012
Other Short-term Assets	$12,954	$18,345	$25,000
Total Short-term Assets	$793,370	$1,071,120	$1,316,551
Long-term Assets			
Capital Assets	$302,009	$328,540	$353,972
Accumulated Depreciation	$30,189	$39,097	$51,945
Total Long-term Assets	$271,820	$289,443	$302,027
Total Assets	$1,065,190	$1,360,563	$1,618,578

Capital and Liabilities

	1996	1997	1998
Accounts Payable	$176,091	$204,325	$223,897
Short-term Notes	$110,000	$54,032	$90,000
Other ST Liabilities	$23,401	$34,067	$18,398
Subtotal Short-term Liabilities	$309,492	$292,424	$332,295
Long-term Liabilities	$310,098	$290,212	$284,862
Total Liabilities	$619,590	$582,636	$617,157
Paid-in Capital	$500,000	$500,000	$500,000
Retained Earnings	($188,967)	$43,829	$426,769
Earnings	$134,567	$234,098	$74,652
Total Capital	$445,600	$777,927	$1,001,421
Total Capital and Liabilities	$1,065,190	$1,360,563	$1,618,578

Comments

The past performance table charts two sets of past numbers: the first six are most important for the benchmarks chart (more on that later), which tracks performance on five key variables. The rest are used mainly for a quick view of the balance sheet, three years running. The Business Plan Pro sofware uses the ending balance of the series to establish the starting balance of the balance sheet.

There is a final section of this table that is hidden for formatting purposes. It wasn't strictly needed, but made the table break over into the following page. AMT used the Hide Row command (in the Format menu) to hide those bottom rows. To see them, just go to the table, select to the bottom, and use the Show Row command.

AMERICAN MANAGEMENT TECHNOLOGIES (AMT), INC.

Past Financial Performance

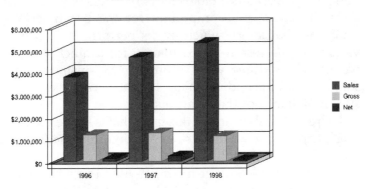

2.3 Company Locations and Facilities

We have one location—a 7,000-square-foot store in a suburban shopping center located conveniently close to the downtown area. It includes a training area, a service department, offices, and a showroom area.

3.0 Products

AMT provides both computer products and services to make them useful to small business. We are especially focused on providing network systems and services to small and medium-sized business. The systems include both PC-based LAN systems and minicomputer server-based systems. Our services include design and installation of network systems, training, and support.

Comments

Like the Highlights chart included with the Executive Summary, this chart gives the reader a quick view of the scale of the company, in sales, gross margin, and profits.

This is a simple list, much more important when a plan is part of a sale of a company, loan application, or investment, than in this case. It is included for completeness, but not really needed.

This first topic is a summary. More detail will follow. A well-written plan uses these first topics as summaries so they can be included in the investment summary memo or loan application documents, which are abbreviated versions. Business Plan Pro prepares those summaries automatically.

AMERICAN MANAGEMENT TECHNOLOGIES (AMT), INC.

3.1 Product Description

In personal computers, we support three main lines:

The Super Home is our smallest and least expensive line, initially positioned by its manufacturer as a home computer. We use it mainly as a cheap workstation for small business installations. Its specifications include . . .[additional specifics omitted]

The Power User is our main up-scale line. It is our most important system for high-end home and small business main workstations, because of . . . Its key strengths are . . . Its specifications include . . . [additional specifics omitted]

The Business Special is an intermediate system, used to fill the gap in the positioning. Its specifications include . . . [additional specifics omitted]

In peripherals, accessories, and other hardware, we carry a complete line of necessary items from cables to forms to mousepads . . . [additional specifics omitted]

In service and support, we offer a range of walk-in or depot service, maintenance contracts and on-site guarantees. We have not had much success selling service contracts. Our networking capabilities . . . [additional specifics omitted]

In software, we sell a complete line of . . . [additional specifics omitted]

In training, we offer . . . [additional specifics omitted]

3.2 Competitive Comparison

The only way we can hope to differentiate well is to define the vision of the company to be an information technology ally to our clients. We will not be able to compete in any effective way with the chains using boxes or products as appliances. We need to offer a real alliance.

The benefits we sell include many intangibles: confidence, reliability, knowing that somebody will be there to answer questions and help at the important times.

Comments

The detail is omitted here because it doesn't matter. In truth, for an internal plan like this one, there is no business reason to list products and services in detail unless there is a significant change intended as a component of the plan. In AMT's case, the people who will use the plan presumably know the products and services quite well.

In this topic, AMT comes to terms with the increasing problems it faces. The arrival of major chain stores threatens the core of its business, selling computers. It's encouraging to see the plan facing the real problems.

AMERICAN MANAGEMENT TECHNOLOGIES (AMT), INC.

These are complex products, products that require serious knowledge and experience to use, and our competitors sell only the products themselves.

Unfortunately, we cannot sell the products at a higher price just because we offer services; the market has shown that it will not support that concept. We have to also sell the service and charge for it separately.

3.3 Sales Literature

Copies of our brochure and advertisements are attached as appendixes. Of course, one of our first tasks will be to change the message of our literature to make sure we are selling the company, rather than the product.

3.4 Sourcing

Our costs are part of the margin squeeze. As competition on price increases, the squeeze between manufacturers' price into channels and end-users' ultimate buying price continues.

With the hardware lines, our margins are declining steadily. We generally buy at . . . Our margins are thus being squeezed from the 25% of five years ago to more like 13–15% at present. In the main-line peripherals a similar trend shows, with prices for printers and monitors declining steadily. We are also starting to see that same trend with software. . . .

In order to hold costs down as much as possible, we concentrate our purchasing with Hauser, which offers 30-day net terms and overnight shipping from the warehouse in Dayton. We need to concentrate on making sure our volume gives us negotiating strength.

In accessories and add-ons we can still get decent margins, 25–40%.

For software, margins are . . .

Comments

This topic is often included just so a company can include sales literature for a banker, buyer, or investor. In this case, however, there is a reason for substantive discussion, since AMT needs to adjust its sales communications to reflect its new strategy.

The AMT plan is not just listing or describing its sources here, it is dealing with some real problems. This is a direct reflection of the margin squeeze that is changing the nature of the business.

AMERICAN MANAGEMENT TECHNOLOGIES (AMT), INC.

3.5 Technology

We have for years supported both Windows and Macintosh technology for CPUs, although we've switched vendors many times for the Windows (and previously DOS) lines. We are also supporting Novell, Banyon, and Microsoft networking, Xbase database software, and Claris application products.

3.6 Service and Support

Our strategy hinges on providing excellent service and support. This is critical. We need to differentiate on service and support, and to therefore deliver as well.

1. Training: details would be essential in a real business plan, but not in this sample plan.

2. Upgrade offers: details would be essential in a real business plan, but not in this sample plan.

3. Our own internal training: details would be essential in a real business plan, but not in this sample plan.

4. Installation services: details would be essential in a real business plan, but not in this sample plan.

5. Custom software services: details would be essential in a real business plan, but not in this sample plan.

6. Network configuration services: details would be essential in a real business plan, but not in this sample plan.

3.7 Future Products

We must remain on top of the new technologies, because this is our bread and butter. For networking, we need to provide better knowledge of cross platform technologies. Also, we are under pressure to improve our understanding of direct-connect internet and related communications. Finally, although we have a good command of desktop publishing, we are concerned about getting better at the integration of technologies that creates fax, copier, printer, and voice mail as part of the computer system.

Comments

This topic reflects a change in technology. Although the plan is presented here with updated dates, it was actually written in 1995, when the Macintosh was still a major player in the AMT market. A more up-to-date plan would have to address the huge change in communications and the explosion of the Internet.

Details are omitted because technology has changed and the details are irrelevant to the plan's value as a realistic example. However, it was critical to the real content of the real plan, because this was one of the most important focuses of the new strategy.

This section is too brief. AMT is a technology-driven company, in a technology market. The real plan had a detailed analysis of specific strategic and tactics regarding new technologies for communications, training, etc.

AMERICAN MANAGEMENT TECHNOLOGIES (AMT), INC.

4.0 Market Analysis Summary

AMT focuses on local markets, small business and home office, with special focus on the high-end home office and the 5–20 unit small business office.

The home offices in Tintown are an important growing market segment. Nationally, there are approximately 30 million home offices, and the number is growing at 10% per year. Our estimate in this plan for the home offices in our market service area is based on an analysis published four months ago in the local newspaper.

Home offices include several types. The most important, for our plan's focus, are the home offices that are the only offices of real businesses, from which people make their primary living. These are likely to be professional services such as graphic artists, writers, and consultants, some accountants and the occasional lawyer, doctor, or dentist. There are also part-time home offices with people who are employed during the day but work at home at night, people who work at home to provide themselves with a part-time income, or people who maintain home offices relating to their hobbies; we will not be focusing on this segment.

Small business within our market includes virtually any business with a retail, office, professional, or industrial location outside of someone's home, and fewer than 30 employees. We estimate 45,000 such businesses in our market area.

The 30-employee cutoff is arbitrary. We find that the larger companies turn to other vendors, but we can sell to departments of larger companies, and we shouldn't be giving up leads when we get them.

4.1 Market Segmentation

The segmentation allows some room for estimates and non-specific definitions. We focus on a small to medium level of small business, and it is hard to find information to make an exact classification. Our target companies are large enough to need the high-quality information technology management we

Comments

This is a remarkably good summary, very brief, but still covers the main information needed.

The segmentation here is practical and useful. The plan pays due respect to more classic market research, then goes to the business core. Although the high-end home office and small business markets are a bit hard to define, all the users of this plan understand what they are and how they impact the strategy, the sales, and the marketing.

AMERICAN MANAGEMENT TECHNOLOGIES (AMT), INC.

offer, but too small to have a separate computer management staff such as an MIS department. We say that our target market has 10–50 employees and needs 5–20 workstations tied together in a local area network; the definition is flexible.

Defining the high-end home office is even more difficult. We generally know the characteristics of our target market, but we can't find easy classifications that fit into available demographics. The high-end home office business is a business, not a hobby. It generates enough money to merit the owner's paying real attention to the quality of information technology management, meaning that there are both budget and concerns that warrant working with our level of quality service and support. We can assume that we aren't talking about home offices used only part-time by people who work elsewhere during the day, and that our target market home office wants to have powerful technology and a lot of links between computing, telecommunications, and video.

Market Analysis

Potential Customers	Growth	1999	2000	2001	2002	2003	CAGR
Consumer	2%	12,000	12,240	12,485	12,735	12,990	2.00%
Small Business	5%	15,000	15,750	16,538	17,365	18,233	5.00%
Large Business	8%	33,000	35,640	38,491	41,570	44,896	8.00%
Government	−2%	36,000	35,280	34,574	33,883	33,205	−2.00%
Other	0%	19,000	19,000	19,000	19,000	19,000	0.00%
Total	2.78%	115,000	117,910	121,088	124,553	128,324	2.78%

Potential Market by Segment

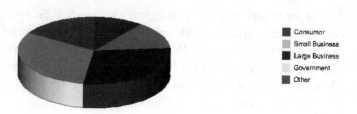

Consumer
Small Business
Large Business
Government
Other

Comments

AMERICAN MANAGEMENT TECHNOLOGIES (AMT), INC.

4.2 Target Market Segment Strategy

Our choice of target markets is strategic. We assume that it definitely reflects our strengths and weaknesses. We are not selling to the self-reliant users, because they buy computers as appliances on the basis of features and price. Instead, we are selling to the service-seeking users whose needs match our strengths.

We don't want to compete in the low-end or even medium home office market, because we realize that all except the high-end home buyer is going to look at computers as boxed prices and buy mainly on the basis of price. This market belongs to the chain stores and office stores.

Regarding the small business segment, we are looking for the types of small business that appreciate our value added enough to pay for it, but aren't big enough to have expertise in house. The small business that is very comfortable with computers and doesn't want our added value is going to buy at price with the chains, and the larger businesses will buy in volume direct.

4.2.1 Market Needs

Because our target market is the service seeker, the most important market needs are support, service, training, and installation, in that order. One of the key points of our strategy is the focus on target segments that know and understand these needs and are willing to pay to have them filled.

All personal computer users need support and service. The self-reliant ones, however, supply those needs themselves. In home offices, these are the knowledgeable computer users who like to do it themselves. Among the businesses, these are businesses that have people on staff.

4.2.2 Market Trends

The most obvious and important trend in the market is declining prices. This has been true for years, but the trend seems to be accelerating. We see the major brand-name manufacturers putting systems together with amazing specs—more power,

Comments

Where the previous topic defines the segmentation, this one explains the strategy behind it. Why does AMT want to focus on these two market segments? How does that work into the strategy?

Good marketing always begins with market needs. It's not what you have to sell, but what needs you fill. What are your customers' needs? This is the first topic of the third level of topics, hence the outline numbering to 4.2.1. We are in a subset of topic 4.2.

The market trends certainly justify the development of the AMT strategy.

AMERICAN MANAGEMENT TECHNOLOGIES (AMT), INC.

more speed, more memory, more disk storage—at amazing prices. The major chain shops are selling brand-name powerful computers for less than $1,000.

This may be related to a second trend, which is the computer as throw-away appliance. By the time a system needs upgrading, it is cheaper to buy completely new. The increasing power and storage of a sub-$1000 system means buyers are asking for less service.

A third trend is ever greater connectivity. Everybody wants onto the internet, and every small office wants a LAN. A lot of small offices want their LAN connected to the internet.

4.2.3 Market Growth

As prices fall, unit sales increase. The published market research on sales of personal computers is astounding, as the U.S. market alone is absorbing more than 30 million units per year, and sales are growing at more than 20% per year. We could quote Dataquest, Infocorp, IDC, or others; it doesn't matter, they all agree on high growth of CPU sales.

Where growth is not as obvious is the retail market. A report in CRW says Dell is now selling $5 million monthly over the web, and we assume Gateway and Micron are both close to that. Direct mail has given way to the web, but catalogs are still powerful, and the non-retail sale is more accepted every day. The last study we saw published has retail sales growing at 5% per year, while web sales and direct sales are growing at 25% or 30% per year.

4.3 Industry Analysis

We are part of the computer reselling business, which includes several kinds of businesses:

1. Computer dealers: storefront computer resellers, usually less than 5,000 square feet, often focused on a few main brands of hardware, usually offering only a minimum of software, and variable amounts of service and support. These are usually old-fashioned (1980s-style) computer

Comments

This section could be better. It talks about the underlying computer market, but what about the growth in the target market? How about the high-end home office and small business markets, and their need for training, support, and service? Those are AMT's real markets.

This is another summary topic. The details follow in the subtopics.

AMERICAN MANAGEMENT TECHNOLOGIES (AMT), INC.

stores and they usually offer relatively few reasons for buyers to shop with them. Their service and support is not usually very good and their prices are usually higher than the larger stores.

2. Chain stores and computer superstores: these include major chains such as CompUSA, Computer City, and Future Shop. They almost always have more than 10,000 square feet of space, usually offer decent walk-in service, and are often warehouse-like locations where people go to find products in boxes with very aggressive pricing, and little support.

3. Mail order: the market is served increasingly by mail order businesses that offer aggressive pricing of boxed product. For the purely price-driven buyer, who buys boxes and expects no service, these are very good options.

4. Others: there are many other channels through which people buy their computers, usually variations of the main three types above.

4.3.1 Industry Participants

1. The national chains are a growing presence. CompUSA, Computer City, Incredible Universe, Babbages, Egghead, and others. They benefit from national advertising, economies of scale, volume buying, and a general trend toward name-brand loyalty for buying in the channels as well as for products.

2. Local computer stores are threatened. These tend to be small businesses, owned by people who started them because they liked computers. They are under-capitalized and under-managed. Margins are squeezed as they compete against the chains, in a competition based on price more than on service and support.

4.3.2 Distribution Patterns

Small business buyers are accustomed to buying from vendors who visit their offices. They expect the copy machine vendors, office products vendors, and office furniture vendors, as well as the local graphic artists, freelance writers, or whomever, to visit their office to make their sales.

Comments

This topic is a review of the kinds of businesses that operate in this industry, how big are they, and what are they like.

Although this discussion is valuable, it belongs more in the target market analysis than industry analysis. Ultimately, however, what's important is to cover the main concepts and make sure your plans are properly explained.

AMERICAN MANAGEMENT TECHNOLOGIES (AMT), INC.

There is usually a lot of leakage in ad-hoc purchasing through local chain stores and mail order. Often the administrators try to discourage this, but are only partially successful.

Unfortunately our Home Office target buyers may not expect to buy from us. Many of them turn immediately to the superstores (office equipment, office supplies, and electronics) and mail order to look for the best price, without realizing that there is a better option for them at only a little bit more.

4.3.3 Competition and Buying Patterns

The small business buyers understand the concept of service and support, and are much more likely to pay for it when the offering is clearly stated.

There is no doubt that we compete much more against all the box pushers than against other service providers. We need to effectively compete against the idea that businesses should buy computers as plug-in appliances that don't need ongoing service, support, and training.

Our focus group sessions indicated that our target Home Offices think about price but would buy based on quality service if the offering were properly presented. They think about price because that's all they ever see. We have very good indications that many would rather pay 10–20% more for a relationship with a long-term vendor providing back-up and quality service and support; they end up in the box-pusher channels because they aren't aware of the alternatives.

Availability is also very important. The Home Office buyers tend to want immediate, local solutions to problems.

4.3.4 Main Competitors

Chain stores:

We have Store 1 and Store 2 already within the valley, and Store 3 is expected by the end of next year. If our strategy works, we will have differentiated ourselves sufficiently to not have to compete against these stores.

Comments

This is a good treatment of why the target market will look toward AMT with the new strategy.

The competitive analysis is in another topic and so is the nature of the competition. This topic lists the specific competitors in AMT's market. This one has been reduced a great deal because of the need to not mention specific names of real competitors.

AMERICAN MANAGEMENT TECHNOLOGIES (AMT), INC.

Strengths: national image, high volume, aggressive pricing, economies of scale.

Weaknesses: lack of product, service, and support knowledge; lack of personal attention.

Other local computer stores:

Store 4 and Store 5 are both in the downtown area. They are both competing against the chains in an attempt to match prices. When asked, the owners will complain that margins are squeezed by the chains and customers buy on price only. They say they tried offering services and that buyers didn't care, instead preferring lower prices. We think the problem is also that they didn't really offer good service, and also that they didn't differentiate from the chains.

5.0 Strategy and Implementation Summary

Our AMT strategy is based on playing toward our strengths and away from our weaknesses, with a nice angle regarding serving target market needs. We are not going to fight our competition on their playing field, selling products on the basis of price and brand names, as off-the-shelf appliances. Instead, we move toward our strengths, which are know-how and reliability, staying power, and relationships. To do that well we also shift strategy toward a better-focused target market, specifically, those segments that are most likely to perceive the need and understand the benefits at the core of our strategy.

5.1 Strategy Pyramids

For placing emphasis on service and support, our main tactics are networking expertise, excellent training, and developing our own proprietary software/network administrative system. Our specific programs for networking include mailers and internal training. Specific programs for training include direct mail promotion and train-the-trainers programs. For developing our own proprietary systems, our programs are company direct mail marketing, and working with VARs.

Comments

This is a very good, concise summary of the main elements of strategy. It serves as an excellent introduction to the topics that follow.

The strategy pyramid is a framework for analysis, one of my favorites, not necessarily the best and certainly not the only one. AMT uses this framework well.

AMERICAN MANAGEMENT TECHNOLOGIES (AMT), INC.

Our second strategy is emphasizing relationships. The tactics are marketing the company (instead of the products), more regular contacts with the customer, and increasing sales per customer. Programs for marketing the company include new sales literature, revised ad strategy, and direct mail. Programs for more regular contacts include call-backs after installation, direct mail, and sales management. Programs for increasing sales per customer include upgrade mailings and sales training.

5.1.1 Service and Support

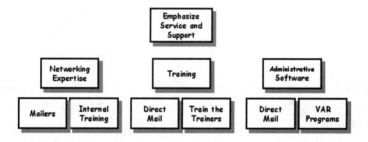

5.1.2 Company, Not Products

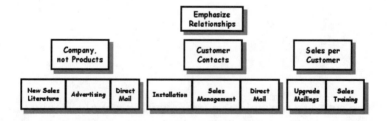

5.2 Value Proposition

Our value proposition has to be different from the standard box-oriented retail chain. We offer our target customer, who is service seeking and not self reliant, a vendor who acts as a strategic ally, at a premium price that reflects the value of reassurance that systems will work.

Comment

This topic was added to the outline specifically to allow the addition of a graphic in Business Plan Pro. The graphic was created with the organization chart software built into Microsoft Powerpoint™. It was transferred to a graphic file ending in .bmp, then imported in Business Plan Pro using the text manager tab in the topic, from text mode. The illustration is a simple illustration of the strategy pyramid.

This illustration was also produced with Powerpoint and copied to a graphic file that was imported into the topic.

This simple statement is probably redundant at this point, but the value proposition is another good framework for articulating strategy. This is based on value-based marketing, a conceptual framework developed by Lynn Phillips at Stanford's Graduate School of Business.

AMERICAN MANAGEMENT TECHNOLOGIES (AMT), INC.

5.3 Competitive Edge

Our competitive edge is our positioning as strategic ally with our clients, who are clients more than customers. By building a business based on long-standing relationships with satisfied clients, we simultaneously build defenses against competition. The longer the relationship stands, the more we help our clients understand what we offer them and why they need it.

5.4 Marketing Strategy

The marketing strategy is the core of the main strategy:

1. Emphasize service and support.

2. Build a relationship business.

3. Focus on small business and high-end home office as key target markets.

5.4.1 Positioning Statement

For businesspeople who want to be sure their computer systems are always working reliably, AMT is a vendor and trusted strategic ally that makes sure their systems work, their people are trained, and their down time is minimal. Unlike the chain retail stores, it knows the customer and goes to his or her site when needed, offering proactive support, service, training, and installation.

5.4.2 Pricing Strategy

We must charge appropriately for the high-end, high-quality service and support we offer. Our revenue structure has to match our cost structure, so the salaries we pay to assure good service and support must be balanced by what we charge.

We cannot build the service and support revenue into the price of products. The market can't bear the higher prices, and the buyers feel ill-used when they see the same product priced lower at the chains. Despite the logic behind this, the market doesn't support this concept.

Comments

This is a simple but eloquent statement of the competitive edge that AMT wants to develop. The potential is there, although much depends on AMT's ability to develop the advantages it hopes it has.

At this point the marketing strategy is already well articulated. AMT's overall strategy is driven by its marketing strategy.

The positioning statement is a good discipline. Here you see a good example of an overall company positioning statement. Positioning more often applies to products, not companies. In this case it fits quite well.

The pricing strategy fits perfectly with the overall strategy.

AMERICAN MANAGEMENT TECHNOLOGIES (AMT), INC.

Therefore, we must make sure that we deliver and charge for service and support. Training, service, installation, networking support—all of this must be readily available and priced to sell and deliver revenue.

5.4.3 Promotion Strategy

We depend on newspaper advertising as our main way to reach new buyers. As we change strategies, however, we need to change the way we promote ourselves:

1. Advertising

We'll be developing our core positioning message: "24 Hour On-Site Service—365 Days a Year With No Extra Charges" to differentiate our service from the competition. We will be using local newspaper advertising, radio, and cable TV to launch the initial campaign.

2. Sales Brochure

Our collaterals have to sell the store, and visiting the store, not the specific book or discount pricing.

3. Direct Mail

We must radically improve our direct mail efforts, reaching our established customers with training, support services, upgrades, and seminars.

4. Local Media

It's time to work more closely with the local media. We could offer the local radio a regular talk show on technology for small business, as one example.

5.5 Sales Strategy

1. We need to sell the company, not the product. We sell AMT, not Apple, IBM, Hewlett-Packard, or Compaq, or any of our software brand names.

Comments

Promotion in this context includes everything from advertising to public relations, press relations, and everything else involved in getting the marketing message to the potential users.

The sales strategy has been laid out clearly enough in the previous topics, so that by this time there are no surprises.

AMERICAN MANAGEMENT TECHNOLOGIES (AMT), INC.

2. We have to sell our service and support. The hardware is like the razor, and the support, service, software services, training, and seminars are the razor blades. We need to serve our customers with what they really need.

3. The Yearly Total Sales chart summarizes our ambitious sales forecast. We expect sales to increase from $5.3 million last year to $6.5 million next year and to more than $9 million in the last year of this plan.

Projected Sales

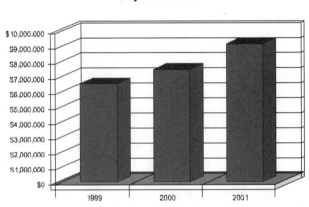

5.5.1 Sales Forecast

The important elements of the sales forecast are shown in the Total Sales by Month in Year 1 table. The nonhardware sales increase to about $2 million total in the third year.

Sales Forecast

Unit Sales	1999	2000	2001
Systems	2,255	2,500	2,800
Service	3,128	6,000	7,500
Software	3,980	5,000	6,500
Training	2,230	4,000	8,000
Other	2,362	2,500	3,000
Total Unit Sales	13,955	20,000	27,800

Comments

The illustration automatically charts the projected increase in sales.

The text here merely introduces the sales forecast to follow.

The table prints just the annual values as part of the main plan document, because of the formatting. The plan document is laid out vertically, but most of the detailed monthly tables are essentially horizontal. Business Plan Pro handles this problem by printing just annual values in the main document, leaving the horizontal monthly tables to be printed automatically in the appendixes, in horizontal instead of vertical format.

AMERICAN MANAGEMENT TECHNOLOGIES (AMT), INC.

Unit Prices	1999	2000	2001
Systems	$1,980.80	$1,984.50	$1,980.80
Service	$68.47	$84	$87
Software	$212.86	$195	$180
Training	$46.58	$72	$79
Other	$384.64	$300	$385

Sales	1999	2000	2001
Systems	$4,466,708	$4,961,240	$5,546,245
Service	$214,159	$504,000	$652,500
Software	$847,183	$975,000	$1,170,000
Training	$103,865	$288,000	$632,000
Other	$908,520	$750,000	$1,153,920
Total Sales	$6,540,434	$7,478,240	$9,154,665

Direct Unit Costs	1999	2000	2001
Systems	1,700.00	$1,686.82	$1,683.68
Service	58.08	$33.60	$34.80
Software	$120.00	$117.00	$108.00
Training	$11.10	$21.60	$23.70
Other	$244.11	$90.00	$118.26

Direct Cost of Sales	1999	2000	2001
Systems	$3,833,500	$4,217,054	$4,714,308
Service	$181,680	$201,600	$261,000
Software	$477,600	$585,000	$702,000
Training	$24,753	$86,400	$189,600
Other	$576,580	$225,000	$354,792
Subtotal Direct Cost of Sales	$5,094,113	$5,315,054	$6,221,700

Comments

You should turn to the AMT appendixes to see how the Sales Forecast accommodates an inventory program in the first month of the plan. This shows a sale of several hundred thousand dollars of inventory for less than cost. It produces a cost of sales much higher than sales for the first month, as it corrects an inventory problem that had been accumulating.

AMERICAN MANAGEMENT TECHNOLOGIES (AMT), INC.

Projected 1999 Sales by Month

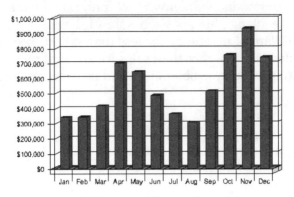

5.5.2 Sales Programs

1. Direct mail: Use great detail to describe your company's programs here.

2. Seminars: Use great detail to describe your company's programs here.

5.6 Milestones

Our important milestones are shown in the following table. Row by row, they track the need to follow up on strategy with specific activities. Most of the activities on the list can be easily tied to our strategic goals of selling more service and enhancing the relationship with the customer.

Comments

The chart provides a nice compromise to the problem of horizontal vs. vertical page formats and display information. Although the detailed monthly sales forecast is left for the appendixes, this monthly chart gives a good simple view of the sales forecast in the chart.

This is my personal favorite portion of a business plan because it gets into real specifics. A plan shouldn't be vague and intangible. It needs to include specific dates and specific milestones. This is where the managers commit to real action and real programs.

AMERICAN MANAGEMENT TECHNOLOGIES (AMT), INC.

Business Plan Milestones

Milestone	Manager	Planned Date	Department	Budget
Corporate Identity	TJ	12/17/98	Marketing	$10,000
Seminar implementation	IR	1/10/99	Sales	$1,000
Business Plan Review	RJ	1/10/99	GM	$0
Upgrade mailer	IR	1/16/99	Sales	$5,000
New corporate brochure	TJ	1/16/99	Marketing	$5,000
Delivery vans	SD	1/25/99	Service	$12,500
Direct mail	IR	2/16/99	Marketing	$3,500
Advertising	RJ	2/16/99	GM	$115,000
X4 Prototype	SG	2/25/99	Product	$2,500
Service revamp	SD	2/25/99	Product	$2,500
6 Presentations	IR	2/25/99	Sales	$0
X4 Testing	SG	3/6/99	Product	$1,000
3 Accounts	SD	3/17/99	Sales	$0
L30 Prototype	PR	3/26/99	Product	$2,500
Tech95 Expo	TB	4/12/99	Marketing	$15,000
VP S&M hired	JK	6/11/99	Sales	$1,000
Mailing system	SD	7/25/99	Service	$5,000
Totals				$181,500

6.0 Management Summary

Our management philosophy is based on responsibility and mutual respect. People who work at AMT want to work at AMT because we have an environment that encourages creativity and achievement.

6.1 Organizational Structure

1. The team includes 22 employees, under a president and four managers.

2. Our main management divisions are sales, marketing, service, and administration. Service handles service, support, training, and development.

Comments

The table keeps track of implementation specifics. It also includes plan-vs.-actual columns that are not printed in the document but are useful for implementation later on.

This is not much of a summary. The plan would be better off summarizing the number of employees, breaking down between part-time and full-time, and talking about the amount of total payroll.

This is also weak. In this case AMT is not presenting the plan to buyers or investors, and organizational changes are not part of the main strategy; so for this internal-use-only plan the brevity is acceptable.

AMERICAN MANAGEMENT TECHNOLOGIES (AMT), INC.

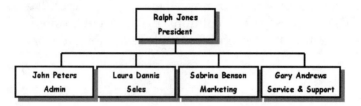

6.2 Management Team

Ralph Jones, President, 46 years old, founded AMT in 1989 to focus on reselling high-powered personal computers to small business. He has a degree in computer science and spent 15 years with Large Computer Company, Inc. in positions ending with project manager. Ralph has been attending courses at the local Small Business Development Center for more than six years now, steadily adding business skills and business training to his technical background.

Sabrina Benson, VP Marketing, 36 years old, joined us last year after a very successful career with Continental Computers. Her hiring was the culmination of a long recruiting search. With Continental she managed the VAR marketing division. She is committed to re-engineering AMT to be a service and support business that sells computers, not vice-versa. She has an MBA and an undergraduate degree in history.

Gary Andrews, VP Service and Support, 48 years old, has 18 years with Large Computers, Inc. in programming and service-related positions, 7 years with AMT. He has an M.S. in computer science and a B.S. in electrical engineering.

Laura Dannis, VP Sales, 32 years old and a former teacher, joined AMT part-time in 1991 and went full-time in 1992. She has very high people skills and a B.A. in elementary education. She has taken several sales management courses at the local SBDC.

John Peters, Director of Administration, 43 years old, started with AMT as a part-time bookkeeper in 1987 and has become the full-time administrative and financial backbone of the company.

Comments

The management team section is especially important in a business plan related to sale of a company or communications to investors. A company must be judged by the quality of its management team. Most plans will include real information here, and many refer to résumés included in the appendixes.

AMERICAN MANAGEMENT TECHNOLOGIES (AMT), INC.

6.3 Management Team Gaps

At present we believe we have a good team for covering the main points of the business plan. The addition of Sabrina Benson was important as a way to cement our fundamental re-positioning and re-engineering.

Currently, we are weakest in the area of technical capabilities to manage the database marketing programs and upgraded service and support, particularly with cross-platform networks. We also need to find a training manager.

6.4 Personnel Plan

The Personnel Plan reflects the need to bolster our capabilities to match our positioning. Our total headcount should increase to 22 this first year, and to 30 by the third year. Detailed monthly projections are included in the appendixes.

Personnel Plan

Production	1999	2000	2001
Manager	$12,000	$13,000	$14,000
Assistant	$36,000	$40,000	$40,000
Technical	$12,500	$35,000	$35,000
Technical	$12,500	$35,000	$35,000
Technical	$24,000	$27,500	$27,500
Fulfillment	$18,000	$22,000	$50,000
Other	$0	$0	$0
Subtotal	$115,000	$172,500	$201,500

Sales and Marketing Personnel

Manager	$72,000	$76,000	$80,000
Technical sales	$60,000	$63,000	$85,000
Technical sales	$45,500	$46,000	$46,000
Salesperson	$40,500	$55,000	$64,000
Salesperson	$40,500	$50,000	$55,000
Salesperson	$31,000	$38,000	$45,000
Salesperson	$21,000	$30,000	$33,000
Salesperson	$0	$30,000	$33,000
Other	$0	$0	$0
Subtotal	$310,500	$388,000	$441,000

Comments

Most companies have team gaps at one time or another. It is much better to recognize gaps in the plan than to have outsiders point them out. To recognize a gap is to take the first step toward filling it.

This plan says relatively little about personnel because it is an internal plan and personnel changes are not significant.

Like the Sales Forecast, this table is actually a detailed monthly table but only the annual values appear in the main document.

AMERICAN MANAGEMENT TECHNOLOGIES (AMT), INC.

General and Administrative Personnel

President	$66,000	$69,000	$95,000
Finance	$28,000	$29,000	$30,000
Admin Assistant	$24,000	$26,000	$28,000
Bookkeeping	$18,000	$25,000	$30,000
Clerical	$12,000	$15,000	$18,000
Clerical	$7,000	$15,000	$18,000
Clerical	$0	$0	$15,000
Other	$0	$0	$0
Subtotal	$155,000	$179,000	$234,000
Programming	$36,000	$40,000	$44,000
Other	$0	$0	$0
Subtotal	$36,000	$40,000	$44,000
Total Payroll	$616,500	$779,500	$920,500
Payroll Burden	$98,640	$124,720	$147,280
Total Payroll Expenditures	$715,140	$904,220	$1,067,780

6.5 Other Management Considerations

Our attorney, Frank Dudley, is also a co-founder. He invested significantly in the company over a period of time during the 1980s. He remains a good friend of Ralph's and has been a steady source of excellent legal and business advice.

Paul Karots, public relations consultant, is also a co-founder and co-owner. Like Dudley, he invested in the early stages and remains a trusted confidant and vendor of public relations and advertising services.

7.0 Financial Plan

The most important element in the financial plan is the critical need for improving several of the key factors that impact cash flow:

Comments

This is a good example of why other management considerations matter. Many companies depend on professionals or the board of directors for additional management functions.

This is a very solid financial plan summary, well suited to being included in a summary memo. It covers the key points quite well.

AMERICAN MANAGEMENT TECHNOLOGIES (AMT), INC.

1. We must at any cost stop the slide in inventory turnover and develop better inventory management to bring the turnover back up to 8 turns by the third year. This should also be a function of the shift in focus toward service revenues to add to the hardware revenues. Therefore, we are going to do a major inventory sell-off in January, selling several hundred thousand dollars worth of goods at well below cost.

2. We must also bring the gross margin back up to 25%. This too is related to improving the mix between hardware and service revenues, because the service revenues offer much better margins. Our annual results for 1999 won't show the improvement because of the huge negative gross margin for the inventory sell off, but after January the gross margin should improve notably, even if the annual figure is low.

3. We plan to borrow another $100,000 long-term this year, although payment of old loans makes the net amount about $65,000. The amount seems in line with the balance sheet capabilities.We will increase our short-term borrowing as needed to manage cash flow as sales ramp up in Spring and to finance improved equipment.

4. We are also financing major improvements in our own equipment for in-house, most of which is booked as short-term assets. We need this upgrade to stay competitive and to fulfill our value proposition with our customers.

7.1 Important Assumptions

The financial plan depends on important assumptions, most of which are shown in Table 7.1. The key underlying assumptions are:

1. We assume a slow-growth economy, without major recession.

2. We assume, of course, that there are no unforeseen changes in technology to make products immediately obsolete.

On our General Assumptions table, the most ambitious and also the most questionable assumption is our projected improvement in inventory turnover. This is critical to healthy cash flow, but will also be difficult.

Comments

This topic is included mainly to explain the general assumptions table. AMT also includes some other general assumptions, beyond the specific tables, that are part of the plan.

AMERICAN MANAGEMENT TECHNOLOGIES (AMT), INC.

General Assumptions

	1999	2000	2001
Short-term Interest Rate %	8.00%	8.00%	8.00%
Long-term Interest Rate %	8.50%	8.50%	8.50%
Payment Days Estimator	45	45	45
Collection Days Estimator	45	45	45
Inventory Turnover Estimator	6.00	7.00	8.00
Tax Rate %	20.00%	20.00%	20.00%
Expenses in Cash %	14.00%	14.00%	14.00%
Sales on Credit %	70.00%	70.00%	70.00%
Personnel Burden %	16.00%	16.00%	16.00%

7.2 Key Financial Indicators

The Benchmark Comparison chart highlights our ambitious plans to correct declining gross margin and inventory turnover. The chart illustrates why we think the ambitious sales increases we plan are reasonable. We have had similar increases in the recent past.

Benchmark Comparison

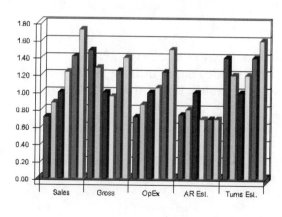
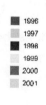

Comments

The general assumptions table includes several assumptions that are important for other tables.

This topic is included for explanations of the important Benchmarks chart, which follows. The plan document properly notes some of the questions inherent in the plan benchmarks.

The Benchmarks chart offers a very valuable comparison of past performance to future plans in a visible way. It sets an index value of 1 for the the last full year value of each of the key indicators, then compares the change, past and present, as a function of that index. You can see that the sales and operating expenses seem to be increasing at a believable pace, but the other three indicators generate questions. The gross margin has been declining steadily, and AMT plans to bring it back up. The collection days have been increasing, and AMT plans to decrease them. Inventory turnover has been decreasing, and AMT plans to increase it. These indicators should make you want to look back at the plan and see how AMT intends to accomplish some of these turnarounds in specific areas.

AMERICAN MANAGEMENT TECHNOLOGIES (AMT), INC.

7.3 Break-even Analysis

For our break-even analysis, we assume running costs of approximately $96,000 per month, which includes our full payroll, rent, and utilities, and an estimation of other running costs. Payroll alone, at our present run rate, is only about $55,000.

Margins are harder to assume. Our overall average of $343/248 is based on past sales. We hope to attain a margin that high in the future.

The chart shows that we need to sell about $350,000 per month to break even, according to these assumptions. This is about half of our planned 1999 sales level, and significantly below our last year's sales level, so we believe we can maintain it.

Break-even Analysis:

Monthly Units Break-even   824
Monthly Sales Break-even $352,336

Assumptions:

Average Per-Unit Revenue	$427.69
Average Per-Unit Variable Cost	$311.41
Estimated Monthly Fixed Cost	$95,792

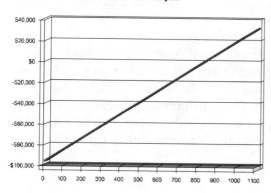

Break-even Analysis

Comments

The break-even analysis is included in this business plan because most people expect it. It takes a look at the built-in risk from the point of view of this classic financial analysis.

The table shows the assumptions behind the chart that follows. Break-even always involves a hard set of assumptions because one has to assume a standard month of fixed costs and a standard single-product set of variable costs and price. This is not easy to do in a complex business.

This chart shows the classic break-even analysis that crosses the line at the point of break-even.

AMERICAN MANAGEMENT TECHNOLOGIES (AMT), INC.

7.4 Projected Profit and Loss

The most important assumption in the Projected Profit and Loss statement is the gross margin, which is supposed to increase. This is up from barely 21% in the last year. The increase in gross margin is based on changing our sales mix, and it is critical. However, the increase doesn't show in the next year because we need to sell off nearly half a million dollars of excess inventory, most of it at a loss. The gross margin is so negative for January that it brings the rest of the year average down to 19%, when it would otherwise be closer to 25%. We have a negative gross margin of several hundred thousand dollars in the first month.

All results are affected by the important action regarding inventory, to take place at the beginning of the year, when we sell off as much as half a million dollars' worth of inventory. This increases our sales and short-term cash but is extremely unprofitable and reduces our annual gross margin a great deal. However, it is necessary to adjust our inventory, because we've allowed ourselves to accumulate too much inventory. Furthermore, a lot of that is either obsolete or will be obsolete if we leave it in inventory.

Month-by-month assumptions for profit and loss are included in the appendixes. You can see how the inventory sale completely affects our results for the first month, then in the rest of the year the gross margin is back up.

Profit and Loss (Income Statement)

	1999	2000	2001
Sales	$6,540,434	$7,478,240	$9,154,665
Direct Cost of Sales	$5,094,113	$5,315,054	$6,221,700
Production payroll	$115,000	$172,500	$201,500
Other	$6,000	$6,600	$7,260
Total Cost of Sales	$5,215,113	$5,494,154	$6,430,460
Gross Margin	$1,325,321	$1,984,086	$2,724,205
Gross Margin %	20.26%	26.53%	29.76%
Operating Expenses:			

Comments

The profit and loss statement introduces AMT's planned inventory action, which affects results for the first year. AMT is going to sell off several hundred thousand dollars of inventory in the first month to correct inventory problems that have been accumulating for years. It is worth turning to the appendixes to look at the specifics of how this was handled. First, the sales forecast has to show the sales of goods at below cost, then the profit and loss also shows the same impact. The inventory sale was necessary for AMT, but also had negative impact on profitability.

AMERICAN MANAGEMENT TECHNOLOGIES (AMT), INC.

	1999	2000	2001
Sales and Marketing Expenses			
Sales and Marketing			
Payroll	$310,500	$388,000	$441,000
Ads	$125,000	$140,000	$175,000
Catalog	$25,000	$19,039	$19,991
Mailing	$113,300	$120,000	$150,000
Promo	$16,000	$20,000	$25,000
Shows	$20,200	$25,000	$30,000
Literature	$7,000	$10,000	$12,500
PR	$1,000	$1,250	$1,500
Seminar	$31,000	$45,000	$60,000
Service	$10,250	$12,000	$15,000
Training	$5,400	$7,000	$15,000
Total Sales and			
Marketing Expenses	$664,650	$787,289	$944,991
Sales and Marketing %	10.16%	10.53%	10.32%
General and Administrative Expenses			
General and			
Administrative			
Payroll	$155,000	$179,000	$234,000
Payroll Burden	$98,640	$124,720	$147,280
Depreciation	$12,681	$13,315	$13,981
Leased Equipment	$30,000	$31,500	$33,075
Utilities	$9,000	$9,450	$9,923
Insurance	$6,000	$6,300	$6,615
Rent	$84,000	$88,200	$92,610
Other	$0	$0	$0
Other	$6,331	$6,648	$6,980

Comments

AMERICAN MANAGEMENT TECHNOLOGIES (AMT), INC.

	1999	**2000**	**2001**
Total General and Administrative Expenses	$401,652	$459,133	$544,464
General and Administrative %	6.14%	6.14%	5.95%
Other Expenses			
Other Payroll	$36,000	$40,000	$44,000
Contract/Consultants	$1,500	$5,000	$30,000
Other	$3,000	$6,000	$10,000
Total Other Expenses	$40,500	$51,000	$84,000
Other %	0.62%	0.68%	0.92%
Total Operating Expenses	$1,106,802	$1,297,422	$1,573,455
Profit Before Interest and Taxes	$218,519	$686,664	$1,150,750
Interest Expense Short-term	$10,167	$12,000	$12,000
Interest Expense Long-term	$29,628	$26,833	$21,162
Taxes Incurred	$35,745	$129,566	$223,518
Net Profit	$142,979	$518,265	$894,071
Net Profit/Sales	2.19%	6.93%	9.77%

7.5 Projected Cash Flow

The cash flow depends on assumptions for inventory turnover, payment days, and accounts receivable management. Our projected 45-day collection days is critical, and it is also reasonable. We need $100,000 in new long-term financing in March to get through a cash flow dip as we build up for mid-year sales. Our credit line borrowing increases to more than $350,000 in May, but decreases to zero by August and ends the year at $150,000.

Comments

This critical section depends much more on numbers than words. These are just brief explanations of the tables. The most important element is in the appendixes, the monthly detail.

AMERICAN MANAGEMENT TECHNOLOGIES (AMT), INC.

Pro Forma Cash Flow

	1999	2000	2001
Net Profit	$142,979	$518,265	$894,071
Plus:			
Depreciation	$12,681	$13,315	$13,981
Change in Accounts Payable	$537,079	$38,082	$142,345
Current Borrowing (repayment)	$60,000	$0	$0
Increase (decrease) Other Liabilities	$0	$0	$0
Long-term Borrowing (repayment)	$63,292	($64,953)	($68,484)
Capital Input	$0	$0	$0
Subtotal	$816,031	$504,709	$981,913
Less:	1999	2000	2001
Change in Accounts Receivable	$449,771	$121,144	$216,557
Change in Inventory	$319,188	($112,533)	$25,266
Change in Other ST Assets	($150,000)	$0	$0
Capital Expenditure	$90,000	$200,000	$400,000
Dividends	$0	$0	$0
Subtotal	$708,959	$208,610	$641,822
Net Cash Flow	$107,072	$296,099	$340,090
Cash Balance	$162,504	$458,603	$798,693

Comments

The important immediate message in the chart is that the cash flow can obviously go above or below zero, but the cash balance must always be positive.

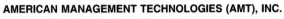

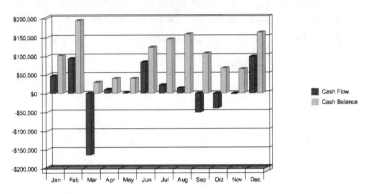

7.6 Projected Balance Sheet

The Projected Balance Sheet is quite solid. We do not project any real trouble meeting our debt obligations—as long as we can achieve our specific objectives.

Pro forma Balance Sheet
Assets

	Starting Balances	1999	2000	2001
Short-term Assets				
Cash	$55,432	$162,504	$458,603	$798,693
Accounts Receivable	$395,107	$844,878	$966,022	$1,182,579
Inventory	$841,012	$1,160,200	$1,047,667	$1,072,933
Other Short-term Assets	$25,000	($125,000)	($125,000)	($125,000)
Total Short-term Assets	$1,316,551	$2,042,582	$2,347,292	$2,929,204

Comments

The printed plan shows just the annual numbers, which are not the most important. You should refer to the appendixes to see the detailed cash flow.

The topic is really a placeholder for the balance sheet table.

The most interesting numbers are in the monthly balance sheet, in the appendixes.

AMERICAN MANAGEMENT TECHNOLOGIES (AMT), INC.

	Starting Balances	1999	2000	2001
Long-term Assets				
Capital Assets	$353,972	$443,972	$643,972	$1,043,972
Accumulated Depreciation	$51,945	$64,626	$77,941	$91,922
Total Long-term Assets	$302,027	$379,346	$566,031	$952,050
Total Assets	$1,618,578	$2,421,928	$2,913,323	$3,881,254
Liabilities and Capital				
Accounts Payable	$223,897	$760,976	$799,058	$941,403
Short-term Notes	$90,000	$150,000	$150,000	$150,000
Other Short-term Liabilities	$18,398	$18,398	$18,398	$18,398
Subtotal Short-term Liabilities	$332,295	$929,374	$967,456	$1,109,801
Long-term Liabilities	$284,862	$348,154	$283,201	$214,717
Total Liabilities	$617,157	$1,277,528	$1,250,657	$1,324,518
Paid-in Capital	$500,000	$500,000	$500,000	$500,000
Retained Earnings	$426,769	$501,421	$644,400	$1,162,666
Earnings	$74,652	$142,979	$518,265	$894,071
Total Capital	$1,001,421	$1,144,400	$1,662,666	$2,556,737
Total Liabilities and Capital	$1,618,578	$2,421,928	$2,913,323	$3,881,254
Net Worth	$1,001,421	$1,144,400	$1,662,666	$2,556,737

Comments

AMERICAN MANAGEMENT TECHNOLOGIES (AMT), INC.

7.7 Business Ratios

The table follows with our main business ratios. We do intend to improve gross margin, collection days, and inventory turnover.

Ratio Analysis

Profitability Ratios	1999	2000	2001
Gross Margin	20.26%	26.53%	29.76%
Net Profit Margin	2.19%	6.93%	9.77%
Return on Assets	5.90%	17.79%	23.04%
Return on Equity	12.49%	31.17%	34.97%

Activity Ratios	1999	2000	2001
AR Turnover	5.42	5.42	5.42
Collection Days	49	63	61
Inventory Turnover	5.21	4.98	6.06
Accts Payable Turnover	6.34	6.34	6.34
Total Asset Turnover	2.70	2.57	2.36

Debt Ratios	1999	2000	2001
Debt to Net Worth	1.12	0.75	0.52
Short-term Liab. to Liab.	0.73	0.77	0.84

Liquidity Ratios	1999	2000	2001
Current Ratio	2.20	2.43	2.64
Quick Ratio	0.95	1.34	1.67
Net Working Capital	$1,113,208	$1,379,836	$1,819,404
Interest Coverage	5.49	17.68	34.70

Comments

This text is really just a placeholder for the ratios analysis.

As always, the important message in the business ratios is the change. You can also note here how the ratios in this table are different from the ratios in the assumptions table. The assumptions ratios are used as predictors, inputs in calculating the month-by-month estimates. The ratios shown in the ratio tables are calculated after the fact, using annual balances, the way they would normally be calculated in financial analysis. These are very different numbers, used for very different purposes.

AMERICAN MANAGEMENT TECHNOLOGIES (AMT), INC.

Additional Ratios	1999	2000	2001
Assets to Sales	0.37	0.39	0.42
Debt/Assets	53%	43%	34%
Current Debt/Total Assets	38%	33%	29%
Acid Test	0.04	0.34	0.61
Asset Turnover	2.70	2.57	2.36
Sales/Net Worth	5.72	4.50	3.58

CHAPTER 15
EXAMPLE: BRIARPATCH
DEVELOPS A PLAN

This section chronicles the development of a business plan for Briarpatch Furniture Specialties, a hypothetical sample company. For the sake of illustration, we talk of this plan as it would have been developed by business owners Jim and Susan Morgan with help from Ted, their accountant.

PLANNING MEETING

The plan process starts with an initial meeting. In about two hours, with Ted's help, Jim and Susan and their managers go through a good review of the company. The managers are Jan, their sales manager; Terry, marketing manager; Kelly, finance manager; and Robin, production manager.

They had no mission statement, but agreed to write one. "That's really just fluff," Jim said, looking around for approval. Susan and most of the others disagreed.

"We're different from a lot of companies," said Jan, the sales manager. "We believe in things, starting with some things you and Susan believe in. You believe in giving value to your customers, and you believe in treating employees fairly." As they went on with the discussion, there were some jokes and breaks of laughter, and at the same time it was a useful discussion. Briarpatch needed to explicitly record its owners' sense of value in business. It needed a mission statement that made its values explicit, especially regarding value for customers, the employee community, and customer satisfaction.

Most of the rest of the discussion was also useful. They all looked for a while at the business in terms of the underlying benefit offered to its target customers. Benefits included satisfaction, quality, and the essence of workmanship and design. The best of Briarpatch was custom furniture done so well it felt like craftsmanship, almost art.

"We're really not selling office furniture, not even computer office furniture. We're selling a look and feel, an environment," said Robin. "People don't buy our furniture just because they need furniture. It is always part of a larger sense of the office space as personality." The managers all agreed that Briarpatch needed to maintain its sense of quality and its positioning.

An open discussion of the keys to success in the business and the main priorities for the next year followed. The managers seemed to find significant areas of agreement, but several at the meeting felt as if much of what was said hadn't really been discussed before. It was almost like team building just to ask the right questions.

As the meeting ended, Ted, the Grahams, and their managers agreed on some follow-up steps. They agreed that Susan would produce the mission statement, keys to success, and business objectives for a business plan. They also asked each of the managers to suggest specific programs (business activities) and forecasts (sales, personnel, costs, and expenses) for their specific areas.

This meeting took three hours of CPA-billable time. Jim and Susan were encouraged by the quality of the discussion and looked forward to moving ahead with the plan. They purchased their business plan software and were ready to start working.

BUDGET AND PROGRAMS MEETING

The budget and programs meeting took place a week later. It took half a day and required an LCD projector that connects to a laptop computer. Susan took program and budget suggestions from the managers, plus an initial sales forecast, and input them into the sales forecast and milestones tables of the business plan.

Figure 15–1 shows the milestones table as it appeared at the beginning of the meeting. The projector displays specific programs and specific budgets. Jan, Terry, and Jim have followed up on the first meeting with suggested programs to be put into the milestones table for the business

Milestone	Mngr	Date	Dept.	Budget
Our in-house catalog plan	Terry	1/31/98	Other	$0
New distributor	Jan	3/15/98	Travel	$5,000
New distributor	Jan	3/15/98	PR	$3,000
New distributor	Jan	3/15/98	Ads	$25,000
In-house catalog design	Terry	4/1/98	Other	$5,000
In-house catalog mailing	Terry	5/1/98	Other	$15,000
Third catalog placement	Jan	5/15/98	Ads	$150,000
Spring trade show	Terry	5/15/98	PR	$10,000
Spring trade show	Terry	5/15/98	Events	$20,000
Spring trade show	Terry	5/15/98	Travel	$6,000
Laptop product test	Jim	6/15/98	Other	$5,000
Summer trade show	Terry	7/15/98	PR	$8,000
Summer trade show	Terry	7/15/98	Events	$20,000
Summer trade show	Terry	7/15/98	Travel	$6,000
Laptop product release	Terry	10/15/98	PR	$35,000
Fall trade show	Terry	10/15/98	Travel	$6,000
Fall trade show	Terry	10/15/98	PR	$8,000
Fall trade show	Terry	10/15/98	Events	$20,000
Second catalog	Jan	n.a.	Ads	$125,000
First catalog placement	Jan	n.a.	Ads	$175,000
General ads	Jan	n.a.	Ads	$200,000
Computer mag ads	Jan	n.a.	Ads	$200,000
Other	n.a.	n.a.	n.a	$0
Totals				**$1,047,000**

Figure 15–1. The milestones table as it appeared at the beginning of the budget and programs meeting.

plan. Susan took that information and put it into a draft business plan.

The budget and program proposals were unrealistic. As the end of 1997 neared, Briarpatch would have had about $1.8 million in gross sales. Its total operating expenses would have been about $900,000, including payroll of $675,000.

Therefore, the proposed budget of more than $1 million in sales and marketing expenses was about three times as high as it should have been.

The sales forecast was just as unrealistic, as the meeting started. Susan asked Jan, as sales manager, to project sales as well as specific programs. Sales managers tend to be quite optimistic, and Jan was no exception. "All we have to do is spend more money and we can triple sales." Three times the normal budget—Jan's proposed programs sum to almost $900,000—would supposedly produce three times the sales. Jan projected sales at $4.8 million, about three times 1997 sales. Figure 15–2 summarizes Jan's sales forecast.

As the group looked at those numbers, the discussion became more realistic. Figure 15–3 shows the Business Plan Pro

Unit Sales	1998	1999	2000
Executive desk oak	786	970	1,200
Executive desk cherry	546	680	840
Other furniture oak	786	970	1,200
Other furniture cherry	546	680	840
Other	546	680	840
Total Unit Sales	6,375	9,030	13,020
Unit Prices			
Executive desk oak	$1,600	$1,600	$1,600
Executive desk cherry	$1,750	$1,750	$1,750
Other furniture oak	$900	$900	$900
Other furniture cherry	$1,000	$1,000	$1,000
Other	$2,500	$2,500	$2,500
Total Sales			
Executive desk oak	$1,257,600	$1,552,000	$1,920,000
Executive desk cherry	$955,500	$1,190,000	$1,470,000
Other furniture oak	$707,400	$873,000	$1,080,000
Other furniture cherry	$546,000	$680,000	$840,000
Other	$1,365,000	$1,700,000	$2,100,000
Total Sales	$4,831,500	$5,995,000	$7,410,000

Figure 15–2. Jan's sales forecast.

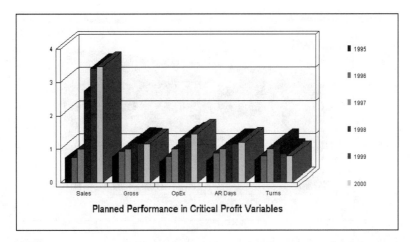

Figure 15–3. The Business Plan Pro benchmarks chart related to the preliminary numbers.

benchmarks chart related to these preliminary numbers. The benchmarks chart compares the past with the present and future, so you can visually see the suggested change. The benchmarks chart takes five key factors and displays them in relative numbers, with the last full year set as 1.0, and the two years before that and the next three years showing according to their relationship with the last full year. If sales in 1997 (the last real year) were 5 million and sales in 1998 were 10 million, then 1997 would show up as 1 and 1998 as 2. If sales were 2 million in 1997 and expected to hit 2.5 million in 1998, then the 1993 value is 1.25. The key is the visual comparison. Obviously, the sales bar goes way up from 1997 to 1998. Would this be realistic? Would it be possible? Probably not.

Another clue on realism was the shape of the sales by month chart, shown in Figure 15–4. In the past Briarpatch sales always went up from January through March, then down into the summer, then back up in the fall and down in December. The group relaxed and joked a bit about Jan's enthusiasm, but eventually everybody agreed that budgets and forecasts needed to come down to about a third of what Jan had started out with.

Then there was some serious discussion. Nobody wanted to lower budget, but everybody agreed sales and expenses

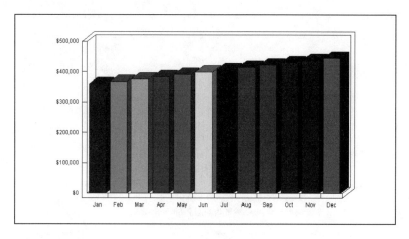

Figure 15–4. Total sales by month in Year 1.

were too high. Jan defended the proposals for major new spending in advertising and trade shows, but the group prevailed and projections were lowered. In the meantime, Jan won a much higher advertising budget than Briarpatch had ever had. Terry successfully defended plans for increased trade show participation, but agreed to drop the summer show to save budget for spring and fall.

This budgeting process generates commitment. Terry argued with peers about the need for trade shows. Jan argued for advertising. They both talked about how much sales would result, and the value for the business. They were both committed to completing and implementing their programs and making them work. This kind of personal commitment is vital to business planning.

By the end of the meeting, the main sales and marketing programs summed to $365,000, as shown in Figure 15–5. The sales forecast went down to a much more realistic $2.15 million—a strong 20% growth, but also more believable. Figure 15–6 shows the forecast. The monthly forecast reflects seasonality, as you can see in Figure 15–7. These projections are the ones included in the final plan, which may be found in Chapter 13 and included on your disk. Figure 15–8 illustrates the revised benchmarks chart, which shows a more orderly flow from year to year. Notice how the index of change in all five

Milestone	Mngr	Date	Dept.	Budget
Our in-house catalog plan	Terry	1/31/98	Other	$0
New distributor	Jan	3/15/98	Travel	$5,000
New distributor	Jan	3/15/98	Ads	$3,000
In-house catalog design	Terry	4/1/98	Other	$2,000
In-house catalog mailing	Terry	5/1/98	Other	$5,000
Third catalog placement	Jan	5/15/98	Ads	$64,000
Spring trade show	Terry	5/15/98	Events	$20,000
Spring trade show	Terry	5/15/98	PR	$10,000
Spring trade show	Terry	5/15/98	Travel	$6,000
Laptop product test	Jim	6/15/98	Other	$1,000
Laptop product release	Terry	10/15/98	PR	$5,000
Fall trade show	Terry	10/15/98	Events	$20,000
Fall trade show	Terry	10/15/98	PR	$8,000
Fall trade show	Terry	10/15/98	Travel	$6,000
Second catalog	Jan	n.a.	Ads	$85,000
First catalog placement	Jan	n.a.	Ads	$125,000
Other	n.a.	n.a.	n.a.	$0
Totals				**$365,000**

Figure 15–5. The milestones table as it appeared at the end of the budget and programs meeting.

variables shows more orderly change in this revised chart. This is a good measure of built-in realism.

FINISHING UP

After the budgets meeting, there were two other follow-up meetings between Ted and the Briarpatch people. Before each of these meetings, Susan sent Ted the business plan as a Business Plan Pro *.BPZ file, an attachment to an e-mail message. When the e-mail was down they sent it on floppy disk,

Unit Sales	1998	1999	2000
Executive desk oak	615	710	820
Executive desk cherry	312	330	350
Other furniture oak	424	450	470
Other furniture cherry	109	110	120
Other	54	60	70
Total Unit Sales	**1,514**	**1,660**	**1,830**
Unit Prices			
Executive desk oak	$1,600	$1,600	$1,600
Executive desk cherry	$1,750	$1,750	$1,750
Other furniture oak	$900	$900	$900
Other furniture cherry	$1,000	$1,000	$1,000
Other	$2,500	$2,500	$2,500
Total Sales			
Executive desk oak	$984,000	$1,136,000	$1,312,000
Executive desk cherry	$545,825	$577,500	$612,500
Other furniture oak	$381,600	$405,000	$423,000
Other furniture cherry	$109,000	$110,000	$120,000
Other	$135,000	$150,000	$175,000
Total Sales	**$2,155,425**	**$2,378,500**	**$2,642,500**

Figure 15–6. The new sales forecast.

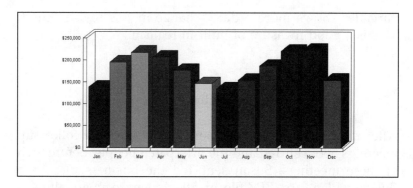

Figure 15–7. The new monthly forecast, reflecting seasonality.

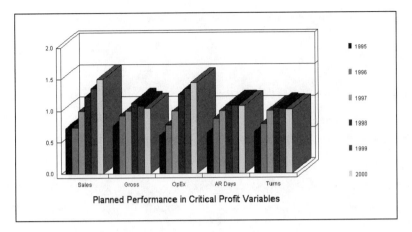

Figure 15–8. The revised benchmarks chart.

by courier. The accountant went over the file on a computer, and then discussed it during the meetings. Any projections printed in Ted's office were stamped "for internal use only." Some projections were also just viewed on the computer screen and discussed. The forecasts were always Briarpatch's forecast, their intellectual work, not Ted's.

Ted did, however, go over the forecasts, the assumptions, the output, and even the wording of the plan. Ted is an accountant, not an editor, but he carefully read the business plan and then reassured Jim and Susan that the plan looked good enough for the bank.

FOLLOWING UP

When the plan and the people were ready, the plan went to the bank. The loan application was approved, and Briarpatch's credit line went up. Two months later, Susan asked Ted to work with her and Kelly to analyze plan-vs.-actual results for the first two months of the plan. The business plan was done, and implementation was under way.

CHAPTER 16
BRIARPATCH FURNITURE
SPECIALTIES, INC. SAMPLE PLAN

This sample business plan has been made available to users of Business Plan Pro™, business-planning software published by Palo Alto Software. Our sample plans were developed by existing companies or new business start-ups as research instruments to determine market viability or funding availability. Names, locations, and numbers may have been changed, and substantial portions of text may have been omitted to preserve confidentiality and proprietary information

You are welcome to use this plan as a starting point to create your own, but you do not have permission to reproduce, publish, distribute, or even copy this plan as it exists here.

Requests for reprints, academic use, and other dissemination of this sample plan should be addressed to the marketing department of Palo Alto Software.

Briarpatch Furniture Specialities, Inc.

1.0 Executive Summary

Briarpatch Furniture has been riding a growth spurt, having discovered the high-end direct mail channel that gave us a push to new potential volumes through channels. Bolstered by appearances in specialty catalogs, we were able to develop an additional channel through distributors of office equipment that sell directly to corporations.

This annual business plan calls for another year of 20% + growth, followed by two years of consolidation. Because our sales growth has brought some working capital implications, we are carefully planning to manage growth and provide for steady cash flow.

We also expect to be profitable as never before. In all, this plan is a healthy company with good growth prospects, looking to manage its orderly growth in the near future.

This chapter shows a sample plan from Briarpatch Furniture Company as it would be created and printed with the help of Business Plan Pro.

Briarpatch Furniture Specialities, Inc.

Business Plan Highlights

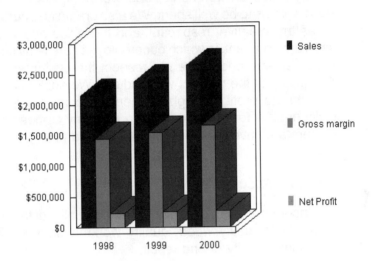

1.1 Objectives

1. Sales passing $2 million in 1998, and $2.5 million in 2000.
2. Gross margin of 65% or more.
3. Net profit above 10% of sales.

1.2 Mission

Briarpatch helps create pleasant, productive office environments with well-designed furniture that incorporates new technology into the classic office mode, in which real people can work happily. We are sensitive to the look and feel of good wood and fine furniture as well as to high-powered personal computing. We always provide the best possible value to our customers, who care about

Briarpatch Furniture Specialities, Inc.

quality office environments, and we want every dollar spent with us to be well spent. We also create and nurture a healthy, creative, respectful, and fun office and work-shop environment, in which our employees are fairly compensated and encouraged to respect the customer and the quality of the product we produce. We seek fair and responsible profit, enough to keep the company financially healthy for the long term and to fairly compensate owners and investors for their money and risk.

1.3 Keys to Success

1. Uncompromising commitment to the quality of the end product: quality wood, quality workmanship, quality design, quality of end result.

2. Successful niche marketing: we need to find the quality-conscious customer in the right channels, and we need to make sure that customer can find us.

3. Almost-automatic assembly: we can't afford to ship fully assembled desks, but assembly must be so easy and automatic that it makes the customer feel better about the quality, not worse.

2.0 Company Summary

Briarpatch is a privately owned specialty manufacturer of high-end office furniture for computer users who care about elegant office space. Our customers are in all levels of business that can afford high quality office furniture, plus a growing portion of high-end home offices.

Briarpatch Furniture Specialities, Inc.

2.1 Company Ownership

Briarpatch is an Oregon corporation, subchapter S, owned entirely by Jim and Susan Graham. It was created in 1992. At that time the product line and industrial property rights (including trademarks) were purchased from the heirs to the Briarpatch Association, which was a 1970s commune in rural Oregon.

2.2 Company History

Briarpatch had actually existed since the 1970s as a commune, but its present existence began in 1992 when the furniture line was purchased by Jim and Susan Graham. The Grahams moved to Oregon from California and purchased the business as part of the move.

Sales took a big jump in 1996, when we reached more effective channels of distribution. The key was winning a place in the Premier Executive office furniture catalog, which led to winning the interest of the Needham furniture distributors, and display space in several hundred stores.

Profitability and working capital were problems during our recent growth, but we believe we now have costs and cash flow under control.

Briarpatch Furniture Specialities, Inc.

Past Performance

	1995	1996	1997
Sales	$1,278,090	$1,305,678	$1,757,899
Gross margin	$583,806	$723,737	$1,052,454
Gross % (calculated)	45.68%	55.43%	59.87%
Operating expenses	$546,021	$698,011	$901,245
Collection period (days)	35	47	54
Inventory turnover	4	4.7	6
Balance sheet			1997
Short-term assets			
Cash			$14,381
Accounts receivable			$176,054
Inventory			$101,405
Other short-term assets			$23,751
Total short-term assets			$315,591
Long-term assets			
Capital assets			$32,097
Accumulated depreciation			$17,204
Total long-term assets			$14,893
Total assets			$330,484
Debt and equity			
Accounts payable			$61,907
Short-term notes			$25,000
Other short-term liabilities			$18,031
Subtotal short-term liabilities			$104,938
Long-term liabilities			$10,000
Total liabilities			$114,938
Paid in capital			$45,000
Retained earnings			$45,793
Earnings	$11,329	$1,870	$124,753

Briarpatch Furniture Specialities, Inc.

Past Performance, cont.

	1995	1996	1997
Total equity			$215,546
Total debt and equity			$330,484
Other inputs			1997
Payment days			35
Sales on credit			$1,404,344
Receivables turnover			7.98

Past Financial Performance

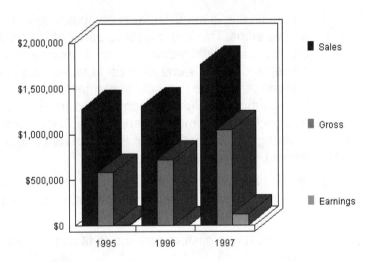

2.3 Company Locations and Facilities

Briarpatch is located in a single facility in the West Eleventh industrial district in Eugene, Oregon. The facility includes office and workshop space, access to the local bus route, and good parking.

Briarpatch Furniture Specialities, Inc.

3.0 Products

Briarpatch offers high quality office furniture designed to effectively incorporate computer machinery into the executive office or home office. The key to the line is an ergonomically effective desk that still looks like an executive desk, looks attractive in a high-end home office, but is intended to accommodate the personal computer.

3.1 Product Description

1. Our main line is the Briarpatch computer desk in several versions. This is an elegant piece of office furniture designed to look attractive in executive office or home office, and at the same time be ideal for real use of the computer. The two critical elements of ergonomics—keyboard height and angle and monitor height and angle—are completely adjustable. Cable runs and shelving add to the utility of the executive computer, without sacrificing elegance.

2. In addition, we make complementary pieces to fill out the office suite, including file cabinets, printer stands, and bookcases.

3. We also make custom designs to fit exact measurements.

3.2 Competitive Comparison

Within our niche we have two significant competitors, Acme Computer Furniture and ABC Manufacturing. Acme is a bigger company, operating mainly in our same

Briarpatch Furniture Specialities, Inc.

niche, whose marketing is better than its product quality. ABC is a subsidiary of Haines Furniture, a major furniture manufacturer, which has recently targeted our niche.

In general, however, our competition is not in our niche. We compete against generalized furniture manufacturers, cheaper computer-related furniture, and the mainstream merchandise in the major furniture channels and office supply stores. People do not choose our competitors instead of our product, rather, they choose lesser quality, mainstream materials instead of the higher quality furniture we offer.

3.3 Sales Literature

Sales literature is attached as an appendix to the plan.

For 1998 we plan to develop a company catalog, which would include some other products for the same target customers. The focus will be the executive office catalog, with furniture, lamps, and other accessories.

3.4 Sourcing

Our Oregon location is a distinct advantage for local wood. We can buy higher quality oak and cherry than either of our competitors (one in California, and one in New York). Because our sales increased over the past two years, we have been able to buy at better prices, because of higher volumes.

We work with three wood suppliers, all local. Bambridge supplies most of our oak and a bit of cherry and some

Briarpatch Furniture Specialities, Inc.

other specialty woods. Bambridge has been in business for as long as we have and has given us good service and good prices. This is a good, stable supplier. Duffin Wood Products is a good second source, particularly for cherry and specialty woods. We've used Merlin supplies as well, frequently, for filling in when either of our two main suppliers was short.

We also work with a number of specialty manufacturers for furniture fittings, drawer accessories, glass, shelving accessories, and related purchases.

Although we are not a major player compared with the major furniture manufacturers, we are one of the biggest buyers of the custom materials we need. Most of our suppliers sell through channels to hobbyists and carpenters, so they treat us as a major account.

3.5 Technology

We depend on our dominance of the latest in technology of ergonomics, combined with classic design elements of fine furniture. We must remain on top of new technologies in display, input and output, and communications. For example, our latest models already assume the desktop digital scanner as a frequent accessory, and audio for use in creating presentations, e-mail attachments, and so on.

Our assembly patents are an important competitive edge. No competitor can match the way we turn a drawback—having to assemble the product—into a feature. Our customer surveys confirm that customers view the interlocking assembly system as an enhancement to quality.

Briarpatch Furniture Specialities, Inc.

3.6 Future Products

In 1988 we will introduce the new line based on the executive laptop computer, with docking station to connect to a network. The new furniture has a different configuration to assume easy access to the docking station and better use of the space that doesn't have to be dedicated the the CPU case.

We are also going to accommodate larger monitors, the 17" and 21" sizes that are becoming much more common, particularly in our high-end market. As we do, we will also be watching for the new technology providing wall-mounted flat screens, the liquid plasma, and similar technologies.

4.0 Market Analysis Summary

Our target market is a person who wants to have fine furniture with the latest in technology, combined with an old-fashioned sense of fine woods and fine woodworking. This person may be in the corporate towers, a small or medium-sized business, or in a home office. The common bond is the appreciation of quality and the lack of price constraints.

4.1 Market Segmentation

- Corporate executives: our market research indicates about 2.5 million potential customers who are managers in corporations of more than 100 employees. The target customer is going to be at a high executive level, in most cases, because the purchase price is relatively steep compared to standard office furniture.

Briarpatch Furniture Specialities, Inc.

- Small business owners: our customer surveys indicate a strong market among the owners of businesses with fewer than 100 employees. There are 11 million such businesses in this country, most of them with concentrated ownership that makes the owners potential customers.

- Home offices: the home office business has proliferated during the 1990s, and we also have home offices for people employed outside the home. This is a big market, some 36 million home offices, growing faster than other markets.

Market Analysis

Potential Customers	Customers	Growth rate
Corporate executives	2,500,000	1%
Small business owners	11,000,000	4%
Home offices	36,000,000	10%
Other	1,000,000	3%
Total	50,500,000	8.23%

Potential Market

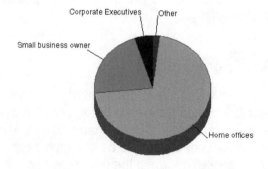

Briarpatch Furniture Specialities, Inc.

4.2 Industry Analysis

The office furniture industry has undergone a great deal of change in this decade. The growth of the office super-stores made a few large brands dominant. They produce relatively inexpensive furniture that makes compromises in order to stay at the low price level.

Makers of higher quality furniture are in general shuffling for niches to hide in. Although Briarpatch was essentially developed around a niche, many of the more traditional furniture makers are looking for niches, trying to deal with declining sales as the main volume goes elsewhere.

4.2.1 Industry Participants

The main volume in the industry is now concentrated in four main brands, all of which compete for retail sales through the major retail chain stores (Office Depot, Office Max, Staples, and others). These same four are also concentrating efforts as well in the major club discount stores (Price Club, Costco, Sams, etc.).

Designs are similar and quite competitive, costs and cost control is critical, and channel management and channel marketing are the keys to these business' continued success.

In mainstream office furniture, the rise of the office store channel has siphoned a great deal of volume from the older and more traditional manufacturers. The channels that sold the more traditional lines are also suffering. What's left are smaller brands, smaller companies, and divisions of more traditional furniture companies.

Briarpatch Furniture Specialities, Inc.

Some traditional manufacturers still make desks as part of furniture lines focused primarily on home furnishings. Some of these have looked at times at our niche and are competing for the same dollars.

4.2.2 Distribution Patterns

The four main manufacturers sell direct to the office superstores and buying discount clubs. This accounts for the main volume of distribution. The office furniture customer seems to be growing steadily more comfortable with the retail buy in the chain store.

The major corporate purchases are still made directly with manufacturers. Although this is still a major channel for some of the more traditional manufacturers, it is essentially closed to new competition. The direct channel is dominated by two manufacturers and two distributors. The distributors will occasionally take on a new line— happily, this has helped Briarpatch—but the main growth is in retail.

Published research indicates that 51% of the total sales volume in the market goes through the retail channel, most of that major national chains. Another 23% goes through the direct sales channel, although in this case direct sales includes sales by distributors who are buying from multiple manufacturers. Most of the remainder, 18%, is sold directly to buyers by catalogs.

Briarpatch Furniture Specialities, Inc.

4.2.3 Competition and Buying Patterns

In the mainstream business, channels are critical to volume. The manufacturers that have impact in the national sales win display space in the store, and most buyers seem content to pick their product off the store floor. Price is critical, because the channels take significant margins. Buyers are willing to settle for laminated quality and serviceable design.

In direct sales to corporations, price and volume are critical. The corporate buyer wants trouble-free buying in volume, at a great price. Reliable delivery is as important as reliable quality.

In the high-end specialty market, particularly in our niche, features are quite important. Our target customer does not make selections on the basis of price. The ergonomics, design, and accommodation of the computer features within the high-quality feel of good wood are much more important than mere price. We are also seeing that assembly is critical to shipping and packing, but our customer doesn't accept any assembly problems. We need to make sure that the piece comes together almost like magic, and as it does, it presents a greater feel of quality than if it hadn't required assembly at all.

4.2.4 Main Competitors

Acme Computer Furniture

Operating since the mid 1980s, Acme grew up with computer-related furniture. It was one of the first, certainly the first we are aware of, to develop personal computer

Briarpatch Furniture Specialities, Inc.

desks and market through advertising in computer magazines. Today they are about twice our size. They have a nicely produced catalog and good relationships with two distributors.

Strengths: good marketing, strong advertising budget, relationships with distributors, strong direct sales.

Weaknesses: the product is more standardized and of lesser quality, with less sense of design and materials and workmanship.

ABC Manufacturing is a division of Haines Furniture, the second largest manufacturers of mainstream home furnishings. Haines bought ABC three years ago and is focusing on our niche. We see good quality product and an excellent sense of design, but little movement in channels or catalogs.

Strengths: financial backing, product quality.

Weaknesses: ABC has not seemed to understand our niche, where to find the buyers, how to market as a specialty niche instead of through the more traditional furniture channels.

5.0 Strategy and Implementation Summary

We focus on a special kind of customer, the person who wants high quality office furniture customized to work beautifully with modern technology, including personal computers, scanners, internet connections, and other high-tech items. Our customer might be in a larger corpo-

Briarpatch Furniture Specialities, Inc.

ration, a small or medium-sized business, or in a home office with or without a home-office business. What is important to the customer is elegance, fine workmanship, ease of use, ergonomics, and practicality.

Our marketing strategy assumes that we need to go into specialty channels to address our target customer's needs. The tie-in with the high-end quality catalogs like Sharper Image is perfect, because these catalogs cater to our kind of customers. We position as the highest quality, offering status and prestige levels of purchase.

The product strategy is also based on quality, in this case the intersection of technical understanding with high quality woodworking and professional materials and workmanship.

Our most important competitive edge is our assembly strategy, which is based on interlocking wood pieces of such high quality that assembly is not only a pleasure for our customers, but it is actually a feature that enhances the sense of quality.

5.1 Marketing Strategy

Our product is positioned carefully: this is high-quality office furniture combining workmanship and ergonomics for the customer who understands quality, is a user of high technology equipment, and is willing to spend money on the best. Unlike the mainstream products, we do not use laminates or cheap manufacturing technology.

Briarpatch Furniture Specialities, Inc.

Our marketing strategy is based mainly on making the right information available to the right target customer. We can't afford to sell people on our expensive products, because most don't have the budget. What we really do is make sure that those who have the budget and appreciate the product know that it exists and know where to find it.

The marketing must convey the sense of quality in every picture, every promotion, and every publication. We can't afford to appear in second-rate catalogs with poor illustrations that make the product look less than it is. We also need to leverage our presence using high-quality catalogs and specialty distributors.

5.1.1 Pricing Strategy

We will maintain our pricing position as a premier provider. We are the best product available, for the most discriminating consumer. We intend to maintain our separation from the price competition at the lower end of the business. Our plan calls for no significant changes in pricing.

5.1.2 Promotion Strategy

Our most important vehicle for sales promotion is the direct mail catalog published by the specialty retailer such as Sharper Image and its competitors. Our advertising budget of $264 million goes mainly for space in the specialty catalog.

Briarpatch Furniture Specialities, Inc.

We also participate in major industry events, including both the Spring and Fall national computer furniture shows and the fall computer show. Our total budget for events is $40,000, plus about half of the $31,000 travel budget.

This year we will also promote our products with an in-house catalog showing our own products plus related merchandise of interest to the same target market.

5.2 Sales Strategy

Our strategy focuses first on maintaining the identity with the high-end buyer who appreciates the best available quality but is also very demanding regarding computer systems and technology. We've been able to find these customers using a combination of direct mail catalogs and direct sales to distributors.

For the next year we will continue to focus on a growing presence in the high-end direct mail catalog that finds our specialty customer. We will work with Sharper Image and Broadview more than ever, and we expect to gain position in the major airline catalogs as well. Specialty retail is a new channel that could become important for us.

Our work with distributors has been promising. We hope to continue the relationship with distributors selling directly to larger corporations, even though this takes working capital to support receivables.

Briarpatch Furniture Specialities, Inc.

Yearly Total Sales

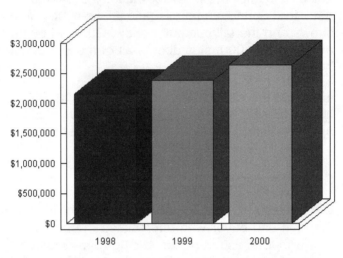

5.2.1 Sales Forecast

Our sales forecast assumes no change in costs or prices, which is a reasonable assumption for the past few years.

We are expecting to increase sales from $1.76 million to $2.16 million in the next year, which is slightly more than 20% growth. The growth forecast is in line with our last year and is relatively high for our industry because we are developing new channels. In 1999 and 2000 we expect growth closer to 10% per year, to a projected total of $2.64 million in 2000.

We are not projecting significant change in the product line or in the proportion between different lines.

Briarpatch Furniture Specialities, Inc.

Our seasonality, as shown in the chart, is still a factor in the business. We tend to sell much better in Spring and Fall, and sales drop in the summer.

Sales Forecast

Unit Sales		1998	1999	2000
Executive desk oak	15.00%	615	710	820
Executive desk cherry	5.00%	312	330	350
Other furniture oak	5.00%	424	450	470
Other furniture cherry	5.00%	109	110	120
Other	20.00%	54	60	70
Total Unit Sales		1,514	1,660	1,830
Unit Prices				
Executive desk oak		$1,600	$1,600	$1,600
Executive desk cherry		$1,750	$1,750	$1,750
Other furniture oak		$900	$900	$900
Other furniture cherry		$1,000	$1,000	$1,000
Other		$2,500	$2,500	$2,500
Total Sales				
Executive desk oak		$984,000	$1,136,000	$1,312,000
Executive desk cherry		$545,825	$577,500	$612,500
Other furniture oak		$381,600	$405,000	$423,000
Other furniture cherry		$109,000	$110,000	$120,000
Other		$135,000	$150,000	$175,000
Total Sales		$2,155,425	$2,378,500	$2,642,500
Direct Unit costs				
Executive desk oak	25.00%	$400	$400	$400
Executive desk cherry	30.00%	$525	$525	$525
Other furniture oak	20.00%	$180	$180	$180

Briarpatch Furniture Specialities, Inc.

Sales Forecast, cont.

		1998	1999	2000
Other furniture cherry	30.00%	$300	$300	$300
Other	25.00%	$625	$625	$625
Total direct cost of Sales				
Executive desk oak		$246,000	$284,000	$328,000
Executive desk cherry		$163,748	$173,250	$183,750
Other furniture oak		$76,320	$81,000	$84,600
Other furniture cherry		$32,700	$33,000	$36,000
Other		$33,750	$37,500	$43,750
Subtotal Direct Costs		$552,518	$608,750	$676,100

Total Sales by Month in Year 1

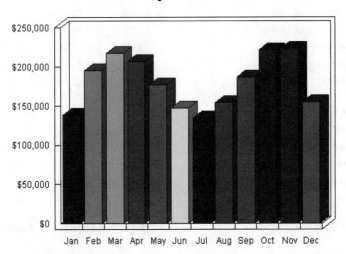

5.2.2 Sales Programs

Specific sales programs:

1. Catalog sales: develop placement with one additional catalog catering to the high-end office executive, pay-

Briarpatch Furniture Specialities, Inc.

ing for space and positioning. The budget is $10,000 for this program, due March 15, with Jan responsible.

2. Distributor sales: we need to develop at least new distributors, spending for copromotion as required and making direct sales calls. The specific responsibility is Jan, and due date is May 15, with a budget of $15,000.

3. Direct sales: we mail a new in-house catalog, developed by the marketing department, to add to our direct telephone sales. Jan will be responsible, without a budget or a deadline because the catalog is a marketing program.

5.3 Milestones

The accompanying table shows specific milestones, with responsibilities assigned, dates, and (in most cases) budgets. We are focusing in this plan on a few key milestones that should be accomplished.

Business Plan Milestones

Milestone	Mngr.	Date	Dept.	Budget
Third catalog placement	Jan	5/15/98	Sales	$10,000
New distributor	Jan	3/15/98	Sales	$15,000
Our in-house catalog plan	Terry	1/31/98	Marketing	$0
In-house catalog design	Terry	4/1/98	Marketing	$2,000
In-house catalog mailing	Terry	5/1/98	Marketing	$10,000
Laptop product test	Jim	6/15/98	Design	$1,000
Laptop product release	Terry	10/15/98	Marketing	$5,000

Briarpatch Furniture Specialities, Inc.

Business Plan Milestones, cont.

Milestone	Mngr.	Date	Dept.	Budget
Spring trade show	Terry	5/15/98	Marketing	$10,000
Fall trade show	Terry	10/15/98	Marketing	$10,000
Other		1/1/95	Sales	$0
Totals				$63,000

6.0 Management Summary

We are a small company owned and operated by Jim and Susan Graham, husband and wife, as a Subchapter S corporation. Jim is the developer and designer of the products, and Susan manages the company as president.

Management style reflects the participation of the owners. The company respects its community of co-workers and treats all workers well. We attempt to develop and nurture the company as community. We are not very hierarchical.

6.1 Organizational Structure

Susan Graham, President, is responsible for overall business management. Our managers of finance, marketing, and sales report directly to Susan.

Jim Graham, designer, is responsible for product design and development, assembly, and manufacturing. Our workshop manager reports directly to Jim.

Briarpatch Furniture Specialities, Inc.

As co-owners, Jim and Susan jointly develop business strategy and long-term plans. Jim is strong on product know-how and technology, and Susan is strong on management and business know-how.

6.2 Management Team

Susan Graham, 43, president, had a successful career in retail management before becoming half owner of Briarpatch. She has an MBA degree from Stanford and was Marketing Manager of Ross Stores, a buyer for Macy's, and merchandising manager for Sears and Roebuck.

Jim Graham, 44, designer, designed furniture for Haines Manufacturing before becoming half owner of Briarpatch. He was responsible for one of the first executive desks designed to include customized fittings for personal computers, and was one of the first to design the monitor inside the desk under glass. He has a B.S. and M.S. in industrial design, from Stanford University and the University of Oregon, respectively.

Kelly Weber, 37, finance manager, was administrative manager at the Wings Seminars before joining us and had done bookkeeping and administrative management at other companies prior to that. Kelly has a degree in history from the University of North Carolina, and an M.B.A. from the University of Oregon.

Jan Stevens, 38, sales manager, was a store manager for Office Depot before joining Briarpatch. Jan had been with Office Depot for 12 years, working in the direct sales group before taking over the local store in Eugene.

Briarpatch Furniture Specialities, Inc.

Terry Hatcher, 34, is marketing manager. Terry joined Briarpatch from the marketing department of the Thomasville Furniture chain, having been in charge of national catalog production and catalog advertising. Terry also managed direct sales at one of the furniture distributors that has since died as a result of industry consolidation. Terry has a B.A. degree in literature from the University of Washington.

Leslie Williams, 46, is workshop manager. Leslie is a master furniture builder with a great knack for managing people and an instinctive sense of the right way to work with wood.

6.3 Management Team Gaps

As we grow we will need to develop more manufacturing technique, more mass production. Leslie grew up with the hand-made and custom furniture business and knows fine woodworking well, but admits a weakness in establishing standardized assembly.

6.4 Personnel Plan

The personnel table assumes slow growth in employees, and 5% per annum pay raises. We already have a strong benefits policy (with fully paid medical, dental, and life insurance, plus a profit sharing and 401k plan) and low turnover.

Salaries are generally in line with market pay for the Eugene area, although our benefits are above standard

Briarpatch Furniture Specialities, Inc.

market level, so we ultimately pay a bit more for our people than what might be considered standard in our market. Eugene, however, is on average a lower wage location than most of the more developed industry areas.

Personnel Plan

Production		1998	1999	2000
Workshop manager	5.00%	$36,000	$38,000	$40,000
Cutting/fitting	5.00%	$30,000	$64,000	$100,500
Assembly	5.00%	$33,000	$70,000	$111,000
Other	5.00%	$54,000	$57,000	$60,000
Subtotal		$153,000	$229,000	$311,500

Sales and Marketing Salaries

Marketing manager	5.00%	$60,000	$63,000	$66,000
Sales manager	5.00%	$60,000	$63,000	$66,000
Support/admin	5.00%	$36,000	$38,000	$40,000
Other	5.00%	$12,000	$13,000	$14,000
Subtotal		$168,000	$177,000	$186,000

General and Administrative Salaries

President	5.00%	$90,000	$95,000	$100,000
Finance	5.00%	$72,000	$76,000	$80,000
Admin	5.00%	$48,000	$50,000	$53,000
Other	5.00%	$60,000	$63,000	$66,000
Subtotal		$270,000	$284,000	$299,000

Other Salaries

Design	5.00%	$48,000	$50,000	$53,000
Other	5.00%	$12,000	$13,000	$14,000
Subtotal		$60,000	$63,000	$67,000

Briarpatch Furniture Specialities, Inc.

Personnel Plan, cont.

	1998	1999	2000
Total Headcount	16	17	19
Total Payroll	$651,000	$753,000	$863,500
Payroll Burden	$97,650	$112,950	$129,525
Total Payroll Expenditures	$748,650	$865,950	$993,025

7.0 Financial Plan

The financial picture is quite encouraging. We have been slow to take on debt, but with our increase in sales we do expect to apply for a credit line with the bank, to a limit of $150,000. The credit line is easily supported by assets.

We do expect to be able to take some money out as dividends. The owners don't take overly generous salaries, so some draw is appropriate.

7.1 Important Assumptions

The accompanying table lists our main assumptions for developing our financial projections. The most sensitive assumption is the collection days. We would like to improve collection days to take pressure off of our working capital, but our increasing sales through channels makes the collection time a cost of doing business.

We do expect to see a decline in our inventory turnover ratio, another unfortunate side effect of increasing sales through channel. We find ourselves having to buy earlier and hold more finished goods in order to deal with sales through the channel.

Briarpatch Furniture Specialities, Inc.

General Assumptions

	1998	1999	2000
Short-term Interest Rate	10.00%	10.00%	10.00%
Long-term Interest Rate	9.00%	9.00%	9.00%
Payment days	35	35	35
Collection days	58	58	58
Inventory turnover	5	5.00	5.00
Tax rate percent	25.00%	25.00%	25.00%
Expenses in cash %	10.00%	10.00%	10.00%
Sales on credit	75.00%	75.00%	75.00%

Note: Ratios in assumptions are used as estimators and may therefore have different values than ratios calculated in the ratios section.

7.2 Key Financial Indicators

The following chart shows changes in key financial indicators: sales, gross margin, operating expenses, collection days, and inventory turnover. The growth in sales goes above 20% for the second year in a row, but then settles. We expect to keep gross margin higher than before, but our projections show a slight decline as we go into new product areas and face new competition.

The projections for collection days and inventory turnover show that we are already expecting a decline in these indicators, because of increasing sales through channels.

Briarpatch Furniture Specialities, Inc.

Benchmark Comparison

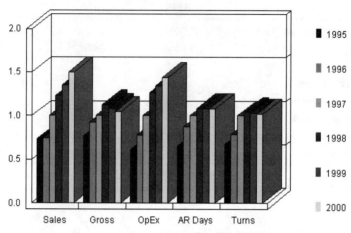

Planned Performance in Critical Profit Variables

7.3 Break-even Analysis

Our break-even analysis is based on running costs, the "burn-rate" costs we incur to keep the business running, not on theoretical fixed costs that would be relevant only if we were closing. Between payroll, rent, utilities, and basic marketing costs, we think $40,000 is a good estimate of fixed costs.

Our assumptions on average unit sales and average per-unit costs depend on averaging. We don't really need to calculate an exact average, this is close enough to help us understand what a real break-even point might be.

The essential insight here is that our sales level seems to be running comfortably above break-even.

Briarpatch Furniture Specialities, Inc.

Break-Even Analysis:

Monthly Units Break-even	67
Monthly Sales Break-even	$80,000

Assumptions:

Average Unit Sale	$1,200.00
Average Per-Unit Cost	$600.00
Fixed Cost	$40,000

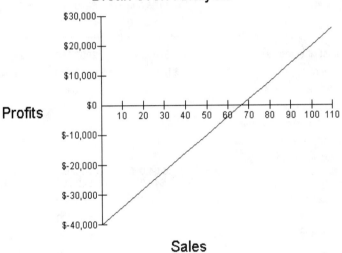

Break-even Analysis

7.4 Projected Profit and Loss

We do expect a significant increase in profitability this year, and in the future, because we have learned how to deal with the increasing sales levels of selling through channels. Despite the lower profitability levels of recent years, we expect to pass 10% in 1998, and remain at that level through 2000.

Briarpatch Furniture Specialities, Inc.

Our higher sales volume has lowered our cost of goods and increased our gross margin. This increase in gross margin is important to profitability.

Pro-forma Income Statement

		1998	1999	2000
Sales		$2,155,425	$2,378,500	$2,642,500
Direct cost of sales		$552,518	$608,750	$676,100
Production		$153,000	$229,000	$311,500
Other		$0	$0	$0
Total cost of sales		$705,518	$837,750	$987,600
Gross margin		$1,449,908	$1,540,750	$1,654,900
Gross margin percent		67.27%	64.78%	62.63%
Operating expenses:				
Sales and marketing expenses				
Sales and marketing salaries		$168,000	$177,000	$186,000
Advertising/promotion	10.00%	$264,000	$280,000	$310,000
Events	5.00%	$40,000	$42,000	$44,000
Public relations	5.00%	$36,000	$38,000	$40,000
Travel	5.00%	$31,000	$33,000	$35,000
Miscellaneous	5.00%	$24,000	$25,000	$26,000
Other	5.00%	$12,000	$13,000	$14,000
Total sales and marketing expenses		$575,000	$608,000	$655,000
Sales and marketing percent		26.68%	25.56%	24.79%
General and Administrative Expenses				
General and Administrative Salaries		$270,000	$284,000	$299,000
Leased equipment		$36,000	$36,000	$36,000

Briarpatch Furniture Specialities, Inc.

Pro-forma Income Statement, cont.

	1998	1999	2000
Utilities	$12,000	$12,000	$12,000
Insurance	$6,000	$6,000	$6,000
Rent	$30,000	$30,000	$30,000
Depreciation	$3,000	$3,000	$3,000
Payroll burden	$97,650	$112,950	$129,525
Profit sharing	$20,000	$25,000	$30,000
Other	$12,000	$12,000	$12,000
Total General and Administrative Expenses	$486,650	$520,950	$557,525
General and Administrative Percent	22.58%	21.90%	21.10%
Other expenses			
Other salaries	$60,000	$63,000	$67,000
Contract/consultants	$12,000	$12,000	$12,000
Other	$6,000	$6,000	$6,000
Total Other Expenses	$78,000	$81,000	$85,000
Other Percent	3.62%	3.41%	3.22%
Total Operating Expenses	$1,139,650	$1,209,950	$1,297,525
Profit Before Interest and Taxes	$310,258	$330,800	$357,375
Interest Expense ST	$3,833	$0	$0
Interest Expense LT	$900	$450	$0
Taxes Incurred	$76,381	$82,588	$89,344
Net Profit	$229,143	$247,763	$268,031
Net Profit/Sales	10.63%	10.42%	10.14%

Briarpatch Furniture Specialities, Inc.

7.5 Projected Cash Flow

Although we expect to be more profitable in 1988, we still have drains on the cash flow. We need to invest $65,000 in new assembly and manufacturing equipment, plus $25,000 in new computer equipment, and another $10,000 in miscellaneous short-term assets, including office equipment.

Because of our increased sales through channels, and necessary increase in inventory levels, we need to increase working capital. We plan to extend our credit line to cover as much as $150,000 in short-term credit, backed by receivables and inventory. Our maximum extension looks like $125,000 in March, and it is well covered by an estimated $300,000 in receivables and $165,000 in inventory that same month.

Pro-Forma Cash Flow

	1998	1999	2000
Net profit:	$229,143	$247,763	$268,031
Plus:			
Depreciation	$3,000	$3,000	$3,000
Change in accounts payable	$33,991	$7,454	$9,651
Current borrowing (repayment)	($25,000)	$0	$0
Increase (decrease) other liabilities	$16,381	$0	$0
Long-term borrowing (repayment)	$0	($10,000)	$0
Capital Input	$0	$0	$0
Subtotal	$257,515	$248,217	$280,682
Less:			
Change in accounts receivable	$95,921	$28,148	$33,312
Change in inventory	$23,035	$23,323	$26,431
Change in other ST assets	$10,000	$25,000	$40,000
Capital expenditure	$65,000	$40,000	$50,000

Briarpatch Furniture Specialities, Inc.

Pro-Forma Cash Flow, cont.

	1998	1999	2000
Dividends	$50,000	$150,000	$300,000
Subtotal	$243,956	$266,471	$449,743
Net cash flow	$13,559	($18,255)	($169,061)
Cash balance	$27,940	$9,686	($159,375)

Cash Analysis

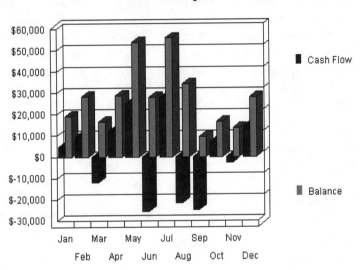

7.6 Projected Balance Sheet

Our projected balance sheet shows an increase in net worth to more than $1 million in 2000, at which point we expect to be making 13% profit on sales of $2.5 million. With the present financial projections we have no trouble supporting our working capital credit line, and we are growing assets both because we want to—new equipment — and because we have to grow receivables and inventory to support growth in sales through channels.

Briarpatch Furniture Specialties, Inc.

Pro-forma Balance Sheet

	Starting Balances	1998	1999	2000
Short-term assets				
Cash	$14,381	$27,940	$9,686	($159,375)
Accounts receivable	$176,054	$271,975	$300,123	$333,435
Inventory	$101,405	$124,440	$147,763	$174,194
Other short-term assets	$23,751	$33,751	$58,751	$98,751
Total short-term assets	$315,591	$458,106	$516,323	$447,005
Long-term assets				
Capital assets	$32,097	$97,097	$137,097	$187,097
Accumulated depreciation	$17,204	$20,204	$23,204	$26,204
Total long-term assets	$14,893	$76,893	$113,893	$160,893
Total Assets	$330,484	$534,999	$630,216	$607,898
Debt and equity				
Accounts payable	$61,907	$95,898	$103,352	$113,003
Short-term notes	$25,000	$0	$0	$0
Other ST liabilities	$18,031	$34,412	$34,412	$34,412
Subtotal short-term liabilities	$104,938	$130,310	$137,764	$147,415
Long-term liabilities	$10,000	$10,000	$0	$0
Total liabilities	$114,938	$140,310	$137,764	$147,415
Paid in capital	$45,000	$45,000	$45,000	$45,000
Retained earnings	$45,793	$120,546	$199,689	$147,452
Earnings	$124,753	$229,143	$247,763	$268,031
Total equity	$215,546	$394,689	$492,452	$460,483
Total debt and equity	$330,484	$534,999	$630,216	$607,898
Net worth	$215,546	$394,689	$492,452	$460,483

Briarpatch Furniture Specialities, Inc.

7.7 Business Ratios

Our ratios look healthy and solid. Gross margin is projected to stay above 65%, return on assets at 40%, and return on equity at 50% or better. Debt and liquidity ratios also look very good, with debt to net worth running at about one fifth, no more than one quarter. The projections, if we make them, are those of a very solid company.

Ratio Analysis

Profitability Ratios:	1998	1999	2000
Gross margin	67.27%	64.78%	62.63%
Net profit margin	10.63%	10.42%	10.14%
Return on Assets	42.83%	39.31%	44.09%
Return on Equity	58.06%	50.31%	58.21%
Activity Ratios:			
AR turnover	5.94	5.94	5.94
Collection days	51	59	58
Inventory turnover	6.25	6.16	6.13
Accts payable turnover	10.29	10.29	10.29
Total asset turnover	4.03	3.77	4.35
Debt Ratios:	1998	1999	2000
Debt to net worth	0.36	0.28	0.32
Short-term debt to liab.	0.93	1.00	1.00
Liquidity Ratios:			
Current Ratio	3.52	3.75	3.03
Quick Ratio	2.56	2.68	1.85
Net Working Capital	$327,796	$378,559	$299,590

Briarpatch Furniture Specialities, Inc.

Ratio Analysis, cont.

	1998	1999	2000
Interest Coverage	65.55	735.11	0.00

Additional ratios:	1998	1999	2000
Assets to sales	0.25	0.26	0.23
Debt/Assets	26%	22%	24%
Current debt/Total Assets	24%	22%	24%
Acid Test	0.47	0.50	-0.41
Asset Turnover	4.03	3.77	4.35
Sales/Net Worth	5.46	4.83	5.74

Chapter 16 Appendix: Briarpatch Furniture Specialties, Inc.

Appendix: Projected Balance Sheet
Pro-forma Balance Sheet

	Starting Balances	Jan-98	Feb-98	Mar-98	Apr-98	May-98	Jun-98	Jul-98	Aug-98	Sep-98	Oct-98	Nov-98	Dec-98
Short-term Assets													
Cash	$14,381	$18,996	$28,431	$16,404	$28,643	$53,760	$28,080	$55,878	$34,348	$9,558	$16,404	$13,652	$27,940
Accounts receivable	$176,054	$197,931	$279,592	$311,412	$307,675	$277,388	$233,605	$203,345	$209,510	$247,825	$296,459	$321,968	$271,975
Inventory	$101,405	$115,752	$151,740	$165,420	$158,760	$139,992	$120,348	$111,804	$124,380	$146,016	$167,430	$167,160	$124,440
Other Short-term Assets	$23,751	$23,751	$23,751	$28,751	$28,751	$33,751	$33,751	$33,751	$33,751	$33,751	$33,751	$33,751	$33,751
Total Short-term Assets	$315,591	$356,430	$483,514	$521,988	$523,829	$504,891	$415,784	$404,778	$401,989	$437,150	$514,043	$536,530	$458,106
Long-term Assets													
Capital Assets	$32,097	$47,097	$47,097	$47,097	$47,097	$47,097	$72,097	$72,097	$97,097	$97,097	$97,097	$97,097	$97,097
Accumulated Depreciation	$17,204	$17,204	$17,204	$17,204	$17,204	$17,204	$17,204	$17,204	$17,204	$17,204	$17,204	$17,204	$20,204
Total Long-term Assets	$14,893	$29,893	$29,893	$29,893	$29,893	$29,893	$54,893	$54,893	$79,893	$79,893	$79,893	$79,893	$76,893
Total Assets	$330,484	$386,323	$513,407	$551,881	$553,722	$534,784	$470,677	$459,671	$481,882	$517,043	$593,936	$616,423	$534,999
Debt and Equity													
		Jan-98	Feb-98	Mar-98	Apr-98	May-98	Jun-98	Jul-98	Aug-98	Sep-98	Oct-98	Nov-98	Dec-98
Accounts Payable	$61,907	$68,330	$99,393	$105,296	$96,209	$100,538	$70,313	$71,804	$72,053	$86,567	$142,410	$126,759	$95,898
Short-term Notes	$25,000	$65,000	$125,000	$125,000	$85,000	$45,000	$15,000	$0	$0	$0	$0	$0	$0
Other ST Liabilities	$18,031	$20,385	$29,390	$22,533	$35,265	$39,448	$23,478	$24,103	$29,594	$19,756	$25,018	$34,553	$34,412
Subtotal Short-term Liabilities	$104,938	$153,715	$253,783	$252,829	$216,474	$184,986	$108,791	$95,908	$101,647	$106,323	$167,428	$161,312	$130,310
Long-term Liabilities	$10,000	$10,000	$10,000	$10,000	$10,000	$10,000	$10,000	$10,000	$10,000	$10,000	$10,000	$10,000	$10,000
Total Liabilities	$114,938	$163,715	$263,783	$262,829	$226,474	$194,986	$118,791	$105,908	$111,647	$116,323	$177,428	$171,312	$140,310
Paid in Capital	$45,000	$45,000	$45,000	$45,000	$45,000	$45,000	$45,000	$45,000	$45,000	$45,000	$45,000	$45,000	$45,000
Retained Earnings	$45,793	$170,546	$170,546	$170,546	$170,546	$170,546	$170,546	$170,546	$170,546	$170,546	$170,546	$170,546	$120,546
Earnings	$124,753	$7,062	$34,078	$73,506	$111,703	$124,252	$136,340	$138,217	$154,689	$185,174	$200,962	$229,565	$229,143
Total Equity	$215,546	$222,608	$249,624	$289,052	$327,249	$339,798	$351,886	$353,763	$370,235	$400,720	$416,508	$445,111	$394,689
Total Debt and Equity	$330,484	$386,323	$513,407	$551,881	$553,722	$534,784	$470,677	$459,671	$481,882	$517,043	$593,936	$616,423	$534,999
Net Worth	$215,546	$222,608	$249,623	$289,052	$327,249	$339,798	$351,886	$353,763	$370,235	$400,720	$416,508	$445,111	$394,689

Appendix: Projected Cash Flow

Pro-Forma Cash Flow

	Jan-98	Feb-98	Mar-98	Apr-98	May-98	Jun-98	Jul-98	Aug-98	Sep-98	Oct-98	Nov-98	Dec-98
Net Profit:	$7,062	$27,016	$39,428	$38,197	$12,549	$12,088	$1,877	$16,472	$30,486	$15,788	$28,603	($422)
Plus:												
Depreciation	$0	$0	$0	$0	$0	$0	$0	$0	$0	$0	$0	$3,000
Change in Accounts Payable	$6,423	$31,063	$5,903	($9,088)	$4,329	($30,224)	$1,491	$249	$14,514	$55,843	($15,651)	($30,861)
Current Borrowing (repayment)	$40,000	$60,000	$0	($40,000)	($40,000)	($30,000)	($15,000)	$0	$0	$0	$0	$0
Increase (decrease) Other Liabilities	$2,354	$9,005	($6,857)	$12,732	$4,183	($15,971)	$626	$5,491	($9,838)	$5,263	$9,534	($141)
Long-term Borrowing (repayment)	$0	$0	$0	$0	$0	$0	$0	$0	$0	$0	$0	$0
Capital Input	$0	$0	$0	$0	$0	$0	$0	$0	$0	$0	$0	$0
Subtotal	$55,839	$127,084	$38,474	$1,842	($18,939)	($64,107)	($11,006)	$22,211	$35,162	$76,893	$22,487	($28,424)
Less:	Jan	Feb	Mar	Apr	May	Jun	Jul	Aug	Sep	Oct	Nov	Dec
Change in Accounts Receivable	$21,877	$81,661	$31,821	($3,737)	($30,288)	($43,783)	($30,260)	$6,165	$38,315	$48,634	$25,509	($49,993)
Change in Inventory	$14,347	$35,988	$13,680	($6,660)	($18,768)	($19,644)	($8,544)	$12,576	$21,636	$21,414	($270)	($42,720)
Change in Other ST Assets	$15,000	$0	$5,000	$0	$5,000	$25,000	$0	$0	$0	$0	$0	$0
Capital Expenditure	$0	$0	$0	$0	$0	$25,000	$0	$25,000	$0	$0	$0	$0
Dividends	$0	$0	$0	$0	$0	$0	$0	$0	$0	$0	$0	$50,000
Subtotal	$51,224	$117,649	$50,501	($10,397)	($44,056)	($38,427)	($38,804)	$43,741	$59,951	$70,048	$25,239	($42,713)
Net Cash Flow	$4,615	$9,435	($12,027)	$12,239	$25,117	$25,680	$27,798	($21,530)	($24,789)	$6,845	($2,752)	$14,289
Cash balance	$18,996	$28,431	$16,404	$28,643	$53,760	$28,080	$55,878	$34,348	$9,558	$16,404	$13,652	$27,940

Appendix: Important Assumptions
General Assumptions

	Jan-98	Feb-98	Mar-98	Apr-98	May-98	Jun-98	Jul-98	Aug-98	Sep-98	Oct-98	Nov-98	Dec-98
Short-term Interest Rate	10.00%	10.00%	10.00%	10.00%	10.00%	10.00%	10.00%	10.00%	10.00%	10.00%	10.00%	10.00%
Long-term Interest Rate	9.00%	9.00%	9.00%	9.00%	9.00%	9.00%	9.00%	9.00%	9.00%	9.00%	9.00%	9.00%
Payment days	35	35	35	35	35	35	35	35	35	35	35	35
Collection days	58	58	58	58	58	58	58	58	58	58	58	58
Inventory turnover	5.00	5.00	5.00	5.00	5.00	5.00	5.00	5.00	5.00	5.00	5.00	5.00
Tax rate percent	25.00%	25.00%	25.00%	25.00%	25.00%	25.00%	25.00%	25.00%	25.00%	25.00%	25.00%	25.00%
Expenses in cash%	10.00%	10.00%	10.00%	10.00%	10.00%	10.00%	10.00%	10.00%	10.00%	10.00%	10.00%	10.00%
Sales on credit	75.00%	75.00%	75.00%	75.00%	75.00%	75.00%	75.00%	75.00%	75.00%	75.00%	75.00%	75.00%
Personnel burden %	15.00%	15.00%	15.00%	15.00%	15.00%	15.00%	15.00%	15.00%	15.00%	15.00%	15.00%	15.00%

Note: Ratios in assumptions are used as estimators and may therefore have different values than ratios calculated in the ratios section.

Appendix: Personnel Plan

		Jan-98	Feb-98	Mar-98	Apr-98	May-98	Jun-98	Jul-98	Aug-98	Sep-98	Oct-98	Nov-98	Dec-98
Production													
Workshop manager	5.00%	$3,000	$3,000	$3,000	$3,000	$3,000	$3,000	$3,000	$3,000	$3,000	$3,000	$3,000	$3,000
Cutting/fitting	5.00%	$2,500	$2,500	$2,500	$2,500	$2,500	$2,500	$2,500	$2,500	$2,500	$2,500	$2,500	$2,500
Assembly	5.00%	$2,750	$2,750	$2,750	$2,750	$2,750	$2,750	$2,750	$2,750	$2,750	$2,750	$2,750	$2,750
Other	5.00%	$4,500	$4,500	$4,500	$4,500	$4,500	$4,500	$4,500	$4,500	$4,500	$4,500	$4,500	$4,500
Subtotal		$12,750	$12,750	$12,750	$12,750	$12,750	$12,750	$12,750	$12,750	$12,750	$12,750	$12,750	$12,750
Sales and Marketing Salaries													
Marketing manager	5.00%	$5,000	$5,000	$5,000	$5,000	$5,000	$5,000	$5,000	$5,000	$5,000	$5,000	$5,000	$5,000
Sales manager	5.00%	$5,000	$5,000	$5,000	$5,000	$5,000	$5,000	$5,000	$5,000	$5,000	$5,000	$5,000	$5,000
Support/admin	5.00%	$3,000	$3,000	$3,000	$3,000	$3,000	$3,000	$3,000	$3,000	$3,000	$3,000	$3,000	$3,000
Other	5.00%	$1,000	$1,000	$1,000	$1,000	$1,000	$1,000	$1,000	$1,000	$1,000	$1,000	$1,000	$1,000
Subtotal		$14,000	$14,000	$14,000	$14,000	$14,000	$14,000	$14,000	$14,000	$14,000	$14,000	$14,000	$14,000
General and Administrative Salaries													
President	5.00%	$7,500	$7,500	$7,500	$7,500	$7,500	$7,500	$7,500	$7,500	$7,500	$7,500	$7,500	$7,500
Finance	5.00%	$6,000	$6,000	$6,000	$6,000	$6,000	$6,000	$6,000	$6,000	$6,000	$6,000	$6,000	$6,000
Admin	5.00%	$4,000	$4,000	$4,000	$4,000	$4,000	$4,000	$4,000	$4,000	$4,000	$4,000	$4,000	$4,000
Other	5.00%	$5,000	$5,000	$5,000	$5,000	$5,000	$5,000	$5,000	$5,000	$5,000	$5,000	$5,000	$5,000
Subtotal		$22,500	$22,500	$22,500	$22,500	$22,500	$22,500	$22,500	$22,500	$22,500	$22,500	$22,500	$22,500
Other Salaries													
Design	5.00%	$4,000	$4,000	$4,000	$4,000	$4,000	$4,000	$4,000	$4,000	$4,000	$4,000	$4,000	$4,000
Other	5.00%	$1,000	$1,000	$1,000	$1,000	$1,000	$1,000	$1,000	$1,000	$1,000	$1,000	$1,000	$1,000
Subtotal		$5,000	$5,000	$5,000	$5,000	$5,000	$5,000	$5,000	$5,000	$5,000	$5,000	$5,000	$5,000
Total Headcount		16	16	16	16	16	16	16	16	16	16	16	16
Total Payroll		$54,250	$54,250	$54,250	$54,250	$54,250	$54,250	$54,250	$54,250	$54,250	$54,250	$54,250	$54,250
Payroll Burden		$8,138	$8,138	$8,138	$8,138	$8,138	$8,138	$8,138	$8,138	$8,138	$8,138	$8,138	$8,138
Total Payroll Expenditures		$62,388	$62,388	$62,388	$62,388	$62,388	$62,388	$62,388	$62,388	$62,388	$62,388	$62,388	$62,388

Appendix: Projected Profit and Loss

	Jan-98	Feb-98	Mar-98	Apr-98	May-98	Jun-98	Jul-98	Aug-98	Sep-98	Oct-98	Nov-98	Dec-98
Sales	$138,400	$195,500	$217,750	$207,000	$176,650	$146,600	$134,300	$154,000	$186,700	$221,025	$223,000	$154,500
Direct Cost of Sales	$35,480	$50,475	$56,175	$53,400	$45,580	$37,395	$33,835	$39,075	$48,090	$57,013	$56,900	$39,100
Production	$12,750	$12,750	$12,750	$12,750	$12,750	$12,750	$12,750	$12,750	$12,750	$12,750	$12,750	$12,750
Other	$0	$0	$0	$0	$0	$0	$0	$0	$0	$0	$0	$0
Total Cost of Sales	$48,230	$63,225	$68,925	$66,150	$58,330	$50,145	$46,585	$51,825	$60,840	$69,763	$69,650	$51,850
Gross margin	$90,170	$132,275	$148,825	$140,850	$118,320	$96,455	$87,715	$102,175	$125,860	$151,263	$153,350	$102,650
Gross margin percent	65.15%	67.66%	68.35%	68.04%	66.98%	65.79%	65.31%	66.35%	67.41%	68.44%	68.77%	66.44%
Operating expenses:												
Sales and Marketing Expenses												
Sales and Marketing Salaries	$14,000	$14,000	$14,000	$14,000	$14,000	$14,000	$14,000	$14,000	$14,000	$14,000	$14,000	$14,000
Advertising/Promotion	$15,000	$25,000	$30,000	$24,000	$20,000	$15,000	$15,000	$15,000	$20,000	$40,000	$30,000	$15,000
Events					$10,000					$15,000	$15,000	
Public Relations	$3,000	$3,000	$3,000	$3,000	$3,000	$3,000	$3,000	$3,000	$3,000	$3,000	$3,000	$3,000
Travel	$0	$5,000	$0		$6,000	$0	$5,000	$0	$0	$10,000	$5,000	$0
Miscellaneous	$2,000	$2,000	$2,000	$2,000	$2,000	$2,000	$2,000	$2,000	$2,000	$2,000	$2,000	$2,000
Other	$1,000	$1,000	$1,000	$1,000	$1,000	$1,000	$1,000	$1,000	$1,000	$1,000	$1,000	$1,000
Total Sales and Marketing Expenses	$35,000	$50,000	$50,000	$44,000	$56,000	$35,000	$40,000	$35,000	$40,000	$85,000	$70,000	$35,000
Sales and Marketing Percent	25.29%	25.58%	22.96%	21.26%	31.70%	23.87%	29.78%	22.73%	21.42%	38.46%	31.39%	22.65%
General and Administrative Expenses												
General and Administrative Salaries	$22,500	$22,500	$22,500	$22,500	$22,500	$22,500	$22,500	$22,500	$22,500	$22,500	$22,500	$22,500
Leased Equipment	$3,000	$3,000	$3,000	$3,000	$3,000	$3,000	$3,000	$3,000	$3,000	$3,000	$3,000	$3,000
Utilities	$1,000	$1,000	$1,000	$1,000	$1,000	$1,000	$1,000	$1,000	$1,000	$1,000	$1,000	$1,000
Insurance	$500	$500	$500	$500	$500	$500	$500	$500	$500	$500	$500	$500
Rent	$2,500	$2,500	$2,500	$2,500	$2,500	$2,500	$2,500	$2,500	$2,500	$2,500	$2,500	$2,500
Depreciation	$0	$0	$0	$0	$0	$0	$0	$0	$0	$0	$0	$3,000
Payroll Burden	$8,138	$8,138	$8,138	$8,138	$8,138	$8,138	$8,138	$8,138	$8,138	$8,138	$8,138	$8,138
Profit sharing												$20,000
Other	$1,000	$1,000	$1,000	$1,000	$1,000	$1,000	$1,000	$1,000	$1,000	$1,000	$1,000	$1,000
Total General and Administrative Expenses	$61,638	$38,638	$38,638	$38,638	$38,638	$38,638	$38,638	$38,638	$38,638	$38,638	$38,638	$38,638

Appendix: Projected Profit and Loss, cont.

Pro-Forma Income Statement	Jan-98	Feb-98	Mar-98	Apr-98	May-98	Jun-98	Jul-98	Aug-98	Sep-98	Oct-98	Nov-98	Dec-98
General and Administrative Percent	27.92%	19.76%	17.74%	18.67%	21.87%	26.36%	28.77%	25.09%	20.69%	17.48%	17.33%	39.89%
Other Expenses												
Other Salaries	$5,000	$5,000	$5,000	$5,000	$5,000	$5,000	$5,000	$5,000	$5,000	$5,000	$5,000	$5,000
Contract/Consultants	$1,000	$1,000	$1,000	$1,000	$1,000	$1,000	$1,000	$1,000	$1,000	$1,000	$1,000	$1,000
Other	$500	$500	$500	$500	$500	$500	$500	$500	$500	$500	$500	$500
Total Other Expenses	$6,500	$6,500	$6,500	$6,500	$6,500	$6,500	$6,500	$6,500	$6,500	$6,500	$6,500	$6,500
Other Percent	4.70%	3.32%	2.99%	3.14%	3.68%	4.43%	4.84%	4.22%	3.48%	2.94%	2.91%	4.21%
Total Operating Expenses	$80,138	$95,138	$95,138	$89,138	$101,138	$80,138	$85,138	$80,138	$85,138	$130,138	$115,138	$103,138
Profit Before Interest and Taxes	$10,033	$37,138	$53,688	$51,713	$17,183	$16,318	$2,578	$22,038	$40,723	$21,125	$38,213	($488)
Interest Expense ST	$542	$1,042	$1,042	$708	$375	$125	$0	$0	$0	$0	$0	$0
Interest Expense LT	$75	$75	$75	$75	$75	$75	$75	$75	$75	$75	$75	$75
Taxes Incurred	$2,354	$9,005	$13,143	$12,732	$4,183	$4,029	$626	$5,491	$10,162	$5,263	$9,534	($141)
Net Profit	$7,062	$27,016	$39,428	$38,197	$12,549	$12,088	$1,877	$16,472	$30,486	$15,788	$28,603	($422)
Net Profit/Sales	5.10%	13.82%	18.11%	18.45%	7.10%	8.25%	1.40%	10.70%	16.33%	7.14%	12.83%	-0.27%

Appendix: Sales Forecast

		Jan-98	Feb-98	Mar-98	Apr-98	May-98	Jun-98	Jul-98	Aug-98	Sep-98	Oct-98	Nov-98	Dec-98
Unit Sales													
Executive desk oak	15.00%	40	55	60	60	50	45	40	45	50	60	65	45
Executive desk cherry	5.00%	20	30	33	30	27	20	16	20	30	36	30	20
Other furniture oak	5.00%	26	35	40	35	31	29	32	35	38	43	45	35
Other furniture cherry	5.00%	6	11	13	12	9	6	6	8	10	11	11	6
Other	20.00%	4	5	6	6	5	3	3	3	4	5	6	4
Total Unit Sales		96	136	152	143	122	103	97	111	132	155	157	110
Unit Prices													
Executive desk oak		$1,600	$1,600	$1,600	$1,600	$1,600	$1,600	$1,600	$1,600	$1,600	$1,600	$1,600	$1,600
Executive desk cherry		$1,750	$1,750	$1,750	$1,750	$1,750	$1,750	$1,750	$1,750	$1,750	$1,750	$1,750	$1,750
Other furniture oak		$900	$900	$900	$900	$900	$900	$900	$900	$900	$900	$900	$900
Other furniture cherry		$1,000	$1,000	$1,000	$1,000	$1,000	$1,000	$1,000	$1,000	$1,000	$1,000	$1,000	$1,000
Other		$2,500	$2,500	$2,500	$2,500	$2,500	$2,500	$2,500	$2,500	$2,500	$2,500	$2,500	$2,500
Total Sales													
Executive desk oak		$64,000	$88,000	$96,000	$96,000	$80,000	$72,000	$64,000	$72,000	$80,000	$96,000	$104,000	$72,000
Executive desk cherry		$35,000	$52,500	$57,750	$52,500	$47,250	$35,000	$28,000	$35,000	$52,500	$62,825	$52,500	$35,000
Other furniture oak		$23,400	$31,500	$36,000	$31,500	$27,900	$26,100	$28,800	$31,500	$34,200	$38,700	$40,500	$31,500
Other furniture cherry		$6,000	$11,000	$13,000	$12,000	$9,000	$6,000	$6,000	$8,000	$10,000	$11,000	$11,000	$6,000
Other		$10,000	$12,500	$15,000	$15,000	$12,500	$7,500	$7,500	$7,500	$10,000	$12,500	$15,000	$10,000
Total Sales		$138,400	$195,500	$217,750	$207,000	$176,650	$146,600	$134,300	$154,000	$186,700	$221,025	$223,000	$154,500
Direct Unit costs													
Executive desk oak	25.00%	$400	$400	$400	$400	$400	$400	$400	$400	$400	$400	$400	$400
Executive desk cherry	30.00%	$525	$525	$525	$525	$525	$525	$525	$525	$525	$525	$525	$525
Other furniture oak	20.00%	$180	$180	$180	$180	$180	$180	$180	$180	$180	$180	$180	$180
Other furniture cherry	30.00%	$300	$300	$300	$300	$300	$300	$300	$300	$300	$300	$300	$300
Other	25.00%	$625	$625	$625	$625	$625	$625	$625	$625	$625	$625	$625	$625
Total direct cost of Sales													
Executive desk oak		$16,000	$22,000	$24,000	$24,000	$20,000	$18,000	$16,000	$18,000	$20,000	$24,000	$26,000	$18,000
Executive desk cherry		$10,500	$15,750	$17,325	$15,750	$14,175	$10,500	$8,400	$10,500	$15,750	$18,848	$15,750	$10,500
Other furniture oak		$4,680	$6,300	$7,200	$6,300	$5,580	$5,220	$5,760	$6,300	$6,840	$7,740	$8,100	$6,300
Other furniture cherry		$1,800	$3,300	$3,900	$3,600	$2,700	$1,800	$1,800	$2,400	$3,000	$3,300	$3,300	$1,800
Other		$2,500	$3,125	$3,750	$3,750	$3,125	$1,875	$1,875	$1,875	$2,500	$3,125	$3,750	$2,500
Subtotal Direct Costs		$35,480	$50,475	$56,175	$53,400	$45,580	$37,395	$33,835	$39,075	$48,090	$57,013	$56,900	$39,100

CHAPTER 17
ABC PARTNERS SAMPLE PLAN

This sample business plan has been made available to users of Business Plan Pro™ business-planning software published by Palo Alto Software. Our sample plans were developed by existing companies or new business start-ups as research instruments to determine market viability or funding availability. Names, locations, and numbers may have been changed, and substantial portions of text may have been omitted to preserve confidentiality and proprietary information.

You are welcome to use this plan as a starting point to create your own, but you do not have permission to reproduce, publish, distribute, or even copy this plan as it exists here.

Requests for reprints, academic use, and other dissemination of this sample plan should be addressed to the marketing department of Palo Alto Software.

ABC Partners

1.0 Executive Summary

ABC Partners is a successful and growing CPA firm in the Ourtown area. We have an excellent reputation and an excellent team, plus solid financial results. This is an annual plan intended to help us focus on priorities, develop and implement strategy, and therefore maximize the business elements of our accounting practice.

Business Plan Highlights

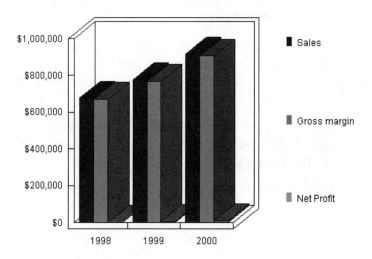

1.1 Objectives

1. Increase total fees to $680K in 1998 and to more than $950K in 2000.

ABC Partners

2. Increase partner salaries to $144K in 1998, $155K in 1999, and $170K in 2000, without producing a net loss for S-Corp income.

3. Add one new associate before the end of next year, with enough sales to pay for the additional salary.

1.2 Mission

ABC Partners offers its clients the best of professional accounting and related business financial advice on a long-term basis with a combination of professional ethics, expertise, hard work, and good advice. ABC seeks financial stability for its partners and fair compensation for its employees in an environment built on trust, respect, fairness, and teamwork. This should always be a good place to work, for employees as well as partners. Our clients should always be better off for our advice and expertise.

1.3 Keys to Success

1. Excellence in fulfilling the promise—completely reliable expertise and information. We take this for granted, of course, because we are professionals. Still, it is one of our keys to success.

2. Developing visibility to generate new business leads.

3. Leveraging from a single pool of expertise into multiple revenue generation opportunities—not just tax work and bookkeeping, but business planning and technology consulting as well.

ABC Partners

2.0 Practice Summary

ABC Partners is a professional partnership providing accounting services to businesses and individuals in the Ourtown area. We have three CPA partners and a professional bookkeeper on staff, plus one administrative employee. Our practice has more than 1,000 clients, including more than 900 individuals and more than 100 businesses. Our individual clients account for about half of our billing hours. A business client absorbs on average six times the hours that an individual client absorbs.

2.1 Practice Ownership

ABC Partners is a subchapter S corporation (S Corp) owned in equal shares by three partners: Frank Abbott, Laura Baker, and Terry Collins.

2.2 Practice History

ABC Partners was formed in 1994 as an S Corp. Each of the three founders contributed $25K to paid-in capital.

The accompanying table illustrates the highlights of the past three years, in which billings hovered around half a million dollars. Business has been growing steadily but not spectacularly. We concentrate on compensation more through salary than profits.

ABC Partners

Past Performance

	1995	1996	1997
Sales	$523,456	$567,098	$609,876
Gross	$515,032	$553,055	$606,591
Gross % (calculated)	98.39%	97.52%	99.46%
Operating Expenses	$514,143	$545,098	$604,034
Collection period (days)	38	42	48

Past Performance

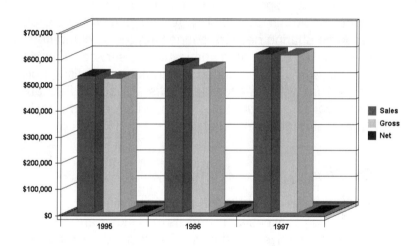

2.3 Practice Services

As with most CPA practices, our practice depends on tax-related services, including reporting and preparation and tax planning. As part of this practice we bill at different rates for services fulfilled by partners, by other professional staff, or by support staff. We also bill for some research projects.

ABC Partners

Although most of what we do is related to tax and reporting, this business plan calls for a definite increase in related consulting services. We want our clients to call on us for help with planning and budgeting, general business administration, and most particularly financial planning and capital planning.

2.4 Practice Locations and Facilities

Our offices occupy approximately 900 square feet of A-quality office space in the main business center of Ourtown. Within that facility we have a Windows 95 resource-sharing network connecting seven computers, plus copying and related administrative services. Our file and storage space includes off-site long-term filing purchased from Acme Storage Vaults. All active files are kept available in our main offices, with long-term back-up and storage farmed out.

3.0 Services

ABC Partners provides the highest-quality professional accounting services for clients as individuals and in small and medium-sized business. This includes a range of tax and tax planning functions, plus some financial and administrative consulting. As part of this plan we intend to broaden our services to include more business planning and more technological consulting services. The latter will focus mainly on helping clients select and install bookkeeping and accounting software on Windows 95 systems.

ABC Partners

3.1 Billable Services Offered

1. *Personal tax reporting and tax planning.* This is by far our most important service, the mainstay of the practice. We serve more than 900 clients, who account for half of our professional hours. Although the individual work is more concentrated on tax season and less per client than our work for small business, we still depend on the individuals who have been our clients for years.

2. *Business tax reporting and tax planning.* For those of our clients that are companies, we need to provide timely advice and planning several times per year to meet the payroll reporting requirements of the IRS and the state.

3. *Personal financial planning.* We want to help our clients grow, which means we want to provide them with expert advice and consulting on how to grow.

4. *Business planning and consulting.* We intend to offer much more business planning and consulting for our clients, particularly advisory services related to the client's development of business plans. We do not intend to develop business plans for clients but rather to help clients develop their own business plans.

5. *Technological consulting.* "Technological consulting" may be too broad or too ambitious a description. We help our clients select and install bookkeeping and accounting-related software on Windows95 systems.

3.2 Professional Qualifications

All three of our partners are highly respected CPAs, with good standing in the local business community. Among

ABC Partners

them they have more than 25 years of experience and tradition. Frank Abbott has been president of the local chamber of commerce, Terry Collins has been treasurer, and Laura Baker is active in such organizations as the country club and Kiwanis. Frank and Terry participate in the local business school foundation as well.

Detailed résumés are included in the appendixes to this plan.

Our present associate has been recruited with careful attention to quality of services. All future associates we take on staff must be of high enough quality and background to become partners as we grow. We expect to add one new associate within the next two years, and he or she will be selected for the potential to become a partner.

3.3 Competitive Comparison

Our competition comes in several forms:

1. One kind of competition comes from smaller CPA firms and combinations of CPAs attempting to serve our clients. The one-person accounting business, or one-CPA accounting business, is often trying to pick up clients already working with ABC Partners. Generally we hold our own quite well against this kind of competition, but the extremely cost-sensitive clients will occasionally wander to a smaller provider. We don't feel particularly threatened by this competition, since we have a high retention rate. Last year we lost fewer than 5% of existing clients, and we picked up more than that as new clients.

ABC Partners

2. The more significant competition comes from the seven larger firms operating in the Ourtown area. Growing companies are too frequently tempted by a larger partnership with more partners and other services they can provide under one roof. They too frequently think a growing company needs a larger CPA firm.

3. The third general kind of competitor is not relevant today but could become so in the future as we broaden our services to include more business planning and technology consulting. This is the management consulting business, particularly business planning and financial consultants. We are quite concerned with the tendency of our clients to turn to consultants for their business planning and seeking investment capital. We can give them better and more professional advice.

3.4 Technology

We are obviously a smaller firm with limited technology, but we are nonetheless growing in capabilities as technology becomes steadily more critical in the management of business information. As we look to develop our future position, there are three main points on which we intend to leverage our technology management to provide more and better services to our clients.

1. We intend to develop a business planning practice that provides our advice and assistance to clients completing their own business plans. We believe this can help us increase the number of businesses in our client base, as opposed to individuals. The client will purchase the software and develop the plan on his or her own, presenting us with interim files we can

ABC Partners

examine. We will provide commentary and advice relating to the plan. This accommodates the clients' need for help and sensitivity to costs, because the client spends the bulk of the hours involved. Furthermore, it will also help our clients understand the budgeting process and the mechanics of financials, especially cash flow.

2. Our clients will turn to us for advice on selecting, installing, and working with the bookkeeping and accounting packages that most individuals and small businesses use to balance checkbooks and manage basic bookkeeping information. Already we can take their Quicken and Microsoft Money files for individuals, for tax purposes, and we have worked with several clients to install and operate Quickbooks. We will broaden slightly from this base, giving our clients additional advice and consultation within our capability levels.

3.5 Future Services

We see an important trend toward more non-compliance-based services (business planning, working with accounting and bookkeeping software) from professional accountants, in addition to the traditional compliance services (tax reporting and tax planning). As we look forward for our practice, we have the expertise to provide for our clients more accounting-related advice beyond our compliance-based services.

If we view our future as serving our clients' needs, we have an enormous opportunity to provide additional service and help our clients more. The vast majority of our clients are successful in business because they offer

ABC Partners

products or services their customers want, not because they are great financial managers. We can fill their gaps for them in economic ways.

To build this new practice, we emphasize business planning and raising capital. We are going to develop a service that helps our clients develop their own business plans, while we provide additional expertise as advisors, as if we were looking over their shoulder. When they do their own plans, using competent software to help, we can advise without taking on the legal responsibility and potential liability of doing their plans ourselves.

4.0 Market Analysis Summary

ABC Partners focuses on the local area. More than 900 or our 1,050 clients are individuals, who average three hours per year of billing. Only 150 clients are businesses, but these account for about 40% of our billing hours. The local market includes approximately 5,000 small businesses employing 1–50 employees.

Our most important group of potential customers are existing small businesses. Although they generally do not have large budgets for accounting services, they are also the source of future growth and future business.

4.1 Market Segmentation

Aside from individuals, our main potential market is the small business in the local market. We are not looking for business with government agencies or larger compa-

ABC Partners

nies. We divide our small business clients into several types:

1. ***Local retail business***. In a market like ours one of the main sources of business is the local retail store, normally home-owned, normally a business large enough to require accounting services and small enough to look for a local firm. Our research indicates approximately 1,200 retail firms in our area. We now serve 58 retail firms, including our two largest clients, AMT (computer retail) and Burke's Market.

2. ***Local consumer service business***. These businesses include the auto repair shops, cleaners, and other local services. Their businesses tend to be quite similar to the retail businesses. We estimate 1,850 such service businesses in our market, of which we now serve 57.

3. ***Professional services***. These services include local attorneys, physicians, accountants, and consultants. We see a growing number of technical and internet services in this group as well. We estimate there are 750 such businesses in the Ourtown area, and we serve 41 of them. We are also one of these businesses.

4. ***Personal accounts***. We estimate 12,500 households of $50K or more annual income. We currently serve almost 1,000 of these households. The most interesting, for us are the owners of our business clients who want their tax work done in a single house. This is particularly important for Subchapter S companies, whose numbers automatically appear on their owners' personal taxes.

ABC Partners

Market Analysis

Potential Customers	Customers	Growth rate
Local retail	1,200	5%
Local service	1,850	5%
Professional services	750	10%
Personal accounts	12,500	5%
Other	100	2%
Total	16,400	5.23%

Potential Market

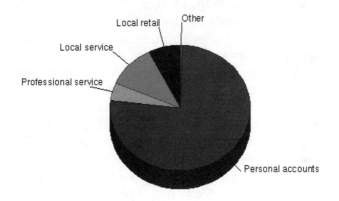

4.2 Market Analysis

The market for accounting services includes a wide range of participants, from the professional accounting firms to bookkeepers and, when taken in the broadest sense, bookkeeping software and software-related and internet-related services. Professional accounting firms range from major international big four firms to tens of thousands of individuals. We need to understand the business of accounting, including changes in the nature

ABC Partners

and structure of professional participants, marketing trends, the way clients select accountants, and the nature of competition.

4.2.1 Professional Participants

The providers of accounting services include thousands of smaller accounting practices and individual accountants for every one of the few dozen well-known companies.

At the highest level are the few well-established major names in accounting. Most of these are organized as partnerships established in major markets around the world, linked together by interconnecting directors and sharing the name and corporate wisdom. Some evolved from accounting companies (e.g. Arthur Anderson, Touche Ross) into that plus management consulting. These companies charge high rates and maintain relatively high overhead structures and fulfillment structures based on partners selling and junior associates fulfilling. They are not a factor in our local market, although our town has some subsidiary offices of larger companies, which presumably deal with these major players.

In Ourtown we have almost 40 accountant listings in the yellow pages. Of those, only 12 are larger than ABC, 10 or 15 are about the same size, and the rest are smaller. The 12 larger firms include eight local and four regional firms. We have no direct representation of the six major international firms, although three of our larger competitors have correspondence relationships.

ABC Partners

4.2.2 Marketing Trends

Accounting service is sold and purchased mainly on a word-of-mouth basis, with relationships and previous experience being by far the most important factor. The most important new trend is marketing toward more non-compliance services, and toward the younger entrepreneurial businesses, with services such as business planning and assistance with accounting and bookkeeping software.

In recent years, we see a trend toward more marketing through seminars, speaking opportunities, newspaper editorial contribution, events sponsorship, relationships with banks, and with educational institutions. We expect to see more attention paid to internet presence.

The major name-brand houses have locations in major cities and major markets, and executive-level managers or partners develop new business through industry associations, business associations, and chambers of commerce and industry, even in some cases such social associations as country clubs.

The medium-level houses are generally area-specific or function-specific and are not easily able to leverage their business through marketing technique.

Smaller practices depend entirely on word of mouth recommendation. Leads are generated through contacts, banking relations, and participation in civic affairs, Rotary, Lion's, and other clubs.

Throughout professional accounting, sales and marketing technique is constrained by the need to maintain a

ABC Partners

professional decorum. There are no discount accounting firms advertising on late-night cable TV, and even newspaper advertising is suspect.

Our local market is no exception to the rule. We see our fellow accountants at business development functions, such as the chamber of commerce and local civic groups.

4.2.3 Selection Patterns

The most important factor in selecting a professional, unfortunately, is who gets there first. In small businesses people tend to stick with their provider unless a particular problem occurs, such as overbilling or a tax problem. Satisfied clients rarely seek new accounting relationships. This means, of course, that to grow we need to find the new growing companies.

The second factor is word of mouth. This is why we need to maintain our presence in civic organizations, event sponsorship, and relationships with banks, attorneys, and other business leaders. Recommendations are very important.

Our understanding is that our clients choose us because they expect completely trustworthy advice and reliable accounting services. We are not selected for low rates or low cost, and we have lost clients to smaller firms to reduce their total cost.

In the business as a whole, we do see some categorization in selection patterns. People generally choose the larger firms because they want more reliability and assurance and are willing to pay more. They generally choose

ABC Partners

smaller firms and single accountants because they want to reduce costs.

We are all convinced that the key to keeping clients is to give excellent advice and completely reliable service. We are selling peace of mind. Our clients don't think we are the cheapest provider, but they expect that our tax advice will be the best compromise between minimizing taxes and minimizing legal risk.

4.2.4 Main Competitors

The 12 larger firms:

Strengths: Multiple locations managed by owner-partners with a high level of presentation and understanding of general business. Enviable reputations, which make choice of accountants an easy decision for a manager, despite the high prices.

Weaknesses: Not generally able to provide detailed service in local markets, because of overhead and cost structure. Also, fees are extremely expensive, and work is generally done by very junior-level accountants, even though it is sold by high-level partners.

The same-sized local firms:

Strengths: Good local market knowledge, permanent staff developing services and support on a permanent basis, good relationships with potential client companies.

ABC Partners

Weaknesses: Too costly for the newer start-up and entrepreneurial businesses but not prestigious enough for the growing medium-sized local businesses.

Single-CPA and other small firms:

Strengths: Low overhead, low cost.

Weaknesses: Lack of support structure, variability of professional quality. Some of these professionals are excellent, but the local business has a hard time telling good services from bad.

5.0 Strategy Summary

Our business strategy begins with maintaining our existing strengths. Then we add business planning and consulting on bookkeeping software and systems on personal computers and small networks, with some attention to growing capital needs of small entrepreneurial firms.

We want to maintain our strengths, maintaining our strong position with loyal individuals and increasing our relationships with existing small businesses in the local market. As we push to develop our business further, we must not lose sight of the most important foundation of the business, which is to never lose a good client.

Beyond that, we hope to develop the business further by selling more billable hours per client to our existing clients. The first push is to help our clients develop and manage business planning and bookkeeping software.

ABC Partners

5.1 Professional Services Strategy

1. We start with maintaining our strengths in professional accounting, including reporting and tax planning, tax preparation, and personal financial planning. This is our main strength.

2. We add a broader sense of business service for our clients, including the business plan program using off-the-shelf software. The business planning service puts us into an expanded advisory role. We help our clients develop their own plans, rather than develop plans for them. In our advisory capacity we help the clients help themselves and give more value, optimize the client's own time, and minimize our liability and professional risk.

3. We build in the base of the business plan and technology consulting business to provide attractive seminars for small business. This puts us in front of the eyes of the local companies that will provide us with future growth.

5.2 Marketing Strategy

Our marketing strategy shouldn't involve much change. We need to be consistent. Our main marketing strategy is based on dignified professional expertise in the public eye via selected occasions, events, newspaper columns, and seminars. To refine that strategy we have some new wrinkles:

1. Focus more attention on business planning and technology consulting through a combination of seminars, newspaper articles, and events.

ABC Partners

2. Continue to participate in selected business groups and events, such as the annual new venture contest at the university, the chamber of commerce, and the annual marketing events.

3. Always remember that the best marketing technique for a professional service company is not losing the clients we already have. We must always do excellent work and give excellent advice.

5.3 Pricing Strategy

ABC Partners needs to maintain billing rates at the medium-high level of what the market will bear, competing with the larger firms. We cannot be more expensive than the top names, but we don't want to compete with the one-person practices on the basis of billing rates. We need to bill at the level commensurate with our professional expertise.

The pricing fits with the general positioning of ABC as high-level expertise.

Billing should remain at $125 per hour for partners, increasing to $90 per hour for the new associate planned for 1999, and $45 per hour for the existing associate.

5.4 Billings Forecast

The following billings forecast shows the annual projections for 1998, 1999, and 2000. We expect to increase our billings to more than $950K in 2000. The main bulk of billings will still depend on direct billings of our three

ABC Partners

main partners, as the table indicates, but we also expect to increase billings from two associates.

The forecast depends on assumptions and marketing strategy. We do not foresee increased billing rates, although we do expect a small increase in billing hours.

A monthly billings forecast summary is included in the appendix. The annual sales projections are included in the following table.

Sales Forecast

Billing units		1998	1999	2000
A billing hours	0%	1,735	1,800	1,900
B billing hours	2%	1,675	1,800	1,900
C billing hours	2%	1,665	1,800	1,900
Associate hours	25%	960	1,600	2,600
Other	10%	6,000	6,600	7,300
Total Billings		12,035	13,600	15,600

Billing rates			
A billing hours	$125	$125	$125
B billing hours	$125	$125	$125
C billing hours	$125	$125	$125
Associate hours	$40	$60	$75
Other	$1	$1	$1

Total billings			
A billing hours	$216,875	$225,000	$237,500
B billing hours	$209,375	$225,000	$237,500
C billing hours	$208,125	$225,000	$237,500
Associate hours	$38,400	$96,000	$195,000

ABC Partners

Sales Forecast, cont.

	1998	1999	2000
Other	$6,000	$6,600	$7,300
Total Billing	$678,775	$777,600	$914,800

Billing Direct Costs

	1998	1999	2000
A billing hours	$0.00	$0.00	$0.00
B billing hours	$0.00	$0.00	$0.00
C billing hours	$0.00	$0.00	$0.00
Associate hours	$0.00	$0.00	$0.00
Other	$1.00	$1.00	$1.00

Total Direct Costs

	1998	1999	2000
A billing hours	$0	$0	$0
B billing hours	$0	$0	$0
C billing hours	$0	$0	$0
Associate hours	$0	$0	$0
Other	$6,000	$6,600	$7,300
Subtotal Direct Cost of Billings	$6,000	$6,600	$7,300

Total Sales by Month in Year 1

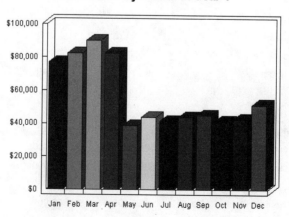

ABC Partners

5.5 Strategic Alliances

At this writing strategic alliances with Smith and Jones are possibilities, given the content of existing discussions. Given the background of prospective partners, we might also be talking to regional firms, including Siemens and Olivetti and others, but only to keep our options open.

We should maintain our good relationships with local banks, attorneys, and the chambers of commerce. These relationships are crucial to developing new business. That also means participation in local events such as the Small Business Development Center marketing fair and others.

5.6 Implementation Milestones

The most important milestones for our plan are the business plan seminars, which are scheduled to take place in May, September, and October. We expect the seminars to lay the cornerstone for our new practice in helping our clients run their businesses by developing their own business plans.

The milestones also include an important redesign of our internet presence, plus a new brochure for the business planning business, a marketing event, and office equipment. We are also planning a new office upgrade in late 1998, because our office furniture is looking worn, and computer upgrades in February.

ABC Partners

Milestone	Mngr.	Date	Dept.	Budget
Website logistics	FA	1/15/98	Website	$1,500
Office equipment	LB	2/15/98	Admin	$15,000
Business plan seminar	TC	5/15/98	Busdev	$500
Client mailing 1	LB	6/1/98	BusDev	$1,500
Website redesign	FA	6/15/98	Website	$3,000
Brochure program	LB	6/15/98	BusDev	$2,000
Business plan seminar	TC	9/15/98	BusDev	$500
Business plan seminar	TC	11/5/98	Busdev	$500
Office upgrade	LB	11/15/98	Admin	$4,000
Other				
Totals				$28,500

6.0 Management Summary

Present management depends mainly on the three partners for executive management, with the three dividing
responsibility for other functions including marketing, administration, and technical management. Key decisions
are made by all three.

As we grow we will take on an additional associate, plus
additional administrative help.

6.1 Organizational Structure

ABC is managed by working partners, whose résumés
are included in the appendix. Most critical or strategic
decisions are made by all three partners.

For day-to-day management, Laura manages marketing,
Terry manages administration, and Frank manages the

ABC Partners

computers and website. This division seems to work comfortably.

We also maintain our associate and administrative positions. Résumés are included in the appendixes.

6.2 Management Team

The ABC Partners practice is managed by its three professional partners, who divide key management responsibilities as explained in the previous topic. The team also includes one associate, whose detailed résumé is included in the appendixes. We also have four other administrative employees.

6.3 Personnel Plan

Personnel is by far our most important investment and makes up the bulk of our cost of sales and operating expenses. The personnel plan shows how we intend to add two partners while maintaining our professional staff. Our total headcount will increase from 5 this year to 7 in 2000.

The detailed monthly personnel plan for the next year is included in the appendixes. The annual personal estimates are included here in the following table. Total personnel cost will increase from $506K next year, to $582K and then $685K.

ABC Partners

Personnel Plan

	1998	1999	2000
Abbott	$144,000	$155,000	$170,000
Baker	$144,000	$155,000	$170,000
Collins	$144,000	$155,000	$170,000
Associate 1	$42,000	$45,000	$50,000
Associate 2	$0	$22,000	$70,000
Admin 1	$26,400	$30,000	$33,000
Admin 2	$0	$20,000	$22,000
Other	$6,000	$0	$0
Subtotal	**$506,400**	**$582,000**	**$685,000**

7.0 Financial Plan

The financial plan is based on solid growth and conservative financial planning. We are paying down our small long-term debt and financing growth mainly through existing business. We do have a short-term credit line backed by receivables, which we use to fill seasonal gaps in cash flow.

For the three-year period we project maintaining the firm's net worth at around $100K. We try to manage for cash flow and dependable salaries, more than for S-Corp profits.

The detailed monthly personnel plan for the first year is included in the appendixes. The annual personal estimates are included here.

ABC Partners

7.1 Important Assumptions

The following table summarizes key financial assumptions, including 45-day average collection days, 35 days on average for payment of invoices, and present-day interest rates.

General Assumptions

	1998	1999	2000
Short-term interest rate	8.00%	8.00%	8.00%
Long-term interest rate	10.00%	10.00%	10.00%
Payment days	35	35	35
Collection days	45	45	45
Inventory turnover	6.00	6.00	6.00
Tax rate percent	25.00%	25.00%	25.00%
Expenses in cash%	5.00%	5.00%	5.00%
Sales on credit	100.00%	100.00%	100.00%
Personnel burden %	18.00%	18.00%	18.00%

Note: Ratios in assumptions are used as estimators and may therefore have different values than ratios calculated in the ratios section.

7.2 Key Financial Indicators

The following benchmark chart indicates our key financial indicators for the next three years. The chart includes sales, gross margin, operating expenses, and maintaining 45 collection days, set as index values to display changes over time. The fifth area in the chart, set aside for inventory turns, is set at zero because we do not manage inventory.

ABC Partners

We foresee major growth in sales and operating expenses, and little change in our collection days as we spread the business during expansion.

Benchmark Comparison

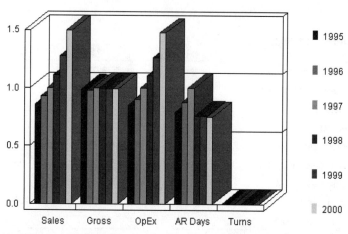

Planned Performance in Critical Profit Variables

7.3 Break-even Analysis

The following table summarizes our simple break-even analysis, based on fixed costs of about $45,000 per month, most of which is payroll. Our variable costs are negligible, because our cost is predominantly fixed cost. The break-even point is at about the same $45,000 as our fixed costs, because we have little or no variable cost per dollar of sales. We do well above break-even during the tax season and about break-even thereafter.

ABC Partners

Break-Even Analysis:

Monthly units break-even	45,455
Monthly sales break-even	$45,455
Assumptions:	
Average unit sale	$1.00
Average per-unit cost	$0.01
Fixed cost	$45,000

Break-even Analysis

7.4 Projected Profit and Loss

As long as we remain profitable enough to support growth, we are an S-Corp entity that doesn't want to distribute excess profits. Our projection calls for generally low profitability, because maintaining steady salary levels is more important. This level maintains our stability and supports growth.

The detailed monthly pro-forma income statement for the first year is included in the appendixes. The annual estimates are included here.

ABC Partners

Pro-forma Income Statement

		1998	1999	2000
Sales		$678,775	$777,600	$914,800
Cost of sales		$6,000	$6,600	$7,300
Other		$1,200	$1,500	$1,750
Total cost of sales		$7,200	$8,100	$9,050
Gross margin		$671,575	$769,500	$905,750
Gross margin percent		98.94%	98.96%	99.01%
Operating expenses:				
Continuing education	10.00%	$14,500	$16,000	$18,000
Travel	10.00%	$12,500	$14,000	$15,000
Business development		$6,900	$7,500	$9,000
Website	10.00%	$4,500	$5,000	$6,000
Payroll expense		$506,400	$582,000	$685,000
Leased equipment	5.00%	$2,640	$3,000	$3,000
Utilities	5.00%	$9,000	$9,000	$9,000
Insurance	5.00%	$3,600	$4,000	$4,000
Rent	5.00%	$14,400	$15,000	$16,000
Depreciation		$1,800	$2,000	$2,000
Payroll burden		$91,152	$104,760	$123,300
Other		$1,200	$1,000	$1,000
Total operating expenses		$668,592	$763,260	$891,300
Profit before interest and taxes		$2,983	$6,240	$14,450
Interest expense ST		$237	$1,000	$3,000
Interest expense LT		$1,383	$916	$473
Taxes incurred		$341	$1,081	$2,744
Net profit		$1,023	$3,243	$8,232
Net profit/sales		0.15%	0.42%	0.90%

ABC Partners

7.5 Projected Cash Flow

Cash flow projections are critical to our success. We project a steady cash flow picture over the next 12 months, with the balance growing predictably in relation to the tax season. We will have enough cash to take our credit line back to zero and to continue paying down our long-term debt.

The monthly cash flow is shown in the illustration, with one bar representing the cash flow per month and the other the monthly balance. The annual cash flow figures are included in the following table. Detailed monthly numbers are included in the appendixes.

Pro-Forma Cash Flow

	1998	1999	2000
Net Profit:	$1,023	$3,243	$8,232
Plus:			
Depreciation	$1,800	$2,000	$2,000
Change in accounts payable	($8,964)	$475	$556
Current borrowing (repayment)	($5,000)	$25,000	$0
Increase (decrease) other liabilities	$3	$0	$0
Long-term borrowing (repayment)	($1,285)	($3,967)	($4,426)
Capital input	$0	$0	$0
Subtotal	($12,423)	$26,751	$6,363
Less:	1905	1905	1905
Change in accounts receivable	($1,612)	$10,545	$14,639
Change in inventory	$0	$0	$0
Change in other ST assets	$0	($5,000)	$0
Capital expenditure	$19,000	$15,000	$15,000
Dividends	$0	$0	$0

ABC Partners

Pro-Forma Cash Flow, cont.

	1998	1999	2000
Subtotal	$17,388	$20,545	$29,639
Net cash flow	($29,811)	$6,206	($23,276)
Cash balance	$2,260	$8,466	($14,810)

Cash Analysis

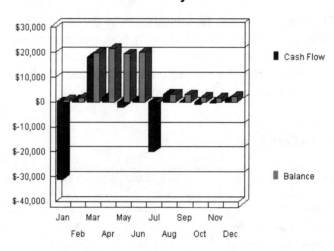

7.6 Projected Balance Sheet

Our pro-forma balance sheet shows healthy stability financial position. Our debt is decreasing, and capitalization is holding steady. The monthly estimates are included in the appendixes.

ABC Partners

Pro-forma Balance Sheet

	Starting Balances	1998	1999	2000
Short-term assets				
Cash	$32,071	$2,260	$8,466	($14,810)
Accounts receivable	$74,037	$72,425	$82,970	$97,609
Other short-term assets	$12,089	$12,089	$7,089	$7,089
Total short-term assets	$118,197	$86,774	$98,525	$89,888
Long-term assets				
Capital assets	$13,801	$32,801	$47,801	$62,801
Accumulated depreciation	$3,901	$5,701	$7,701	$9,701
Total long-term assets	$9,900	$27,100	$40,100	$53,100
Total assets	$128,097	$113,874	$138,625	$142,988
Accounts payable	$14,807	$5,843	$6,318	$6,874
Short-term notes	$5,000	$0	$25,000	$25,000
Other ST liabilities	$1,971	$1,974	$1,974	$1,974
Subtotal short-term liabilities				
	$21,778	$7,817	$33,292	$33,848
Long-term liabilities	$14,412	$13,127	$9,160	$4,734
Total Liabilities	$36,190	$20,944	$42,452	$38,583
Paid in capital	$75,000	$75,000	$75,000	$75,000
Retained earnings	$14,350	$16,907	$17,930	$21,173
Earnings	$2,557	$1,023	$3,243	$8,232
Total equity	$91,907	$92,930	$96,173	$104,405
Total debt and equity	$128,097	$113,874	$138,625	$142,988
Net worth	$91,907	$92,930	$96,173	$104,405

ABC Partners

7.7 Business Ratios

The following table shows the projected businesses ratios. We expect to maintain healthy ratios for profitability, risk, and return.

Ratio Analysis

Profitability Ratios:	1998	1999	2000
Gross margin	98.94%	98.96%	99.01%
Net profit margin	0.15%	0.42%	0.90%
Return on assets	0.90%	2.34%	5.76%
Return on equity	1.10%	3.37%	7.89%
Activity Ratios:			
AR Turnover	9.37	9.37	9.37
Collection days	39	36	36
Inventory turnover	0.00	0.00	0.00
Accts payable turnover	12.72	12.72	12.72
Total asset turnover	5.96	5.61	6.40
Debt Ratios:	1998	1999	2000
Debt to net worth	0.23	0.44	0.37
Short-term debt to liab.	0.37	0.78	0.88
Liquidity Ratios:			
Current ratio	11.10	2.96	2.66
Quick ratio	11.10	2.96	2.66
Net working capital	$78,957	$65,233	$56,040
Interest coverage	1.84	3.26	4.16
Additional Ratios:	1998	1999	2000
Assets to sales	0.17	0.18	0.16

ABC Partners

Ratio Analysis, cont.

	1998	1999	2000
Debt/assets	18%	31%	27%
Current debt/total assets	7%	24%	24%
Acid test	1.84	0.47	-0.23
Asset turnover	5.96	5.61	6.40
Sales/net worth	7.30	8.09	8.76

Chapter 17 Appendix: ABC Partners

Appendix: Projected Balance Sheet

Pro-forma Balance Sheet

	Starting Balances	Jan-98	Feb-98	Mar-98	Apr-98	May-98	Jun-98	Jul-98	Aug-98	Sep-98	Oct-98	Nov-98	Dec-98	1998	1999	2000
Short-term Assets																
Cash	$32,071	$888	$1,753	$19,683	$21,553	$19,330	$20,087	$26	$3,037	$2,927	$1,953	$1,654	$2,260	$2,260	$8,466	($14,810)
Accounts Receivable	$74,037	$113,659	$121,981	$133,077	$127,425	$79,925	$63,050	$63,050	$64,300	$66,800	$63,675	$63,050	$72,425	$72,425	$82,970	$97,609
Other Short-term Assets	$12,089	$12,089	$12,089	$12,089	$32,089	$62,089	$72,089	$72,089	$57,089	$42,089	$37,089	$22,089	$12,089	$12,089	$7,089	$7,089
Total Short-term Assets	$118,197	$126,636	$135,823	$164,848	$181,067	$161,344	$155,226	$135,165	$124,426	$111,816	$102,717	$86,793	$86,774	$86,774	$98,525	$89,888
Long-term Assets																
Capital Assets	$13,801	$13,801	$28,801	$28,801	$28,801	$28,801	$28,801	$28,801	$28,801	$28,801	$28,801	$28,801	$32,801	$32,801	$47,801	$62,801
Accumulated Depreciation	$3,901	$3,901	$3,901	$3,901	$3,901	$3,901	$3,901	$3,901	$3,901	$3,901	$3,901	$3,901	$5,701	$5,701	$7,701	$9,701
Total Long-term Assets	$9,900	$9,900	$24,900	$24,900	$24,900	$24,900	$24,900	$24,900	$24,900	$24,900	$24,900	$24,900	$27,100	$27,100	$40,100	$53,100
Total Assets	$128,097	$136,536	$160,723	$189,748	$205,967	$186,244	$180,126	$160,065	$149,326	$136,716	$127,617	$115,693	$113,874	$113,874	$138,625	$142,988

Debt and Equity	Starting Balances	Jan-98	Feb-98	Mar-98	Apr-98	May-98	Jun-98	Jul-98	Aug-98	Sep-98	Oct-98	Nov-98	Dec-98	1998	1999	2000
Accounts Payable	$14,807	$3,766	$3,766	$9,232	$3,766	$6,499	$16,337	$9,232	$10,325	$4,859	$7,592	$4,312	$5,843	$5,843	$6,318	$6,874
Short-term Notes	$5,000	$7,000	$9,500	$9,500	$9,500	$0	$0	$0	$0	$0	$0	$0	$0	$0	$25,000	$25,000
Other ST Liabilities	$1,971	$1,972	$1,974	$1,974	$1,974	$1,974	$1,974	$1,974	$1,974	$1,974	$1,974	$1,974	$1,974	$1,974	$1,974	$1,974
Subtotal Short-term Liabilities	$21,778	$12,738	$15,240	$20,706	$15,240	$8,473	$18,311	$11,206	$12,299	$6,833	$9,566	$6,286	$7,817	$7,817	$33,292	$33,848
Long-term Liabilities	$14,412	$14,328	$14,242	$14,156	$14,069	$13,982	$13,893	$13,804	$13,714	$13,623	$13,531	$13,439	$13,127	$13,127	$9,160	$4,734
Total Liabilities	$36,190	$27,065	$29,482	$34,862	$29,309	$22,455	$32,204	$25,010	$26,013	$20,456	$23,097	$19,725	$20,944	$20,944	$42,452	$38,583
Paid in Capital	$75,000	$75,000	$75,000	$75,000	$75,000	$75,000	$75,000	$75,000	$75,000	$75,000	$75,000	$75,000	$75,000	$75,000	$75,000	$75,000
Retained Earnings	$14,350	$16,907	$16,907	$16,907	$16,907	$16,907	$16,907	$16,907	$16,907	$16,907	$16,907	$16,907	$16,907	$16,907	$17,930	$21,173
Earnings	$2,557	$17,563	$39,334	$62,979	$84,751	$71,883	$56,015	$43,148	$31,407	$24,353	$12,613	$4,061	$1,023	$1,023	$3,243	$8,232
Total Equity	$91,907	$109,470	$131,241	$154,886	$176,658	$163,790	$147,922	$135,055	$123,314	$116,260	$104,520	$95,968	$92,930	$92,930	$96,173	$104,405
Total Debt and Equity	$128,097	$136,536	$160,723	$189,748	$205,967	$186,244	$180,126	$160,065	$149,326	$136,716	$127,617	$115,693	$113,874	$113,874	$138,625	$142,988
Net Worth	$91,907	$109,470	$131,241	$154,886	$176,658	$163,790	$147,922	$135,055	$123,314	$116,260	$104,520	$95,968	$92,930	$92,930	$96,173	$104,405

Appendix: Projected Cash Flow

	Jan-98	Feb-98	Mar-98	Apr-98	May-98	Jun-98	Jul-98	Aug-98	Sep-98	Oct-98	Nov-98	Dec-98	1998	1999	2000
Net Profit:	$17,563	$21,770	$23,646	$21,771	($12,868)	($15,868)	($12,867)	($11,741)	($7,053)	($11,740)	($8,552)	($3,038)	$1,023	$3,243	$8,232
Plus:															
Depreciation	$0	$0	$0	$0	$0	$0	$0	$0	$0	$0	$0	$1,800	$1,800	$2,000	$2,000
Change in Accounts Payable	($11,041)	$0	$5,466	($5,466)	$2,733	$9,838	($7,105)	$1,093	($5,466)	$2,733	($3,279)	$1,530	($8,964)	$475	$556
Current Borrowing (repayment)	$2,000	$2,500	$0	$0	($9,500)	$0	$0	$0	$0	$0	$0	$0	($5,000)	$25,000	$0
Increase (decrease) Other Liabilities	$1	$2	$0	$0	$0	$0	$0	$0	$0	$0	$0	$0	$3	$0	$0
Long-term Borrowing (repayment)	($84)	($85)	($86)	($87)	($88)	($88)	($89)	($90)	($91)	($92)	($93)	($311)	($1,285)	($3,967)	($4,426)
Capital Input	$0	$0	$0	$0	$0	$0	$0	$0	$0	$0	$0	$0	$0	$0	$0
Subtotal	$8,439	$24,187	$29,025	$16,219	($19,723)	($6,118)	($20,062)	($10,738)	($12,610)	($9,099)	($11,924)	($19)	($12,423)	$26,751	$6,363
	Jan	Feb	Mar	Apr	May	Jun	Jul	Aug	Sep	Oct	Nov	Dec	1998	1999	2000
Less:							1905		1905			1905	1905	1905	1905
Change in Accounts Receivable	$39,622	$8,322	$11,096	($5,652)	($47,500)	($16,875)	$0	$1,250	$2,500	($3,125)	($625)	$9,375	($1,612)	$10,545	$14,639
Change in Inventory	B3	$0	$0	$0	$0	$0	$0	$0	$0	$0	$0	$0	$0	$0	$0
Change in Other ST Assets	$0	$0	$0	$20,000	$30,000	$10,000	$0	($15,000)	($15,000)	($5,000)	($15,000)	($10,000)	$0	($5,000)	$0
Capital Expenditure	$0	$15,000	$0	$0	$0	$0	$0	$0	$0	$0	$4,000	$0	$19,000	$15,000	$15,000
Dividends	$0	$0	$0	$0	$0	$0	$0	$0	$0	$0	$0	$0	$0	$0	$0
Subtotal	$39,622	$23,322	$11,096	$14,348	($17,500)	($6,875)	$0	($13,750)	($12,500)	($8,125)	($11,625)	($625)	$17,388	$20,545	$29,639
Net Cash Flow	($31,183)	$865	$17,930	$1,870	($2,223)	$757	($20,062)	$3,012	($110)	($974)	($299)	$606	($29,811)	$6,206	($23,276)
Cash balance	$888	$1,753	$19,683	$21,553	$19,330	$20,087	$26	$3,037	$2,927	$1,953	$1,654	$2,260	$2,260	$8,466	($14,810)

Appendix: Important Assumptions

	Jan-98	Feb-98	Mar-98	Apr-98	May-98	Jun-98	Jul-98	Aug-98	Sep-98	Oct-98	Nov-98	Dec-98	1998	1999	2000
Short Term Interest Rate 8.00%	8.00%	8.00%	8.00%	8.00%	8.00%	8.00%	8.00%	8.00%	8.00%	8.00%	8.00%	8.00%	8.00%	8.00%	
Long Term Interest Rate 10.00%	10.00%	10.00%	10.00%	10.00%	10.00%	10.00%	10.00%	10.00%	10.00%	10.00%	10.00%	10.00%	10.00%	10.00%	
Payment days	35	35	35	35	35	35	35	35	35	35	35	35	35	35	35
Collection days	45	45	45	45	45	45	45	45	45	45	45	45	45	45	45
Inventory Turnover	6.00	6.00	6.00	6.00	6.00	6.00	6.00	6.00	6.00	6.00	6.00	6.00	6.00	6.00	6.00
Tax Rate Percent	25.00%	25.00%	25.00%	25.00%	25.00%	25.00%	25.00%	25.00%	25.00%	25.00%	25.00%	25.00%	25.00%	25.00%	25.00%
Expenses in cash%	5.00%	5.00%	5.00%	5.00%	5.00%	5.00%	5.00%	5.00%	5.00%	5.00%	5.00%	5.00%	5.00%	5.00%	5.00%
Sales on credit	100.00%	100.00%	100.00%	100.00%	100.00%	100.00%	100.00%	100.00%	100.00%	100.00%	100.00%	100.00%	100.00%	100.00%	100.00%
Personnel Burden %	18.00%	18.00%	18.00%	18.00%	18.00%	18.00%	18.00%	18.00%	18.00%	18.00%	18.00%	18.00%	18.00%	18.00%	18.00%

Note: Ratios in assumptions are used as estimators and may therefore have different values than ratios calculated in the ratios section.

Appendix: Personnel Plan

	Jan-98	Feb-98	Mar-98	Apr-98	May-98	Jun-98	Jul-98	Aug-98	Sep-98	Oct-98	Nov-98	Dec-98	1998	1999	2000
Abbott	$12,000	$12,000	$12,000	$12,000	$12,000	$12,000	$12,000	$12,000	$12,000	$12,000	$12,000	$12,000	$144,000	$155,000	$170,000
Baker	$12,000	$12,000	$12,000	$12,000	$12,000	$12,000	$12,000	$12,000	$12,000	$12,000	$12,000	$12,000	$144,000	$155,000	$170,000
Collins	$12,000	$12,000	$12,000	$12,000	$12,000	$12,000	$12,000	$12,000	$12,000	$12,000	$12,000	$12,000	$144,000	$155,000	$170,000
Associate 1	$3,500	$3,500	$3,500	$3,500	$3,500	$3,500	$3,500	$3,500	$3,500	$3,500	$3,500	$3,500	$42,000	$45,000	$50,000
Associate 2	$0	$0	$0	$0	$0	$0	$0	$0	$0	$0	$0	$0	$0	$22,000	$70,000
Admin 1	$2,200	$2,200	$2,200	$2,200	$2,200	$2,200	$2,200	$2,200	$2,200	$2,200	$2,200	$2,200	$26,400	$30,000	$33,000
Admin 2	$0	$0	$0	$0	$0	$0	$0	$0	$0	$0	$0	$0	$0	$20,000	$22,000
Other	$500	$500	$500	$500	$500	$500	$500	$500	$500	$500	$500	$500	$6,000	$0	$0
Subtotal	$42,200	$42,200	$42,200	$42,200	$42,200	$42,200	$42,200	$42,200	$42,200	$42,200	$42,200	$42,200	$506,400	$582,000	$685,000

Appendix: Projected Profit and Loss

	Jan-98	Feb-98	Mar-98	Apr-98	May-98	Jun-98	Jul-98	Aug-98	Sep-98	Oct-98	Nov-98	Dec-98	1998	1999	2000
Sales	$76,825	$82,450	$89,950	$82,450	$38,700	$43,700	$41,200	$43,700	$44,950	$41,200	$42,450	$51,200	$678,775	$777,600	$914,800
Cost of Sales	$500	$500	$500	$500	$500	$500	$500	$500	$500	$500	$500	$500	$6,000	$6,600	$7,300
Other	$100	$100	$100	$100	$100	$100	$100	$100	$100	$100	$100	$100	$1,200	$1,500	$1,750
Total Cost of Sales	$600	$600	$600	$600	$600	$600	$600	$600	$600	$600	$600	$600	$7,200	$8,100	$9,050
Gross margin	$76,225	$81,850	$89,350	$81,850	$38,100	$43,100	$40,600	$43,100	$44,350	$40,600	$41,850	$50,600	$671,575	$769,500	$905,750
Gross margin percent	99.22%	99.27%	99.33%	99.27%	98.45%	98.63%	98.54%	98.63%	98.67%	98.54%	98.59%	98.83%	98.94%	98.96%	99.01%
Operating expenses:															
Continuing education	$0	$0	$2,000	$0	$0	$4,000	$2,000	$3,000	$0	$3,500	$0	$0	$14,500	$16,000	$18,000
Travel	$0	$0	$3,000	$0	$0	$3,000	$3,000	$3,000	$500	$0	$0	$0	$12,500	$14,000	$15,000
Business development	$150	$150	$150	$150	$650	$3,650	$150	$150	$650	$150	$650	$250	$6,900	$7,500	$9,000
Website	$125	$125	$125	$125	$2,125	$1,125	$125	$125	$125	$125	$125	$125	$4,500	$5,000	$6,000
Payroll expense	$42,200	$42,200	$42,200	$42,200	$42,200	$42,200	$42,200	$42,200	$42,200	$42,200	$42,200	$42,200	$506,400	$582,000	$685,000
Leased Equipment	$220	$220	$220	$220	$220	$220	$220	$220	$220	$220	$220	$220	$2,640	$3,000	$3,000
Utilities	$750	$750	$750	$750	$750	$750	$750	$750	$750	$750	$750	$750	$9,000	$9,000	$9,000
Insurance	$300	$300	$300	$300	$300	$300	$300	$300	$300	$300	$300	$300	$3,600	$4,000	$4,000
Rent	$1,200	$1,200	$1,200	$1,200	$1,200	$1,200	$1,200	$1,200	$1,200	$1,200	$1,200	$1,200	$14,400	$15,000	$16,000
Depreciation	$0	$0	$0	$0	$0	$0	$0	$0	$0	$0	$0	$1,800	$1,800	$2,000	$2,000
Payroll Burden	$7,596	$7,596	$7,596	$7,596	$7,596	$7,596	$7,596	$7,596	$7,596	$7,596	$7,596	$7,596	$91,152	$104,760	$123,300
Other	$100	$100	$100	$100	$100	$100	$100	$100	$100	$100	$100	$100	$1,200	$1,000	$1,000
Total Operating Expenses	$52,641	$52,641	$57,641	$52,641	$55,141	$64,141	$57,641	$58,641	$53,641	$56,141	$53,141	$54,541	$668,592	$763,260	$891,300
Profit Before Interest and Taxes	$23,584	$29,209	$31,709	$29,209	($17,041)	($21,041)	($17,041)	($15,541)	($9,291)	($15,541)	($11,291)	($3,941)	$2,983	$6,240	$14,450
Interest Expense ST	$47	$63	$63	$63	$0	$0	$0	$0	$0	$0	$0	$0	$237	$1,000	$3,000
Interest Expense LT	$119	$119	$118	$117	$117	$116	$115	$114	$114	$113	$112	$109	$1,383	$916	$473
Taxes Incurred	$5,854	$7,257	$7,882	$7,257	($4,289)	($5,289)	($4,289)	($3,914)	($2,351)	($3,913)	($2,851)	($1,013)	$341	$1,081	$2,744
Net Profit	$17,563	$21,770	$23,646	$21,771	($12,868)	($15,868)	($12,867)	($11,741)	($7,053)	($11,740)	($8,552)	($3,038)	$1,023	$3,243	$8,232
Net Profit/Sales	22.86%	26.40%	26.29%	26.41%	-33.25%	-36.31%	-31.23%	-26.87%	-15.69%	-28.50%	-20.15%	-5.93%	0.15%	0.42%	0.90%

Appendix: Billings Forecast

	Jan-98	Feb-98	Mar-98	Apr-98	May-98	Jun-98	Jul-98	Aug-98	Sep-98	Oct-98	Nov-98	Dec-98	1998	1999	2000
Billing units															
A billing hours	195	210	230	210	100	120	100	110	120	100	110	130	1,735	1,800	1,900
B billing hours	195	210	230	210	90	100	100	110	110	100	100	120	1,675	1,800	1,900
C billing hours	195	210	230	210	90	100	100	100	100	100	100	130	1,665	1,800	1,900
Associate hours	80	80	80	80	80	80	80	80	80	80	80	80	960	1,600	2,600
Other	500	500	500	500	500	500	500	500	500	500	500	500	6,000	6,600	7,300
Total Billings	1,165	1,210	1,270	1,210	860	900	880	900	910	880	890	960	12,035	13,600	15,600
Billing rates															
A billing hours	$125	$125	$125	$125	$125	$125	$125	$125	$125	$125	$125	$125	$125	$125	$125
B billing hours	$125	$125	$125	$125	$125	$125	$125	$125	$125	$125	$125	$125	$125	$125	$125
C billing hours	$125	$125	$125	$125	$125	$125	$125	$125	$125	$125	$125	$125	$125	$125	$125
Associate hours	$40	$40	$40	$40	$40	$40	$40	$40	$40	$40	$40	$40	$40	$60	$75
Other	$1	$1	$1	$1	$1	$1	$1	$1	$1	$1	$1	$1	$1	$1	$1
Total billings															
A billing hours	$24,375	$26,250	$28,750	$26,250	$12,500	$15,000	$12,500	$13,750	$15,000	$12,500	$13,750	$16,250	$216,875	$225,000	$237,500
B billing hours	$24,375	$26,250	$28,750	$26,250	$11,250	$12,500	$12,500	$13,750	$13,750	$12,500	$12,500	$15,000	$209,375	$225,000	$237,500
C billing hours	$24,375	$26,250	$28,750	$26,250	$11,250	$12,500	$12,500	$12,500	$12,500	$12,500	$12,500	$16,250	$208,125	$225,000	$237,500
Associate hours	$3,200	$3,200	$3,200	$3,200	$3,200	$3,200	$3,200	$3,200	$3,200	$3,200	$3,200	$3,200	$38,400	$96,000	$195,000
Other	$500	$500	$500	$500	$500	$500	$500	$500	$500	$500	$500	$500	$6,000	$6,600	$7,300
Total Billing	$76,825	$82,450	$89,950	$82,450	$38,700	$43,700	$41,200	$43,700	$44,950	$41,200	$42,450	$51,200	$678,775	$777,600	$914,800
Billing Direct Costs															
A billing hours	$0.00	$0.00	$0.00	$0.00	$0.00	$0.00	$0.00	$0.00	$0.00	$0.00	$0.00	$0.00	$0.00	$0.00	$0.00
B billing hours	$0.00	$0.00	$0.00	$0.00	$0.00	$0.00	$0.00	$0.00	$0.00	$0.00	$0.00	$0.00	$0.00	$0.00	$0.00
C billing hours	$0.00	$0.00	$0.00	$0.00	$0.00	$0.00	$0.00	$0.00	$0.00	$0.00	$0.00	$0.00	$0.00	$0.00	$0.00
Associate hours	$0.00	$0.00	$0.00	$0.00	$0.00	$0.00	$0.00	$0.00	$0.00	$0.00	$0.00	$0.00	$0.00	$0.00	$0.00
Other	$1.00	$1.00	$1.00	$1.00	$1.00	$1.00	$1.00	$1.00	$1.00	$1.00	$1.00	$1.00	$1.00	$1.00	$1.00
Total Direct Costs															
A billing hours	$0	$0	$0	$0	$0	$0	$0	$0	$0	$0	$0	$0	$0	$0	$0
B billing hours	$0	$0	$0	$0	$0	$0	$0	$0	$0	$0	$0	$0	$0	$0	$0
C billing hours	$0	$0	$0	$0	$0	$0	$0	$0	$0	$0	$0	$0	$0	$0	$0
Associate hours	$0	$0	$0	$0	$0	$0	$0	$0	$0	$0	$0	$0	$0	$0	$0
Other	$500	$500	$500	$500	$500	$500	$500	$500	$500	$500	$500	$500	$6,000	$6,600	$7,300
Subtotal Direct Cost of Billings	$500	$500	$500	$500	$500	$500	$500	$500	$500	$500	$500	$500	$6,000	$6,600	$7,300

CHAPTER 18
SAMPLE SOFTWARE COMPANY
SAMPLE PLAN

This sample business plan has been made available to users of Business Plan Pro™, business-planning software published by Palo Alto Software. Our sample plans were developed by existing companies or new business start-ups as research instruments to determine market viability or funding availability. Names, locations, and numbers may have been changed, and substantial portions of text may have been omitted to preserve confidentiality and proprietary information.

You are welcome to use this plan as a starting point to create your own, but you do not have permission to reproduce, publish, distribute, or even copy this plan as it exists here.

Requests for reprints, academic use, and other dissemination of this sample plan should be addressed to the marketing department of Palo Alto Software.

Sample Software Company

Confidentiality Agreement

The undersigned reader acknowledges that the information provided by _____ in this business plan is confidential; therefore, reader agrees not to disclose it without the express written permission of _____.

It is acknowledged by reader that information to be furnished in this business plan is in all respects confidential in nature, other than information which is in the public domain through other means, and that any disclosure or use of same by reader may cause serious harm or damage to _____.

Upon request, this document is to be immediately returned to _____.

_____   _____
Signature   Date

_____
Name (typed or printed)

This is a business plan. It does not imply an offering of securities.

Sample Software Company

1.0 Executive Summary

We want to take Sample Software to the next level.

Sample is a profitable S-corporation based in Ourtown. It has grown from a one-man consulting company started in 1993 to a $1-million software company whose main product, Product X™, is sold through major retail channels.

Growth has come from patience, hard work, and quality of product and service. The company has never had outside investment. It has been financed by owner house equity, sweat equity, profits, and small bank lines of credit.

As we grow, we want to grow right. For example, we have to recognize the unique capital requirements of a successful software publisher: our business is working-capital intensive. We will always have to support two and three months' worth of sales as receivables, because that is the nature of the channels we deal with. Also, we need to build our management team correctly. We need the right people in the right place at the right time. We also need to develop our team so that our people can grow as the company grows.

1.1 Objectives

1. To increase sales to $1.9 million in 1999 and $3.8 million in 2000.

2. To increase gross margin to 70% and net profit margin to more than 9.75%.

Sample Software Company

Highlights

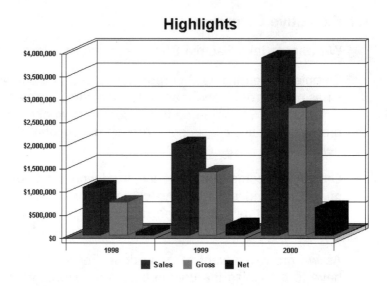

3. To hold personnel to one full-time person for every $250K in revenues.

4. To maintain at least 30% market share of Product X, as measured by PC Data.

1.2 Mission

Sample Software develops, publishes, and markets business tools and business know-how together in a software product that includes software and documentation. It makes business techniques accessible to millions of business users who would otherwise not have the knowledge to use them. It makes a profit and generates cash. It provides a rewarding work environment and fair compensation to its employees, a fair return to its owners, and a fair royalty to its authors.

Sample Software Company

1.3 Keys to Success

1. Marketing power. We need to have our products on the shelves with attractive packaging and enough marketing power to maintain a 30% or more market share, as measured by PC Data.

2. Product quality and customer satisfaction. Everything we sell is guaranteed, so the product has to do what we promise and do it well.

3. Long-term customer satisfaction is critical to our survival.

4. The right management team, with strong foundations in marketing, management, finance, and product development, is essential. We need enough working capital to survive in the working-capital-intensive retail channel.

2.0 Company Summary

Sample Software was founded in 1993 by Ralph Smith to market his Product X software. Originally installed in a home office, it moved into its present space in 1996. It has added several new products and has acquired shelf space in the retail market.

2.1 Company Ownership

Sample Software, Inc. is now a Subchapter S corporation owned entirely by founder Ralph Smith and his wife, Mabel. It elected to go Subchapter S at the beginning of the 1996 tax year, after having been Subchapter C from founding until then. Its fiscal year is the calendar year. The Oregon corporation was established with 100 shares issued, 51 to Ralph Smith and 49 to Mabel Smith.

Sample Software Company

2.2 Company History

Sample Software, Inc. was founded in Ourtown in 1993 as Infoplan, a sole proprietorship. In 1994 it was incorporated in Delaware as Infoplan, Inc. In 1996 it was incorporated in California as Sample Software, Inc. Infoplan, Inc. was dissolved.

For most of its existence, this was a one-man consulting company supporting a product company. It kept a very conservative stance on products, advertising with slim budgets, with marketing depending mainly on published reviews and direct sales, until the market grew.

In 1995 we introduced a new, breakthrough product, Product X, that was the first effective task X software with bundled spreadsheet and word processor along with automatic charts.

Past Performance

	1995	1996	1997
Sales	$384,113	$464,592	$695,136
Gross margin	$270,062	$342,824	$480,163
Gross % (calculated)	70.31%	73.79%	69.07%
Operating expenses	$251,471	$290,145	$513,144
Collection period (days)	65	65	95
Inventory turnover	7	6	6

Balance sheet			
Short-term Assets	1995	1996	1997
Cash	$0	$0	$625
Accounts receivable	$0	$0	$124,056
Inventory	$0	$0	$28,623
Other short-term assets	$0	$0	$431
Total short-term assets	$0	$0	$153,735

Sample Software Company

Past Performance, cont.

	1995	1996	1997
Long-term Assets			
Capital assets	$0	$0	$35,577
Accumulated depreciation	$0	$0	$24,247
Total long-term assets	$0	$0	$11,330
Total assets	$0	$0	$165,065

Capital and Liabilities			
	1995	1996	1997
Accounts payable	$0	$0	$36,557
Short-term notes	$0	$0	$22,336
Other short-term liabilities	$0	$0	$25,526
Subtotal short-term liabilities	$0	$0	$84,419
Long-term liabilities	$0	$0	$0
Total liabilities	$0	$0	$84,419
Paid in capital	$0	$0	$76,960
Retained earnings	$0	$0	$36,668
Earnings	$0	$0	($32,982)
Total capital	$0	$0	$80,646
Total capital and liabilities	$0	$0	$165,065

Other Inputs	1995	1996	1997
Payment days	0	0	30
Sales on credit	$0	$0	$660,379
Receivables turnover	0.00	0.00	5.32

Sample Software Company

Past Performance

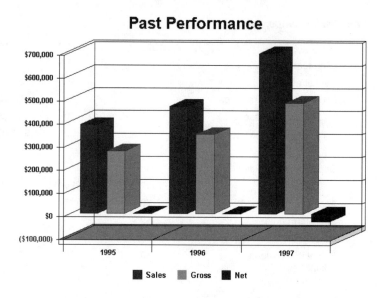

■ Sales	■ Gross	■ Net	

2.3 Company Locations and Facilities

The company is located in Ourtown, with offices at 100 Main Street. We were started in a home office, but we moved to the present space in 1996. We rent 750 square feet for $900 per month. We have a two-year contract limiting rent increases.

3.0 Products

Our products are prescriptive software, more than just tools, because they instruct and empower the user with know-how as well as tools. Our best-selling flagship product, Product X, is the key. We are also shipping Product Y for Windows.

People don't buy these products for the software itself. They buy them for the benefit they provide, the step-by-step solution to a problem. They buy them for the

Sample Software Company

reassurance that they've covered all the bases, that the job is done right, that they won't be embarrassed when they show the plan to banker, boss, or partner. They don't want the software, they want the software's task completed. They want it done and done well.

The company name is well known, and its products are respected. We have sold more than 70,000 units through distribution, and we have names and addresses of more than 40,000 direct buyers and registered users. Our products are sold through several major mail order houses and several computer retail chains, and they are listed in most available product databases. We are now distributed through the major distributors who reach the most important retail channels. Throughout, Sample Software has maintained a high professional standard and a reputation as the quality provider.

3.1 Product Description

- Product X: Suggested Retail Price $XX, street price $XX, the second-leading Windows task X software in the U.S. market, according to PC Data, and the quality leader according to prestigious publications ranging from *PC Magazine* to *Home Office Computing* and even *Journal of Business Strategy* (copies are included in the appendices). This is the best task X application on the market, according to the objective analysis of most published reviews. It combines an easy-to-use, step-by-step interface full of guidance, help, and glossaries, with a powerful business analysis model, complete financial analysis, and very strong cash flow analysis. Sales literature and texts of reviews are included in the appendices.

Sample Software Company

- Product Y: Suggested Retail Price $XX, street price $XX, a stand-alone task Y application for Windows. This product is more than just that, because it also includes complete [omitted]. It is the best product available for performing task Y, and the only product for day-to-day management of the [omitted] function. Reviews and sales literature are included with this plan.

- Product Z: Suggested Retail Price $XX, street price $XX, a stand-alone task Y application for Windows. This product is more than just that, because it also includes complete [omitted]. It is the best product available for performing task Y, and the only product for day-to-day management of the [omitted] function. Reviews and sales literature are included with this plan.

3.2 Competitive Comparison

In the broader sense, our competition is books, magazines, courses, seminars, consultants, and assorted experts—anything that helps our target market get through the tasks on which we focus. The bulk of the target market wants an easy way to successfully complete a difficult task, along with assurance that the end result will look competent. Our part of the market is the software component, Windows-based software to develop [omitted], sold through retail at $XX per unit.

At present we compete mainly against three other task X packages sold through retail: The traditional leader is Product A, by Competitor A. Third place is held by Competitor B, with a product called Product B. The fourth competitor is Product C, by Company C. The appendices include charts illustrating complete data on market share, in units and dollars, for the past year.

Sample Software Company

Company A is a formidable competitor. It is also privately owned, but it is apparently well financed. Company A started just a few months after we did, with a similar but inferior product and better marketing. Company A has consistently been more aggressive with sales and marketing expenses and plain better at marketing than we have been. The company imitated our early template products and since then built a line of template-based products including not just Product A and Marketing Builder, but also Employee Manual Maker, Safety Plan, Publicity Builder, Loan Builder, Living Trust Builder, and Agreement Builder. Despite the broad product line, however, it still depends as much on Product A as we do on Product X. The company's other products add bulk to its ads, but only the business plan, marketing plan, and occasionally the employee handbook appear on the retail shelves.

Company A's Product A has been the market leader, with 45% unit share as measured by PC Data, the leading source of retail market data. First into retail, Product A is advertised aggressively in some small business magazines and in Skymall catalogs in airlines. In 1995 Product X appeared on the market as the first stand-alone product (meaning that it included everything needed in an all-in-one application) when Product A was still just templates (meaning data files to work with other applications such as word processors or spreadsheets). Our product won warm praise from reviewers everywhere, as well as a lot of shelf space, so Product X rose quickly to a brief stay as the top seller before Company A mustered its marketing skills and fought back with new packaging, aggressive advertising, and a lot of spending on in-store programs. Last November Company A finally introduced what it calls "interactive" Product A, which is finally better than a template. However, it is very hard to work with and doesn't appear to pose a serious threat to our superiority in terms of product quality and reviews.

Sample Software Company

Third in the market, behind us, Company B seems to be fading. Its product, Product B, is clumsy and old fashioned, text-based, weak on tables, and has no charts. It has reasonably good-looking packaging and a lot of inertia from years in the market. Its 1996 market share was 22%, according to PC Data.

The fourth-place competitor last year had 3% but could still become a serious competitor. Company C publishes Product C, which is a poor imitation of our first version of Product X. Company C is well funded by a shipping magnate worth several hundred million dollars and is not a public institution. Company C has embarked on an ambitious product plan to create not only Product X, but also Product Y, and a series of others. It is marketing these products in a way that promotes its bundled word processor and spreadsheet as general business productivity tools. This approach brings potentially huge problems in product development and support and pits Company C against productivity giants, including Microsoft, Lotus, and Corel. Sample Software, in contrast, includes similarly bundled word processing and spreadsheet software in its task-oriented applications but sells only the benefit of the specific task solution.

The appendices also include data on sales of marketing products. Company A has a Task Y Product, which is reasonably successful. Company B had a Task Y, but dropped the product. Company C has announced a Task Y product but has not released it.

3.3 Sales Literature

Sales literature and collaterals are attached to this plan as appendices. The literature shows how we have devel-

Sample Software Company

oped the Product X and Product Y packaging and advertising, with consistent look and "seven easy steps" theme.

3.4 Sourcing

This detailed discussion of vendors of packaging, programming, disk duplication, and assembly has been omitted.

3.5 Technology

Both Product X and Product Y are enhancements of previous products, copyrighted since the 1980s by Ralph Smith and Sample Software.

We have a software development engine, that we own, that brings together guided text, spreadsheet tables, and charts in a user-friendly environment with wizards, help files, and on-line coaching. This is a powerful competitive edge.

- [This discussion omitted. It deals with product and company specifics not useful for sample purposes.]
- [This discussion omitted. It deals with product and company specifics not useful for sample purposes.]

3.6 Future Products

The most important factor in developing future products is market need. Our understanding of the needs of our target market segment is one of our competitive advantages. It is critical to our effort to develop the right new products. We also have what we call a "core product

Sample Software Company

engine" that we own (previous section), which should be the foundation of future products.

Our next big product will [material omitted]. We can also make it compatible with both Product X and Product Y future versions, to create a true management system that can become vital to small businesses that use it. We have created an in-house system that could be the prototype. Businesses need to manage cash and budgets, and there is no effective software available.

Our second major product development effort—pending further research on customer needs—might be the [this discussion omitted].

We are also considering a new product [discussion omitted].

4.0 Market Analysis Summary

Our market includes millions of people in this country and others who deal with Tasks X, Y, and Z. We find them in home offices and small offices everywhere, plus business schools and professional offices. The trends only favor our business with growing needs for people performing these tasks.

According to research published last year by [source omitted], the market for [product area] is worth an estimated $3.8 billion at end-customer value in 19__ and is projected to grow at 20% per year, according to professional forecasts published in [xxxxxxxx] in August of 19__. Sources included Ralph Research and Infocorp. The [industry] Association estimates total retail sales of $3.075 billion in 19__.

Sample Software Company

4.1 Market Segmentation

The target customer in this segment is adult, male or female. Our customers have a wide range of computer and business skills, but our most important target customers are relatively unsophisticated at computing. In many cases, our customers are also unsophisticated about business management and business analysis.

We find this target customer by focusing on small business and home office market segments, called SOHO by many market watchers. The SOHO market segment is one of the fastest growing in the U.S. market, being given increasing attention by many marketers. We fit perfectly into the SOHO trend.

In both the home office and the small office segment, our most important target customer is a smart, well-educated, and self-reliant adult in a small-business setting who requires a broad range of business tasks, including the nuts and bolts of daily business as well as strategic planning, business planning, marketing, sales, and administration. This person is a generalist, not a functional expert in the areas our products cover, such as task X, but does want a do-it-yourself product that will help him or her get the job right without having to turn to (and pay) an expert.

Business schools, including teachers and students, use our products for their teaching power. Our products are excellent for helping people learn by doing. We refer to this group as the academic market.

Consultants, accountants, and experts with the good sense to value their own time use our products to maximize their productivity. These people have the knowledge to do their own, but they understand that working with

Sample Software Company

our products instead can save them dozens of valuable hours. We refer to these as the expert market.

Market Analysis

Potential Customers	Growth	1998	1999	2000	2001	2002	CAGR
Home office	2%	22,000	22,440	22,889	23,347	23,814	2.00%
Small office	5%	15,000	15,750	16,538	17,365	18,233	5.00%
Professionals	8%	10,000	10,800	11,664	12,597	13,605	8.00%
Academic	0%	12,000	12,000	12,000	12,000	12,000	0.00%
Other	0%	10,000	10,000	10,000	10,000	10,000	0.00%
Total	3.00%	69,000	70,990	73,091	75,309	77,652	3.00%

Market Analysis (Pie)

■ Home office
□ Small office
■ Professionals
□ Academic
■ Other

4.2 Target Market Segment Strategy

[This should be a very thoughtful discussion of why we have chosen the topics we've chosen, but of course this is a sample business plan, not a real plan.]

There is already a sense of segment strategy in the way we define our target markets. We are choosing to compete in areas that lend themselves to local competition

Sample Software Company

and product and channel areas that match our strengths and avoid our weaknesses.

For this reason, we operate in only two channels, the mainstream XXX and YYY. We don't feel that we can compete without higher prices and better margins than what would be acceptable in the mainstream grocery and main-market store channels. We are much better positioned in the smaller [omitted], both stores and chains, where the customer base is sensitive to politics of environment and the community, concerned about the ethics of buying, consuming, and producing, and in tune with our vision.

4.2.1 Market Needs

Our target small businesses are very dependent on reliable information technology. They use the computers for a complete range of functions, beginning with the core administration information such as accounting, shipping, and inventory. They also use them for communications within the business and outside of the business, and for personal productivity. They are not, however, large enough to have dedicated computer personnel such as the MIS departments in large businesses. Ideally, they come to us for a long-term alliance, looking to us for reliable service and support to substitute for their in-house people.

These are not businesses that want to shop for rock-bottom price through chain stores or mail order. They want to have reliable providers of expertise.

Our standard small businesses will be 5- to 20-unit installations, critically dependent on local-area networks. Back-up, training, installation, and ongoing support are very

Sample Software Company

important. They require database and administrative software as the core of their systems.

4.2.2 Market Trends

One important trend is the one toward greater international sales in personal computing products. Although the U.S. market is still the biggest, all the major manufacturers are recording more gains in the non-U.S. market than in the U.S. market. This is true for the main CPU lines and related lines, including peripherals, software, and accessories.

Another important trend is the one toward greater use of specialized and focused consultants instead of in-house resources. Companies are looking for more out-sourcing and, in general, a preference for variable costs over fixed costs.

4.2.3 Market Growth

The market for non-U.S. personal computers has been growing at approximately 22% per year during the past three years, according to a study by InfoQuest published in the *Wall Street Journal* earlier this year. This level of growth presumably applies to related products as well. It is considerably higher than growth in the U.S. market.

It is more difficult to gauge the more important growth rate, which would be the growth in specialty international marketing consulting. John Doe, an expert in marketing-related consulting, estimated the growth in focused marketing consulting at 40% per year, according to a report published in the *San Jose Chronicle*.

Sample Software Company

In our market analysis, we suggest growth in the number of potential customers between 6 and 7% per year.

4.3 Industry Analysis

The software industry is frequently segmented according to product type. The important division between designs and systems software is only the beginning. Some analysts split software into leverages, types of designs, and so on, ad infinitum.

We prefer segmentation by economics and buying patterns. This incorporates some of the product type differences but in a more practical sense:

- OEM software development: software sold through others. A great deal of systems software and communications software is sold by hardware manufacturers or bundled together into packages. The economic model is like custom consulting or engineering; buying decisions are major events, made by committee, covering significant amounts for significant lengths of time.

- Mainline packaged software: software sold at $50–$700 through direct sales to large buyers, direct response via advertising or direct mail promotion, catalogs, and retail blippo and software stores. Whether it's systems or design software, the economic model is essentially the same. It's an industry still settling down to realistic prices.

- Specialty or vertical market software: sold outside the main software channels with careful target marketing, often through trade shows and magazines unrelated to industrial blippos.

Sample Software Company

Another useful segmentation divides the market by the various buyer/user types:

- Consumer: users of industrial blippos, commonly known as home blippos. A market mainly for playing games, sold often through toy, hobby, or consumer channels, and, not infrequently, by discounters or mass merchandisers.

- Small business: some 10 million businesses in the United States, plus several million professionals and home offices. Companies may be segmented by revenues, employee size, or some other category. The division between small business and large business is more a matter of buying patterns and product needs than a specific division between categories.

- Large business: The key distinctions between large and small business include:

  —Product needs: large business needs are much more complex.

  —Buying patterns: large business demands different channels.

- K–12: elementary and middle schools. However you divide education, the K–12 market tends to be dominated by Litmus Development.

- Higher education: universities, colleges, teacher training, junior colleges, and so on.

4.3.1 Industry Participants

Industrial Blippo software is an immature industry characterized by high growth rates, low barriers to entry, and many small competitors. Born in the last 10 years as part of the industrial blippo revolution, it is now beginning to

Sample Software Company

settle into the process of maturation. Despite the pulverized complexion of the industry, leaders have emerged. Several have revenues in the hundreds of millions of dollars annually:

- Malcom Corporation (Really, Penn.): manufacturer of MWARK widget system, a complete line of programming languages, and solid lines of designs software for both the Groolo, the ZOOLT, and compatible industrial blippos. Revenues of $300.9 million in 19___, 33% above 19___.

- Arrog International: (Los Angeles, Calif.) manufacturer of rillwell management software. Has acquired several other leading products through acquisition of its companies. Revenues of $267.3 million in 19___, growth of 27%.

- Litmus Development Corporation: (Collex, Ohio) manufacturer of Litmus and other products. Revenues of $395.6 million in 19___, growth of 39%.

The market for software is worth an estimated $3.8 billion at end-user value in 19___ and is projected to grow at 20% per year, according to professional forecasts published in *Widget Reseller News* in August of 19___. Sources included Ralph Research and Infocorp. The Widget Manufacturers' Association (WMA) estimates total retail sales of $3.075 billion in 1987; $274 million of that was bleep software, and $2.4 billion of that was blap software.

Market leaders are Malcom Corporation, Arrog International, and Litmus Development Corporation. However, the industry is highly pulverized; its top 10 companies account for less than one-third of the total market.

Sample Software Company

4.3.2 Distribution Patterns

Distribution channels are a serious bottleneck. The country's 7,000 retail outlets are swamped with product, completely unable to deal with the thousands of titles published. This has several repercussions:

- The cost of marketing a new product is becoming a serious barrier to entry. The channels won't accept a new product without major advertising and promotion expenses.

- Brand name carries more weight. The channels are dominated by existing brands. Retailers don't have to experiment when they carry name brands.

- Developers are turning more often to produce their work with major brands instead of marketing it themselves. So the big names get bigger, and smaller names have it so tough that they often end up as inventors whose work is published by the industry leaders.

Royalties run well below the bleep industry, as low as 1–2% for very high profile manufacturing, 5–10% for most contracts, and higher for some low volume, low profile manufacturing.

There are exceptions to the rule. Beerland International faced practically the same barriers to entry when it started in 1983, but a combination of good product and good marketing broke through those barriers. There is still enough market to provide ample opportunity to the right combination.

4.3.3 Competition and Buying Patterns

The single most important factor in software is the bandwagon. The rich get richer, and the poor get poorer. How-

Sample Software Company

ever, there is still a lot of room for new products and new companies outside the main designs types.

- In the main design types, market share generates more market share. Rillwell 3, for example, is not the best rillwell, but it is the market leader. More people know it better than any other rillwell. There are more books, add-on packages, and training programs available for rill3 than for any other. Most important, the retailers feature it. So it continues to dominate. Despite the existence of better products, it is the wisest choice for the buyer.

- Buyers want brand names. Quality of software is hard to measure. Brand names assure quality. However, brand names operate only in mainstream product types; there is plenty of room for smaller names with specific solutions that appeal to buyers.

- Buyers are willing to pay high prices for solutions that work. While competitors chip away at market leaders for lower prices, the leaders continue to command high prices. Javelin failed with a high-quality dealio product priced at $700, and it continued to fail when the company dropped the price to $99. Although the product was much better than Litmus 1-2-3, the price didn't make enough difference.

- Channels discount heavily. Brand name, packaged software becomes a commodity and is bought on price. Buyers will pay a heavy premium for Rillwell 3 over a lesser-known knockoff, but they happily pay $250 in a discount store instead of $500 at a full-price retail store.

- There is no consensus about software copying. Estimates of its revenue impact vary from 10% to 60% of the theoretical revenue manufacturers would receive if copying were impossible. Illegal software copying is a fact of life that manufacturers live with because they

Sample Software Company

have no other choice. There is evidence, however, that wholesale copying of Rillwell 3 and Litmus kooo helped those products build their market share leads, which became their key strengths.

- Impulse buying goes on with products below $100. Buyers have discovered products like _____ and _____ that are low priced and extremely useful. There is a great deal more freedom in the lower end of the market.

- Distribution channels are clogged. Lack of channels is a serious barrier to industry growth. Industrial Blippo and software stores are insufficient for the wealth of products available and the constant flood of new products.

- Support becomes a serious factor at higher price levels. Companies that charge hundreds of dollars for software are expected to answer user questions. Those that don't will suffer from bad reviews and poor word of mouth. However, neither Litmus nor Arrog International has had a reputation for good support, and both are successful.

4.3.4 Main Competitors

Sample Software Company is staking out a new area in software. We handle specific business tasks in a way unlike that which other software companies or software products do. We identify competition in terms of specific products that fill the same needs that we fill. The main competitors are:

Cheap dealio software:

Sellers of cheap software for business applications. The most successful is _____ of _____, __, which has

Sample Software Company

established itself as a 'xxxxxxxx' for xxxxxxx for _____, and _____. There are a few others.

Strengths:

The main strength of the cheap software packages is their price. In a price-sensitive area, such products can be very strong.

Weaknesses:

_____'s weakness is common to all vendors of low-cost _____: the product is not very useful. Buyers get what they pay for—a cheap widget model with no documentation.

5.0 Strategy and Implementation Summary

Our strategy is based on serving niche markets well. The world is full of small and medium-sized businesses that can't get good products or services from the major vendors who focus on high-volume orders only.

Also:

- What begins as a customized version of a standard product, tailored to the needs of a local business, can eventually become a niche product that will fit the needs of similar businesses across the country.
- We are building our marketing infrastructure so that we can eventually reach specific kinds of businesses across broad geographic lines.
- We focus on satisfying the needs of small and medium-sized business.

Sample Software Company

- We focus on follow-on technology that we can take to the masses, not leading-edge technology that aims at the experts and volume leaders.

5.1 Strategy Pyramids

Our main strategy at Sample is to position ourselves at the top of the quality scale, featuring our combination of superb technology and fine old-fashioned programming, for the buyer who wants the best quality regardless of price. Tactics underneath that strategy include research and development related to new designs and new technology, choosing the right channels of distribution, and communicating our quality position to the market. Programs are mainly those listed in the milestones table, including new design programs, new equipment to keep up with design, channel development, channel marketing programs, our direct sales, and our continued presence in high-end catalog channels and new presence in the Mall.

5.2 Value Proposition

Sample Software gives the discriminating personal computer user, who cares about design and quality and needs to complete Tasks X, Y, and Z, a combination of the highest quality software and the latest technology, at a fair price.

5.3 Competitive Edge

Our competitive edge is our software engine, our knowledge of the product area, and our long-term commitment to customer satisfaction.

[Major discussion omitted from this sample plan.]

Sample Software Company

5.4 Marketing Strategy

Our marketing strategy emphasizes focus. This is the key. We are a small company with limited resources, so we must focus on certain kinds of products with certain kinds of users. More specifically:

- We focus on the [discussion omitted].

- We focus our [discussion omitted].

- We focus on the kind of product quality that produces good, quotable reviews, which can then generate sales at the retail level because of quotes on boxes. We must always have a relatively heavy PR component to our marketing, because reviews are critical. Ralph Smith has always been active in maintaining personal relationships with the key writers in the field, which is easier for him than for his counterparts because his background includes years in journalism. He is very involved in our relationship with the trade and business press.

- We are building image and awareness through consistency and distinctiveness in our packaging. The yellow pushpin and red box of the Product X and the "serious software for serious business" theme will be repeated consistently throughout our marketing.

- We are focusing advertising on several key media, and this discussion is omitted also.

5.4.1 Positioning Statement

For business owners and managers who need to deal with Task X, Product X is software that creates and helps manage professional Task X. Unlike [name omitted] from [name omitted], Product X provides a system for schedul-

Sample Software Company

ing and tracking the entire Task X process from plan to action.

For business people in all levels of management who make decisions that impact the success of their companies, [name omitted] is software that analyzes almost any type of strategic or tactical problem and guides the user to choose the best course of action. Unlike [name omitted], [name omitted] features an easy-to-use intuitive interface and step-by-step online guide system that enables all users—from novice to expert—to make smart decisions easily and confidently.

For small businesses, professionals, and the self-employed who recognize that managing cash flow can be the difference between success and failure, [name omitted] is financial software that handles all the essential bookkeeping functions including checkbook management, check printing, expense tracking, and report printing. Unlike [name omitted] and other complex accounting programs, [name omitted] focuses on cash flow management to avoid cash shortages, which are the leading cause of business failure.

5.4.2 Pricing Strategy

Our pricing is determined by our focus on retail sales. We aim at the consumer market with prices intended to generate street prices in the high two-digits, such as the $XX street price of Product X. A suggested list of $XX seems perfectly satisfactory to us and the customers. We do not expect to change prices on any existing products.

Sample Software Company

5.4.3 Promotion Strategy

- [Discussion omitted. This is very specific to the real sample company, not to be presented here.]
- Ralph Smith must also make as many [discussion omitted].
- We need to plan our co-promotion efforts to take full advantage of [discussion omitted].
- Our advertising is focusing on [discussion omitted].

5.4.4 Distribution Strategy

1. We are concentrating our image and awareness marketing by focusing on the [discussion omitted].
2. Our display advertising is leveraged through [discussion omitted].
3. We watch for interesting [discussion omitted], and others.

5.4.5 Marketing Programs

Our most important marketing program is [specifics omitted]. Leslie Doe will be responsible, with a budget of $XX,XXX and a milestone date of the 15th of May. This program is intended to [objectives omitted]. Achievement should be measured by [specific concrete measurement].

Another key marketing program is [specifics omitted]. [Name] will be responsible, with a budget of $XX,XXX and a milestone date of [date]. This program is intended

Sample Software Company

to [objectives omitted]. Achievement should be measured by [specific concrete measurement].

5.5 Sales Strategy

Sales strategy shouldn't change. We will continue to work with XXX and to focus on retail sales. During 1999 we should focus not on changing strategy but on improving our implementation, by working on key objectives and much better coordination of marketing efforts related to sales channels.

For the short term at least, the selling process depends on point-of-purchase decisions, impacted by boxes on shelves and quotes on boxes. Our marketing does not intend to affect the perception of need as much as knowledge and awareness of the product category.

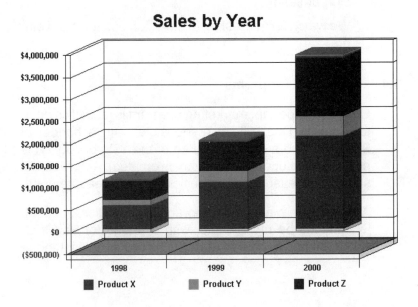

Sales by Year

Sample Software Company

5.5.1 Sales Forecast

The sales forecast for 1998 depends on Product X for the bulk of our sales, an estimated 15,000 units. We expect Product Y to maintain a ratio of 2/10 against Product X, for sales of 3,000 units.

The table that follows shows unit sales of more than 15,000 Product X in 1998. The related monthly sales table in the appendices shows our sales for 1998 in monthly detail. Sales discounts, discontinued products, and future product sales go into the "Other" sales category.

The Monthly Sales Chart that follows indicates that we have some seasonality in the business. Also, since January–April are the strongest months shown on the chart, the chart indicates that our forecasts are conservative. Although on the chart we show our strongest months as February and April, our strongest period has been September–November in past years.

Sales Forecast

Unit Sales	1998	1999	2000
Product X	15,100	30,000	60,000
Product Y	2,976	6,000	10,000
Product Z	1,320	2,000	4,000
Old version returns	(900)	(1,200)	(1,800)
OEM & customization	9	25	35
Other	12	15	20
Total unit sales	18,517	36,840	72,255

Unit Prices	1998	1999	2000
Product X	$35.00	$35.00	$35.00
Product Y	$45.00	$45.00	$45.00
Product Z	$325.00	$325.00	$325.00
Old version returns	$95.00	$35.00	$35.00
OEM & customization	$1,000.00	$1,000.00	$1,000.00

Page 30

Sample Software Company

Sales Forecast, cont.

	1998	1999	2000
Other	$1,500.00	$1,500.00	$1,500.00

Sales

	1998	1999	2000
Product X	$528,500	$1,050,000	$2,100,000
Product Y	$133,920	$270,000	$450,000
Product Z	$429,000	$650,000	$1,300,000
Old version returns	($85,500)	($42,000)	($63,000)
OEM & customization	$9,000	$25,000	$35,000
Other	$18,000	$22,500	$30,000
Total sales	$1,032,920	$1,975,500	$3,852,000

Direct Unit Costs	1998	1999	2000
Product X	$7.82	$8.50	$8.00
Product Y	$8.39	$8.39	$8.39
Product Z	$0.00	$0.00	$0.00
Old version returns	$0.00	$0.00	$0.00
OEM & customization	$0.00	$0.00	$0.00
Other	$0.00	$8.50	$8.00

Direct Cost of Sales	1998	1999	2000
Product X	$118,082	$255,000	$480,000
Product Y	$24,969	$50,340	$83,900
Product Z	$0	$0	$0
Old version returns	$0	$0	$0
OEM & customization	$0	$0	$0
Other	$0	$128	$160
Subtotal direct cost of sales	$143,051	$305,468	$564,060

5.5.2 Sales Programs

We continue to work with [omitted] (XXX) to develop, maintain, and consolidate our retail channel sales. XXX, is based in Ourtown. Despite the coincidence of a nearby

Sample Software Company

location, XXX operates as a national sales rep firm. It is dependent on XXXX, but it also has an office in Southern California and a sales representative in Canada, and it has good relations with all three of our major distributors. XXX receives a 6% commission on sales to major distributors, which is payable only after we receive our payments.

We have asked XXX to focus first on four key tasks for 1998:

- Increase our access to sell-through numbers
- Increase our channels' shelf stocking levels
- Get our products into XXX
- Get our products into YYY

As of April, we had won entry into XXX, and stocking levels seem to have improved. We are still not in YYY, and although our sell-through information is good, it is not good enough.

Sales Monthly

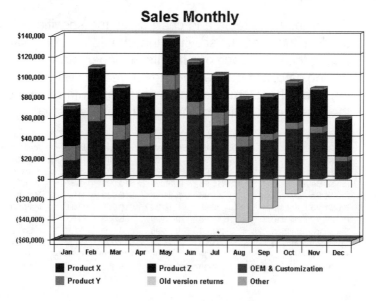

Sample Software Company

We need to improve our relationship with XXX, which is second to XXX among [omitted] of personal computer software to retail channels.

5.6 Strategic Alliances

Product development: The emphasis in this plan is on getting products developed and into the market, especially the new versions of Product X and Product Y.

Marketing: We need to watch sell-through and performance very carefully to measure the results of our 1997 marketing push. Our first sales review in May seemed to indicate a successful launch, but we need to keep watching.

Finance: We are also looking to enhance our capital structure and management team.

5.7 Milestones

The milestones table and chart show the specific detail about actual program activities that should be taking place during the year. Each one has its manager, starting date, ending date, and budget. During the year we will be keeping track of implementation against plan, with reports on the timely completion of these activities as planned.

Milestones	Plan				
Milestone	Start Date	End Date	Budget	Manager	Department
ProdX V3	2/1/98	6/1/98	$5,000	ABC	ProdDev
ProdY V2	6/15/98	7/15/98	$15,000	DEF	ProdDev
ProdZ Beta	9/15/98	11/30/98	$10,000	DEF	ProdDev
ProdX Packaging	2/1/98	3/31/98	$15,000	HIJ	Marketing
ProdX V3 Release	4/30/98	6/16/98	$10,000	HIJ	Marketing
ProdY V2 Release	8/15/98	9/30/98	$5,000	HIJ	Marketing
Seminar Promotion	3/1/98	5/15/98	$10,000	KLM	Sales
Upgrade promotion	7/1/98	8/15/98	$50,000	KLM	Sales
Year-end promotion	11/1/98	12/15/98	$25,000	OPQ	Sales
Channel rebate program	10/14/98	12/15/98	$5,000	ABC	Admin
Totals			$150,000		

Sample Software Company

Milestones

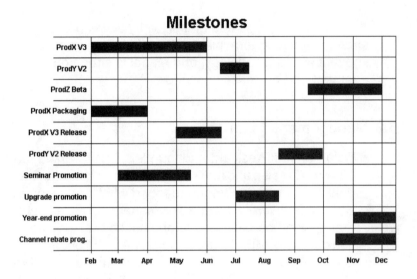

6.0 Management Summary

We are a small company owned and operated by Ralph and Mabel Smith, husband and wife, as a Subchapter S corporation. Ralph is the developer and designer of the products, and Mabel manages the office.

Management style reflects the participation of the owners. The company respects its community of co-workers and treats all workers well. We attempt to develop and nurture the company as community. We are not very hierarchical.

6.1 Organizational Structure

Ralph Smith, President, is responsible for overall business management. Our managers of finance, marketing, and sales report directly to Ralph.

Jim Graham, programmer, is responsible for product design and development.

Sample Software Company

As co-owners, Ralph and Mabel jointly develop business strategy and long-term plans. Ralph is strong on product know-how and technology, and Mabel is strong on management and business know-how.

6.2 Management Team

- Ralph Smith: President and founder. Smith worked for 10 years in sales and marketing with Arrog International before returning to Oregon to found what has become Sample Software. He was sales manager of the eastern region when he founded the original software distribution company. MBA from Stanford, MA with honors from University of Oregon, BA magna cum laude from the University of Notre Dame. Forty years old, married, five children.

- Allen Lombard: on board of directors. ____, ____. Previously General Manager for ____, where sales increased during his 1982–1987 management from less than $3 million to $29 million annually. MBA Harvard Business School, BS Stanford.

- Mabel Smith: Consultant, general manager. Was the manager of XYZ Lumber in Standard before being hired by Acme six years ago. BA in Business Administration, University of North Carolina.

- Henry Callahan: on board of directors. Well-known and respected public relations and advertising consultant based in Blank.

- Perry Masonjar: attorney and secretary of board. Founding attorney of _____, _____, Austec, and other start-ups.

- Linda Wilson: Marketing Coordinator. 25 years old. BA Marketing, _____.

Sample Software Company

6.3 Management Team Gaps

- The present team is quite weak on professional sales.

- The present team, though strong on how to market at a high level, is short on practical front-line marketing experience.

- Product development requires a stable of entrepreneurial inventors willing to work for royalties.

6.4 Personnel Plan

Our people are compensated well, for the Ourtown market. Compensation includes complete HMO health care for the employee and all dependents, plus a dental plan, plus a 401(k) with generous profit sharing, plus two weeks of vacation every year. The atmosphere at work is enhanced by team-building activities including river rafting, roller skating, and pizza parties.

We do expect to increase personnel significantly as sales increase.

Monthly personnel details for 1998 are in the appendices as Table 6.4.

Personnel Plan

Production Personnel	1998	1999	2000
Technical Support Mgr.	$33,300	$37,000	$41,000
Technical Support	$0	$25,000	$50,000
Other	$0	$0	$0
Other	$0	$0	$0
Subtotal	$33,300	$62,000	$91,000
Sales and Marketing Personnel			
Marketing Manager	$48,000	$53,000	$58,000
Name or title	$0	$0	$0

Sample Software Company

Personnel Plan, cont.

Sales and Marketing Personnel	1998	1999	2000
Name or title	$0	$0	$0
Other	$0	$0	$0
Subtotal	$48,000	$53,000	$58,000

General and Administrative Personnel			
President	$60,000	$66,000	$73,000
Office Manager	$30,000	$33,000	$36,000
Name or title	$0	$0	$0
Other	$0	$0	$0
Subtotal	$90,000	$99,000	$109,000

Other Personnel			
Development	$30,300	$50,000	$100,000
Name or title	$0	$0	$0
Name or title	$0	$0	$0
Other	$0	$0	$0
Subtotal	$30,300	$50,000	$100,000

Total headcount	0	0	0
Total payroll	$201,600	$264,000	$358,000
Payroll burden	$19,656	$25,740	$34,905
Total payroll expenditures	$221,256	$289,740	$392,905

7.0 Financial Plan

Ideally, we would want to bring in as much as $1 million of equity investment from investors compatible with our growth plan, management style, and vision, in return for some equity ownership. We are not going to discuss specifics of a deal until we have met the right partners. This plan does not call for equity from outside investors.

Sample Software Company

If and when the time comes for outside investors, we want compatible investors or no investors at all. Compatibility means (1) a fundamental respect for giving our customers value, and for maintaining a healthy and happy workplace; (2) respect for realistic forecasts, and conservative cash flow and financial management; (3) cash flow as first priority, growth second, profits third; (4) located in Oregon or the Northwest; and (5) willingness to follow the company carefully and contribute valuable input to strategy and implementation decisions. Of these, only the last two are flexible.

We want to establish a mechanism for employees to acquire fair stock options that can become valuable as the company grows.

7.1 Important Assumptions

The financial plan depends on important assumptions, most of which are shown in the following table. The key underlying assumptions are:

- We assume a slow-growth economy, without major recession.

- We assume, of course, that there are no unforeseen changes in technology to make products immediately obsolete.

- We assume access to equity capital and financing sufficient to maintain our financial plan as shown in the tables.

General Assumptions

	1998	1999	2000
Short-term interest rate %	10.50%	10.50%	10.50%
Long-term interest rate %	11.00%	11.00%	11.00%

Sample Software Company

General Assumptions, cont.

	1998	1999	2000
Payment days estimator	40	40	40
Collection days estimator	75	75	75
Inventory turnover estimator	7.00	7.00	7.00
Tax rate %	25.00%	25.00%	25.00%
Expenses in cash %	10.00%	10.00%	10.00%
Sales on credit %	60.00%	60.00%	60.00%
Personnel burden %	9.75%	9.75%	9.75%

7.2 Key Financial Indicators

The chart shows changes in key financial indicators: sales, gross margin, operating expenses, collection days, and inventory turnover. The growth in sales is the most obvious change and operating expenses with sales. We believe the growing market for our products, the larger potential market, justifies the growth projections.

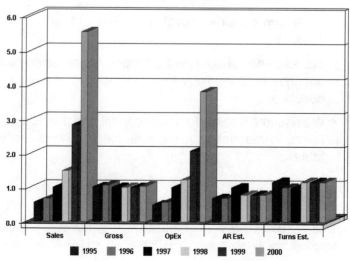

Benchmarks

Sample Software Company

We expect to maintain gross margin at about the 70% level, or close to that, without major changes.

The projections for collection days and inventory turnover show that we are already expecting improvements as our increasing sales give us greater economies of scale and greater negotiation strength with our channel partners.

7.3 Break-even Analysis

Our break-even analysis is based on our cost and price structure at present. As we grow, the fixed costs will grow in proportion to our employee numbers.

Break-even Analysis:

Monthly units break-even	520
Monthly sales break-even	$29,019
Assumptions:	
Average per-unit revenue	$55.78
Average per-unit variable cost	$7.73
Estimated monthly fixed cost	$25,000

7.4 Projected Profit and Loss

The following table shows that we expect to maintain gross margin but increase net profit margin during the next three years. The single most important factor in the improving profit margin is the economies of scale in our general and administrative expenses. These expenses should decline as a percentage of sales, from more than 15% of sales in 1998 to less than 9% in 2000.

We do not expect to decrease sales and marketing expenses as a percent of sales. The packaged software business requires heavy marketing expenses.

Sample Software Company

Break-Even Analysis

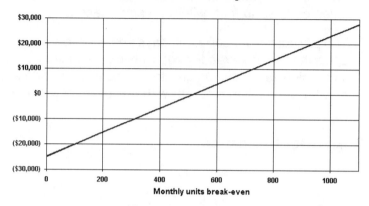

Monthly units break-even

Units break-even point = where line intersects with $0

We also intend to maintain and increase the percent of revenue spent on development. By 2000 we will be spending almost 7% of sales on product development. This is the key to our future.

The bottom line should increase from 5% to about 10% on sales by 2000.

The following table shows just the annual numbers. The detailed monthly projections for 1988 are included in the appendices.

Profit and Loss (Income Statement)

	1998	1999	2000
Sales	$1,032,920	$1,975,500	$3,852,000
Direct cost of sales	$143,051	$305,468	$564,060
Production payroll	$33,300	$62,000	$91,000
Freight	$20,547	$29,000	$33,800
Fulfillment	$20,333	$17,578	$19,064
Royalties	$103,292	$197,550	$385,200
Total cost of sales	$320,522	$611,596	$1,093,124

Sample Software Company

Profit and Loss (Income Statement), cont.

	1998	1999	2000
Gross margin	$712,398	$1,363,905	$2,758,876
Gross margin %	68.97%	69.04%	71.62%
Operating Expenses:			
Sales and Marketing Expenses			
Sales and Marketing payroll	$48,000	$53,000	$58,000
Advertising	$210,000	$400,000	$770,000
Sales commissions	$61,975	$118,530	$231,120
Graphics and collaterals	$35,000	$70,000	$140,000
Printing	$28,700	$57,000	$114,000
Public relations	$14,400	$29,000	$58,000
Research	$2,000	$4,000	$8,000
Tollfree telephone	$6,000	$12,000	$24,000
Trade shows and events	$6,000	$12,000	$24,000
Meals	$4,300	$9,000	$18,000
Travel	$12,800	$26,000	$52,000
Miscellaneous	$12,000	$24,000	$48,000
Total Sales and Marketing Expenses	$441,175	$814,530	$1,545,120
Sales and Marketing %	42.71%	41.23%	40.11%
General and Administrative Expenses			
General and Administrative payroll	$90,000	$99,000	$109,000
Payroll burden	$19,656	$25,740	$34,905
Depreciation	$1,000	$1,250	$1,563
Online services	$3,600	$4,500	$5,625
Contributions	$300	$375	$469
Dues and subscriptions	$600	$750	$938
Insurance	$6,000	$7,500	$9,375
Maintenance and repairs	$1,800	$2,250	$2,813
Office supplies	$1,200	$1,500	$1,875

Sample Software Company

Profit and Loss (Income Statement), cont.

	1998	1999	2000
Postage	$2,400	$3,000	$3,750
Professional fees	$6,000	$7,500	$9,375
Telephone	$9,000	$11,250	$14,063
Rent	$10,800	$13,500	$16,875
Other	$3,000	$3,750	$4,688
Total General and Administrative Expenses	$155,356	$181,865	$215,311
General and Administrative %	15.04%	9.21%	5.59%
Other Expenses			
Other payroll	$30,300	$50,000	$100,000
Product development	$1,200	$15,000	$100,000
Total Other Expenses	$31,500	$65,000	$200,000
Other %	3.05%	3.29%	5.19%
Total Operating Expenses	$628,031	$1,061,395	$1,960,431
Profit before interest and taxes	$84,367	$302,510	$798,445
Interest expense short-term	$1,820	$245	$245
Interest expense long-term	$0	$0	$0
Taxes incurred	$20,637	$75,566	$199,550
Net profit	$61,910	$226,698	$598,650
Net profit/sales	5.99%	11.48%	15.54%

7.5 Projected Cash Flow

The following chart is most important for illustrating our cash projections for the next 12 months. Because of our dependence on sales through channels, and the channels' tendency to pay slowly, there are wide variations that must be supported with working capital acquired through short-term credit on receivables and inventory.

Sample Software Company

Cash

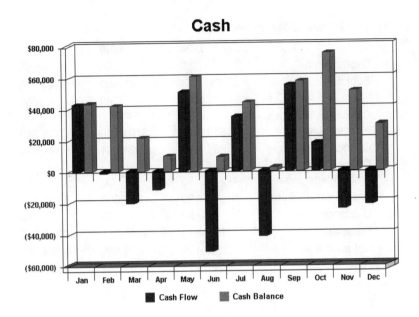

Legend: Cash Flow, Cash Balance

The table shows just the annual results, which are less significant. The key to our business plan is the monthly cash flow table, in the appendices, which also shows up as the key numbers of the following chart.

Pro-Forma Cash Flow

	1998	1999	2000
Net profit	$61,910	$226,698	$598,650
Plus:			
Depreciation	$1,000	$1,250	$1,563
Change in accounts payable	($15,689)	$20,642	$40,566
Current borrowing (repayment)	($20,000)	$0	$0
Increase (decrease) other liabilities	($9,487)	$0	$0
Long-term borrowing (repayment)	$0	$0	$0

Sample Software Company

Pro-Forma Cash Flow, cont.

	1998	1999	2000
Capital input	$0	$0	$0
Subtotal	$17,734	$248,590	$640,778
Less:	1998	1999	2000
Change in accounts receivable	($10,187)	$103,910	$206,866
Change in inventory	($1,269)	$24,841	$41,094
Change in other short-term assets	$0	$0	$0
Capital expenditure	$0	$50,000	$100,000
Dividends	$0	$0	$0
Subtotal	($11,456)	$178,751	$347,960
Net cash flow	$29,189	$69,839	$292,817
Cash balance	$29,815	$99,654	$392,472

7.6 Projected Balance Sheet

The table shows the annual balance sheet results, with a healthy projected increase in net worth. Detailed monthly projections are in the appendices.

Pro-Forma Balance Sheet

Assets

Short-term Assets	1998	1999	2000
Cash	$29,815	$99,654	$392,472
Accounts receivable	$113,870	$217,780	$424,646
Inventory	$27,354	$52,195	$93,289
Other short-term assets	$431	$431	$431
Total short-term assets	$171,469	$370,060	$910,837
Long-term Assets			
Capital assets	$35,577	$85,577	$185,577
Accumulated depreciation	$25,247	$26,497	$28,060
Total long-term assets	$10,330	$59,080	$157,518
Total assets	$181,799	$429,140	$1,068,355

Sample Software Company

Pro-Forma Balance Sheet, cont.

Liabilities and Capital

	1998	1999	2000
Accounts payable	$20,868	$41,510	$82,076
Short-term notes	$2,336	$2,336	$2,336
Other short-term liabilities	$16,040	$16,040	$16,040
Subtotal short-term liabilities	$39,243	$59,886	$100,451
Long-term liabilities	$0	$0	$0
Total liabilities	$39,243	$59,886	$100,451
Paid in capital	$76,960	$76,960	$76,960
Retained earnings	$3,686	$65,596	$292,294
Earnings	$61,910	$226,698	$598,650
Total capital	$142,556	$369,254	$967,904
Total liabilities and capital	$181,799	$429,140	$1,068,355
Net worth	$142,556	$369,254	$967,904

7.7 Business Ratios

Standard business ratios are included in the following table. The ratios show a plan for balanced, healthy growth. One of the more important indicators is the increase in working capital, which is critical to our channel sales strategy and our financial health.

The ratios for collection days and inventory turnover are different from the ones in the assumptions table, because those are used as estimators to project balance sheet items for every month, while the ratios shown in this table are calculated on an annual basis, using the same formulas used by our accountants, after the fact.

Sample Software Company

Ratio Analysis

Profitability Ratios:	1998	1999	2000	RMA
Gross margin	68.97%	69.04%	71.62%	0
Net profit margin	5.99%	11.48%	15.54%	0
Return on assets	34.05%	52.83%	56.03%	0
Return on equity	43.43%	61.39%	61.85%	0

Activity Ratios	1998	1999	2000	RMA
AR turnover	5.44	5.44	5.44	0
Collection days	70	51	51	0
Inventory turnover	11.45	15.38	15.03	0
Accts payable turnover	30.80	30.80	30.80	0
Total asset turnover	5.68	4.60	3.61	0

Debt Ratios	1998	1999	2000	RMA
Debt to net worth	0.28	0.16	0.10	0
Short-term liabilities to liabilities	1.00	1.00	1.00	0

Liquidity Ratios	1998	1999	2000	RMA
Current ratio	4.37	6.18	9.07	0
Quick ratio	3.67	5.31	8.14	0
Net working capital	$132,226	$310,174	$810,386	0
Interest coverage	46.35	1233.39	3255.41	0

Additional ratios	1998	1999	2000	RMA
Assets to sales	0.18	0.22	0.28	0
Debt/assets	22%	14%	9%	0
Current debt/total assets	22%	14%	9%	0
Acid test	0.77	1.67	3.91	0
Asset turnover	5.68	4.60	3.61	0
Sales/net worth	7.25	5.35	3.98	0
Dividend payout	$0	0.00	0.00	0

CHAPTER 19
ACME CONSULTING SAMPLE PLAN

This sample business plan has been made available to users of Business Plan Pro™ business-planning software published by Palo Alto Software. Our sample plans were developed by existing companies or new business start-ups as research instruments to determine market viability or funding availability. Names, locations, and numbers may have been changed, and substantial portions of text may have been omitted to preserve confidentiality and proprietary information.

You are welcome to use this plan as a starting point to create your own, but you do not have permission to reproduce, publish, distribute, or even copy this plan as it exists here.

Requests for reprints, academic use, and other dissemination of this sample plan should be addressed to the marketing department of Palo Alto Software.

ACME Consulting

Confidentiality Agreement

The undersigned reader acknowledges that the information provided by Acme Consulting in this business plan is confidential; therefore, reader agrees not to disclose it without the express written permission of Acme Consulting.

It is acknowledged by reader that information to be furnished in this business plan is in all respects confidential in nature, other than information which is in the public domain through other means and that any disclosure or use of same by reader, may cause serious harm or damage to Acme Consulting.

Upon request, this document is to be immediately returned to Acme Consulting.

_____   _____
Signature   Date

_____
Name (typed or printed)

This is a business plan. It does not imply an offering of securities.

ACME Consulting

1.0 Executive Summary

Acme Consulting will be formed as a consulting company specializing in the marketing of high-technology products in international markets. Its founders are former marketers of consulting services, personal computers, and market research, all in international markets. They are founding Acme to formalize the consulting services they offer.

1.1 Objectives

1. Sales of $350,000 in 1995 and $1 million by 1997
2. Gross margin higher than 80%
3. Net income more than 10% of sales by the third year

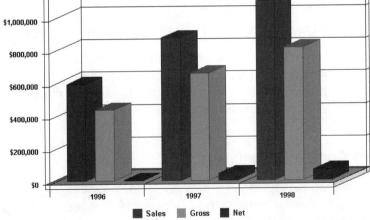

Highlights

ACME Consulting

1.2 Mission

Acme Consulting offers high-tech manufacturers a reliable, high-quality alternative to in-house resources for business development, market development, and channel development on an international scale. A true alternative to in-house resources offers a high level of practical experience, know-how, contacts, and confidentiality. Clients must know that working with Acme is a more professional, less risky way to develop new areas even than working completely in house with their own people. Acme must also be able to maintain financial balance, establishing a high value for its services and delivering an even higher value to its clients. Initial focus will be development in the European and Latin American markets, or for European clients in the U.S. market.

1.3 Keys to Success

1. Excellence in fulfilling the promise—completely confidential, reliable, trustworthy expertise and information

2. Developing visibility to generate new business leads

3. Leveraging from a single pool of expertise into multiple revenue generation opportunities: retainer consulting, project consulting, market research, and market research published reports

2.0 Company Summary

Acme Consulting is a new company providing high-level expertise in international high-tech business development, channel development, distribution strategies, and

ACME Consulting

marketing of high-tech products. It will focus initially on providing two kinds of international triangles:

- Providing U.S. clients with development for European and Latin American markets.
- Providing European clients with development for the U.S. and Latin American markets.

As the company grows it will take on people and consulting work in related markets, such as the rest of Latin America, the Far East, and similar markets. It will also look for additional leverage by taking brokerage positions and representation positions to create percentage holdings in product results.

2.1 Company Ownership

Acme Consulting will be created as a California C corporation based in Santa Clara County, owned by its principal investors and principal operators. As of this writing, it has not yet been chartered and is still considering alternatives of legal formation.

2.2 Start-up Summary

Total start-up expense (including legal costs, logo design, stationery, and related expenses) comes to $18,350. Start-up assets required include $32,000 in short-term assets (office furniture, etc.) and $25,000 in initial cash to handle the first few months of consulting operations as sales and accounts receivable play through the cash flow. The details are included in the following table.

ACME Consulting

Start-up Plan

Start-up Expenses

Legal	$1,000
Stationery, etc.	$3,000
Brochures	$5,000
Consultants	$5,000
Insurance	$350
Expensed equipment	$3,000
Other	$1,000
Total start-up expense	$18,350

Start-up Assets Needed

Cash requirements	$25,000
Other short-term assets	$7,000
Total short-term assets	$32,00
Long-term assets	$0
Total assets	$32,000
Total start-up requirements:	$50,350
Left to finance:	$0

Start-up Funding Plan

Investment

Investor 1	$20,000
Investor 2	$20,000
Other	$10,000
Total investment	$50,000

Short-term Liabilities

Unpaid expenses	$5,000
Short-term loans	$0
Interest-free short-term loans	$0

ACME Consulting

Start-up Plan, cont.

Short-term Liabilities

Subtotal short-term liabilities	$5,000
Long-term liabilities	$0
Total liabilities	$5,000
Loss at start-up	($23,000)
Total capital	$27,000
Total capital and liabilities	$32,000
Checkline	$0

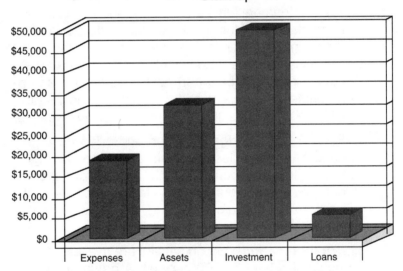

Start-up

2.3 Company Locations and Facilities

The initial office will be established in A-quality office space in the Santa Clara County "Silicon Valley" area of California, the heart of the U.S. high-tech industry.

ACME Consulting

3.0 Services

Acme offers the expertise a high-technology company needs to develop new product distribution and new market segments in new markets. This can be taken as high-level retainer consulting, market research reports, or project-based consulting.

3.1 Service Description

1. **Retainer consulting:** We represent a client company as an extension of its business development and market development functions. This begins with complete understanding of the client company's situation, objectives, and constraints. We then represent the client company, quietly and confidentially sifting through new market developments and new opportunities as appropriate to the client and representing the client in initial talks with possible allies, vendors, and channels.

2. **Project consulting:** Proposed and billed on a per-project and per-milestone basis, project consulting offers a client company a way to harness our specific qualities and use our expertise to solve specific problems, develop and/or implement plans, and develop specific information.

3. **Market research:** Group studies are available to selected clients at $5,000 per unit. A group study is a packaged and published complete study of a specific market, channel, or topic. Examples might be studies of developing consumer channels in Japan or Mexico or implications of changing margins in software.

ACME Consulting

3.2 Competitive Comparison

The competition comes in several forms:

1. The most significant competition is no consulting at all, companies choosing to perform business development, channel development, and market research in house. Their own managers do this on their own as part of their regular business functions. Our key advantage in competition with in-house development is that managers are already overloaded with responsibilities, and they don't have time for additional responsibilities in new market development or new channel development. Also, Acme can approach alliances, vendors, and channels on a confidential basis, gathering information and making initial contacts in ways that the corporate managers can't.

2. The high-level prestige management consulting: McKinsey, Bain, Arthur Andersen, Boston Consulting Group, etc. These are essentially generalists who take their name-brand management consulting into specialty areas. Their other important weakness is the management structure that has the partners selling new jobs and inexperienced associates delivering the work. We compete against them as experts in our specific fields and with the guarantee that our clients will have the top-level people doing the actual work.

3. The third general kind of competitor is the international market research company. Examples are International Data Corporation (IDC), Dataquest, and Stanford Research Institute. These companies are formidable competitors for published market research and market forums but cannot provide the kind of high-level consulting that Acme will provide.

ACME Consulting

4. The fourth kind of competition is the market-specific smaller house. Examples are Nomura Research in Japan and Select S.A. de C.V. in Mexico (now affiliated with IDC).

5. Sales representation, brokering, and deal catalysts are an ad-hoc business form that will be defined in detail by the specific nature of each individual case.

3.3 Sales Literature

The business will begin with a general corporate brochure establishing the positioning. This brochure will be developed as part of the start-up expenses.

Literature and mailings for the initial market forums will be very important.

3.4 Fulfillment

1. The key fulfillment and delivery will be provided by the principals of the business. The real core value is professional expertise, provided by a combination of experience, hard work, and education (in that order).

2. We will turn to qualified professionals for freelance backup in market research and presentation and report development, which are areas that we can afford to sub-contract without risking the core values provided to the clients.

3.5 Technology

Acme Consulting will maintain the latest Windows and Macintosh capabilities including:

ACME Consulting

1. Complete e-mail facilities on the Internet, Compuserve, America Online, and Applelink, for working with clients directly through e-mail delivery of drafts and information.

2. Complete presentation facilities for preparation and delivery of multimedia presentations on Macintosh or Windows machines, in formats including on-disk presentation, live presentation, and video presentation.

3. Complete desktop publishing facilities for delivery of regular retainer reports, project output reports, marketing materials, and market research reports.

3.6 Future Services

In the future, Acme will broaden the coverage by expanding into additional markets (e.g., all of Latin America, the Far East, Western Europe) and additional product areas (e.g., telecommunications and technology integration).

We are also studying the possibility of newsletter or electronic newsletter services and perhaps special on-topic reports.

4.0 Market Analysis Summary

Acme will be focusing on high-technology manufacturers of computer hardware and software, services, and networking, who want to sell to markets in the United States, Europe, and Latin America. These are mostly larger companies and occasionally medium-sized companies.

Our most important potential customers are executives in larger corporations. These are marketing managers,

ACME Consulting

general managers, and sales managers, sometimes charged with international focus and sometimes charged with market or even specific channel focus. They do not want to waste their time or risk their money looking for bargain information or questionable expertise. As they go into markets looking at new opportunities, they are quite sensitive to risking their company's name and reputation.

4.1 Market Segmentation

One market segment consists of large manufacturing corporations. Our most important market segment is the large manufacturer of high-technology products, such as Apple, Hewlett-Packard, IBM, Microsoft, Siemens, and Olivetti. These companies will be calling on Acme for development functions that are better spun off than managed in house, for market research, and for market forums.

A second market segment consists of medium-sized growth companies. Particularly in software, multimedia, and some related high-growth fields, Acme will offer an attractive development alternative to the company that is management constrained and unable to address opportunities in new markets and new market segments.

Market Analysis

Potential Customers	Growth	1996	1997	1998	1999	2000	CAGR
U.S. high tech	10%	5,000	5,500	6,050	6,655	7,321	10.00%
European high tech	15%	1,000	1,150	1,323	1,521	1,749	15.00%
Latin America	35%	250	338	456	616	832	35.07%
Other	2%	10,000	10,200	10,404	10,612	10,824	2.00%
Total	6.27%	16,250	17,188	18,233	19,404	20,726	6.27%

ACME Consulting

Market Analysis (Pie)

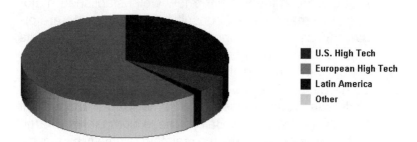

- U.S. High Tech
- European High Tech
- Latin America
- Other

4.2 Target Market Segment Strategy

As indicated by the previous table and illustration, we must focus on a few thousand well-chosen potential customers in the United States, Europe, and Latin America. These few thousand high-tech manufacturing companies are the key customers for Acme.

4.3 Service Business Analysis

The consulting "industry" is pulverized and disorganized, with thousands of smaller consulting organizations and individual consultants for every one of the few dozen well-known companies.

Consulting participants range from major international name-brand consultants to tens of thousands of individuals. One of Acme's challenges will be to establish itself as a *real* consulting company, positioned as a relatively risk-free corporate purchase.

ACME Consulting

4.3.1 Business Participants

At the highest level are the few well-established major names in management consulting. Most of these are organized as partnerships established in major markets around the world, linked together by interconnecting directors and sharing the name and corporate wisdom. Some evolved from accounting companies (e.g. Arthur Andersen, Touche Ross) and some from management consulting (McKinsey, Bain). These companies charge high rates for consulting and maintain relatively high overhead structures and fulfillment structures based on partners selling and junior associates fulfilling.

At the intermediate level are some function-specific or market-specific consultants, such as the market research firms (IDC, Dataquest) and channel development firms (ChannelCorp, Channel Strategies, ChannelMark).

Some kinds of consulting are little more than contract expertise provided by somebody who, while temporarily out of work, offers consulting services.

4.3.2 Distributing a Service

Consulting is sold and purchased mainly on a word-of-mouth basis, with relationships and previous experience being, by far, the most important factor.

The major name-brand houses have locations in major cities and major markets, and executive-level managers or partners develop new business through industry associations, business associations, chambers of commerce and industry, and so on, and in some cases social associations such as country clubs.

ACME Consulting

The medium-level houses are generally area specific or function specific and are not easily able to leverage their business through distribution.

4.3.3 Competition and Buying Patterns

The key element in purchase decisions made at the Acme client level is trust in the professional reputation and reliability of the consulting firm.

4.3.4 Main Competitors

1. High-level prestige management consulting:

Strengths: International locations managed by owner-partners with a high level of presentation and understanding of general business. Enviable reputations, which make purchase of consulting an easy decision for a manager, despite the high prices.

Weaknesses: General business knowledge doesn't substitute for the specific market, channel, and distribution expertise of Acme, focusing on high-technology markets and products only. Also, fees are extremely expensive, and work is generally done by junior-level consultants, even though it is sold by high-level partners.

2. The international market research company:

Strengths: International offices, specific market knowledge, permanent staff developing market research information on permanent basis, good relationships with potential client companies.

Weaknesses: Market numbers are not marketing, not channel development, nor market development. Although these companies compete for some of the business Acme is after, they cannot really offer the same level of business understanding at a high level.

ACME Consulting

3. Market-specific or function-specific experts:

Strengths: Expertise in market or functional areas. Acme should not try to compete with Nomura or Select in their markets with market research or with ChannelCorp in channel management.

Weaknesses: The inability to spread beyond a specific focus, or to rise above a specific focus, to provide actual management expertise, experience, and wisdom beyond the specifics.

4. Companies that do in-house research and development:

Strengths: No incremental cost except travel; also, the general work is done by the people who are entirely responsible, and planning is done by those who will implement it.

Weaknesses: Most managers are terribly overburdened already, unable to find incremental resources in time and people to apply to incremental opportunities. Also, there is a lot of additional risk in market and channel development done in house from the ground up. Finally, retainer-based antenna consultants can greatly enhance a company's reach and extend its position into conversations that might otherwise never have taken place.

5.0 Strategy and Implementation Summary

Acme will focus on three geographic markets (the United States, Europe, and Latin America) and in limited product segments (personal computers, software, networks, telecommunications, personal organizers, and technology integration products).

The target customer is usually a manager in a larger corporation and, occasionally, an owner or president of a medium-sized corporation in a high-growth period.

ACME Consulting

5.1 Pricing Strategy

Acme Consulting will be priced at the upper edge of what the market will bear, competing with the name-brand consultants. The pricing fits with the general positioning of Acme as providing high-level expertise.

Consulting should be based on $5,000 per day for project consulting, $2,000 per day for market research, and $10,000 per month and up for retainer consulting. Market research reports should be priced at $5,000 per report, which will, of course, require that reports be well planned, focused on important topics, and well presented.

5.2 Sales Strategy

The sales forecast monthly summary is included in the appendix. The annual sales projections are included here in the following table.

Sales Forecast

Sales	1996	1997	1998
Retainer consulting	$200,000	$350,000	$425,000
Project consulting	$270,000	$325,000	$350,000
Market research	$122,000	$150,000	$200,000
Strategic reports	$0	$50,000	$125,000
Other	$0	$0	$0
Total sales	$592,000	$875,000	$1,100,000

Direct Cost of Sales	1996	1997	1998
Retainer consulting	$30,000	$38,000	$48,000
Project consulting	$45,000	$56,000	$70,000
Market research	$84,000	$105,000	$131,000
Strategic reports	$0	$20,000	$40,000
Other	$0	$0	$0
Subtotal cost of sales	$159,000	$219,000	$289,000

ACME Consulting

Sales by Year

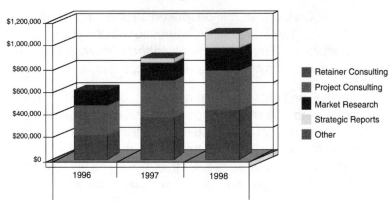

5.3 Strategic Alliances

At this writing, strategic alliances with Smith and Jones are possibilities, given the content of existing discussions. Given the background of prospective partners, we might also be talking to European companies, including Siemens and Olivetti, and to U.S. companies related to Apple Computer. In Latin America we would be looking at the key local high-technology vendors, beginning with Printaform.

5.4 Milestones

Our detailed milestones are shown in the following table and chart. The related budgets are included with the expenses shown in the projected Profit and Loss statement, which is in the financial analysis that comes in Chapter 7 of this plan.

ACME Consulting

Milestones

Milestone	Plan Start Date	End Date	Budget	Manager	Department
Business plan	10/1/95	11/19/95	$5,000	5000	Development
Logo design	1/1/96	2/1/96	$2,000	2000	Marketing
Retainer contracts	2/1/96	12/31/96	$10,000	HM	Sales
Stationery	3/1/96	4/15/96	$500	JD	G&A
Brochures	3/1/96	4/15/96	$2,500	TAJ	Marketing
Financial backing presentations	4/1/96	9/15/96	$10,000	HM	Development
Initial mailing	6/1/96	7/1/96	$5,000	HM	Sales
Office location	1/15/96	2/9/96	$5,000	JD	G&A
Office equipment	1/15/96	2/19/96	$12,500	JD	G&A
Other	1/1/96	12/31/96	$10,000	ABC	Department
Totals			$62,500		

Milestones

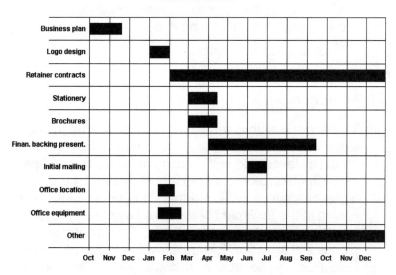

ACME Consulting

6.0 Management Summary

The initial management team depends on the founders themselves, with little backup. As we grow, we will take on additional consulting help, plus graphic/editorial, sales, and marketing.

6.1 Organizational Structure

Acme should be managed by working partners, in a structure taken mainly from Smith Partners. In the beginning, we assume 3–5 partners:

- Ralph Sampson
- At least one, probably two, partners from Smith and Jones
- One strong European partner, based in Paris
- The organization must be quite flat in the beginning, with each of the founders responsible for his or her own work and management
- One other strong partner

6.2 Management Team

The Acme business requires a high level of international experience and expertise, which means that it will not be easily leveraged in the common consulting company mode in which partners run the business and make sales, while associates fulfill. Partners will necessarily be involved in the fulfillment of the core business proposition, providing expertise to the clients. The initial personnel plan is still tentative. It should involve 3–5 partners, 1–3 consultants, one strong editorial/graphic person with

ACME Consulting

good staff support, one strong marketing person, an office manager, and a secretary. Later, we will add more partners, consultants, and sales staff. Founders' résumés are included as an attachment to this plan.

6.3 Personnel Plan

The detailed monthly personnel plan for the first year is included in the appendix. The annual personnel estimates are included here.

Personnel Plan

Personnel	1996	1997	1998
Partners	$144,000	$175,000	$200,000
Consultants	$0	$50,000	$63,000
Editorial/graphic	$18,000	$22,000	$26,000
VP Marketing	$20,000	$50,000	$55,000
Sales people	$0	$30,000	$33,000
Office manager	$7,500	$30,000	$33,000
Secretarial	$5,250	$20,000	$22,000
Other	$0	$0	$0
Other	$0	$0	$0
Total payroll	$194,750	$377,000	$432,000
Total headcount	7	14	20
Payroll burden	$27,265	$52,780	$60,480
Total payroll expenditures	$222,015	$429,780	$492,480

ACME Consulting

7.0 Financial Plan

Our financial plan is based on conservative estimates and assumptions. We will need to plan on initial investment to make the financials work.

7.1 Important Assumptions

The following table summarizes key financial assumptions, including 45-day average collection days, sales entirely on invoice basis, expenses mainly on net 30 basis, 35 days on average for payment of invoices, and present-day interest rates.

General Assumptions

	1996	1997	1998
Short-term interest rate %	8.00%	8.00%	8.00%
Long-term interest rate %	10.00%	10.00%	10.00%
Payment days estimator	35	35	35
Collection days estimator	45	45	45
Tax rate %	25.00%	25.00%	25.00%
Expenses in cash %	25.00%	25.00%	25.00%
Sales on credit %	100.00%	100.00%	100.00%
Personnel burden %	14.00%	14.00%	14.00%

7.2 Key Financial Indicators

The following benchmark chart indicates our key financial indicators for the first three years. We foresee major growth in sales and operating expenses, and a bump in our collection days as we spread the business during expansion.

ACME Consulting

Benchmarks

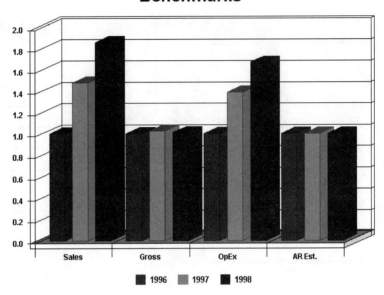

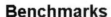

7.3 Break-even Analysis

The following table summarizes the break-even analysis, including monthly units and sales break-even points.

Break-even Analysis

Monthly units break-even	12,500
Monthly sales break-even	$12,500

Assumptions:	
Average per-unit revenue	$1.00
Average per-unit variable cost	$0.20
Estimated monthly fixed cost	$10,000

ACME Consulting

Break-Even Analysis

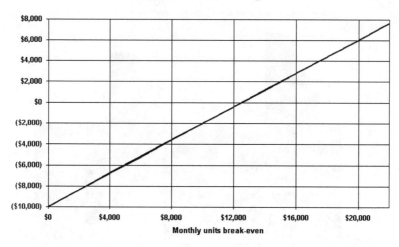

Monthly units break-even

Units break-even point = where line intersects with $0

7.4 Projected Profit and Loss

The detailed monthly pro-forma income statement for the first year is included in the appendix. The annual estimates are included here.

Profit and Loss (Income Statement)

	1996	1997	1998
Sales	$592,000	$875,000	$1,100,000
Direct cost of sales	$159,000	$219,000	$289,000
Other	$0	$0	$0
Total cost of sales	$159,000	$219,000	$289,000
Gross margin	$433,000	$656,000	$811,000
Gross margin %	73.14%	74.97%	73.73%

ACME Consulting

Profit and Loss (Income Statement), cont.

	1996	1997	1998
Operating expenses:			
Advertising/promotion	$36,000	$40,000	$44,000
Public relations	$30,000	$30,000	$33,000
Travel	$90,000	$60,000	$110,000
Miscellaneous	$6,000	$7,000	$8,000
Travel	$0	$0	$0
Payroll expense	$194,750	$377,000	$432,000
Payroll burden	$27,265	$52,780	$60,480
Depreciation	$3,600	$0	$0
Leased equipment	$18,000	$7,000	$7,000
Utilities	$0	$12,000	$12,000
Insurance	$0	$2,000	$2,000
Rent	$0	$0	$0
Other	$0	$0	$0
Contract/consultants	$0	$0	$0
Total operating expenses	$423,615	$587,780	$708,480
Profit before interest and taxes	$9,385	$68,220	$102,520
Interest expense, short-term	$1,800	$6,400	$10,400
Interest expense, long-term	$5,000	$5,000	$5,000
Taxes incurred	$646	$14,205	$21,780
Net profit	$1,939	$42,615	$65,340
Net profit/sales	0.33%	4.87%	5.94%

7.5 Projected Cash Flow

Cash flow projections are critical to our success. The monthly cash flow is shown in the illustration, with one

ACME Consulting

bar representing the cash flow per month and the other representing the monthly balance. The annual cash flow figures are included in the following table. Detailed monthly numbers may be found in the appendix.

Pro-Forma Cash Flow

	1996	1997	1998
Net profit	$1,939	$42,615	$65,340
Plus:			
Depreciation	$3,600	$0	$0
Change in accounts payable	$23,735	$2,698	$10,897
Current borrowing (repayment)	$30,000	$100,000	$0
Increase (decrease) other liabilities	$0	$0	$0
Long-term borrowing (repayment)	$50,000	$0	$0
Capital input	$0	$0	$0
Subtotal	$105,674	$145,313	$76,237
Less:	1996	1997	1998
Change in accounts receivable	$100,000	$47,804	$38,007
Change in other ST assets	$0	$0	$0
Capital expenditure	$0	$0	$0
Dividends	$0	$0	$0
Subtotal	$100,000	$47,804	$38,007
Net cash flow	$5,674	$97,509	$38,231
Cash balance	$30,674	$128,183	$166,414

ACME Consulting

Cash

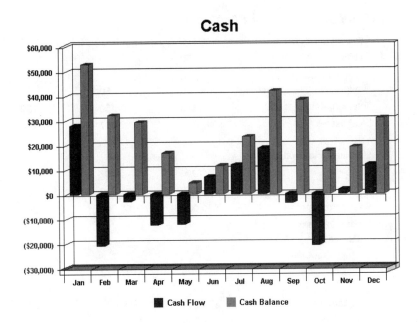

Cash Flow ■ Cash Balance

7.6 Projected Balance Sheet

The balance sheet shows healthy growth of net worth, and strong financial position. The monthly estimates are included in the appendix.

Pro-Forma Balance Sheet

Assets

Short-term assets	1996	1997	1998
Cash	$30,674	$128,183	$166,414
Accounts receivable	$100,000	$147,804	$185,811
Other short-term assets	$7,000	$7,000	$7,000
Total short-term assets	$137,674	$282,987	$359,224

ACME Consulting

Pro Forma Balance Sheet, cont.

Long-term assets	1996	1997	1998
Capital assets	$0	$0	$0
Accumulated depreciation	$0	$0	$0
Total long-term assets	$0	$0	$0
Total assets	$137,674	$282,987	$359,224

Liabilities and capital			
	1996	1997	1998
Accounts payable	$28,735	$31,433	$42,331
Short-term notes	$30,000	$130,000	$130,000
Other short-term liabilities	$0	$0	$0
Subtotal short-term liabilities	$58,735	$161,433	$172,331
Long-term liabilities	$50,000	$50,000	$50,000
Total liabilities	$108,735	$211,433	$222,331
Paid-in capital	$50,000	$50,000	$50,000
Retained earnings	($23,000)	($21,061)	$21,554
Earnings	$1,939	$42,615	$65,340
Total capital	$28,939	$71,554	$136,894
Total liabilities and capital	$137,674	$282,987	$359,224
Net worth	$28,939	$71,554	$136,894

7.7 Business Ratios

The following table shows the projected business ratios. We expect to maintain healthy ratios for profitability, risk, and return.

ACME Consulting

Ratio Analysis

Profitability Ratios	1996	1997	1998	RMA
Gross margin	73.14%	74.97%	73.73%	0
Net profit margin	0.33%	4.87%	5.94%	0
Return on assets	1.41%	15.06%	18.19%	0
Return on equity	6.70%	59.56%	47.73%	0

Activity Ratios	1996	1997	1998	RMA
AR turnover	5.92	5.92	5.92	0
Collection days	31	52	55	0
Inventory turnover	0.00	0.00	0.00	0
Accounts payable turnover	9.61	9.61	9.61	0
Total asset turnover	4.30	3.09	3.06	0

Debt Ratios	1996	1997	1998	RMA
Debt to net worth	3.76	2.95	1.62	0
Short-term liabilities to liabilities	0.54	0.76	0.78	0

Liquidity Ratios	1996	1997	1998	RMA
Current ratio	2.34	1.75	2.08	0
Quick ratio	2.34	1.75	2.08	0
Net working capital	$78,939	$121,554	$186,894	0
Interest coverage	1.38	5.98	6.66	0

Additional ratios	1996	1997	1998	RMA
Assets to sales	0.23	0.32	0.33	0
Debt/assets	79%	75%	62%	0
Current debt/total assets	43%	57%	48%	0
Acid rest	0.64	0.84	1.01	0
Asset turnover	4.30	3.09	3.06	0
Sales/net worth	20.46	12.23	8.04	0
Dividend payout	$0	0.00	0.00	0

BUSINESS PLANNING PROJECT CHECKLIST

Company Name: _____ By inits. __ Date: __/__/__

I. Pre-meeting call.   Date: __/__/____

a. Establish personnel to attend meeting and carry out tasks

Primary contact:

Name:

Title:

Phone:

Area of responsibility:

Other contacts:

Name:	*Name:*
Title:	*Title:*
Phone:	*Phone:*
Area of responsibility:	*Area of responsibility:*
Name:	*Name:*
Title:	*Title:*
Phone:	*Phone:*
Area of responsibility:	*Area of responsibility:*

b. Meeting room, PC, display unit

c. Purchase Business Plan Pro

II. Initial Meeting.   Date: __/__/____

a. Review purpose for meeting

b. Introductions

c. Review steps in process

d. Assignment of responsibilities

   e. Begin training in BPP
      - Initial Assessment
      - Describe Your Company
      - Company History
      - Define the Market
      - Sell Your Team
      - Forecast Your Sales
      - The Bottom Line
      - Cash Plan
      - Finish the Financials
      - Executive Summary

   Steps to be accomplished by: __/__/____

   Draft:

   _____

   _____

   _____

III. Second Meeting.   Date:__/__/__

   a. BPP Training for primary operators

   Steps to be accomplished by date: __/__/____

   _____

   _____

   _____

IV. Third Meeting.   Date:__/__/____

   a. Review drafts

   b. Continued BPP training

   Steps to be accomplished by date: __/__/____

   Draft:

   _____

   _____

   _____

Refine:

_____

_____

_____

V. Fourth Meeting.   Date: __/__/____

a. Review drafts

b. Continued BPP training

Steps to be accomplished by date: __/__/____

Draft:

_____

_____

_____

Refine:

_____

_____

_____

VI. Final Meeting.   Date: __/__/____

a. Review materials

b. Establish time for annual follow up

c. Sign off for "end of project"

We have been pleased to assist your firm with the development of a Business Plan using Business Plan Pro software. At this point, the final phase of this initial project is complete. However, we will look forward to working with you on additional updates and adjustments to this plans.

Plan project completed __/__/__ Noted by _____
<*authorized signature*>

SAMPLE ENGAGEMENT LETTER

<Date>

<Client Name>

<Address>

Dear *<Client Name>*:

It was a pleasure meeting with you to discuss assisting your firm with the business planning advice and technology consulting to satisfy your business objectives. Our proposal is as follows:

Business Plan Pro Installation, Training and Support

Installation, training and support assistance are available at our standard consulting rate, which is currently $*<Rate>*/ hour during normal business hours. Because of the variability in requirements from installation to installation, training and on-site support is billed on an as-needed basis.

Suggested Project Schedule

Project Schedule:

Task List	<Time>
Plan for install	<ASAP>
Equipment Needs	_____
	_____
	_____
	_____
Initial Meeting	<Date 1>
Conference room installation	<Date 2>
Install software on one computer	<Date 3>
Conference room initial meeting	<Date 4 Initial training>
Meetings 2	<Final at 1 week intervals>

Terms and Conditions

Training and support are available at our customary consulting rate, currently $<Rate>/hour during normal business hours. For prepaid agreements of $<Amount> or more, you will receive a discounted rate of $<Discount Rate>/hour during normal business hours, and no-fee phone support from <Support Group> both for a period of 90 days from the original installation or prepaid agreement. Travel and out-of-pocket expenses are extra cost items. This quote is good for sixty days.

You will be billed for actual hours spent at our agreed-upon rate. We will meet with you in advance to discuss alternatives if it looks like actual hours will significantly exceed estimates. Availability of your personnel to actively participate in the efforts as designed above directly affect the level of assistance we will be able to provide and, consequently, the level of our professional fees. Billings are due when rendered.

This engagement is limited to management consulting services and, as such, is not designed to detect errors or irregularities in your accounting system; however, if we become aware of any, we will contact you.

Thank you for your time and letting <Contact Person> assist you in this important project. If you wish to proceed with this proposal, please sign and return a copy of this agreement.

Project agreed to by:

_____

      <Firm name>

Very truly yours,

_____

      <CPA>

PART 2
GUIDE TO BUSINESS PLAN
PRO SOFTWARE VERSION 4.0

PART 2
GUIDE TO BUSINESS PLAN
PRO SOFTWARE VERSION 4.0

Welcome! This section contains instructions on how to install Business Plan Pro 4.0, with explanations and examples on the features in the program, and how to access those features. Business Plan Pro 4.0, the latest and best version on Business Plan pro, is included with this book.

- Chapter 1 guides you through the installation, registration, and how to download updates from our web site.

- Chapter 2 describes how to start *Business Plan Pro*, and the options available from its Welcome screen.

- Chapter 3 explains how to start a new business plan using the Plan Wizard, the Text, Table, and Chart mode screens, and the on-screen help options.

In addition, the program provides on-screen help (F1), help on the tables and mathematical functions (F3), and built-in Wizards. The combination of written instructions and on-screen assistance provides you with more than one method of learning from the software.

NEW FEATURES IN BUSINESS PLAN PRO 4.0

Publish to LivePlan.com

Please review the special insert for instructions on how to use **Publish to LivePlan.com,** our exciting new Internet option! This secure, password-protected website, combined with *Business Plan Pro,* lets you work on your business plan from any computer with Internet access. When the plan is finished, you can selectively make it available for viewing by colleagues, lenders, or anyone else you choose. Publishing to LivePlan.com gives you a full-color presentation right at your fingertips!

Plan Manager

The Plan Manager screen provides easy access to the key resources of *Business Plan Pro,* such as the **Plan Wizard, Print your Plan,** and **Publish to LivePlan.com.** It also includes direct links to our website resources, such as **Ask the Experts, Ask the Authors,** and **Technical Support.**

Improved Plan Outline and Task Manager Screens

The **Plan Outline** screen shows the entire text outline and also lists where tables and charts are linked to a topic for printing. You can see, at a glance, the topic order and move from topic to topic.

The **Task Manager** takes you step by step through the recommended sequence in writing your plan. You can also track your progress by using the status column to mark a step as **skip, in progress,** or **completed.**

Thesaurus

In addition to the spell check, *Business Plan Pro* now provides a Thesaurus.

Enhanced Print Preview Screen

Now the Preview screen lets you view two pages at a time, side by side, and the **Go To Page** button lets you jump to a specific page to view.

Forecaster

The Forecaster provides a visual picture of your 12-month forecast. The chart results can then be adjusted by dragging the lines up and down with your mouse. Once your adjusted forecast is satisfactory, you can apply the revised values back into the active table row.

New Milestones Chart

Now you can see your milestones table in chart format.

Custom Header/Footer

Customize the appearance and location of your header and footer text for printing. Include date, time, and page number codes, or write your own text.

Enhanced Paste for Table Formulas

Copy a cell's contents from a Microsoft Excel file into *Business Plan Pro* and vice-versa. You can copy/paste formulas, formats, values, or a combination.

Additional Export Options

In addition to the export to rich text format (.rtf) option, you now have two more export formats to choose from:

- Export to .DOC format

  You can export your business plan direct as a Microsoft Word™ file (.doc) and preserve all of its original formatting.

- Export to HTML

  Hypertext Markup Language (html) is a system for marking a document so it can be published on the World Wide Web. This option will create separate html pages for each page of your plan.

- Five-Year Plan for Tables

  For those who want to plan farther into the future than a standard three-year forecast, the Plan Wizard lets you include additional yearly columns in your tables to create a five-year forecast.

- Tables (Fit-to-Page)

  The Fit-to-Page feature will adjust to print a large table, like the Balance Sheet, to a single page.

- Table Undo

  This feature lets you reverse the last action performed in table mode.

- ZOOM

  This new function gives you a better view of your text on the screen, without having to increase the actual font size.

- Notes Tab

  The Notes tab gives you a place for reminders, etc. that will *not* print as part of your plan but can be printed separately.

CONTENTS

Chapter 1: Installation

This chapter describes how to install Business Plan Pro, your registration options, and how to obtain product updates from our Internet website.

Requirements

Complete Setup

Custom Setup

Start the Program

Personalize Your Software

Registration

Web Update

Technical Support

Chapter 2: Start-Up Options

This chapter explains the starting options available from the Welcome screen which displays each time you start Business Plan Pro.

The Welcome Screen

Start a Plan

Continue your Last Plan

Open a Plan

Open a Sample Plan

Create a Business Plan File from a Sample Plan

Chapter 3: Starting a New Plan

This chapter explains how to start a new business plan (using the Plan Wizard), the text, table, and chart modes, and the additional help options.

Plan Wizard

Saving New Plan to Disk

Edit Plan Wizard

Plan Manager

Website Resources

Program Resources
Tips
Text Mode
Plan Outline
Task Manager
Instructions Tab
Example Tab
Formatting Tips Tab
Text Manager Tab
Notes Tab
Table Mode
Instructions Tab
Example Tab
Notes Tab
Table Help Tab
Table Manager Tab
Chart Mode
Chart Wizard
Chart Designer
Web Resources and Additional Help

CHAPTER 1
SOFTWARE INSTALLATION

This chapter describes how to install *Business Plan Pro*, your registration options, and how to obtain product updates from the Palo Alto Internet web site.

REQUIREMENTS

To use Business Plan Pro, you'll need:

- A personal computer that runs either Microsoft Windows 95/98/2000™ or Windows NT4SP3™.
- Operating System minimum requirements for RAM.
- 20MB of available hard disk storage space (minimum), or 100MB for the Complete installation, including accessory files (see page 6 for more information on the accessory files).
- 256-color VGA monitor; SVGA recommended.
- Any printer supported by Windows 95/98/2000/NT™.
- Internet access for all Internet features.
- 28,000 bps or higher baud modem for Internet features.
- Sound card for audio help features (optional).

Note: You must run the *Setup* program to install *Business Plan Pro* on to your computer. You cannot install *Business Plan Pro* on a hard disk that doesn't have enough space to expand the compressed files from the CD-ROM.

INSTALLATION

1. Click the **Start** button.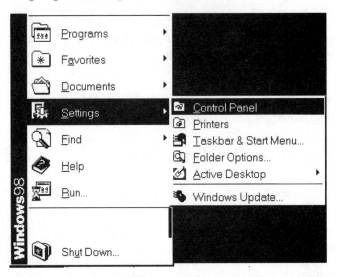

2. Highlight **Settings > Control Panel.**

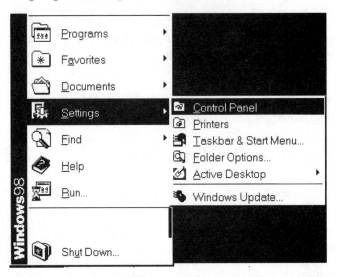

If your CD-ROM drive has an auto-start feature, skip to Step 6 of the installation procedures.

3. Double click on the **Add/Remove Programs** icon in the Control Panel window.

4. The **Add/Remove Programs Properties** dialog box will display:

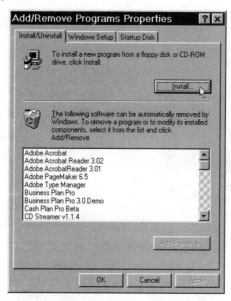

Click on the ▓ Install... ▓ button.

5. The **Install Program from Floppy Disk or CD-ROM** dialog box will display. Insert the CD into the CD-ROM drive.

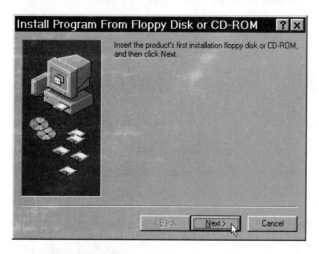

Click the ▓ Next > ▓ button.

6. The *Business Plan Pro* **Welcome** Setup screen will display:

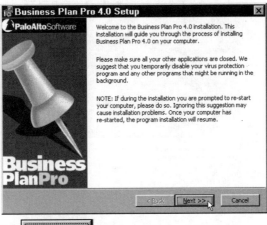

Click the [**Next >**] button.

Special Note: Depending on your system and version of Windows, you may see additional screens prior to this one. Once the other files have been copied, the program installation will continue.

7. The **Electronic License Agreement** screen will display:

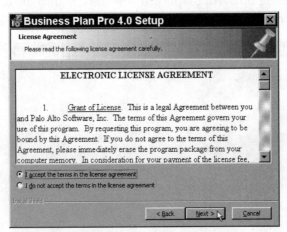

- Please read this agreement carefully!

- If you accept, click the [**Next >**] button.

8. The **Destination Folder** screen will prompt you for the directory in which to install *Business Plan Pro*:

Click **Change...** button to install to another directory

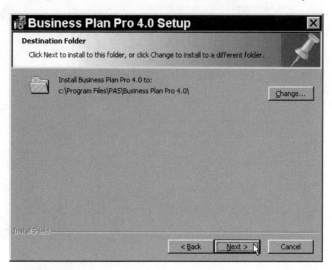

Click the [**Next >**] button to continue.

- The default installation is the **Complete Setup,** which includes the full program and all accessory files. Accessory files are separate from the program files. They include the 30 sample plans, audio files for row-by-row table help, and electronic documentation.

- The **Custom Setup** lets you select which of the accessory files to install. Since accessory files are not required in order to run *Business Plan Pro*, you have the option in the **Custom** setup to either install accessory files to your hard drive or access them from the CD.

9. The **Setup Type** screen will display:

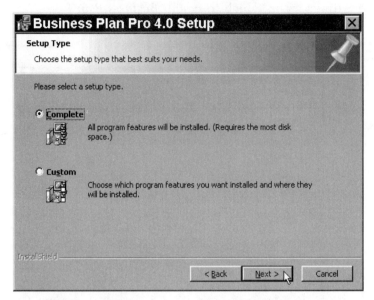

Select your setup option and click the ⎡ Next > ⎤ button.

COMPLETE SETUP

The **Complete Setup** copies the full program and all of the accessory files to your destination folder:

* Audio help files (row-by-row explanations for all tables).

Note: You need approximately 50MB or hard disk space to store the audio files. It is not required to install these files in order to use them. You can access the audio files directly be placing the Business Plan Pro CD-ROM in to your drive whenever you use the program.

---

* Sample Plans (30).
* Electronic Documentation. Portable Document Format (PDF) file for this *Getting Started* manual.

CUSTOM SETUP

The **Custom Setup** copies the full program and lets you choose whether to install the accessory files to your hard drive or access them from the CD-ROM. The **Custom Setup** dialog screen will display:

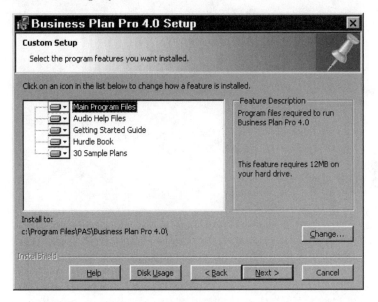

- Highlight the accessory.
- A special pull-down menu will display that lets you choose to install to your local hard drive or run from the CD:

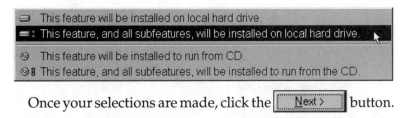

Once your selections are made, click the [Next >] button.

Note: If you make no selecctions from this screen, the default Custom Setup will install all accessory files to your hard drive.

10. The **Ready to Install the Program** screen will now display:

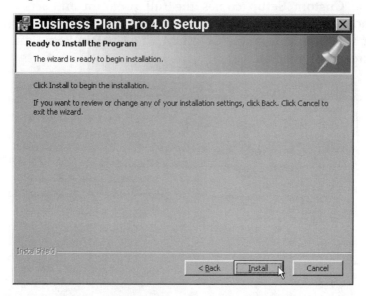

Click the 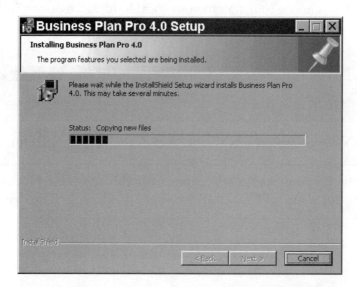 button to begin.

11. The installation process will take a few minutes, depending on which setup you chose. A status screen will display:

12. Once the files are copied, the **following screen** will display:

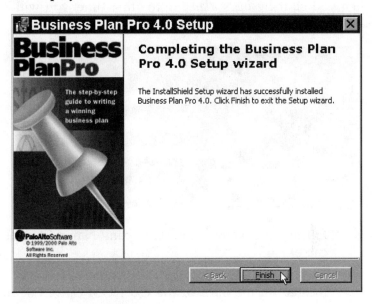

Click the | Finish | button.

This completes the program installation.

START THE PROGRAM

1. Click the **Start** button. |Start|

2. Choose **Programs>Palo Alto Software>Business Plan Pro.**

PERSONALIZE YOUR SOFTWARE

When you start *Business Plan Pro* the first time, you will be asked to personalize your software:

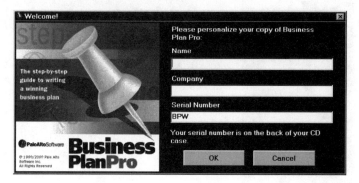

- Fill in your Name and a Company Name (if applicable).

- Type in the serial number (**The serial number is located on the back of the CD-ROM case). Use no spaces when typing; type the number 0, not the letter O.**

- Click the **OK** button to continue.

Note: Once you have completed this step, your serial number and name will display from within *Business Plan Pro.* You can view this information from the **Help** menu, **About** *Business Plan Pro.*

REGISTRATION

Please register your software. You can register from our website or use the registration card included in the program box. The benefits of registration include:

- Notification of software updates.
- Access to special offers.
- Free technical support.

On-Line Registration

Once the installation is completed, you're given the option to register on-line from our website, **www.paloaltosoftware.com.**

- The "required" fields must be completed in order for your registration to be processed.

Click the **Submit** button at the bottom of the screen.

Note: The on-line registration screens can also be accessed at any time from the Help menu.

WEB UPDATE

Periodically, we create updates to our program's current version. The Update file may contain corrections to menu text or a programming change. This update needs to be copied into your installed *Business Plan Pro* directory in order for these corrections to take affect. Updates are free to all registered users.

We have created a **Web Update** function to make this a simple and automated process. The first time you start *Business Plan Pro* (and each month thereafter), the program will ask if you want to download the update file.

Note: This option can also be accessed at any time from the Help menu, **Update Product Now.** If you are unable to download updates, please contact our Technical Support department (see page 434).

The **Web Update** screen will display:

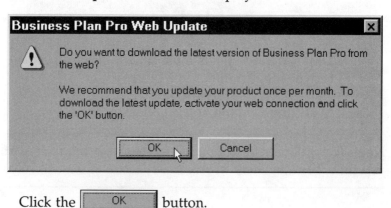

Click the [OK] button.

Note: An Update is different from an Upgrade. Updates deal with optimizing the current version. An upgrade is a new version of the program. For example, *Business Plan Pro 4.0* is an upgrade of *Business Plan Pro 3.0*.

The version number of your copy of *Business Plan Pro* will be compared to the latest update:

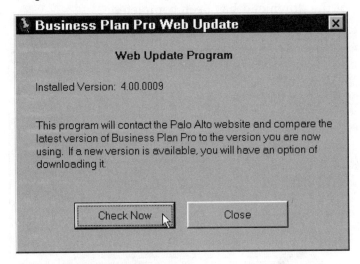

Click the [Check Now] button to continue.

If there is a newer update file, a comparison screen will display:

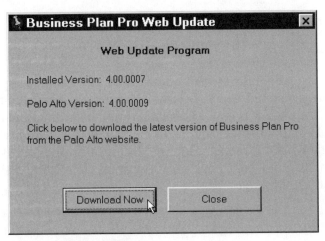

Click the [Download Now] button.

The update files will be copied to your *Business Plan Pro* directory. A **Setup** screen will display showing what percentage of the download has been completed:

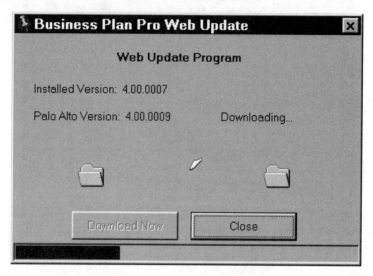

Once the Update is finished, *Business Plan Pro* will re-open to its **Welcome Screen.**

TECHNICAL SUPPORT

We make every effort to provide prompt, professional support for our registered users. Telephone support is available from 8:30 a.m. to 4:30 p.m. (U.S. Pacific time) on normal business days. E-mail messages and faxes are usually answered within a single working day. Our Internet technical support is always available. Answers to our most common technical questions can be found at:

http://www.paloaltosoftware.com/support

Note: The **Plan Manager** screen and the **Resources** menu provide a direct link to the Technical Support database as well as our other website resources.

Telephone Number: 1-541-683-6162

Please be at your computer when you call, have your system on and be ready to work with the software, and have your serial number available.

Fax Number: 1-541-683-6250

Please make sure your fax number is plainly visible on your fax to us. Unless you specify some other fax number, we will send our response to the fax number that sent the original message.

E-Mail Addresses:

Internet: **help@paloaltosoftware.com**

America On-line: **Pasware**

SUPPORT POLICIES AND PHILOSOPHY

Our product support offers registered users professional answers, to the best of our ability, to questions regarding the installation, use, and normal operation of our software. Support focuses mainly on operating the software, such as and including installation, opening, saving, and printing. Support does not deal with the contents of a business plan.

CHAPTER 2
START-UP OPTIONS

This chapter explains the starting options available from the
Welcome screen which displays each time you start *Business
Plan Pro*.

THE WELCOME SCREEN

Choose from one of the four starting options on the Welcome
screen to begin.

Start a Plan

This option walks you through the steps to create a new plan file. (Chapter 3, Start a New Plan, provides more information on the Plan Wizard screens and the different work modes.)

Continue your Last Plan

This option will automatically re-open the last plan file you saved.

Open a Plan

This option lets you open one of your previously saved plan files.

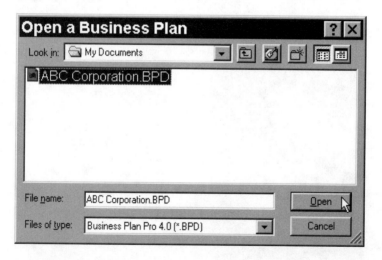

1. Highlight the file name.
2. Click the [Open] button.

Open a Sample Plan

This option lets you view one of the sample plans provided as part of your installation.

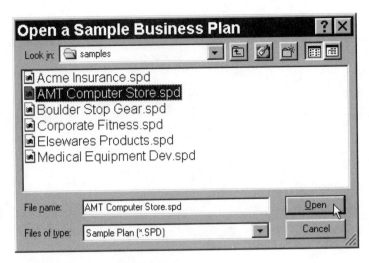

1. Highlight the file name.
2. Click the [Open] button.

Sample plans can be viewed and printed, but no changes will be saved. See the following section on how to convert a sample plan into a standard business plan file.

Create a Business Plan File from a Sample Plan

Sample plans can be saved as a standard business plan file, then modified to include your specific information.

1. Open the sample plan (as described above).
2. From the **File** menu, choose **Save As.**
3. Type the file name you want to save to.
4. Click the [Save] button.

The new file name will have the extension .BPD attached. Text, tables, and charts can now be modified like any other plan file.

Note: You may want to modify the original plan settings to better suit your needs. See **Edit Plan Wizard** in Chapter 3 (page 477) for more information.

CHAPTER 3
STARTING A NEW PLAN

This chapter explains how to start a new business plan (using the **Plan Wizard),** the text, table, and chart modes, and the additional help options.

Choose **Start a Plan** from the **Welcome** screen. Or, if you have already started the program, choose the **File** menu, **New Plan** command.

WELCOME SCREEN

FILE MENU

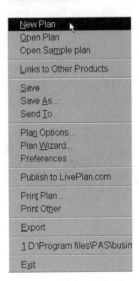

PLAN WIZARD

Business Plan Pro needs to know certain information from you in order to customize the text outline and tables you will be using. The **Plan Wizard** was created to make this an easy, step-by-step process.

The **Plan Wizard** automatically opens when you create a new business plan. The **Introduction** screen will display:

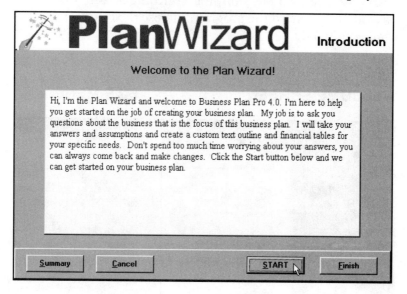

Click the **START** button to begin. A series of screens will ask questions about your business.

Move between the screens by using the following buttons:

Click the **Next >>** button to move to the next screen.

Click the **<< Back** button to return to the previous screen.

- Select the answers to each step that best describe your business.

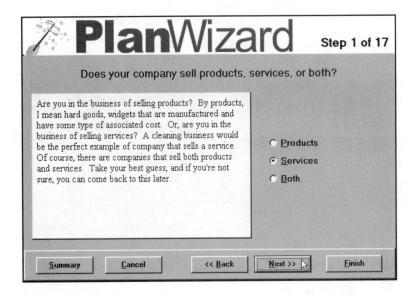

The final step asks for the title of your plan. This can be company name, project title, etc. The plan name will display at the top of each printed page.

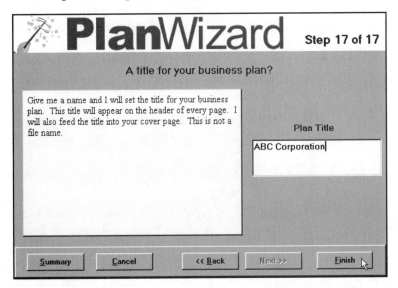

Once the **Plan Wizard** is finished, you are ready to save your plan to disk.

SAVING A NEW PLAN TO DISK

The **Save Business Plan As** dialog box automatically displays after the **Plan Wizard** questions have been completed.

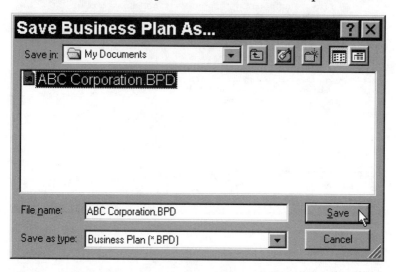

The title of your plan will automatically be entered as the file name to save to. Or, you can type in a different file name. This file name is for storage to your hard drive.

- File names may contain letters, numbers, and other standard file-naming characters. Spaces between words are accepted.

- The software automatically attaches a period and extension to your file name (**.BPD**).

Click the [Save] button.

You are now ready to begin working on your business plan.

EDIT PLAN WIZARD

You can go back to the **Plan Wizard** later and change any of your answers.

1. From the **File** menu, choose **Plan Wizard.**
2. The **Summary** screen will display:

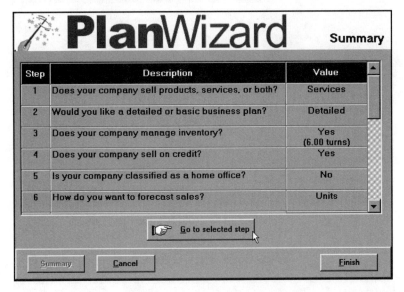

Note: The Summary screen shows only the first plan questions. Use the scroll bar to view additional questions.

3. Click the 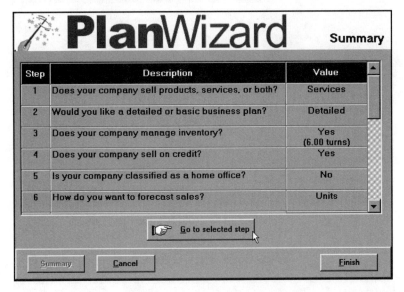 button to re-open the question window.

4. Click the **Finish** button when all changes have been made.

PLAN MANAGER

The Plan Manager links the key resources of *Business Plan Pro*.

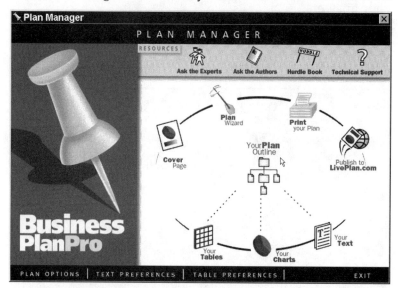

WEBSITE RESOURCES

These resources are located on our website. If you have Internet access, simply click on the icon to connect to the specific resource address.

Ask the Experts—More than 500 answers to questions about business planning. These questions and answers are posted at:

http://www.paloaltosoftware.com/resources/index.cfm

Ask the Authors—Over 400 answers to questions about *Business Plan Pro*. These questions and answers are posted at:

http://www.paloaltosoftware.com/askauthors/index.cfm

Hurdle Book—This is the on-line web version. The address is:

http://www.bizplans.com

Technical Support—This link connects you to common technical questions and answers. The address is:

http://www.palo-alto.com/support/serialcheck.cfm

PROGRAM RESOURCES

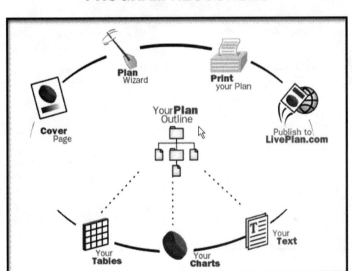

Your Plan Outline—This is your complete topic outline.

Cover Page—Creates a cover page for your plan.

Plan Wizard—Re-opens the Plan Wizard screens to review and edit.

Print Your Plan—Prints the full plan or selected topics.

LivePlan.com—Links your plan to a secure website!

Your Tables—Opens Tables Mode, where you work on your financials.

Your Charts—Opens Chart Mode, for graphics of your numbers.

Your Text—Opens Text Mode, where you type your topics.

TIPS

Each time you start a new plan (or open an existing plan), a **Tips** dialog box will automatically display:

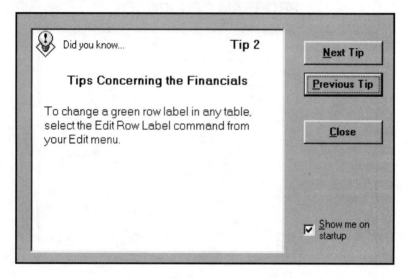

Click the [**Next Tip**] button to read additional tips.

Click the [**Previous Tip**] button to re-display a tip.

Click the [**Close**] button to clear the **Tips** dialog box from the screen.

Note: If you don't want to see the Tips screen each time you start *Business Plan Pro,* clear the check mark from the "Show me on startup" box. The Tips screen can always be opened from the **Help** menu.

WORKING ON YOUR BUSINESS PLAN

The following sections describe the tools available to assist you, the work modes, and additional help options.

Text, Table, and Chart Modes

There are three different screen modes available in *Business Plan Pro*. You can move from one mode to another by clicking on its picture icon, shown at the top of all screens.

 Text Mode provides you with the tools for writing your business plan document. Instructions, examples, and formatting options are available.

 Table Mode provides you with the tools for a complete financial analysis of your plan. Instructions, examples, and row-by-row help are included.

 Chart Mode gives you access to the charts that *Business Plan Pro* automatically creates from the numbers you input to your tables. The **Chart Wizard** and **Chart Designer** let you modify the appearance of these charts.

Note: A complete description of the features in each mode, including menu commands and global preferences for text and tables, can be found in the on-screen **Help**. Press **F1** or click on the **Help** button at the bottom of the screen.

TEXT MODE

The **Text Mode** screen will display when you first start the program. The default text topic is **1.0 Executive Summary.** You can begin with this topic and move through the outline using the Text menu options, the **Next** and **Previous** buttons described below, or jump to a specific topic from the **Plan Outline.**

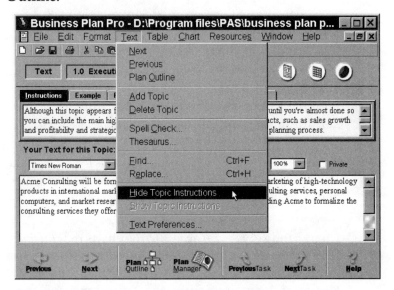

Type your text in the bottom half of the screen. Use the tools from the formatting bar to select font style, size, and appearance.

Next and Previous Buttons

The **Next** button moves you to the next topic in the outline.

The **Previous** button takes you back one topic in the outline.

Plan Outline

If you prefer to work on text topics in your own sequence, you can access the entire topic outline from the **Plan Outline** screen.

The 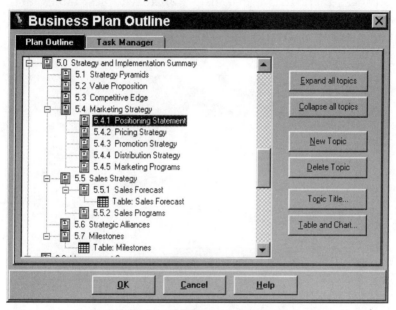 button displays at the bottom of your screen.

A dialog box will display:

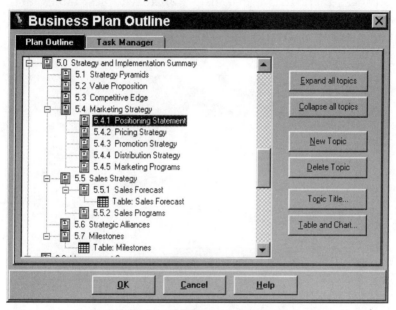

To move to a topic:

- Highlight the topic name.
- Click the OK button.

Task Manager

The **Task Manager** takes you step by step in creating your business plan. It is a task list of all text topics, tables, and charts included in your plan file. As you finish an item, you can mark it as completed. This lets you see at a glance the status of your plan.

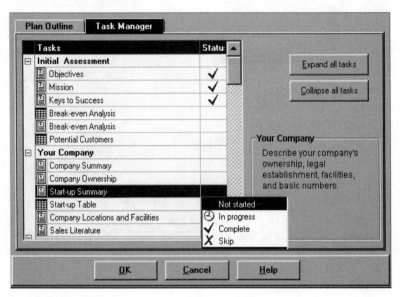

To mark a task:

Click in the Status box for the task. Select the status from the pull-down menu.

Next Task and Previous Task Buttons

These buttons are located at the bottom of the screen in all working modes (Text/Table/Chart).

The **NextTask** button moves you to the next task in the list.

The **PreviousTask** button takes you back one task in the list.

Working in Text Mode

Help features have been included at the top of the **Text Mode** screen. To view any of these areas, click on their tab labels. These tabs can be useful when first learning how to use the program. If you decide later that you want to use more of the screen for your text display, use the **Hide Topic Instructions** command from the **Text** menu.

Instructions Tab

This tab provides specific instructions for completing the current topic.

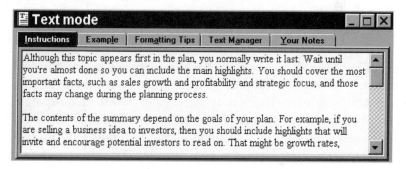

Example Tab

This tab will display actual text taken from a sample plan. It lets you see how another company completed the topic for their business.

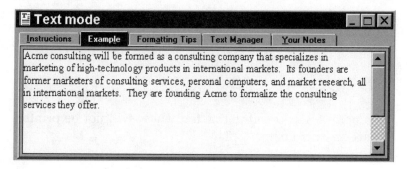

Formatting Tips Tab

This tab explains how the program formats your paragraphs. We recommend you read this information prior to typing in your text.

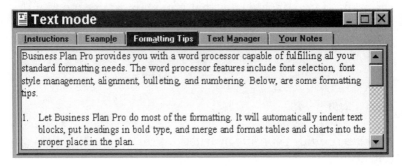

Text Manger Tab

The Text Manager shows what tables and/or charts are linked to a topic. You can jump to a linked table or chart by clicking the **Go to** buttons. There is also an option to attach a separate graphic file created outside of *Business Plan Pro*. The **Text Manager** also provides buttons to access **Spell Check, Text Preferences, Plan Options,** and the **Plan Wizard.**

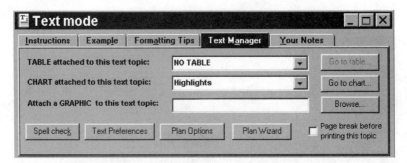

Notes Tab

Keep notes for yourself in this tab. These will not be printed as part of your business plan.

TABLE MODE

If you prefer to work on tables in your own sequence, you can access all tables for your plan from the Table menu.

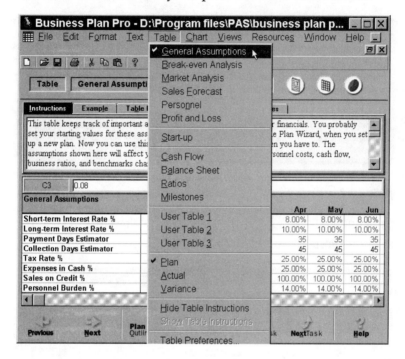

Working in Table Mode

A variety of help features have been included to guide you through the process of entering your table information, including row-by-row help and the optional audio help function from the **Table Help** tab.

These tabs can be useful when first learning how to use the program. If you decide later that you want to use more of the screen for your table display, use the **Hide Table Instructions** command from the Table menu.

Instructions Tab

This tab provides specific instructions for completing the current table.

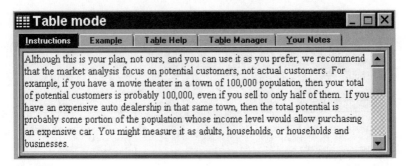

Example Tab

This tab displays table information from one of the available sample plans included with the installation.

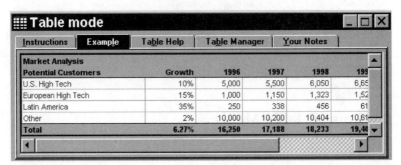

To view other sample plans, use the **Open Sample Plan** option as described in Chapter 2, **Start Up Options.**

Notes Tab

A separate Notes tab for your tables section is also provided.

Table Help Tab

You're not sure exactly what a certain row means. From the **Help** tab, you can read an explanation of whatever row/cell you are on. The optional Audio help function lets you "hear" the row and table definitions!

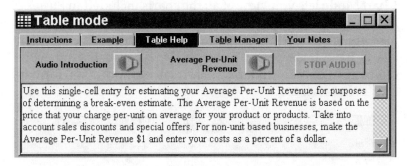

Note: Audio help is available if you installed *Business Plan Pro* from the CD-ROM. Because of the size and number of audio files, they are not available from an Internet download installation.

Table Manager Tab

The **Table Manger** tells you what links, if any, there are between the table you are viewing and the text and charts that make up your plan. The **Table Manager** tab also provides access to the **Calculator, Table Preferences, Plan Options,** and the **Plan Wizard.**

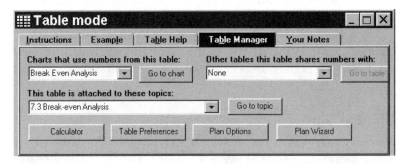

Note: A definition of all buttons can be found by pressing **F1** Help.

CHART MODE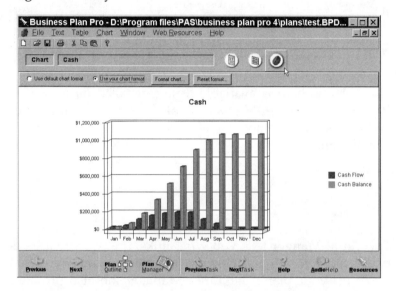

Chart Mode lets you view of all the charts included in *Business Plan Pro*. These charts are linked to their corresponding tables and are generated automatically. The appearance of your charts have been preset to display the numbers from your tables in an easy-to-understand format. No additional formatting is necessary.

However, you can make changes to the main title, the axis titles, and colors, and display the chart in a two- or three-dimensional view.

For a simple, step-by-step approach to chart modification, try the **Chart Wizard.** For more detailed modifications, try the **Chart Designer,** described later in this chapter.

Chart Wizard

The Format chart... button opens the **Chart Wizard.** The following screens let you change the appearance, type, and titles of a chart:

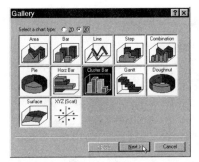

The **Gallery** dialog box lets you decide which type of chart you want. Select the chart type and continue to the next screen.

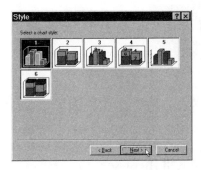

The **Style** dialog box lets you further select how to view your chart.

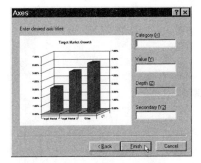

The **Axes** dialog box lets you choose titles for the X and Y axis areas of your chart.

Chart Designer

The Chart Designer gives even more flexibility in changing elements of your chart. From the Chart mode screen, click your right mouse button to display the pull-down menu, and select **Chart Designer.**

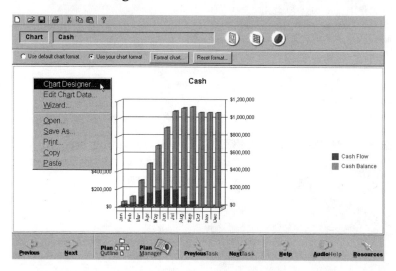

The **Chart Designer** dialog box will display:

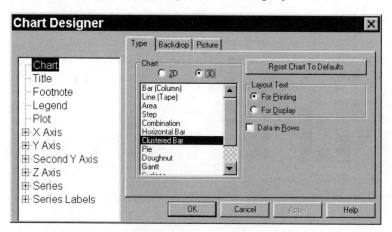

Both the **Chart Wizard** and **Chart Designer** provide you with the ability to modify how your charts will display and print.

WEB RESOURCES AND ADDITIONAL HELP

- Our **Resources** menu and the **Plan Manager** provide links to our Web Resources, which are located at **www.paloaltosoftware.com.** These resources include **Ask the Experts** and **Ask the Authors.** Here you can ask a question about your plan and receive a personal e-mail response. Questions and answers for our most frequently asked questions are posted for your review. Samples of business plans can be viewed and printed. Our Technical Support department includes their own frequently asked questions section and is available for all registered users of our products.

- The on-line version of **Hurdle: The Book on Business Planning** and our latest on-line book, **On Target: The Book on Marketing Plans,** lets you read the chapters on your screen, with full-color graphics!

- *Business Plan Pro* provides on-screen Instructions, Examples, and Help (F1), including context-sensitive help for tables, and mathematical functions for cells containing formulas (F3).

- A table of contents, an index, and a glossary of terms are included within Help.

- If you are in the Table Mode, choosing **Help** will bring context-specific help for the current table. The **Table Help** tab gives help for the current row within the table. And, if you installed *Business Plan Pro* from the CD-ROM, the optional audio files give you table and row help.

The combination of written instructions and on-screen assistance provides you with more than one method of learning the software.

APPENDIXES

APPENDIX A
ERROR MESSAGES

20012   Corrupt database files. Possible causes include:

- Storing or saving files to a disk or diskette with bad sectors.

- Exiting Windows or powering down before closing Business Plan Pro.

- Memory conflicts resulting in data scramble before writeback to disk.

- Opening your Business Plan Pro files in other applications, corrupting their file format.

3026   Not enough disk space. The application needs more disk storage space on the default disk drive (5 megabytes should be enough).

3041   Incompatibility with database utilities related to Microsoft database engine. Most often caused by Microsoft Office installation of earlier version utility with later version date.

Solution: Reinstall VBDB300.DLL from your setup disks by running the setup command as you would normally to install the product, but followed by a space and then a foward slash and an X. For example:

RUN A:\SETUP.EXE /X
RUN B:\SETUP.EXE /X

This will run the installation software in a special mode that gives you a scrolling browse window in which you can select files from the installation set and install them as required, overriding the normal production against writing over existing files.

Select VBDB300.DLL in the scrolling installation file window, and install it to the \WINDOWS \SYSTEM directory, replacing the existing one.

3043 This is apparently a database problem, or a memory management problem in Microsoft Windows. Its most common occurrence is when you have Business Plan Pro open twice, in two separate windows. Check first for two or more incidents of Business Plan Pro open at the same time. Hold the Control key and Escape key at the same time to bring up the Windows 3.1 Task Manager (Alt + Tab in Windows 95). Look at the list of open applications to see whether there is a Business Plan Pro window still open, even after the error message closed one incident.

To solve it, first exit Business Plan Pro and make sure you don't have it opened twice. Second, quit Windows and start up again. Often this access problem is related to Windows memory management, which is cleared when you exit and restart.

3050 Windows file sharing is not properly installed. Refer to your Windows manuals for information about SHARE.EXE and VSHARE.386. Business Plan Pro installs sharing with normal installation, so this should not occur unless there have been changes to the system after installation.

3051 Unable to open a database file. This indicates a conflict between Business Plan Pro and some Windows add-on memory management software, screen saver, or virus utilities.

3078 Text management problems. This usually indicates that the Business Plan Pro application is open twice at the same time. Close one of the two Business Plan Pro windows.

3112 Sometimes caused by having Business Plan Pro open twice in the same Windows session. It is also caused by running Business Plan Pro in a network environment, probably while Microsoft Access files are also running on the same network. Business Plan Pro is not sold as a network compatible product. Although we suspect this is a simple Microsoft Access or network utility problem, you should consult your network manager.

3183 Database unable to open. Check first for two incidents open, and close one of them. Sometimes caused by lack of disk storage space on the temporary disk. Otherwise, Error 3183 indicates a database problem affecting the text database associated with your business plan. Usually it is caused by power failure or otherwise improper database closure.

In the future, please make sure that you exit the Business Plan Pro properly, using the Exit command from the File menu.

3197 Check first for two or more incidents of Business Plan Pro open at the same time. Look at the list of open applications to see whether there is a Business Plan Pro still open, even after the error message closed one incident. Otherwise, Error 3197 indicates a database problem affecting the text database associated with your business plan. Usually it is caused by power failure or otherwise improper database closure.

In the future, please make sure you exit the Business Plan Pro properly, using the Exit command from the File menu.

3271 Invalid Property Value. This error refers to an invalid or outdated .DLL (Windows utilities frequently end in DLL) file operative in your system. Do a Find File search for the utilities included with your installation, according to the list included in the README.TXT file on your distribution disk. If one or more is different, you may force the install from the system disks using the /X mode as explained for Error 3041.

3279 This error is normally caused by Windows not properly closing the database engine at some point, so that later, when the program tries to reinitialize the engine, it causes the error.

To solve this problem, exit and restart Windows. When you exit, it will close the engine and be ready to reinitialize when you start Windows again.

53   This error refers to a Windows 95 problem of opening a database file associated with Business Plan Pro.

This error can be solved by setting your system preferences to show the 16-bit MS-DOS file extensions. To do this, select My Computer. Select the View menu, go down to Options. Select the View tab, and make sure the box labeled "Hide MS-DOS file extensions for file types that are registered" is not checked.

7   Incompatibility with database utilities related to the Microsoft database engine bundled with Business Plan Pro. Most often caused by Microsoft Office installation of earlier version utility with later version date. See the solution suggested for Error 3041.

Cannot load custom control, or custom DLL
This error, followed by the name of the DLL causing it, means improper installation or an error caused by making changes in the system folder (sometimes by other programs) after installation. Refer to the README.TXT file for the names, sizes, and dates of system utilities installed, and use the SETUP /X command as explained under Error 3041 to install the proper utilities.

APPENDIX B
FREQUENTLY ASKED QUESTIONS

BACKING UP YOUR BUSINESS PLAN

To back up a business plan, copy the associated files to a backup medium such as floppy disks or tape.

To transport a business plan from one computer to another and back, copy from hard disk to floppy disk and then from floppy disk to a second hard disk.

Try to always work from the hard disk. This is faster and safer.

You can use the Save As. . . command in the File menu to copy a plan to a floppy disk, but this will make Business Plan Pro look for the plan on the floppy disk drive the next time you open it.

HELP RESOURCES

F1 - Help

In Business Plan Pro, you have context sensitive help. When you press the F1 key while in any Business Plan Pro table, the help for that specific table should pop up. It provides line-by-line details and background.

F3 - Display Formulas Help

Within the Tables mode, many of the formulas used in Business Plan Pro are larger than the normal cell can display. Press F3 to see the complete formula for the selected cell.

TABLE DISPLAY PREFERENCES

Use the Table Display Preferences command in the Tables menu to set your business plan tables to show detailed row and column headers. This helps you read the formulas.

INDEX

This manual has an index. Some of the more important calculations, such as accounts receivable, accounts payable, and inventory, have multiple entries in the index and detailed background in the manual. They are there to help you.

PRINTER PROBLEM TROUBLESHOOTING

Printer Drivers

Frequently, printing problems are caused by outdated printer drivers. The printer drivers you have now are not entirely compatible with Windows 95, unless your printer is extremely new or you have updated the drivers recently. Windows 95 also needs to know that the printer is there, and that it is installed. This solves the majority of printer problems.

To update your printer drivers, contact the printer vendor via its customer service phone number; also, most vendors have World Wide Web sites with FTP capability.

VSVIEW.VBX

The utility named VSVIEW.VBX is critical to printing, print preview, and file export. It has been updated frequently by the vendor Videosoft, and is one of the first things to look for when you have printing problems, particularly if you can't open the print dialog.

Do a file search for VSVIEW.VBX (Windows 3.1 users open File Manager - select File/Search; Windows 95 users click Start - select Find - select Files or Folders) and make sure that the one active is the latest, should be dated Nov. 3 of 1995, 80K, 4:42 p.m. or later. If not, you may force install from the Business Plan Pro system disks.

To force install the VSVIEW.VBX:

- Close all open programs.
- From the Run command, type: "a:setup /x".

- Select VSVIEW.VBX from the menu, and install into the C:\WINDOWS\SYSTEM directory, or whatever your Windows system directory is. Be sure to move any other copies of the VSVIEW.VBX file into a non-Business Plan Pro, non-Windows directory. Also, be careful when moving these critical files around; the importance of backup or system boot disks cannot be stressed enough.

Business Plan Pro does not do anything unusual while printing; it gives the tasks to Windows. Aside from correct printer drivers, check the print settings in Windows from the Control Panel.

OTHER HELPFUL HINTS

- Service companies do not have inventory. All other types do.
- What can affect the Inventory estimate?

The inventory estimate is affected by your cost of sales and inventory turnover assumptions. Cost of sales is in your sales forecast, and inventory turnover is in the general assumptions table. To make inventory greater, decrease the estimated inventory turnover. To make it less, increase the turnover.

- How Inventory affects Cash

Changes in inventory are included in a single row of your cash flow table. Every dollar of increase in inventory results in a dollar less of cash. Every dollar of decrease in inventory results in a dollar more of cash.

- Inventory calculations in Business Plan Pro

The detailed explanation of inventory calculations is in the context-sensitive help files. You can also set your Table Display Preferences to show row and column headings, and then press F3 for the formula in any cell.

- The override facility

When you check the "input balances" box in your Plan Options dialog (accessed via the File menu), then the system turns off protection on the balance sheet rows for accounts payable, accounts receivable, and inventory. You can then type your own balance assumptions into the appropriate cells, overriding the formulas and calculations. The cash flow will be adjusted accordingly.

- Explaining Accounts Receivable in Business Plan Pro

The detailed explanation of accounts receivable calculation is in the context sensitive help files. You can also set your Table Display Preferences to show row and column headings, and then press F3 for the formula in any cell.

- More on Accounts Receivable in Business Plan Pro

A mathematical formula estimates the year-end accounts receivable balances for the second and third year. You don't need to know this complicated formula because you can either use its estimated number or override it with the Input Balances option. It comes from reversing the normal formula that accountants use to determine collection days from the average accounts receivable balance and total sales on credit.
The formula for determining collection days is:

(average accounts receivable * 365) / sales on credit

This formula is implemented exactly in the ratios section of Business Plan Pro, as:

((Starting AR Balance + Ending AR Balance) / 2)

- Sales on Credit

We reverse the formula, because we know collection days (it's an assumption) but we don't know the balance. We estimate the balance by reversing that algebra and solving for the balance, with the collection days as a known amount. The actual formula is:

$$((\text{collection days} * \text{sales on credit} * 2) / 365) - \text{the previous year's balance}$$

The formula we use is financially and algebraically correct, but it doesn't always work for every company because it has to use average balances. The impact of average balances can make the estimated accounts receivable balance go down as sales go up.

There are several simple solutions:

1. Use the Plan Options dialog to turn the Input Balances option on and override these formulas by simply typing balance amounts for accounts receivable for each month. This is perfectly acceptable and will not harm your other calculations. Your cash flow will still be accurate, and so will the collection days.

2. Stick with collection days as the driving assumption, and use trial and error to make the resulting receivables estimate match your intuition. For example, our internal business plan has collection days increasing in 1996 and decreasing in 1997, resulting in a steady relationship between collection days and sales. This is a result of the impact of the averaging built into the standard accounting ratio.

The mathematics and accounting are correct on receivables because of the impact of averaging. We are talking about estimates only; the system allows full flexibility on replacing these estimates with your own estimates.

TELEPHONE SUPPORT

If you have any further questions, contact us via phone, fax, or e-mail, and please have your serial number ready.

Telephone: (541) 683-6162

Fax: (541) 683-6250

World Wide Web: http://www.palo-alto.com

E-mail: help@palo-alto.com

America Online: Pasware

CompuServe: 75755,1000

Unless you specify some other e-mail account, we will reply to the same mail account that sent your original message.

APPENDIX C
GLOSSARY

Accounts payable Bills to be paid as part of the normal course of business.

Accounts receivable Debts owed to your company, usually from sales on credit.

Accumulated depreciation Total accumulated depreciation reduces the formal accounting value (called book value) of assets. Each month's accumulated balance is the same as last month's balance plus this month's depreciation.

Acid test Short-term assets minus accounts receivable and inventory, divided by short-term liabilities. This is a test of a company's ability to meet its immediate cash requirements.

Asset turnover Sales divided by total assets. Important for comparison over time and to other companies of the same industry.

Break-even point The unit sales volumes or actual sales amounts that a company needs to equal its running expense rate and not lose or make money in a given month. Business Plan Pro shows a break-even point based on regular running expenses, which is different from the standard accounting formula based on technical fixed expenses. The formula for the break-even point in units is:

$$= \text{Regular running costs}/(\text{Unit Price} - \text{Unit Variable Cost})$$

The formula for the break-even point in sales amount is:

$$= \text{Regular running costs} /(1 - (\text{Unit Variable Cost}/\text{Unit Price}))$$

Burden rate Refers to personnel burden, the sum of employer costs over and above salaries, including employer taxes and benefits.

Capital assets   Long-term assets, also known as Plant and Equipment.

Capital expenditure   Spending on capital assets (also called plant and equipment, or fixed assets).

Capital input   New money being invested in the business. New capital will increase your cash, and will also increase the total amount of paid-in capital.

Cash   The bank balance, or checking account balance, or real cash in bills and coins.

Collection days   *See* Collection period, below.

Collection period (days)   The average number of days that pass between delivering an invoice and receiving the money. The formula is:

= (Accounts_receivable_balance*360)/(Sales_on_credit*12)

Commissions   Gross margin multiplied by the commissions percentage.

Commissions percent   An assumed percentage used to calculate commissions expense as the product of this percentage multiplied by gross margin.

Cost of sales   The costs associated with producing the sales. In a standard manufacturing or distribution company, this is about the same as the cost of the goods sold. In a services company, this is more likely to be personnel costs for people delivering the service, or subcontracting costs.

Current assets   The same as short-term assets.

Current debt   Short-term debt, short-term liabilities.

Current liabilities   Short-term debt, short-term liabilities.

Debt and equity The sum of liabilities and capital. This should always be equal to total assets.

Depreciation An accounting and tax concept used to estimate the loss of value of assets over time. For example, cars depreciate with use.

Directory A computer term related to the DOS operating system on IBM and compatible computers. Disk storage space is divided into directories.

Dividends Money distributed to the owners of a business as profits.

Earnings Also called income or profits, earnings are the famous "bottom line"—sales less costs of sales and expenses.

EBIT Earnings before interest and taxes.

Equity Business ownership; capital. Equity can be calculated as the difference between assets and liabilities.

Fiscal year Standard accounting practice allows the accounting year to begin in any month. Fiscal years are numbered according to the year in which they end. For example, a fiscal year ending in February of 2001 is Fiscal 2001, even though most of the year takes place in 2000. Business Plan Pro assumes that any plan that doesn't begin in January is based on a fiscal year that begins in the starting month.

Fixed costs Running costs that take time to wind down: usually rent, overhead, some salaries. Technically, fixed costs are those that the business would continue to pay even if it went bankrupt. In practice, fixed costs are usually considered the running costs.

Gross margin Sales minus cost of sales.

Gross margin percent Gross margin divided by sales, displayed as a percentage. Acceptable levels depend on the nature of the business.

Interest expense   Interest is paid on debts, and interest expense is deducted from profits as expenses. Interest expense in Business Plan Pro is either long-term or short-term interest; we make the distinction because interest rates paid are usually higher on long-term debts.

Inventory   Goods in stock, either finished goods or materials to be used to manufacture goods.

Inventory turnover   Total cost of sales divided by inventory. Usually calculated using the average inventory over an accounting period, not an ending inventory value.

Inventory turns   Inventory turnover (above).

Label   The row titles along column A of the tables are called labels, or row labels.

Labor   In Business Plan Pro, labor refers to the labor costs associated with making goods to be sold. This labor is part of the cost of sales, part of the manufacturing and assembly. The row heading refers to fulfillment costs as well, for service companies.

Liabilities   Debts; money that must be paid. Usually debt on terms of less than five years is called short-term liabilities, and debt for longer than five years in long-term liabilities.

Long-term assets   Assets like plant and equipment that are depreciated over terms of more than five years, and are likely to last that long, too.

Long-term interest rate   The interest rate charged on long-term debt. This is usually higher than the rate on short-term debt.

Long-term liabilities   This is the same as long-term loans. Most companies call a debt long-term when it is on terms of five years or more.

Materials   Included in the cost of sales. These are materials involved in the assembly or manufacture of goods for sale.

Net cash flow   This is the projected change in cash position, an increase or decrease in cash balance.

Net profit   The operating income less taxes and interest. The same as earnings, or net income.

Net worth   This is the same as assets minus liabilities, and the same as total equity.

Other short-term assets   These might be securities, business equipment, etc.

Other ST liabilities   These are short-term debts that don't cause interest expenses. For example, they might be loans from founders or accrued taxes (taxes owed, already incurred, but not yet paid).

Paid-in capital   Real money paid into the company as investments. This is not to be confused with par value of stock, or market value of stock. This is actual money paid into the company as equity investments by owners.

Payment days   The average number of days that pass between receiving an invoice and paying it. It is not a simple estimate; it is calculated with a financial formula: =(Accounts_payable_balance*360)/(Total entries to accounts payable*12).

Payroll burden (or Personnel burden)   Payroll burden includes payroll taxes and benefits. It is calculated using a percentage assumption that is applied to payroll. For example, if payroll is $1,000 and the burden rate 10 percent, the burden is an extra $100. Acceptable payroll burden rates vary by market, by industry, and by company.

Personnel burden   *See* Payroll burden.

Plant and equipment   This is the same as long-term, fixed or capital assets.

Product development   Expenses incurred in development of new products: salaries, laboratory equipment, test equipment, prototypes, research and development, etc.

Profit before interest and taxes   This is also called EBIT, for Earnings Before Interest and Taxes. It is gross margin minus operating expenses.

Receivables turnover   Sales on credit for an accounting period divided by the average accounts receivables balance.

Retained earnings   Earnings (or losses) that have been reinvested into the company, and not paid out as dividends to the owners. When retained earnings are negative, the company has accumulated losses.

Return on assets   Net profit divided by total assets. A measure of profitability.

Return on investment   Net profits divided by net worth or total equity; yet another measure of profitability. Also called ROI.

Return on sales   Net profits divided by sales; another measure of profitability.

ROI   Return on investment; net profits divided by net worth or total equity, another measure of profitability.

Sales break-even   The sales volume at which costs are exactly equal to sales. The exact formula is $=$Fixed_costs/(1-(Unit_Variable_Cost/Unit_Price)).

Sales on credit   Sales made on account, shipments against invoices to be paid later.

Short-term   Normally used to distinguish between short-term and long-term, when referring to assets or liabilities.

Definitions vary because different companies and accountants handle this in different ways. Accounts payable is always a short-term liability, and cash, accounts receivable and inventory are always short-term assets. Most companies call any debt of less than five-year terms short-term debt. Assets that depreciate over more than five years (e.g., plant and equipment) are usually long-term assets.

Short-term assets Cash, securities, bank accounts, accounts receivable, inventory, business equipment, assets that last less than five years or are depreciated over terms of less than five years.

Short-term notes These are the same as short-term loans. These are debts with terms of five years or less.

Starting date The starting date for the entire business plan system. You set the starting date by setting starting year and starting month, and other datelines will be reset automatically whenever the spreadsheet calculates changes.

Starting month The starting month is entered in the Set Options dialog.

Starting year The starting year is entered in the Set Options dialog.

Tax rate percent An assumed percentage applied against pre-tax income to determine taxes. In Business Plan Pro we use a single percentage calculation, not a graduated rate or complex formula.

Taxes incurred Taxes owed but not yet paid.

Timeline Business Plan Pro rows that show the months and years. These are called Timeline rows.

Unit variable cost The specific labor and materials associated with a single unit of goods sold. Does not include general overhead.

Units break-even   The unit sales volume at which the fixed and variable costs are exactly equal to sales. The formula is UBE = Fixed_costs/(Unit_Price – Unit_Variable_Cost).

APPENDIX D
TABLE TIPS AND TRAPS

Business Plan Pro was designed to provide all of the functions necessary to create a complete business plan, from typing text to entering numbers in the tables. No experience in working with other programs is necessary to use this software.

Included in this appendix are common errors that occur in the Tables mode and how to troubleshoot those errors. This information is helpful for all users, regardless of their computer background.

Also, for those users who are familiar with spreadsheet software and the creation of special formulas, this appendix also provides some "behind-the-scenes" tips on the formulas that are used and how to create your own within the Tables mode.

COMMON TABLE ERRORS

The most common causes of errors in a formula are:

- Mistyping formula references, or
- Pressing the spacebar when the system expects a number.

This causes several of the errors listed here.

Important: Make sure you enter numbers as numbers only. Do not type in any formatting of your numbers (dollar signs or commas, for example). Business Plan Pro automatically formats the numbers within a cell.

####### This is a column width problem: your columns are too narrow to display the number they should, because your number is too large or your format is too large. Solve this problem using the Column Width command in your tables Format menu.

#DIV/0 Divide by zero. May be caused by a reference to a blank cell or a cell containing zero. Reexamine the table links at the beginning of this chapter to see where the data might be dividing by zero. Trace the formulas back by reading the formulas in the formula edit bar, at the upper left of the spreadsheet screen.

#N/A No value is available. May be caused by inappropriate values in the formula or a reference to a cell containing text (an empty space character is also text) or containing the #N/A value.

#NAME Name is not recognized. May be caused by user entering an improper formula into a cell.

#NUM Number problem. May be caused by user entering a number into a user-defined formula improperly.

#REF Reference error. May be caused by referring to a cell that was deleted.

#VALUE May be caused by entering text where a number was expected, or by an improper user-entered formula.

Fixing These Errors

When you enter numbers into the cells, enter just the numbers and no formatting characters (don't enter the "$", the "%", or other formatting characters). The software formats numbers automatically. Don't ever enter a space character, because this will also be interpreted as text.

To test a value that looks like a number, but seems to be interpreted as text, type it beginning with an equal sign and with no number characters. For example: if the problem seems to be with a cell showing "$999,999" then type =999999 into the cell and see what happens.

To solve these errors, you have to trace the error back through the financial tables. The financials are linked, so a bad cell in one table may create the same value errors in other tables. Here are some tips to locate the error.

1. Look first at the Profit and Loss statement.

- If the error shows up in sales or cost of sales, then your error originated in the Sales Forecast.

- If the error shows up first in a personnel line in the P&L, then the error originated in the Personnel Plan.

- If the error shows up in any other part of P&L, its source is probably right where it shows up in that table.

2. Next look at the Balance Sheet.

- If the error shows in any of the starting balances, then the source is either the Start-Up table or the Past Performance table.

- If it shows up anywhere else, look for an error in your General Assumptions or your cash flow table.

3. For further help, study the linked table information in the chapter on Tables in this Software Guide.

TIPS FOR SPREADSHEET USERS

The Business Plan Pro tables are based on a built-in spreadsheet. They use mathematical formulas tied to individual cells and blocks of cells. These formulas are identified by row and column references. Tables also use formulas based on names defined to represent cells or blocks of cells.

Excel Compatibility

The underlying spreadsheet built in to Business Plan Pro is functionally compatible with Microsoft Excel 4.0. Almost any

Excel formula that doesn't involve functions, and some that do, will also work within Business Plan Pro tables. The Table Display Preferences dialog includes the facility to set tables to show Excel-like row and column headings.

Export to Excel

If you want, you can export all of a business plan's tables into Excel and work with them in Excel instead of in Business Plan Pro. Business Plan Pro creates a complete Excel workbook, in which each of the business plan tables is a separate worksheet. It creates this workbook in Excel 95 format, which Excel will automatically convert into any more recent format. Here are some Excel tips that might help you work with the Excel workbook:

1. The exported workbook doesn't show sheet tabs. Go to your Excel Tools menu, choose the Options command, and set your options to show sheet tabs. That will make the worksheets visible.

2. You should know how Excel hides and shows rows and columns. Business Plan Pro frequently hides rows, and you'll need Excel to unhide them.

3. All the worksheets will be protected but without passwords. You can unprotect using the Excel command for that.

4. Several worksheets have multiple range names with multiple tables, all with similar names and purposes. For example, the personnel plan worksheet has three different personnel plans, and the sales forecast has two different sales forecasts. These are used to select structures that match the specific types of businesses. You'll want to look through them and decide which is relevant to the plan you've been working on.

5. Be very careful when deleting rows, columns, cells, and especially range names and worksheets. Business Plan Pro uses a very complex financial linking structure based on range names. Deleting an odd range name

can cause major errors in the entire set of worksheets. Deleting the worksheet named "logistics," which you never see within Business Plan Pro, can cause major errors.

Of course you won't be able to import Excel worksheets back into Business Plan Pro after you've modified them, but there are still situations in which export may be your preferred option.

Warning: Excel programming is not required for working with Business Plan Pro. If a file is exported and modified outside of Business Plan Pro, *no technical support from Palo Alto Sofware will be provided.*

Reading Spreadsheet Formulas

To read the spreadsheet formula of any cell, click the cell and read its formula in the edit bar on the upper left of the spreadsheet display, to the left of the icons. Some formulas are too long to show completely in the edit bar; press F3 to display them in a dialog box instead.

Cells in Business Plan Pro tables can be programmed with the same mathematical formulas you would use in Microsoft Excel.

The table calculations are based on a row-and-column-naming system that numbers the rows and assigns letters to the columns. You can see the row and column system by using your Table Display Preferences dialog box to show row and column headings. The row label texts are all in column A of the tables, months are in columns C–N, and the years are in columns O, P, and Q.

Sample Formulas

To develop your own formulas using spreadsheet programming, use these tips:

1. Enter a formula into a cell by typing into the formula bar at the top left of the screen, or by selecting a cell and pressing the F2 key.

2. Always start the formula with the = sign.

3. To add, subtract, multiply, or divide cells, use the standard mathematical symbols on your keyboard.

   For example:

   To add the contents of cell C100 to the contents of cell C200, the formula would be: =C100+C200

Some Important Range Names

Most of the range names used are self-explanatory, like the name Profit_before_int_and_taxes for profit before interest and taxes, or General_and_administrative_expense in the more detailed profit and loss by function.

If you are familiar with the concept of range names from work in other spreadsheets, you will want to refer to the range names used in the table formulas:

Collection_days   The collection days estimator value, in the general assumptions table.

Cost_of_sales   Total cost of sales.

Cost_of_unit_sales   Direct cost of sales, the cost of sales from the sales forecast.

Gross_margin   Gross margin.

INC_SM   Used by the system to determine which income statement model is used.

Indexor   An indicator of months into the plan.

Interest_expense_LT   Long-term interest expense, in the profit and loss statement.

Interest_expense_ST Short-term interest expense, in the profit and loss statement.

Inventory_turns The inventory turnover estimator value, in the general assumptions table.

Net_profit Net profit, net earnings.

New_accounts_payable Calculated by the formula: (1-payables_Percent)*(Total_Operating_Expenses + Cost_of_sales-(Payroll + Payroll_burden)).

Option1 Determines type of business, for values 1 through 5, as set by the Plan Options dialog.

Option2 Sets ongoing or start-up company, from Plan Options dialog.

Option3 Sets sales in cash only, or sales on credit.

Option4 Number of sales lines, from 1 to 9.

Option5 Business Plan title, a text string.

Option6 Starting year, a number.

Option7 Starting month, from 1 to 12.

Option8 Sets home office option, from Plan Options dialog.

Option9 Sets inventory.

Option10 Sets long-term option.

Payment_days Payment days estimator value, in the general assumptions table.

Sales Sales.

Sales_on_credit   Sales on credit, calculated by multiplying the sales on credit percent in the assumptions table by the sales, for each time period.

SFCA   Used by system to determine which sales forecast is used.

Taxes_incurred   Taxes calculated near the bottom of the profit and loss statement, per time period.

Total_operating_expenses   Total operating expenses

Index